AMERICA
LEARNS TO PLAY

The End of the Fox Hunt

AMERICA LEARNS TO PLAY

A History of Popular Recreation
1607–1940

by

FOSTER RHEA DULLES

GLOUCESTER, MASS.
PETER SMITH
1963

TO

EDITH

PREFACE

THE GROWTH OF POPULAR RECREATION IN THE UNITED STATES may be compared to a river—its course adapting itself to the nature of the country through which it flows, the main stream continually augmented by tributaries, and the river-bed itself ever growing both broader and deeper. In the early period of settlement it was little more than a thin trickle, forcing its way through a forbidding terrain, but with the eighteenth century it slowly gathered volume and flowed on quietly and steadily. The first half of the nineteenth century saw its course deflected into more narrow channels, and for a time the flow appeared to be almost checked, but after the Civil War scores of new tributaries swelled it to far greater size. The twentieth century transformed it into a riotous torrent, breaking through all barriers as it carved out fresh channels. Sometimes it appeared to sweep almost everything else aside, spreading in full flood over a vast territory.

This book is an attempt to trace the main course of this stream. Recreation is considered in its popular sense—the leisure-time activities that the American people have pursued over three centuries for their own pleasure. At all periods of history men and women have probably spent the greater part of their leisure in informal talk, in visiting and entertaining their friends, in casual walks and strolls, and sometimes in reading for their own amusement. But these more simple activities are hidden in the obscurity that shrouds private lives. Organized, public recreation has consciously been adopted as the basis for this record.

It has been found stupendously difficult to delimit its boundaries. There have always been leisure-time pursuits in which cultural and recreational motives are inextricably mixed, and in

more recent years increasing emphasis has been placed on creative activities. In the main, the cultural and the creative have
been ignored in this account of the people at play. Music and
the dance are treated as entertainment, not art. Where religion,
or rather the church, has impinged on the recreational scene,
there is again no attempt to go beyond the surface implications
of the popular enjoyment of the Sunday meeting or midweek
Great and Thursday of colonial days, the frontier revival, the
small-town church social of the 1890's, or the activities clustering
about the institutionalized church of metropolis.

Even with these limitations recreation includes a wide cate-
gory of amusements ranging from horseshoe-pitching to symphony concerts, from the circus to fox-hunting, from prize-fights
to contract bridge, from lodge night to international polo.
Throughout the book the emphasis has invariably been placed
on those diversions or sports which have reached the greatest
number of people. A century ago a shrewd foreign observer
declared that democracy was too new a comer upon the earth
to have been able as yet to organize its pleasures. America would
be compelled in this field of activity, as in politics, to create
everything fresh. How this challenge has been met is the basic
question that has determined my lines of inquiry. Yachting has
been largely ignored in favor of bicycling and motoring, the
opera neglected to stress the importance of minstrel shows and
vaudeville, and though the popular theatre of the mid-nineteenth
century is described, the rise of the movies has forced the legitimate stage of the twentieth century into the background.

In view of the greatly increased leisure for the masses of
people in the present day and the very real concern as to how
it is being used, it is hoped that an account of changing trends
in recreation during the past three centuries may prove of immediate interest. Two important factors, I think, stand out from the
record. The first is the continuing influence of an inherent puritanism, both rising from and enforcing a dogma of work born
of economic circumstance, which may be traced from the seven-

teenth century to the twentieth. Until recent times it has frowned severely upon what the early settlers called any "mispense of time." If to-day this attitude has somewhat changed, the American tradition still insists that amusements should at least make some pretense of serving socially useful ends. The businessman plays golf to keep fit for business; the woman's club emphasizes its educational program; and reformers would have all popular entertainment directed toward the establishment of higher cultural standards.

The second factor is the paramount influence on recreation of the gradual transformation of our economy from the simplicity of the agricultural era to the complexity of the machine age. No field of human activity has been more deeply affected by this change and the concomitant growth of cities. The machine has greatly increased the leisure of the laboring masses, and it has at the same time made life less leisurely. The traditional patterns of everyday living have been completely altered with an ever-growing need for play that can effectively compensate for the intensity under which we must work. If many of the forms of recreation that have evolved under these circumstances appear far from ideal, the question is nevertheless posed as to what the urban masses, granted the conditions of modern life, would be doing if they did not have their commercial amusements and spectator sports.

Entirely apart from the possible bearing on present-day recreation of the developments of the past, an account of three centuries of play also seems to throw as revealing a light upon how the American people have created the modern society in which we live as many records of more serious activities. Lord Lytton has somewhere stated that the civilization of a people is infallibly indicated by the intellectual character of its amusements. It is more and more widely recognized to-day that what a nation does with its leisure is oftentimes just as significant as how it either maintains itself economically or governs itself. This book is presented with the idea that on these grounds alone there is justification for surveying a phase of human activity which the historian often ignores.

The field is so broad that, with the best will in the world, it has proved impossible to treat many topics comprehensively. I have not tried to give a complete record of any single sport or amusement. The origins of diversions are generally traced in some detail, but once popularly accepted (the tributary joining the main stream), further developments have been noted only as incidental to the general expansion of recreation. Moreover, to write authoritatively of New England husking-bees and the concerts and balls of colonial Charleston; of sailing regattas in the 1830's and the trotting races of county fairs in mid-century; of archery and the roller-skating craze; of surprise parties and the popular melodrama of the 1890's; of automobile motoring, the movies, and radio; of softball and skiing; of jazz, crossword puzzles, and major-league baseball, would demand a familiarity with the social scene through three hundred years of American history which I would be the first to disclaim.

It has taken considerable courage even to attempt to plot a course. The mass of available evidence made a sampling process the only possible procedure. Where other writers have traced the history of some one form of amusement (for there is no comparable earlier book covering the whole subject), I have most gratefully availed myself of the fruits of their labor. The chapter notes and bibliography at the end of the volume will give some measure of my indebtedness. But so far as time and space have allowed, I have used the contemporary evidence of how the American people have amused themselves in their leisure time—the records contained in diaries, autobiographies, travel accounts, magazines, newspapers, playbills and posters, sports manuals and advertisements. I have selected whatever appeared significant, interesting, and sometimes amusing in order to present the kaleidoscopic scene as much as possible through the eyes of those who actually observed it. There can be no scientific exactitude about such a record. It is necessarily colored throughout, though

I have tried to restrain myself, by personal interests and enthusiasms—and also by personal blind-spots.

To acknowledge the aid and assistance I have received from various sources is but a poor return for these favors. The book would probably have never been written except for a fellowship awarded by the John Simon Guggenheim Memorial Foundation. I should also like to express my appreciation of the coöperation of Francis G. Wickware in assembling the illustrations, and of Janet Aaron in compiling the index. The manuscript has been patiently read and criticized by several co-workers or friends, among whom I am particularly indebted to John A. Krout; while the aid, encouragement, and practical assistance of Edith Dulles Snare and Marion Dulles are greatly responsible for whatever virtues the book may claim.

FOSTER RHEA DULLES

CONTENTS

ILLUSTRATIONS

AMERICA
LEARNS TO PLAY

Chapter I

"IN DETESTATION OF IDLENESS"

THE SETTLERS WHO PLANTED THE FIRST ENGLISH COLONIES IN America had the same instinctive drive for play that is the common heritage of all mankind. It suffered no sea change in the long and stormy crossing of the Atlantic. Landing at Jamestown, Sir Thomas Dale found the almost starving colonists playing happily at bowls in 1611.[1] * The first Thanksgiving at Plymouth was something more than an occasion for prayer. Edward Winslow wrote that among other recreations the Pilgrims exercised their arms and for three days entertained and feasted the Indians.[2]

Against the generally somber picture of early New England life may also be set the lively account of those gay and wanton festivities at Merry Mount. To the consternation of "the precise separatists, that lived at new Plymouth," the scapegrace followers of Thomas Morton set up a May-pole, brought out wine and strong waters, and invited the Indians to join them:

> Drinke and be merry, merry, merry boyes,
> Let all your delight be in the Hymens joyes,
> Joy to Hymen now the day is come,
> About the merry Maypole take a Roome.
> Make greene garlons, bring bottles out
> And fill sweet Nectar freely about.
> Uncover thy head and fear no harme,
> For hers good liquor to keepe it warme.[3]

* All numerical symbols throughout the text refer to source references to be found in the notes at the end of the book. They may be ignored by the reader not interested in such material.

They spent several days, in William Bradford's disapproving phrase, "dancing and frisking togither, (like so many fairies or furies rather,) and worse practises." [4]

It was from these beginnings that American recreation grew to the varied and full activities we know to-day. They naturally open any record that would attempt to trace its growth and expansion under the changing conditions of American life. But it would be placing a greatly exaggerated emphasis on these simple sports and festivities to imagine that they were everyday occurrences. The first settlers actually had very little time or opportunity to play. Harsh circumstance fastened upon them the necessity for continual work. In the strange and unfamiliar wilderness that was America, "all things stared upon them with a weather-beaten face." The forest crowded against their little settlements along tidewater, and they felt continually menaced by its lurking dangers. None knew when the eerie war-whoop of the Indians might break the oppressive silence. Starvation again and again thinned their ranks, and disease was a grim specter hovering over each household. Merely to keep alive in a land which to their inexperience was cruel and inhospitable demanded all their energy.

The ruling powers, whether north or south, Puritan or Anglican, consequently found it at once necessary to adopt the strictest regulations "in detestation of idleness," to the end of enforcing work and prohibiting all amusements. Sir Thomas Dale sternly forbade further bowling at Jamestown and decreed that any tradesman unfaithful and negligent in daily attendance upon his occupation should be "condemned to the Galley for three years." [5] Governor Endicott of the Massachusetts Bay Colony cut down the May-pole at Merry Mount, gravely warning the revelers for the future "to looke ther should be better walking," and prepared rigorously to enforce the General Court's law that "no person, householder or other, shall spend his time idly or unprofitably, under paine of such punishment as the Courte shall thinke meet to inflict." [6]

It was the paramount need of a primitive, pioneer society for the whole-hearted coöperation of the entire community that fastened upon the first Americans a tradition of work which still weighs heavily upon their descendants. The common welfare in those difficult and perilous days could not permit any "mispense of time." Those who would not work of their own volition had to be driven to it under the lash of compulsion. Religion provided the strongest moral sanction for every law suppressing amusements. It was one of the vital forces making for a life in which recreation for long played hardly any part. But in all the colonies there was this basic fact: if the settlers did not direct all their energy to their work, they could not hope to survive.

-->>)(<<-

VIRGINIA originally enacted laws fully as restrictive as those of New England.[7] The Assembly in 1619 decreed that any person found idle should be bound over to compulsory work; it prohibited gaming at dice or cards, strictly regulated drinking, provided penalties for excess in apparel, and rigidly enforced Sabbath observance.[8] There was, for example, to be no admission of actors "because we resolve to suffer no Idle persons in Virginia."[9] Court records show that offenses against these laws were dealt with severely.[10] It was only as conditions of life became somewhat easier that enforcement grew lax. Once the colony was firmly established and the need for incessant work began to lessen, Virginians were more generally permitted to make the most of whatever opportunities for recreation their expanding life presented.

In New England, where the stern rule of Calvinism condemned idleness and amusements for their own sake, the tradition that life should be wholly devoted to work ("that noe idle drone bee permitted to live amongst us"[11]) held its ground more firmly. The magistrates attempted to suppress almost every form of recreation long after the practical justification for such an unrelenting attitude had disappeared. The intolerance of Puritanism was superimposed upon economic necessity to confine life in New England within the narrowest possible grooves. Massachusetts and Connecticut banned dice, cards, quoits, bowls, ninepins, "or any other unlawful game in house, yard, garden or backside," singling out for special attention "the Game called Shuffle Board, in howses of Common Interteinment, whereby much precious time is spent unfruitfully." [12] They listed "common Coasters, unprofitable fowlers, and Tobacko takers" as idlers subject to immediate punishment. No smoker in Connecticut could "take any tobacco publiquely in the street, nor shall any take yt in the fyelds or woods." His indulgence in a habit generally condemned as time-wasting was limited to the "ordinary tyme of repast commonly called dynner." [13]

Throughout New England, local ordinances further ordered the constables to "search after all manner of gameing, singing and dancing" and to report "disordered meetings" even when they were held in private homes.[14] John Cotton had condoned dancing under certain circumstances, reserving his disapproval with possible justification for "lascivious dancing to wanton ditties, and in amorous gestures and wanton dalliances," but his successors admitted no such subtle distinctions. The Devil was responsible for all dancing, and especially "Gynecandrical Dancing or that which is commonly called Mixt or Promiscuous Dancing of Men and Women." [15] When the Massachusetts General Court learned that the custom of dancing at weddings was growing up, it flatly decreed that there should be no more of it, then or at any other time.[16]

The theatre was of course absolutely prohibited. Connecticut was prepared to adjudge as common rogues and serve fifteen stripes on the bare back to any one who should attempt to "set up and practice common plays, interludes, or other crafty science." Boston on one occasion refused permission for an exhibition of tight-rope walking "lest the said divertisement may tend to promote idleness in the town and great mispense of time." [17]

These laws represented a determination to promote industry and frugality; they also reflected the Puritan concept of the evil inherent in any frivolous waste of time. In one instance there was a curious conflict between these two motives. Toward the close of the period of the Great Migration, the popularity of the midweek church meeting, known as the Great and Thursday, began keeping many of the country people from their work. "There were so many lectures now in the country," John Winthrop wrote in 1639, "and many poor persons would usually resort to two or three in the week, to the great neglect of their affairs, and the damage of the public." [18] Here was one of the few breaks in the harsh routine of daily life that the early settlers experienced, a social function when there were no others. And while the lecture itself might be wearisome and dreary, at least for those to whom Calvinistic theology was not always completely absorbing, it offered a chance for neighborly gossip after the service and for the pleasure of seeing offenders against the Puritan code properly punished—placed in the stocks or whipped at the cart's tail. Consequently the colony's theocratic rulers found themselves in a difficult quandary. Attendance at these meetings could not be prohibited: it hardly fell under the head of idle or frivolous amusement. None the less it represented, from a utilitarian viewpoint, a serious "mispense" of time.

It was first ruled, to prevent waste of a whole day, that lectures should not begin before one o'clock. Then the ministers were urged to hold fewer midweek meetings. And finally the order went out that the church assemblies should ordinarily break up in time to enable people who lived a mile or two off to get home before dusk. Nothing could be permitted that in any way would impair the spirit expressed in William Wood's dictum that aside from everything else "all New England must be workers in some kind." [19]

No such reason could be advanced to justify the vehement efforts of magistrates and elders to compel that strict observance of the Sabbath which they had made one of the cardinal articles of their stern faith. Religion stood its ground without economic support. The Lord's Day was to be wholly devoted to pious reflection upon the bounties of an all-wise Providence. Puritanism did not admit the idea that this one day free of work might possibly be enjoyed for itself.

Virginia had forbidden Sunday amusements in the early years of settlement. The laws of that colony, as applied by Governor Argall in 1618, made the penalty for failure to attend church service imprisonment in the guard-house ("lying neck and heels on the Corps of Gard ye night following and be a slave ye week following") and strictly banned any Sabbath-day dancing, fiddling, card-playing, hunting, or fishing.[20] But while these laws soon fell into abeyance, New England's holy zeal in trying to turn the day into one of vacuous melancholy was not abated.

The strict prohibition of any Sunday labor, travel, or recreation was supplemented by specific bans on "all unnecessary and unseasonable walking in the streets and fields." [21] Application of this law was graciously limited to children over seven, but the Massachusetts General Court gave warning that this by no means implied that "we approve of younger children in evil." [22] In Connecticut the town of New London found occasion to hale John Lewis and Sarah Chapman into court "for sitting together on the Lord's Day, under an apple tree in Goodman Chapman's Orchard." [23] And there is the well authenticated case, cited by Charles Francis Adams, of the New England minister who refused to baptize children born on the Sabbath in the belief that they had been conceived on the Lord's Day, only to be confounded when his wife gave birth to Sabbath-day twins.[24]

➤➤❯❮❮❮

WHY HAD Puritanism developed such an intense disapproval of sports and games, popular amusements? Where had its stern insistence upon the sanctity of the Sabbath come from? In part these ideas stemmed from the religious dissenters of fourteenth-century England. The revolt of Wycliffe and the Lollards against the worldliness of the Anglican Catholic Church had been directed against all those diversions which the Church of that day freely countenanced. They symbolized in the eyes of these reformers the triumph of evil impulses over truly spiritual values; they could have no place in consecrated lives. But there was also a social bias, a class-conscious protest, in this condemnation of pleasure. The Lollards came from the lower classes—poor, hardworking, struggling to improve their position. They resented the pleasures of the rich—the landed nobility, the dissolute court circle, and the wealthier classes in the towns. It was an easy rationalization of this natural feeling to condemn as sinful the amusements they could not themselves enjoy.[25]

Some two centuries later the Puritans found themselves in very much the same position. They too were a party of reform, condemning the worldliness of the Church and damning as sinful many of the pleasures that the Church countenanced. They too resented the amusements of the more wealthy, leisured classes, making a moral issue of their discontent. These two influences, spiritual reform and economic envy, can never be disentangled. They were both present in the sixteenth and seventeenth centuries, and they have been present in every later-day manifestation of the Puritan spirit. The popular conception of this attitude is expressed in Macaulay's often quoted phrase that the Puritans forbade bear-baiting, not because of the pain it caused the bear, but because of the pleasure it afforded the spectators. But it was rooted in the belief of a people who could not afford to waste time (they were dominated by their middle-class ideals of money-making, getting ahead) that any frivolous use of it was inherently sinful.

There was nothing in the original Calvinistic creed to justify the stern attitude that the Puritans assumed. John Knox once came upon Calvin himself playing at bowls, on a Sunday. So sincere a Puritan as Milton expressed again and again the most lively appreciation of all the joyous aspects of life in Merry England—the sports and games, the holidays

When the merry bells ring round,
And the jocund rebecks sound,
To many a youth and many a maid,
Dancing in the chequered shade.

But as the Puritans struggled to bring about the reforms they thought essential, they grew more and more scornful of the way of life of those who opposed them. Their disapproval of the moral laxity of the leisured classes of society soon covered all their diversions. Their foes jeered at them. On the anvil of persecution, disapproval was hammered into fanatical intolerance.

One of the most bitter sources of conflict between the Puritans and James I revolved around sports and Sabbath observance. Compulsory church attendance was a general rule in the early seventeenth century—not a Puritan invention; but after service the day was often given over to recreation—rough-and-tumble sports, morris-dances, interludes. Obsessed by an Old Testament interpretation of the meaning of the Sabbath, the Puritans took it upon themselves to condemn utterly this carefree enjoyment on the Lord's Day. There should be no sports or games, no dancing or interludes, no amusements whatsoever. They ascribed to God rules for keeping His day holy which were entirely born of their own intolerance.[26]

King James took up this challenge. In 1618 he issued a pronouncement, since known as the Book of Sports, declaring it to be the royal pleasure "that after the end of Divine Service, our good people be not disturbed, letted, or discouraged from any lawfull Recreation; Such as dauncing, either men or women, Archeries for men, leaping, vaulting, or other harmless Recreation, nor from having of May-games, Whitson Ales, and Morris-dances, and the setting up of Maypoles and other sports therewith used. ... But withall We doe accompt still as prohibited all unlawfull games to be used upon Sundayes onely, as Beare and Bull-baiting, Interludes, and at all times in the meaner sort of people by Law prohibited, Bowling." [27]

THE KINGS
MAIESTIES
Declaration to His
Subiects,

CONCERNING
lawfull Sports to
be vsed.

LONDON
Printed by BONHAM NORTON,
and IOHN BILL, Deputie Printers
for the Kings most Excellent
Maiestie.

M.DC.XVIII.

Title-Page of King James I's "Book of Sports"
London, 1618. Courtesy of the New York Public Library.

These were among the pastimes that Englishmen, and among them many of the prospective settlers of Jamestown and Plymouth, Maryland and Massachusetts Bay, were accustomed to enjoy. King James would have encouraged them by annulling Sabbath bans. "For when shall the common people," he asked, "have leave to exercise if not upon the Sundayes and Holidays, seeing they must apply their labour, and winne their living in all working days?" Nevertheless, when their day of power came in England, the Puritans had the Book of Sports publicly burned by the common hangman.[28]

In America, as we have seen, the Puritans took an equally intolerant stand. They had sought out the New World to escape persecution, abandoning the program of reform at home to found a Utopia across the seas. They were determined that here there should be no trace of worldliness. "God hath sifted a nation," William Stoughton declared, "that he might send choice grain into this wilderness."[29] Among these chosen people the pagan festivities, the licentious plays and spectacles, the violations of the Sabbath, the generally dissolute ways which were bringing ruin on England, would not be tolerated. There could be no evil in Zion. From the moment of their first landing on the shores of New England, the leaders of this seventeenth-century exodus set themselves implacably against the slightest infringement of their austere code.

So long as these ideals were allied with the practical necessities of life, so long as the condemnation of idle sports and games conformed to that paramount need for day-long labor on which the very survival of the early settlements depended, Puritanism served the colonies well. The strict rule of magistrates and ministers, for which they generously acknowledged the inspiration of God, emphasized the importance of work during a period when any turning aside toward an easier life might well have doomed New England. This debt to Puritanism is a primary fact in American history. But the rulers of Massachusetts Bay and Connecticut, unlike those of the other colonies, became more and more strict in their insistence upon these rigid rules of conduct as their economic justification gradually lessened.

Suppression became a fetish of the Calvinist mind in the New World. Having convinced themselves that all idle pursuits were a Satanic trap to lure the godly from the path of duty, strict followers of the New England way could no more tolerate frivolity than heresy. Their conscience would not let them enjoy worldly pleasures themselves; it would not let them permit others such enjoyment. The compulsion was equal in either instance. On Christmas Day of 1621, when the greater number of Plymouth colonists had gone about their usual tasks, Governor Bradford was shocked to discover a group of newcomers to that godly community "in the streete at play, openly; some pitching the barr and some at stoole-ball, and such-like sports." He promptly took away their "implements," telling them that while it might be against *their* conscience to work on Christmas, it was against *his* conscience that they should play.[30] New England's magistrates took it upon themselves to control with conspicuous zeal every activity of the people given over to their moral and spiritual guidance. When an opportunity to interfere in any way with other people's lives presented itself, they joyfully answered the still, small voice of duty.

->>)<((-

The attitude of one member of this ruling hierarchy is graphically portrayed in the intimately self-revealing diary kept by Samuel Sewall in the last decade of the seventeenth century and opening years of the eighteenth.[31] Magistrate and elder, Judge Sewall was continually busy with moral problems, counseling others on what they should do and sorrowing over their departure from the narrow path of righteousness. "I was grieved," we find him writing a friend on one occasion, "... when I heard and saw you had drunk to excess; so that your head and hand were rendered less useful than at other times.... I mention this that you may believe I write not of prejudice, but kindness; and out of a sense of duty as indeed I do." Another time, when a party of revelers were drinking the Queen's health with too much enthusiasm, he went out in the middle of the night to remonstrate with them. They refused to go home. He took down their names in his little book—or rather, as he tells us, "not knowing how to spell their names, they themselves of their own accord writ them." [32]

Sewall thoroughly approved when Cotton Mather "struck at the Root, speaking against mixt Dances." He maintained an obdurate stand against the scandalous suggestion of allowing play-acting in Boston and vigorously combated the idea of any holiday festivities: "I took occasion to dehort mine from Christmas-keeping and charged them to forebear." When a dancing-master named Francis Stepney attempted to hold classes, he took a leading part in seeing that they were immediately prohibited. With testy ill-humor he noted "the great disorder in the town" when the English introduced the old sport of cock-skailing, or throwing sticks at a cock. "Jos. Mayhem carries a cock at his back, with a Bell in's hand, in the Main Street," he wrote scornfully; "several follow him blindfold, and under pretence of striking him or's cock, with great cart whips strike passengers, and make great disturbance." [33]

Nevertheless he had his own simple pleasures. He thoroughly enjoyed good food and wine: his diary bears frequent witness to his fondness for "rost Beef and minc'd Pyes, good Cheese and Tarts," and he had a special liking for black-cherry brandy with a lump of sugar in it. His appreciation of nature was surprising. We find him noting happily that "the Singing of Birds is come," and of seeing "Six Swallows flying together and chipering very rapturously." Another time he speaks of walking in a friend's orchard and getting quiet enjoyment out of "pushing Catterpillars off the Appletrees." It is also suddenly revealing to find in the memorable account of his courtship of Madame Winthrop the passage where he tells his lady that he came to see her only every other night for fear he would drink too deep draughts of pleasure—"She had talk'd Canary, her kisses were to me better than the best Canary." [34]

Other diversions more generally centered about the good judge's religious life. He often went to service, gladly riding several miles to the Great and Thursday at some outlying town, taking his wife, or perhaps his mother-in-law, on the pillion behind him. He led what went for singing at his own meeting-house. There were only a few mournful repetitive tunes in the Puritan repertory, to which were sung such strange distortions of the Psalms as

> Within their mouths doe thou their teeth
> break out O God most strong,
> Doe thou Jehovah, the great teeth
> break, of the lions young.

'I set York tune and the congregation went out of it into St. David's in the very 2nd. going over," Sewall wrote in his diary one day. "This seems to me an intimation and a call for me to resign the precentor's place to a better voice. I have through the Divine long suffering and favor done it for 24 years." [35]

This upright man found real enjoyment in seeing punishments properly administered, whether it was a whipping or a hanging, and he had that morbid preoccupation with death which was one of the most unpleasing of Puritan characteristics. He took a melancholy pleasure in serving as a pall-bearer at funerals, making a great collection of the gloves and rings with which custom decreed the pall-bearer should be rewarded. He was always happy to undertake this congenial task—unless he disapproved of the deceased's morals. But the obsession with death found most startling expression in his account of how he spent one Christmas. One of his daughters had recently died. Sewall passed the day in the family tomb: "I was entertained with a view of, and converse with the coffins. . . . 'Twas an awful yet pleasing Treat." [36]

—»x«—

IN THESE varied pleasures—spying upon one's neighbors, upholding public morals, going to church meetings, morbidly contem-
plating death—the Puritan leaders might find some compensation
for the amusements of which they deprived themselves. But they
could not possibly satisfy the needs of the humbler members
of the community whose instinct for play could not so easily be
eradicated. Even when these men and women in the ordinary
walks of life were wholly in sympathy with the rule of the
church, it was not enough for them to attend service and go to
funerals. And increasingly large numbers of New Englanders
were not Puritans. During the Great Migration even, between
1630 and 1640, only some four thousand out of sixteen thousand
arrivals in Massachusetts Bay were church members. The rigid
requirements for membership made it entirely possible for a
majority even of the non-members to be in sympathy with the
church, but nevertheless there was a dissident element in the
colony from the very first. And it steadily grew as more and
more people poured into New England whose motives for
seeking the New World had nothing to do with religion.

In their zeal to maintain godliness, to enforce general con-
formity with their own principles of conduct, the magistrates
failed signally to take this group into consideration. Whatever
may be said for the first generation of Puritan leaders, their
successors' inability to recognize the need of the people as a
whole for a freer outlet to the normal urge for recreation was
continually adding fuel to the discontent of the non-Puritans.
They began to consider the restraints imposed upon them an
intolerable burden. Worn out by the endless work on their little
farms, discouraged by poor harvests, fearful of famine, plague,
or Indian attack, they had to have some release for pent-up
emotions, some way to forget the world.

Many of them—and this was true not only in New England
but in all the colonies—found it in drinking. The tavern sprang
up as naturally as the meeting-house, and the conviviality of the
tap-room met a genuine need. They came of good drinking stock,

these New World pioneers, and the early lack of malt and spirituous liquors had been for a time a great cause for complaint. It is revealing to find how proud one godly minister was because he had learned to drink water, and to note another worthy writing home that while he did not yet prefer water to good beer as some professed to do, "any man would choose it before Bad Beere, Wheay, or Buttermilk." [37] Nevertheless the Puritans did not allow any pernicious habit of water-drinking to take hold. Beer and cider were soon plentiful; rum became a New England staple. The taverns and ordinaries everywhere offered an engaging selection of drinks to gratify every taste.[38]

Drunkenness was a frequent consequence of their growing popularity. The early records show many cases of fines, confinement in the stocks, and public whippings for an overindulgence which the lower classes (the indentured servants, the apprentices, the laborers) could hardly avoid with rum at two shillings a gallon. Sometimes the penalty of public scorn was administered. "Robert Cole, having been oft punished for drunkenness," John Winthrop reports in his history of Plymouth (an anything but isolated case even for that sober community), "was now ordered to wear a red D about his neck for a year." [39]

The increase in drinking and its attendant evils was largely due to the lack of other entertainment and to the promotion by tavern-keepers of what was a very profitable business. By the middle of the seventeenth century the General Court was compelled to recognize that it had created a serious social problem. "How has Wyne and Cider, but most of all Rum debauched Multitudes of People," exclaimed the redoubtable Increase Mather. Viewing the fearful circumstances into which Connecticut had been brought, Cotton Mather somewhat later declared somberly that "the consequences of the affected Bottel, in that Colony, as well as in ours, are beyond Imagination." [40]

Many other instances might be cited to show the extent to which tavern drinking took the place of other amusements in these days of Puritan repression. One law deplored the growing

custom whereby on pretext of going to midweek church meetings, men and women rode from town to town "to drinke and
revell in ordinarys and tavernes." An irate clergy thundered the
warning that "the Riots that have too often accompanied our
Huskings have carried in them fearfull Ingratitude and Provo-
cation unto the Glorious God." [41]

It may well be noted, however, that it was not in New England but in what has so often been called Cavalier Virginia that
an attempt was made in the seventeenth century to enforce
prohibition. For all his alarms, even Increase Mather accepted
the need for taverns to sell liquor. "No sober Minister," he declared, "will speak against the Licensing of them." [42] But an
Assembly dominated by Nathaniel Bacon passed a law, in 1676,
taking their licenses from all taverns in Virginia except those
at Jamestown and at the two main ferries on the York. These
privileged ordinaries were permitted to sell beer and cider, but
otherwise a fine of one thousand pounds of tobacco was to be
imposed on any one who sold "any sorte of drinke or liquor
whatsoever to be drunke or spent in his or their house or houses,
upon his or their plantations." [43]

It was not only in drinking that New England was breaking
through the bonds of Puritan restraint. The diary of Samuel
Sewall itself affords graphic evidence of the revolt against repression. Its accounts of the pageantry of Joseph Mayhew, parad-
ing through the streets of Boston with cock and bell; of attempts
to stage plays and hold dancing-classes; of the celebration of
Christmas festivities, all reveal a departure from the original
severity of life in New England.

This is shown also in many of the laws that the magistrates
found it necessary to pass after the middle of the seventeenth
century. They are fully as indicative of what certain elements in
the growing towns of New England were actually doing as of
what their rulers were determined they should not do. Laws on
the statute books often have this paradoxical significance. The
future student of twentieth-century legislation will be quite

justified in assuming that our prohibition laws reflected the popularity of drinking quite as much as they represented an authori-
tarian attempt to impose a dry régime. In the same way, much
of the legislation of early New England forbidding tavern
sports, card-playing, and dancing throws a penetrating light on
how a very considerable number of the people were spending
such free time as they had. Not the rulers and magistrates, but
the everyday people of the Puritan world.

This is illustrated in successive edicts with respect to observance of the Sabbath. We learn from the statute books that
on Saturday and Sunday young people were more and more
freely taking "liberty to walk and sport themselves in the streets
and fields . . . and too frequently repair to public houses of
entertainment and there sit drinking." [44] Finally it even became
necessary to forbid, on Sunday and in the neighborhood of
meeting-houses, "all shouting, hollowing, screaming, running,
riding, singing, dancing, jumping, winding horns or the like." [45]
Here are glimpses of a Puritan Sabbath oddly at variance with
copy-book and historical legend. Some of the youths and maidens
of old New England, for all the insistence of the godly that the
Sabbath should be a day of peace and quiet, appear to have
utilized it for a little restrained hell-raising in vociferous protest
against the laws.

Indeed, at no time after the very first years of settlement was
the New England scene actually as devoid of all amusements
as it is so often said to have been. The Puritans have been depicted as a "crowd of sad-visaged people moving duskily through
a dull gray atmosphere"; their social life has been termed "bare
and spiritless beyond the possibility of description." [46] But this
is to take at their face value the repressive edicts of the magis-
tracy. It ignores the place in New England's life of the large
number of its settlers who were non-Puritan in their sympathies
and who could hardly be compelled by magisterial fiat to accept
the idea that pleasure was synonomous with sin.

Those two stern guardians of public morals, Increase and

Cotton Mather, had no doubts as to what was happening in the closing years of the seventeenth century. The iniquities of the younger generation were causing the glory of the Lord to depart from New England. "How many there are amongst us whose Fathers in coming into the Wilderness, designed nothing but Religion," declared Increase. "But *they* are for another Interest. Their Hearts are not but for the World. . . . That there is a general defection in New England from Primitive Purity and Piety in many respects is so plain that it cannot be denied." Cotton labored under no such restraints in characterizing the age. "Some of our Rising Generation," he stated, "have been given up to the most abominable Impieties of Uncleaness, Drunkeness, and a Lewd, Rude Extravagant sort of Behaviour. There are the Children of Belial among them, and Prodigies of Wickedness." [47]

The Mathers often found evil in what another age would freely condone. Many of their "prodigies of wickedness" would to-day go unrecognized under such a description. Their fierce onslaughts against the rising generation reflected a bitterness at their own departing glory as well as at the departing glory of the Lord. At the same time it was inevitable that reaction to the stern rule Puritanism attempted to impose should in some cases lead to extremes. For in forbidding so many forms of normal recreation the elders and magistrates had only served to confuse moral values. When they instituted such strict laws as to forbid, according to one traveler in Connecticut, "even a harmless Kiss or Innocent merriment among Young people," [48] they were asking for trouble. Human nature could not be flouted with impunity, even by professed men of God.

→⟫⟪←

PURITANISM failed to eradicate the early Americans' natural urge for play. It brought on the inevitable revolt against attempted suppression of human impulses. Nevertheless it left a deep imprint on the mind of New England. And for all the growth of more liberal ideas as the power of the clergy and magistrates declined, some part of the old intolerance lingered on. The northern colonies were always more restricted in their diversions than the middle colonies or the South.

The spirit of Puritanism still has an important influence on our recreational life. Conditions have so greatly changed that our whole idea of leisure-time activities has been completely transformed. The suspicion with which church and state three centuries ago viewed all diversions in their common "detestation of idleness" has given way to the active encouragement and promotion of every form of healthful amusement. But there is certainly more than a trace of the old Puritanism, whatever other factors in a capitalistic society may enter the picture, in an attitude which so often views the increase in present-day opportunities for recreation as the "problem of leisure."

Chapter II

HUSKING-BEES AND TAVERN SPORTS

As the economic security of the little communities that stretched along the eastern fringe of America from Maine to South Carolina gradually increased, colonial life took on many new aspects. The opening of the eighteenth century marked a far departure from the first days of settlement. The South had almost completely broken away from earlier restraints; New England's outlook was beginning to broaden. The colonists generally sought out and developed opportunities for recreation they had not before had time to enjoy. Among the common people, the great mass of yeomanry who made up nine-tenths of the population, the English love of games and sports was reasserting itself. An eager welcome was accorded all possible amusements.

It is not always easy to discover just what form this recreation took. The short and simple annals of the poor are no more revealing on this phase of their life than of other aspects. But there is sufficient evidence to show that they found many ways to enjoy themselves. And the common experience of colonial farmers in hunting and in shooting contests, in simple country sports, in the communal activities of training days and barn-raisings, played its part in the welding of a nation. These phases of colonial recreation more truly reflect the life of eighteenth-century America than the social activities of Boston's wealthy merchants, the dancing assemblies of New York, or the fox-hunts of Virginia.

Rural life in New England was still hard and laborious. It was back-breaking to induce crops to grow in that stony soil. Nevertheless there were compensations which other farming communities in this country have not always enjoyed. The original settlers had taken up their land in townships, close to one another, with communal pasturage for their stock. And the town had its meeting-house, its tavern, and later its town hall. The people from the surrounding countryside could easily gather for their Sunday church services and midweek lectures; they could meet on more festive occasions at the tavern. There was no isolation in the life of colonial New England comparable to that in the Middle West a century and more later when the pioneers of the prairie states were so widely scattered on their far-separated quarter-sections.

The middle colonies, despite their large trading towns, were also a primarily agricultural community. But in addition to farms comparable to those of New England, there were the great estates of the Dutch patroons along the Hudson, and in Pennsylvania and western New York many rough frontier settlements. Conditions were more varied than in New England, and the population with its infiltration of Scotch-Irish and Germans much more mixed. Consequently we find amusements and diversions greatly restricted in some sections and in others freely enjoyed. The influence of Dutch Calvinists and Pennsylvania Quakers was offset by the greater liberalism of other groups in the population.

In the South highly distinctive economic and social conditions prevailed. While the land to a great extent was held in small farms during the seventeenth century and the staple crops of tobacco or rice were grown by as independent and self-respecting a yeomanry as that of the North, the growth of slavery with its substitution of Negro labor for white indentured servants wrought a gradual transformation during the next century. It led to the creation of large plantations which made it more and more difficult for the small farmers to maintain their position. Slave competition, exhaustion of the soil, and lower prices for tobacco drove many of them to the new lands in the west and tended to reduce those who remained near tidewater to the status of poor whites. Nevertheless the southern yeomanry continued to make up the bulk of southern population, sometimes themselves owning one or two slaves with whom they worked in the tobacco fields. Their rôle in colonial life was still an important one.

Recreation for this class corresponded in many respects to that of the comparable class in the North. But the farms were more widely separated, without centralizing townships as in New England. The small planters often led a more lonely life. On the other hand, a warmer climate and more productive soil made possible greater leisure, while the institution of slavery, tending to deprive work of the nobility with which the Puritans clothed it, was a further influence contributing to an easy-going attitude in the use of this leisure.

->>|<<-

Now THAT the early Americans were beginning to feel at home in field and forest, hunting and fishing could be enjoyed as sport. The wealth of game drew out the townsman as well as the farmer, the New Englander as well as the Carolinian. Deer were plentiful everywhere, and the wild-fowl so numerous that account after account describes flocks of wild turkeys or pigeons darkening the skies. Moose ranged through the still unbroken forests of New England; wolves preyed upon the outlying settlements of Connecticut; bear and panther were hunted in the backwoods of Virginia, and buffalo could be found in the western parts of South Carolina.

"Bears, Deer, Beavers, Otters, Foxes, Racounes (almost as big as a Fox, as good meat as a lamb) Hares, wild cats, musk rats, Squirrels (flying and other sorts) and Apossumes of the bignesse and likenesse of a Pigge of a month old . . ." reads Ralph Hamor's list of early Virginia's game. "Eagles, wild Turkeys (much larger than our English), Cranes, Herons (white and russet), Hawks, wild pigeons (in winter beyond number or imagination, myself have seen three or four hours together flocks

Bear-Baiting

English tavern sports transplanted in America. From *The Sporting Magazine*, London, 1795 and 1801.

Skittles

"The Hill Tops," a New Hunting Song

The first sporting picture in an American periodical. *Royal American Magazine*, 1774.

in the air, so thick that even they have shadowed the sky from us), Turkey Buzzards, Partridges, Snipers, Owls, Swans, Geese, Brants, Ducks, and Mallards, Divers, Shel Drakes, Cormorants, Teale, Widgeon, Curlews, Puits, besides other small birds, as, Blackbird, hedge sparrows, oxeies, woodpeckers, and in winter about Christmas many flocks of Parakertoths.... For Fish—the Rivers are plentifully stored, with Sturgeon, Porpasse, Base, Rockfish, Carpe, Shad, Herring, Ele, Catfish, Perch, Flat-fish, Trout, Sheepshead, Drummers, Jarfish, Crevises, Crabs, Oysters and diverse other kinds." [1]

Farmers of Massachusetts and Connecticut enjoyed squirrel hunts, went out often after raccoons and also banded together to hunt wolves. In New London ten to forty men met together every autumn to beat up the swamps and kill these "pernicious creatures."

There was a great deal of fishing. John Rowe, an enthusiastic angler, noted in his diary a day's catch of five dozen large trout— "extraordinary sport." It had been vouchsafed religious approval in Joseph Seccombe's discourse "utter'd in part at Ammauskeeg-Falls, in the Fishing-season, 1739." "If I may eat them [fish] for Refreshment," this worthy divine contended, "I may as well catch them if this recreate and refresh me. It's as lawful to delight the Eye as the Palate." [2] Even Cotton Mather fished. Samuel Sewall tells of the time when the stern old Puritan went out with line and tackle and fell into the water at Spy Pond, "the boat being ticklish."

Long Island was a veritable fish and game paradise. New Yorkers "went out a shooting" regularly at the opening of the century, as the journal of the Reverend John Sharp reveals, [3] and somewhat later we find the sport lending an element of considerable hazard to the lives of the island's settlers. In 1734 a woman was shot accidentally when taken for a fox. "The fatal mistake," reads the old record, "was occasioned by her wearing an Orange Brown Wast-Coat. The man is in a very melancholy condition." The newspaper account of the incident advised shortsighted hunters to go farther west where their mistakes might not be so costly.[4]

"They have hunting, fishing and fowling, with which they entertain themselves in an hundred ways," Robert Beverly wrote of Virginians.[5] The farmers joined in moonlight excursions after opossum as they have done ever since, but a far more exciting sport was hunting the wild horses which ranged through the backwoods. In the Carolinas deer were hunted on horseback, the planters taking a stand and having their beaters drive the deer past them. Sometimes such expeditions were held at night, the huntsmen well fortified with brandy and accompanied by Negroes carrying pans of burning charcoal to serve as flares. In 1784 they were made a misdemeanor because of the inadvertent slaughter of so many cows and horses.[6]

How general hunting was in the South is shown in a statement in George Alsop's seventeenth-century account of life in Maryland: "For every Servant has a Gun, Powder and Shot allowed him, to sport withall on all Holidays and leasurable times. . . ." [7]

⤐⤏ ⤜⤛

Although they were relatively rare, gatherings at training days and elections, at country fairs, corn-huskings, and barn-raisings, provided welcome breaks in the monotony of farm life. Folk-dancing and folk-music were enjoyed on these occasions, with the singing of the popular English ballads which were being hawked through the countryside, even of Massachusetts, as early as 1680. There were sports—shooting at a mark, foot-races, wrestling matches—and a great deal of convivial drinking. "Possibly this leafe may last a century," reads an entry for October 14, 1766, in the diary of Nathaniel Ames, a young man living in Dedham, Massachusetts, "and fall into the hands of some inquisitive Person for whose Entertainment I will inform him that now there is the custom amongst us of making an Entertainment at husking of Indian Corne whereunto all the neighboring Swains are invited, and after the Corn is finished they, like the Hottentots, give three cheers or huzzas, but cannot carry in the husks without a Rhum bottle. They feign great exertion, but do nothing until the Rhum enlivens them, when all is done in a trice; then, after a hearty meal about 10 at night, they go to their pastimes." [8]

There is a somewhat unpuritanic record of certain of these pastimes in a poem of another countryman, Jacob Bailey, probably written when he was teaching school at Kingston, New Hampshire, about 1755:

> The chairs in wild disorder flew quite round the room.
> Some threatened with firebrands, some brandished a broom,
> While others, resolved to increase the uproar,
> Lay tussling the girls in wide heaps on the floor.[9]

It was the custom at the "frolic scene," as is well known, for the young man who might find a red ear of corn to claim a kiss from whatever damsel he chose. On one occasion—it was in a day when strict Puritan supervision was responsible for the story being spread on the town records—difficulties arose over the interpretation of this genial law of the husking-bee. James Chicester found a red ear and promptly kissed Bette Scudder. But the young lady objected and somewhat bluntly told him she "would whip his brick." In the ensuing scuffle Goody Scudder came to her daughter's defense, and the unfortunate James was fined twelve shillings for his temerity.[10]

Quite different is the story of Sarah Tuttle, similarly honored by one Jacob Murline. "They sat down together," we learn again from the court records, "his arm being about her, and her arm upon his shoulder or about his neck, and hee kissed her and shee kissed him, or they kissed one another, continuing in this posture about half an hour." This was too much for the elders, and Jacob was hailed before the magistrate on a charge of "inveigling" Sarah. But Sarah promptly owned up that there had been no inveigling: she had wanted to be kissed. The shocked magistrate thereupon denounced her for a "Bould Virgin," and although she demurely acknowledged her error, expressing the hope that

"God would help her to Carry it Better for time to come," a heavy fine was imposed.[11]

The flirtations and love-affairs of young people naturally suggest the curious custom of bundling, widely prevalent in New England and Pennsylvania. Its origin was supposedly found (although the custom has also been noted among other peoples) in the premium placed on heat and light in those early days of settlement when the whole family had to roll up together in front of the open fire on cold winter evenings. A visitor could be offered only such hospitality as the house afforded, and consequently bundling became among country people a natural and accepted form of courtship. Andrew Burnaby, writing as late as 1775, describes how the young folk in a home he was visiting got into bed together—"but without pulling off their undergarments, in order to prevent scandal." On a tour through Pennsylvania at the close of the century, John Bernard also noted the custom under the name of "tarrying." He reported that in extending the hospitality of her bed it was customary for the girl to take the thoughtful precaution of "confining her petticoat to her ankles." [12]

Bundling was not always as safe as these measures would suggest. The approving Mr. Burnaby wrote that pregnancy was "an accident that seldom happens," but at times all precautions failed. In the case of engaged couples, however, public disapproval of premarital relations was tempered, even in the strictest circles, by the desirability of large families in a primitive farming community. Marriage expiated all guilt. In 1722 there was nothing out of the way in a Harvard student society's publicly debating "Whether it be Fornication to lye with ones Sweetheart (after contract) before Marriage?" [13]

Nevertheless bundling of itself certainly did not imply any improper relationship. It was perhaps the eighteenth-century equivalent of the buggy drive of the next century, or of the evening automobile ride of our present age. Abigail Adams refers casually to it in several of her letters. There is a comfortable description

of bucolic life in Royall Tyler's play *The Contrast:* "twenty acres
of rock, the Bible, Tabitha, and a little peaceable bundling." A
young Connecticut girl gaily records in her 1775 diary how sister
Ellen bundled "till sun about 3 hours high," adding

> If I won't take my sparks to bed
> A laughing stock I shall be made.[14]

→≫≪←

"THEIR DIVERSIONS in this part of the Country," wrote Madame
Sarah Knight, as that "fearfull female travailer," journeyed
through Connecticut in 1704, "are on Lecture days and Training
days mostly: on the former there is Riding from town to town. . . .
And on Training dayes the Youth divert themselves by Shooting
at the Target, as they call it, (but it very much resembles a
pillory,) when hee that hitts neerest the white has some yards
of Red Ribbin presented him, which being tied to his hattband,
the two ends streaming down his back, he is led away in
Triumph, with great applause, as the winners of the Olympiack
Games." [15]

No less a one than Judge Sewall used to attend training days
in Boston, where upwards of a thousand men would gather on
the Common to drill, practise markmanship, and then celebrate
the day in more lively fashion. "Go to prayer. March down and
shoot at a mark," was his usual laconic description of this great
event. But he also records that on one occasion he presented
his company, as a prize for marksmanship, with a pike headed
and shod with silver, which he supposed would stand him some
forty shillings. On another he had the entire company to his
house and treated them with bread, beer, and wine syllabub. A
third time, after some recent bereavement, he gives a pathetic
picture of marching sadly off to muster: "I put on my mourning
rapier, and put a black ribbon in my little cane." [16]

The celebration of training days, as of election days and court
days, almost invariably ended in a general descent upon the local
tavern. There was no other occasion when colonial neighbors so

much enjoyed passing around a friendly bottle. At the opening
of the eighteenth century, Cotton Mather was already thundering against "Training Days become little other than Drinking
Dayes," but though his voice reached throughout New England,
it was more and more ignored. And going south, through the
middle colonies into Virginia and the Carolinas, it would have
been hard to say whether there was more or less drinking. There
is, for instance, the evidence of Ebenezer Cook, from his
memorable "Sot-Weed Factor," which relates the traveler's experience on seeking out the tavern on a Maryland court day:

> A Herd of Planters on the ground,
> O'er-whelmed with Punch, dead drunk we found.[17]

Country fairs drew crowds of merrymakers. The social gatherings in New England were more likely to be associated with
useful communal work—house-raisings, sheep-shearings, log-
rollings, or husking-bees; but Virginia more naturally had meetings where there was little pretense of utility and a wide variety
of diversions. Here was in evidence more of the spirit of Merry
England than Puritans could easily express—horse-racing, chasing
a greased pig, dancing on green lawns.

An advertisement in the *Virginia Gazette* for October, 1737,
tells of some of these sports and the prizes offered for them. It
was proposed that a pair of silver buckles be wrestled for; that a
pair of handsome shoes be danced for; that a hat of the value of
twenty shillings be cudgeled for; that a violin be played for by
twenty fiddlers; that a quire of Ballads be sung for by a number
of songsters; and "that a pair of handsome Silk Stockings of one
Pistole value be given to the handsomest young country maid
that appears in the field." In the case of the songsters it was
announced that they would be allowed "liquor sufficient to clear
their wind pipes," but the advertisement closed with the admoni-
tion that "as this mirth is designed to be purely innocent and void
of offence, all persons resorting there are desired to behave themselves with decency and sobriety." [18]

Still another colonial holiday was the college commencement. At Harvard, Yale, and Princeton, graduation exercises drew not only "a vast concourse of the politest company" to listen to the day's oratory and debates, but also crowds of simple country folk who made the occasion one for horse-racing, games, dancing, and drinking. "Fe-o, whiraw, whiraw, hi, fal, lal, fal, lal, lal, de lal dal, a fine song: commencement is over whiraw I say again whiraw whiraw," wrote one exuberant graduate of Nassau Hall who would appear to have confused those phases of commencement intended for the student body with the more general celebration of the day.[19]

At Harvard too the exercises did not always conform to the expected academic traditions. The day's activities were satirically recorded early in the eighteenth century:

> Some spend the Time at Pins (that toilsome Play)
> Others at cards (more silent) pass the Day.
> In rings some Wrestle till they're mad outright,
> And then their Antagonists they fight.
>
> On Horses some to ride full Tilt along
> Are seen; while on each side a Numerous Throng
> Do gaze. . . .
> Others (as brutish) do propagate their Kind:
> Where amorous Lads to shady Groves resort,
> And under Venus with their Misses sport.[20]

The colonial colleges had to change the date of commencement in order to prevent the occasion from turning into too festive a celebration. Nassau Hall shifted it from autumn to spring in the hope that their planting and sowing might keep the farmers at home.

->>>«<-

THESE FÊTE-DAYS were not the only occasion for sports. "This is to give Notice," reads an announcement in the *Boston News-Letter* of August 22-29, 1715, "that at Cambridge on Wednesday the 21st day of September next, will be run for, a Twenty Pound

How to Mount a Horse

Philip Astley, *The Modern Riding Master*, Philadelphia, 1776.

Plate, by any Horse, Mare or Gelding not exceeding Fourteen and half hands high. . . ." [21] There are many records of cockfights —"fought cocks in the Town House" is one surprising entry in the diary of a Salem resident in 1744—and also of New England bull-baitings and bear-baitings.[22] But while members of the Puritan communities appear to have enjoyed these spectacles, they were much more common in the South than in the North. Activities in which the people themselves could take part were the more general rule in Massachusetts and Connecticut. Sleighing was a favorite winter diversion; in the summer men and boys went swimming. Many accounts refer to cricket, "bat & Ball," and football.[23]

"The place we went to was a Town call'd Rowley, where most of the inhabitants had been Clothiers," John Dunton wrote during his New England travels in 1686; "but there was that Day a great game of Foot-Ball to be play'd with their bare feet, which I thought was very odd; but it was upon a broad Sandy Shoar, free from Stones, which made it more easy. Neither were they so apt to trip up one anothers heels and quarrel, as I have seen 'em in England." [24] A century later William Bentley also speaks of football as being played by the fishermen of Marblehead. "The bruising of shins," he adds to his account, "has rendered it rather disagreeable to those of better education, who use a hand ball, thrown up against an house or fence instead of the Foot Ball, which is unfriendly to clothes as well as safety." [25]

In New York the influence of the Dutch settlers made bowling the most popular pastime, and on the basis of Sabbath-day regulations forbidding certain amusements during the hours of service (not for the entire day as in the case of New England), there were "Dancing, Card-playing, Tick-tacking [a type of backgammon], Playing at ball, at bowls, at ninepins; taking jaunts in Boats, Wagons or Carriages." [26] Another regulation, passed in the days when New York was still New Amsterdam, prohibited picking strawberries on Sunday, and it would seem to merit description as a Long Island sport.

"Such abundance of strawberries is in June," Daniel Denton wrote, "that the fields and woods are dyed red; which the country people perceiving, instantly arm themselves with bottles of wine, cream and sugar, and instead of a coat of Mail every one takes a Female upon his Horse behind him, and so rushing violently into the fields, never leave them till they have disrobed them of their colors and turned them into the old habit." [27]

Winter brought out many skaters, a sport for which the Dutch again were primarily responsible. Ice carnivals, where the tradespeople set up little booths selling liquor and sweetmeats, were held with racing and hockey. The children coasted; in Albany regulations had to be passed for the protection of pedestrians. [28]

In the southern colonies the stratified social order based on the ownership of large plantations sometimes led to the drawing of class lines in sports activities. While the diversions of the semiannual fair at Williamsburg in the middle of the eighteenth century were apparently open to all comers, Sir Francis Nicholson had in 1691 instituted a more exclusive series of athletic games. He offered prizes "to be shott for, wrasttled, played at back-swords, & run for by Horse and foott," but expressly provided that "all which prizes are to be shott for and played for by the better sort of Virginians only, who are Batchelors." [29]

One of the earliest records of horse-racing, which was to become Virginia's most popular sport, also has this undemocratic note. A tailor was fined in 1674 for "haveing made a race for his mare to runn with a horse belonging to Mr. Mathew Slader for twoe thousand pounds of tobacco and cash, it being contrary to law for a Labourer to make a race, being a sport for Gentlemen." [30] But the interest of every Virginian—"almost every ordinary person keeps a horse," wrote a traveler early in the next century [31]—made it impossible to restrict racing to the gentry. Entirely apart from the fashionable meets at Williamsburg or Annapolis, with their expensive trophies and heavy betting, it became a universal feature of country life. The wealthy planters might have their blooded horses and imported stock, but the small farmer was ready to make a match with his own riding horse anywhere and any time. Quarter-racing (an informal quarter-mile match) was a leading village sport, one visitor noting on occasion how the course was lined with a "motley multitude of negroes, Dutchmen, Yankee pedlers, and back-woodsmen." [32]

Cock-fighting was another pastime distinctive of plantation life, far more popular than in New England. Its pitched mains attracted spectators of all ranks, plantation owner, poor white, and Negro slave hovering together over the pit. "The roads as we approached the scene," wrote a northern visitor, "were alive with carriages, horses, and pedestrians, black and white, hastening to the point of attraction. Several houses formed a spacious square, in the center of which was arranged a large cock-pit; surrounded by many genteel people, promiscuously mingled with the vulgar and debased." He was enthusiastic over the beauty of the cocks and their amazing gameness, but it was too much for him: "I soon sickened at this barbarous sport, and retired under the shade of a widespread willow." [33]

Many of the visitors to the southern colonies, both those from the North and those from Europe, were shocked by the rôle that horse-racing and cock-fighting appeared to play in the lives of the people. They seemed to have time for nothing else. "The Common Planters," Hugh Jones wrote in 1724 with some asperity, "don't much admire Labour or any other manly exercise except Horse racing, nor diversion, except Cock-Fighting, in which some greatly delight. This easy Way of Living, and the Heat of the Summer make some very lazy, who are then said to be Climate-struck." [34] At the close of the century the Marquis of Chastellux was even more critical. "The indolence and dissipation of the middling and lower classes of white inhabitants of Virginia," he declared, "are such as to give pain to every reflecting mind. Horse racing, cock fighting, and boxing matches are standing amusements, for which they neglect all business." [35]

>>><<<

OTHER AMUSEMENTS common to all the colonies were those associated with the taverns. The bans upon unlawful games imposed by the Puritans have already been noted as indicating diversions which the colonists in New England surreptitiously enjoyed even in the seventeenth century. In later years there was a progressive relaxation in the enforcement of these rules. Instances may be found in which the licenses granted innkeepers still prohibited all cards, dice, ninepins, and shuffle-board, but open advertisements in the colonial newspapers may be set against obsolete statutes. The tavern was a social center, primarily for drinking, but also for all manner of popular pastimes.[36]

"In most country towns," John Adams wrote of New England in 1761, "... you will find almost every other house with a sign of entertainment before it.... If you sit the evening, you will find the house full of people, drinking drams, flip, toddy, carousing, swearing."[37] There were not as many towns to support taverns in the South, and the isolation of the plantations made people of all classes so eager to entertain chance travelers that keepers of ordinaries complained that their business was one hardly worth following. Nevertheless they could always be found at the county-seats and at the frequent ferry crossings.

An advertisement in the *New England Courant* for April 30, 1722, announced that a public house in Charlestown, Massachusetts, had tables for those who "had a Mind to Recreate themselves with a Game of Billiards."[38] Alexander Macraby singled out what he thought a vile practice in the taverns of New York: "I mean that of playing backgammon (a noise I detest) which is going forward in the public coffee-houses from morning till night, frequently ten or a dozen tables at a time."[39] Dicing was even more popular, fines for playing it having to be imposed upon apprentices, journeymen, servants, and sailors. In Virginia a traveler speaks of finding planters at cards and ninepins even in the early morning hours.

Shooting matches, a favorite amusement of the colonial farmer north and south, were often held at the local tavern. With an

eye to trade the landlord would put up prizes, generally the
fowls that were used as marks. He could count on a tidy profit
from the drinking which was such an essential part of the event.
"There will be a Bear, and a Number of Turkeys set up as a
Mark next Thursday Beforenoon," reads an advertisement of
one such contest, "at the Punch Bowl Tavern in Brookline." [40]

In addition to providing games and also serving as headquarters for cock-fights and animal baitings, the tavern was a
popular place for country dances. It was not only the colonial
aristocracy who danced in the eighteenth century. This diversion
was enjoyed by all classes. Although Puritan prejudice was never
entirely dissipated, the rôle of ordination balls in Connecticut
social life indicates how much the attitude had changed. The
tavern-keeper's bill for one of these affairs included seventy-
four bowls of punch, twenty-eight bottles of wine, and eight
bowls cf brandy.[41] At the close of the century a contemporary
historian declared that dancing had become "the principal and
favorite amusement in New England; and of this the young
people of both sexes are extremely fond." [42] Its hold upon the
South may be illustrated by the will of Charles Carter. He carefully stipulated, in 1762, that his daughters should be "brought
up frugally and taught to dance." [43]

Country people did not dance "la minuet de la cour, with the
gavet," or "la minuet ordinaire with pas grave," so popular with
the gentry. Their dances were jigs and reels, gay and boisterous,
the square dances still known in rural communities. They
amazed one sophisticated observer in the South. "These dances
are without method or regularity," he wrote. "A gentleman and
lady stand up, and dance about the room, one of them retiring
and the other pursuing, then perhaps meeting, in an irregular
fantastical manner. After some time another lady gets up, and
then the first lady must sit down, she being, as they term it, cut
out. The second lady acts the same part which the first did, till
somebody cuts her out. The gentlemen perform in the same
manner." He added ungraciously that "in this they discover

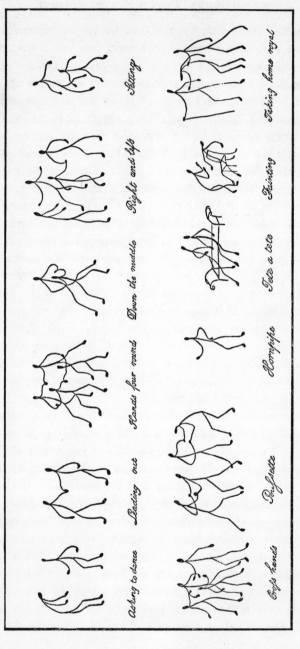

The Square Dance

The Port Folio, 1817.

great want of taste and elegance and seldom appear with the grace and ease which those movements are so calculated to display." [44] To another traveler the "latitude of shuffle" and alternate pursuit of lady and gentleman in these country dances appeared to test "at every turn the respective strength of their sinews." [45]

The music might be a small orchestra of flute, viol, and spinnet, as provided by Benjamin Parker for the dance-hall in his tavern at Medford, Massachusetts. It was more generally furnished by an ancient fiddler or Negro slave with strumming banjo. Farm boys and girls, in leather jerkins and homespun gowns, asked only that the tune be lively. Often they danced until dawn, and sometimes they appear to have spent all their substance on the flips and toddy so obligingly sold by the tavern-keeper. There is a plea in one colonial paper respectfully asking those who had attended a recent dance "to pay the honest fiddler for his trouble and wearing out of his strings, for he gathered but 12d. among the whole company." [46]

Occasionally a traveling performer—acrobat, tight-rope dancer, juggler, the exhibitor of a learned dog or sapient pig—appeared at the tavern to provide the villagers with amusement of a quite different sort. It was a rare event. Such entertainment was seldom found except in the larger towns. Nevertheless there were some forerunners of the traveling wagon shows which in another century were gradually to evolve into the circus.

A wild animal always proved a popular exhibition in town or country. The earliest notice of one appears somewhat mysteriously in Samuel Sewall's diary, in 1714: "May 12. In a piece of Gazett, mentioned, a large Dromedary seven foot high, and 12 foot long, taken from the Turks at the Siege of Vienna, to be sold." [47] Was this dromedary actually in America? If so, it must have been an appalling apparition as it soberly paraded through the twisted lanes of puritan Boston at the opening of the eighteenth century. A few years later a lion was taken on tour throughout the northern colonies, royally caged in an ox cart.

His progress may be traced from Boston to Philadelphia. Somewhat later he appears again in New London, having in the meantime been as far north as Albany. Nor did he neglect Long Island. The *New York Gazette* in May, 1728, stated in its announcement of the Jamaica fair, "It is expected that the Lyon will be there to be seen." [48]

There was a white bear on tour in 1733—"a sight far preferable to the Lion in the Judgment of all Persons who have seen them both"—and also "a very strange & Wonderful Creature called a Sea Lion." One advertisement tells of a "wild animal lately brought from the Mississippi, called a Buffalo," and another of what must have been a monkey—"a creature called a Japanese about 2 feet high, his body resembling a human body in all parts except the feet and tail." The first elephant to visit America was brought from Bengal by Captain David Crowninshield in 1796. It was immediately taken on tour, the Reverend William Bentley looking it over while on exhibition at Salem. He recorded in his diary that the elephant could pull out the cork and drink a bottle of port. [49]

More ambitious showmen than these wandering animal trainers staged various exhibits from elaborate panoramas to acrobatic performances. They reached the village tavern even more rarely than the peripatetic bears and lions, but their appeal was to the same class in colonial society. Their shows were for the common man. Again Samuel Sewall's diary provides one of the earliest records of such entertainment. The magistrates had trouble, in 1687, with a tavern-keeper who set aside one of his rooms "for a man to shew tricks in." He was persuaded of the error of his ways ("he saith seeing 'tis offensive, he will remedy it"), and the disciplinary meeting broke up with singing the ninetieth psalm. [50]

Apparently more successful was the exhibition, possibly the first advertised in a colonial newspaper, of a "curious and exact Modell of the Czar of Muscovia's Country seat, near Moscow." "Tis the most Ingenious and Compleat piece of Workmanship of

To the CURIOUS.

To be seen at Major Leavenworth's Stable, opposite Mr. Lothrop's, State-Street,

Two CAMELS,

Male and Female, lately imported from

ARABIA.

THESE stupendous Animals are most deserving the Attention of the Curious, being the greatest natural Curiosity ever exhibited to the Public on this Continent. They are Nineteen Hands high; have Necks near Four Feet long; have a large high Bunch on their Backs, and another under their Breasts, in the Form of a Pedestal, on which they support themselves when lying down; they have Four Joints in their hind Legs, and will travel Twelve or Fourteen Days without drinking, and carry a Burden of Fifteen Hundred Weight; they are remarkably harmless and docile, and will lie down and rise at Command.

Price of Admittance for a Gentleman or Lady, NINE-PENCE *each.*

[Abraham was old and well stricken in Age: And the Lord had blessed Abraham in all Things. And Abraham said unto his eldest Servant of his House, that ruled over all that he had, Thou shalt go unto my Country, and to my Kindred, and take a Wife unto my Son Isaac. And the Servant took Ten Camels, of the Camels of his Master, and departed; and went to Mesopotamia, unto the City Nahor. And he made his Camels to kneel down without the City, by a Well of Water, about the Time of the Evening, even the Time that Women go out to draw Water. Pure Wisdom directed the Servant, and succeeded him in obtaining the Consent of the Parents, Brethren and Kindred of REBECCAH, that she should go to the Land of Canaan, and become the Wife of ISAAC. And they sent away Rebeccah, their Sister, with her Damsels, and her Nurse, and Abraham's Servant, and his Men, and they rode upon the Camels. GEN. XXIV.]

Exotic Animals on Show in New England

An advertisement in *The Connecticut Journal,* June 30—July 7, 1790.
Courtesy of the American Antiquarian Society.

this Nature that ever was exposed in Europe or America," its happy proprietor announced in the *American Weekly Mercury* for August 1-8, 1723, inviting the good people of Philadelphia to see it "at Mr. Oliver Galltry Perriwig Maker in the Market Street near the Old Prison." [51]

Mr. and Mrs. Dugee delighted many an audience in mid-eighteenth century. The gentleman member of this team could dance on the stiff rope with iron fetters on his feet; his lady could hold six men standing on her ample breast while lying stretched out between two chairs. She was known as the Female Samson and had performed her unusual feat before H.R.H. the Princess Dowager of Wales.[52] Another acrobatic family brought their act to a stirring climax with the star performer "turning round with swift motion, with seven or eight swords' points at her eyes, mouth and breast, for a quarter of an hour together, to the admiration of all that behold the performance." [53] In Boston a Mr. John Childs announced his plans "to fly off of Dr. Cutler's Church." A few days later the *Gazette* stated that "as the performances led many People from their Business, he is forbid flying any more in the Town." [54]

In the latter part of the century there were also exhibitions of "philosophical optical machines," "magick lanthorns," and on one occasion "a very large moving Mashene or Land and Water Skip." [55] After the French Revolution the democratic followers of Mr. Jefferson applauded heartily the affecting spectacle of the guillotining of Louis XVI—"performed to the life by an invisible machine without any perceivable assistance." It reached its climax, as advertised for a performance at the Sign of the Black Bear in Philadelphia on November 21, 1794, when "the head falls in a basket, and the lips, which are first red, turn blue." [56]

→>><<←

HUNTING and fishing, the sports and games associated with farm festivals, shooting matches and horse-races, country dances, the amusements of the colonial tavern with its convivial social atmosphere and pleasant tippling—these were the characteristic forms of recreation for the colonial yeomanry during the eighteenth century. The sports and games were largely those which their forefathers, or they themselves, had once enjoyed in England. The scene depicted in a sixteenth-century poem addressed to Queen Elizabeth would not have been altogether unfamiliar in eighteenth-century America:

Now, when their dinner once is done, and that they well have fed.
To play they go; to casting of the stone, to runne, or shoote;
To tosse the light and windy ball aloft with hand or foote;
Some others trie their skill in gonnes; some wrastell all the day;
And some to schooles of fence do goe, to gaze upon the play;
Another sort there is, that doe not love abroad to roame,
But, for to passe their time at cardes or tables, still at home.[57]

Yet in many instances colonial amusements had been greatly modified by passage overseas, as were all English institutions transplanted to the New World. The training days and election days, with their democratic atmosphere and general participation in sports, were a product of the new environment, and the barn-raisings and husking-bees grew out of the special circumstances of colonial life. The universal popularity of hunting, with the premium placed upon markmanship as exhibited at shooting matches, was even more directly a frontier phenomenon. In their outdoor recreation the colonists turned from masques and wakes, church-ales and morris-dances, and also from such spectator sports as the animal baitings of eighteenth-century England, to the more homely diversions of a life largely shaped by pioneer conditions.

For a time the Great Awakening exerted a repressive influence, but in general there was increasingly less evidence in the eighteenth century of that puritanic condemnation of all amusements which had characterized the early period of settlement. Recreation played an important rôle in colonial life, and it was taking on distinctively American forms.

Chapter III

THE COLONIAL ARISTOCRACY

"Let no trifling diversion, or amusement . . . ; no girl, no gun, no cards, no flutes, no violins, no dress, no tobacco, no laziness, decoy you from your books." [1]

Writing this stern injunction in his diary, a young man starting life in Braintree, Massachusetts, in the 1750's, a young man destined to be the second President of the United States, was guarding himself against what he considered the growing laxity of the age in which he lived. For in his attitude toward amusements, in his discipline of himself, John Adams was very much the Puritan. The changes that had come over the habits of New England, and especially of what had become the New England aristocracy, were a cause for his anxious, although probably not prayerful, concern.

He was highly scornful of the fashionable vogue for frivolous and idle diversions. "Let others waste their bloom of life at the card or billiard table among rakes and fools." Nor could he tolerate the ball-room: "I never knew a dancer good for anything else." He did not go so far as to "conclude peremptorily against sending sons or daughters to dancing, or fencing, or music," but he declared emphatically that he would rather they should be "ignorant of them all than fond of any one of them." [2]

But John Adams was swimming against that strong tide which we have already seen beating against the crumbling rock of Puritan intolerance. The simple country folk of New England were asserting their right to play, the more wealthy and leisured class was even less restrained by earlier prejudice. Prosperity induced a more liberal attitude, and the barriers which once had blocked almost all worldly pleasures were being let down. An advertisement in the *Boston Gazette* in 1767 took "Persons of Fashion" severely to task for their unashamed attendance at plays, balls, assemblies, and card parties.[3] It was a voice crying in the wilderness after Puritan ideals of conduct which no longer commanded popular sanction.

Thirty years after John Adams' troubled reflections, changes along still more liberal lines are reflected in the diary of John Quincy Adams describing his life at Newburyport. He too suffered from the New England conscience. "I go but little into company," reads one entry which might well have appeared in his father's diary, "and yet I am not industrious. Indolence, indolence, I fear, will be my ruin." Nevertheless Mr. Adams allowed himself many pleasures of which his father would hardly have approved.

"Rather dissipated the whole day," we find him writing on one occasion; "could not study with the proper attention, and indeed gave the matter up in the afternoon. At about seven o'clock we met at the dancing hall, and from that time till between three and four in the morning we were continually dancing. I was unacquainted with almost all the company; but I never saw a collection of ladies where there was comparatively so much beauty. Two or three gentlemen got rather over the bay; but upon the whole the proceedings were as regular and agreeable as might be expected." [4]

He appears to have enjoyed female society, with that condescending air which came so naturally to an Adams. One day the entire afternoon was "employ'd in rigging for the ball," and he spent the better part of the evening in the company of "a young lady with a beautiful countenance, an elegant person, and (I am told) an amiable mind." He called on her the next day and learned to play quadrille. But it was also about this time that he confided to his diary that "there are very few young ladies who talk and yet preserve our admiration." [5]

A popular fashion of that day—as of a good many days since—

obliged young women at an evening party to play on the harpsichord, or the new pianoforte, and to sing to their own accompaniment. This bored John Quincy Adams extremely, especially the long preliminaries before the musician would allow herself to be persuaded to perform. "We had some very agreeable and entertaining conversation," he wrote once, "but singing soon came on the carpet, and then the usual nonsense succeeded." Parlor games—for they too have a hoary antiquity—were even worse. Mr. Adams found himself forced to play "start; what is it like; cross questions; I love my love with an A." One evening it was pawns: "A number of pledges were given all 'round, and kissing was the only condition upon which they were redeem'd. Ah! what kissing! 'tis a profanation of one of the most endearing expressions of love." [6]

There are also references in the diary to sleigh rides, noisy walks, serenades until three in the morning, evenings of whist. One day was spent in reading, shooting birds, and flute-playing. An amiable young man, Mr. Adams, enjoying what had come to be accepted as the normal pleasures of society in a small New England town.

→→→)(←←←

IN NEAR-BY BOSTON, social life was at once gayer and more sophisticated even in the middle of the eighteenth century. If there were still vestiges of Puritan restraint, they were not very much in evidence—less so than in the next century. English visitors found the atmosphere little different from that of other American cities. As early as 1740 one of them was both surprised and delighted to discover the Bostonians not quite as sad-visaged as he had apparently been led to expect. "Notwithstanding plays and such like diversions do not obtain here," he wrote, "they don't seem to be dispirited nor moped for want of them, for both the ladies and gentlemen dress and appear as gay, in common, as courtiers in England on a coronation or birthday. And the ladies here visit, drink tea, and indulge every piece of gentility to the height of the mode and neglect the affairs of their families with as good grace as the finest ladies in London." [7]

In this same year an assembly was established. For all of Puritanism's disapproval of dancing, teachers had been available for the young ladies and gentlemen of Boston from some date prior to 1716, an advertisement in the *News-Letter* of that year announcing lessons in "all sorts of fine works, as Feather-work, Filigre, and Painting on Glass . . . and Dancing cheaper than ever was taught in Boston." [8] An assembly, however, was an innovation. Our observer noted that the ladies who attended it "are looked upon to be none of the nicest in regard to their reputation; and it is thought it will soon be repressed, for it is much taken notice of and exploded by the religious and sober part of the people." [9] He overestimated their influence. Four years later it was reported that "assemblies of the gayer sort are frequent here, the gentlemen and the ladies meeting almost every week at concerts of music and balls." [10] In mid-century another visitor declared that they "consisted of 50 Gentlemen and Ladies and those the Best Fashion in Town."

The record of the visit of this latter traveler, Captain Francis Goelet, gives an unusually gay picture of a Boston enlivened both by the rise of a mercantile class and by the presence of a royal governor and his staff. He ferreted out its amusements with commendable perseverance. "Where very merry" is the constant refrain of the accounts of his lively escapades—evenings with the ladies at whist and with the gentlemen over wine, excursions to country taverns for dinner and dancing.

"After haveing Dined in a very Elegant manner upon Turtle, &," Captain Goelet reported of one party at which some forty gentlemen had gathered at a Mr. Sheppard's, "Drank about the [sic] toasts, and Sang a Number of Songs, and where Exceedingly Merry until 3 o'clock in the morning, from whence Went upon the Rake, going past the Common in Our Way Home, Surprised a company of Country Young Men and Women with a Violin at a Tavern, Danceing and Makeing Merry, upon our

Entering the House they Young Women Fled, we took Possession of the Room, having the Fiddler and the Young Men
with us with the Keg of Sugared Dram, we where very Very
Merry, from thence went to Mr. Jacob Wendells where we were
Obliged to Drink Punch and Wine, and about 5 in the morning
made our Excit and to Bed." [11]

On the eve of the Revolution there were two assemblies in
Boston, one for those with Tory leanings, another the Liberty
Assembly. The letters of a young lady loyalist declare that the
former was reputed to be the best in America.[12] There are frequent references in the diary of John Rowe, friend of John
Adams, to brilliant balls and very good dancing. An account in
the diary of William Pynchon of the festivities in Salem during
the holiday season of 1783 seems wholly modern.[13] Nothing
could afford more striking illustration of how times had changed
since Cotton Mather fumed over "wanton Bacchanallian Christ-
mases," petulantly rebuking young people who might attend
"a Frolick, a revelling Feast, and a Ball, which discovers their
corruption."

Card-playing, especially whist, had won its way into almost
complete favor. Custom-house records of imports of cards from
England fully substantiate references to it in diaries and travel
accounts. "The inhabitants of Boston," the Marquis of Chastellux
wrote just after the Revolution, "are fond of high play, and it is
fortunate perhaps that the war happened when it did, to mod-
erate this passion, which began to be attended with dangerous
consequences." [14] The Revolution had far-reaching social effects,
but it is surprising to find this French observer discovering one
of them to have been the curtailment of the gambling fever in
one-time Puritan Boston.

Attempts to introduce the theatre resulted in one of the few
victories of those still true to earlier traditions. It was not until
the very end of the century that the stage was officially tolerated.
When some English actors tried to put on a play in 1750, there
was a small riot, and the Massachusetts General Court sternly

reaffirmed its traditional ban on "public stage-plays, interludes, and other theatrical entertainments, which not only occasion great and unnecessary expenses, and discourage industry and frugality, but likewise tend generally to increase immorality, impiety, and a contempt for religion." [15]

Now and then something very closely approaching theatricals took place in the guise of public readings or moral lectures, and amateur performances were presented quite openly. The diary of Nathaniel Ames, both as a Harvard student and a resident of Dedham, has frequent references both to attending such plays and to acting in them. To his notice of a performance of *Tancred and Sigismunda*, on April 8, 1760, he adds, "We are likely to be prosecuted." [16] But, still active in these theatricals twelve years later, he reported on April 20, 1772, that "the Farce called The Toy Shop was acted ... before a numerous audience of the most respectable Inhabitants of the First Parish in Dedham both male and female." [17]

Concerts took the place of the theatre to a certain extent. Various musical instruments—virginals and spinets, violins and bass viols, flageolets, flutes, and hautboys—were being imported in 1716 by the organist of King's Chapel in Boston. In another fifteen years, to judge from an advertisement in the *News-Letter* by a Mr. Pelham, who was also a dancing-master and tobacconist, public performances were being given with an admission fee of five shillings. Soon thereafter the approval of the selectmen (although they were careful to make it clear they did not wish to establish any "president") was obtained for a concert in Faneuil Hall. By the 1760's concerts were a regular feature of the social calendar. [18]

The wealthy merchants who had taken the place of the Saints in the social hierarchy of New England fully recognized and thoroughly enjoyed the pleasures of this world. Their recreational life did not include commercial amusements, nor did it extend to active sports. In some respects it was typified by those impressive dinners which everywhere brought colonial society together—tedious except for the gaiety inspired by fine old Madeira and good New England rum. But its limitations were those of the age. Boston in the latter half of the eighteenth century may still have had that atmosphere of sobriety and decorum which has generally distinguished it, but its citizens knew how to amuse themselves.

-->>><<<-

THE SOCIAL LIFE of the colonial aristocracy in the middle colonies was seen at its gayest in New York. Philadelphia was noted for its dancing assembly, its exclusive fishing parties on the Schuylkill, and the epicurean banquets given by its prosperous citizens. It had its concerts and its theatre—also its horse-races and its cock-fights for all the disapproval of the Quakers. But the lively little town of some twelve thousand inhabitants at the lower end of Manhattan Island was by mid-century a pressing rival of Boston and Philadelphia "in its fine buildings, its opulence, and extensive commerce," [19] and the superior of either Puritan or Quaker capital in amusements and entertainment. Trade with the West Indies, supplemented by the important side-line of privateering against the French, had created a class of pleasure-loving citizens of both wealth and leisure whose social life was given a further fillip by the presence of the officers of the English garrison.

They might best be seen, these leaders of colonial society, as they paraded of a late afternoon in the fashionable district about Hanover Square, dressed in the latest London mode. The gentlemen were resplendent in powdered wigs, varicolored coats, lace and ruffles, the young dandies wearing silver-hilted small swords and ostentatiously taking snuff from jeweled boxes. New fashions in hooped petticoats, vivid creations in bright scarlet or glistening green, featured the dress of the women. "One cannot but be troubled," wrote a correspondent of the *New York Mercury*, "to see so many well shaped virgins bloated up, and waddling up and down like big bodied women." [20] Sedan-chairs were carried through the streets by Negro slaves. Occasionally Lieutenant-Governor de Lancey drove by in his gilded chariot, drawn by four white horses, or Abraham de Peyster in his silver-trimmed coach, with liveried outriders in blue coats, yellow capes, and yellow small-clothes.[21] There were marked social distinctions in New York, as there were throughout the colonies. Luxurious display had an important rôle in the world of fashion.

The carriages of the gentry were usually bound for their estates out on the Bowery road or even farther afield in Harlem, and excursions by chair or chaise to near-by country taverns had a great vogue among the socially elect. Ladies and gentlemen were assured of being entertained at these resorts "in the genteelest manner," with rich foods, imported wines, and music. Turtle feasts, the terrapin washed down with well-aged Madeira, and fashionable picnics were held on the banks of the East River.

"Thirty or forty gentlemen and ladies," a traveler in 1760 noted, "meet and dine together, drink tea in the afternoon, fish and amuse themselves till evening, and then return home in Italian chaises...a gentleman and lady in each chaise. In the way there is a bridge, about three miles distant from New York, which you always pass over as you return, called the Kissing Bridge, where it is part of the etiquette to salute the lady who has put herself under your protection."[22] It may be added that the visitor, Andrew Burnaby, found the ladies of New York handsome and agreeable.

"Their Diversions in the Winter," Madame Sarah Knight commented, "is Riding in Sleys about three or four Miles out of Town, where they have Houses of entertainment at a place called the Bowery; and some go to friends houses who handsomely treat them....I believe we mett 50 or 60 slays that day—they fly with great swiftness and some are so furious that they'le turn out of the path for none except a Loaden Cart."[23] Describing one such party in 1768, Alexander Macraby says that the sleighs were preceded by fiddlers on horseback, and the company drove to a country inn "where we danced, sung, romped and eat and drank and kicked away care from morning till night." [24]

Toward the close of the century Long Island was drawing an increasing number of pleasure-seekers, the ferries being busy every pleasant summer afternoon. Hempstead and Salisbury Plains attracted fashionable crowds to the horse-races which had been held there every season since 1665. "Upwards of seventy chairs and chaises were carried over the Brooklyn Ferry the day before," the *Weekly Post-Boy* reported after one race meeting, "besides a far greater number of horses." [25] In the years immediately preceding the Revolution the stables of imported thoroughbreds built up by a number of wealthy New Yorkers gave a wide fame to Salisbury. "These plains were celebrated for their races throughout all the Colonies and even in England," a London race book stated in 1776. "They were held twice a year for a silver cup, to which the gentry of New England and New York resorted." [26]

Other sports enjoyed at least occasionally by wealthy New Yorkers are indicated by contemporary references to pleasure boats, shooting matches, cork swimming-jackets, "gouff clubs," and (as advertised by James Rivington in 1766) "battledores and shuttlecocks, cricket-balls, pillets, best racquets for tennis and fives. . . ." [27] Cock-fighting, to say nothing of animal baitings, had its devotees among the aristocracy as well as among the common people. The diary of the chaplain of the English troops makes frequent references to the mains he attended: "Prayers, visited at night ye fighting cocks," or "I was late at ye fighting cocks." [28]

Balls and assemblies, card parties and evening frolics, were greatly enjoyed. The diary of Elisha Parker in 1747 records his being invited to both the Old Assembly and the Young Assembly. [29] The newspapers always noted the great occasion of the Governor's Ball. "The night was passed in the general satisfaction," stated one such report, "without the least incivility offered or offence taken by any one, which is scarce to be said on the like occasions." In 1762 sixty-nine couples attended a lavish ball given by Sir Jeffrey Amherst which was adjudged the "most elegant ever seen in America." [30]

William Livingstone, later to be governor of New Jersey, has left a record of waffle frolics. When one such entertainment included cards and a magnificent supper, he expressed his surprise that so luxurious a feast should be given this humble name. The evening concluded, he further noted somewhat cryptically, with "*ten sunburnt virgins lately come from Columbia's Newfoundland,* besides a play of my own invention ... kissing constitutes a great part of its entertainment." [31]

New York had its concerts. One for the benefit of Mr. Pachelbel, harpsichord player, was advertised in 1735; weekly performances, with both professional and amateur instrumentalists, were being given in the 1760's, and in the period just before the Revolution there was a great deal of musical activity. It is interesting to trace through these days the career of Mr. Herman Zedwitz, successively concertmaster at "Hull's Assembly Rooms, at the Sign of the Golden Spade," chimney-sweep, and a traitor to the patriot cause.[32] Band music was played at the Vauxhall Gardens kept by Samuel Francis, later steward of General Washington, and open-air concerts were given three times a week at the garden of the Kings Arms.

A more distinctive feature of the city's recreational life was the theatre. New York gave an early welcome to the stage, although just how early cannot be definitely stated. Its historians have had an agreeable time progressively moving farther and farther back the probable occasion of the first American theatrical performance. They may yet arrive at the landing of the Jamestown settlers aboard the *Susan Constant.* For it was a practice early in the seventeenth century for sailors aboard English ships to hold amateur theatricals, and as early as 1607 a Captain Keeling, of the East India Company, reported a showing of *Hamlet* aboard the ship *Dragon.*[33]

However that may be, there is definite evidence of a certain Richard Hunter's petitioning the legislature of New York for a license to act plays about 1699; the English actor Anthony Aston (arriving "full of Lice, Shame, Poverty, Nakedness, and Hunger") has left on record that he was playing in the colonies in 1703-04; there is notice of a performance of *The Recruiting Officer* in New York on December 6, 1732; and seven years later *The Adventures of Harlequin and Scaramouche, or The Spaniard Trick'd,* was staged at Mr. Holt's Long Room with a prologue beginning "This gen'rous Town which nurs'd our infant Stage." [34] If no one of these isolated references to the stage is accepted as marking the real beginning of New York's theatrical history, the *New York Gazette or Weekly Post-Boy* records the brief and somewhat inglorious season ("they met with small encouragement") of a company of comedians, believed to have been a troupe headed by Thomas Kean and Walter Murray, which moved upon New York from Philadelphia and gave a series of plays in the winter of 1749-50. [35]

Three years later a band of professional actors headed by Mr. and Mrs. Lewis Hallam arrived. They had reached this country in 1752 by way of the West Indies and had already acted for almost a year in the South, but their reception in New York was only moderately enthusiastic. They soon returned to the richer harvests to be gleaned in Jamaica. There Lewis Hallam died, his widow married David Douglass, and soon afterwards the reorganized troupe, now known as the American Company of Comedians, made a second and more successful venture to the American mainland. From 1758 until the Revolution forced their temporary withdrawal, they played before colonial audiences from Albany to Charleston.

New York's first permanent theatre was the John Street, opened in 1767. It was a small house, seating perhaps three hundred, and drew its audiences from both the aristocracy and the less polite members of society. The presence of the former is attested by advertisements warning patrons to send their servants by four in the afternoon to reserve their places for them, and to set their carriages down with the horses' heads facing up John

New-York, November 12, 1753.

By a Company of COMEDIANS,

At the New-Theatre, in *Nassau-Street*,

This Evening, being the 12th of *November*, will be presented,

(*By particular Desire*)

An *Historical Play*, call'd,

King RICHARD III.

CONTAINING

The Distresses and Death of King *Henry* the VIth; the artful
Acquisition of the Crown by *Crook-back'd Richard*; the Murder
of the two young Princes in the Tower; and the memorable
Battle of *Bosworth-Field*, being the last that was fought between
the Houses of *York* and *Lancaster*.

Richard,	by	Mr. *Rigby*.
King *Henry*,	by	Mr. *Hallam*.
Prince *Edward*,	by	Master L. *Hallam*.
Duke of *York*,	by	Master A. *Hallam*.
Earl of *Richmond*,	by	Mr. *Clarkson*.
Duke of *Buckingham*,	by	Mr. *Malone*.
Duke of *Norfolk*,	by	Mr. *Miller*.
Lord *Stanley*,	by	Mr. *Singleton*.
Lieutenant,	by	Mr. *Bell*.
Catesby,	by	Mr. *Adcock*.
Queen *Elizabeth*,	by	Mrs. *Hallam*.
Lady *Anne*,	by	Mrs. *Adcock*.
Duchess of *York*,	by	Mrs. *Rigby*.

To which will be added,

A Ballad FARCE call'd,

The DEVIL TO PAY.

Sir *John Loverule*,	by	Mr. *Adcock*.
Jobson,	by	Mr. *Malone*.
Butler,	by	Mr. *Miller*.
Footman,	by	Mr. *Singleton*.
Cook,	by	Mr. *Bell*.
Coachman,	by	Mr. *Rigby*.
Conjurer,	by	Mr. *Clarkson*.
Lady *Loverule*,	by	Mrs. *Adcock*.
Nell,	by	Mrs. *Beccely*.
Lettice,	by	Mrs. *Clarkson*.
Lucy,	by	Miss *Love*.

PRICES: BOX, 6*s.* PIT, 4*s.* GALLERY, 2*s.*

No Persons whatever to be admitted behind the Scenes.

*N. B. Gentlemen and Ladies that chuse Tickets, may have them
at Mr. Parker's and Mr. Gaine's Printing-Offices.*

Money will be taken at the DOOR.

To begin at 6 o'Clock.

Playbill of the Hallam Company of Comedians
November 12, 1753, in their first New York season.

Street; that of the latter by notices requesting the gallery gods not to throw eggs on the stage.[36] Admission ranged from three to eight shillings, however, and the colonial theatre was primarily class entertainment. On one occasion a mob broke in on a performance of *The Twin Rivals* and sent the audience flying as a protest against such extravagance while there was serious distress among the poor.[37]

It was at this theatre that the first American comedy to be regularly produced, Royall Tyler's *The Contrast*, was staged on April 16, 1787. One of its characters, prototype of the country yokel in the big city, describes the playhouse. "As I was going about here and there, to and again, to find it," Jonathan says, "I saw a great crowd of folks going into a long entry that had lanterns over the door.... So I went right in, and they showed me away, clean up to the garret, just like a meeting-house gallery. And so I saw a power of topping folks, all sitting around in little cabins, just like father's corn cribs; and there was such a squeaking with the fiddlers, and such a tarnel blaze with the lights, my head was near turned." [38]

Jonathan was none too comfortable in the gallery, but accommodations for "the power of topping folks" were not much better. The two little rows of boxes and the pit were furnished only with hard wooden benches. Heat for the cold winter nights came from a large stove in the foyer, but the wiser members of the audience brought their own foot-warmers. Candles provided the lighting, often dripping on the powdered wigs of those in the boxes. Although the audience were supposed to keep their seats, the management repeatedly complained in public notices that "gentlemen crowd the stage and very much interrupt the performance."

Staging and scenery were primitive. When the green curtain was raised on the sharp blast of a whistle, the audience saw a few painted flats and a backcloth. Stagehands were liable to appear at any moment to shift the flats or to snuff a candle foot-light—if one of the actors had not in the meantime broken off

his lines to do it himself. The performance was Elizabethan in
its simplicity, but colonial audiences were not over-critical.

The play was the thing. The American Company of Comedians
included in its repertoire not only all the Shakespearean plays,
but the best of Elizabethan and Restoration comedies and popular ballad-operas. Its principal offerings were tempered by farces
played as afterpieces. At the John Street Theatre the social
world of colonial New York saw *Richard the Third, The Beggar's
Opera,* and *Venice Preserved; Hamlet, The Beaux' Strategem,*
and *She Stoops to Conquer; Flora, or Hob in the Well, The
Mock Doctor,* and *High Life Below Stairs.*[39]

->>><<<-

IN THE SOUTHERN colonies, social life was even more varied and
colorful than in the prosperous cities of the North. The planters
rode to hounds through the lush countryside of Virginia and
Maryland in blue coats and scarlet waistcoats; they went to
horse-races and cock-fights, betting heavily in so many pounds
of tobacco or so many slaves; and they flocked to Williamsburg,
Annapolis, or Charleston for the most festive social seasons anywhere in America. Washington Irving, in his *Life of George
Washington,* describes how the young ladies of Maryland rode
to the assembly at Annapolis in scarlet riding-habits thrown
over their satin ball dresses, kerchiefs drawn about the great
masses of their puffed and pomaded hair, and after dancing
through the night rode home again in the shadowy dawn.

Through their immense holdings of lands and slaves, the planters had acquired wealth which set them off completely from
the yeomanry of tidewater and the small farmers of the back
country. Tobacco, rice, and indigo had been transmuted into
riches, and the southern aristocracy seized upon every possible
opportunity for diversion. They were not bothered by the puritanic soul-searching which sometimes still inhibited New England's wealthy merchants. They did not care whether their
amusements were inspired by God or the Devil.

"Indolent, easy and good-natured," was Andrew Burnaby's characterization; "extremely fond of society and much given to convivial pleasures." [40] Somewhat later the Marquis of Chastellux caustically declared that the young men were all gamblers, cock-fighters, and horse jockeys—"to hear them converse, you would imagine that the grand point of all science was properly to fix a gaff and touch with dexterity the tail of a cock while in combat." [41] The planters were not the cavaliers of southern legend, but they lived the life of the English aristocrat on their great plantations, the life of the fox-hunting country squire, just as fully as circumstances would permit. It was the most leisured and pleasure-loving society America has ever known—and it produced some of the country's greatest political leaders.

One of the most engaging descriptions of this life is contained in the diary of Philip Vickers Fithian, a young northerner who acted as tutor for the children of Colonel Robert Carter at Nomini Hall, in Westmoreland County, Virginia. A serious-minded young man (he had studied for the Presbyterian ministry at Nassau Hall), Fithian was somewhat disturbed by the gaiety of the society into which he was thrown—"the Balls, the Fish-Feasts, the Dancing-Schools, the Christenings, the Cock-fights, the Horse-Races. . . ." [42] He could not approve an attitude which placed so high a premium on pleasure and amusement that even the Sabbath was largely given over to diversions. It troubled his Calvinistic conscience that every one should look festive and cheerful on the Lord's Day.[43]

His diary tells of race meets at Richmond where the stakes on a single race were £500, and of cock-fights which created the wildest excitement both in the Great House and in the slave quarters. It records a gala occasion with boat-racing on the Rappahannock, and afternoons with the gentry bowling on the green at Nomini Hall. The generous southern hospitality of Colonel Carter, guests being always present at a table luxuriously supplied with all the varied produce of the plantation and a wealth of wines and liquors, greatly impressed him. And it seemed that the women of the South rode about as freely as the men in their visits to neighboring plantations. "Almost every Lady wears a red Cloak," Fithian reported wonderingly, "and when they ride out they tye a red handkerchief over their Head and face." [44] He thought at first that the toothache was epidemic throughout Virginia.

Nomini Hall was a musical household. One day Fithian came home about candle-light to find "Mrs. Carter in the yard seeing to the Roosting of her Poultry; and the Colonel in the Parlour tuning his guitar." There were many evenings when the Colonel was so disposed—music was his "darling amusement"—and the tutor took part in many informal concerts. Colonel Carter had a harpsichord, a forte-piano, a German flute, and a harmonica. The latter, of course, was not our modern mouth-organ. It was an instrument invented by "Mr. B. Franklin of Philadelphia . . . being the musical glasses without water." Fithian declared that its virtues "far exceed even the swelling Organ." [45]

Of all the diversions of the plantation, the one that most intrigued this conscientious northerner with his Presbyterian scruples was the dancing. There were not only regular classes for the children, Mr. Christian coming over to Nomini Hall after giving his lessons at Mount Vernon, but frequent formal dances. During the Christmas holidays there was talk of little else than "the balls, the Fox-hunts, and fine entertainments."

"The assembly was remarkably numerous; beyond my expectations, and exceedingly polite in general," Fithian wrote of one affair to which he was somewhat unwillingly taken. But while not even Mr. Christian could persuade him to take up dancing himself, he greatly enjoyed watching it, especially the jigs, reels, and country dances—the company "moving easily, to the sound of well-performed Music, and with perfect regularity, tho' apparently in the utmost disorder." He would spend most of the evening wandering about, looking in occasionally at the people in the drawing-rooms drinking and playing cards. Little escaped his observant eye: "There was A short pretty stump of a girl. A young Spark seemed to be fond of her; She seemed to be fond of him; they both were fond, & the Company saw it. . . . The insinuating Rogue waited on her home, in close Hugg too, the moment he left the Ball-Room." [46]

On this first occasion Fithian at length became anxious to get away, yet he could not help being drawn back again and again. "The ladies were dressed Gay and splendid, & when dancing, their skirts & Brocades rustled and trailed behind them!" With what seems to have been a somewhat un-Presbyterian eye, he noticed that Miss Betsy Lee was "pinched up rather too near" in a long pair of the new-fashioned stays which permitted "scarce any view at all of the Ladies Snowy Bosoms," and described Miss Priscilla Hale as "a slim, puny silent Virgin. . . . I dare say from her Character that her Modesty is invincible." He had left his own love in the North. It was she whom he always had in mind when the gentlemen drank their toasts to the ladies of Nomini Hall. So after a time Fithian wandered out to walk alone through the woods. He sadly took out his penknife and "carved Laura's much admired Name upon a smooth beautiful Beech Tree." [47]

—>≫X≪<—

The field sports which were such a distinctive feature of plantation life are illustrated in a somewhat better known diary, that of George Washington. This typical southern gentleman was a great rider and huntsman. He was proud of his horses, his pack of hounds (Pilot, Musick, Countess, Truelove), and his imported fowling-pieces. His riding-frocks, waistcoats of superfine scarlet cloth and gold lace, his elegant buckskin breeches, were all specially made in England. Diary entries under the heading "Where and how my time is spent" bear frequent witness to the days he "went a ducking" or "a Fox hunting in the Neck." During January and February, 1769, for example, he rode to hounds fifteen times, one week on six successive days.[48]

Washington was equally enthusiastic about social activities, especially dancing. His diary usually records attendance at the balls and assemblies at Williamsburg, Annapolis, or Alexandria with the brief note, "Went to the play and Ball." On February 5, 1760, there was an occasion which inspired more extensive comment: "Went to the Ball at Alexandria, where Musick and Dancing was the chief Entertainment. However in a convenient Room detached for the purpose abounded great plenty of Bread and Butter, some biscuits with Tea, and Coffee which the Drinker of could not Distinguish from Hot water sweetened. Be it remembered that pocket handkerchiefs served the purpose of Table Cloths & Napkins and that no apologies were made for either. I shall therefore distinguish this Ball by the Stile and Title of the Bread and Butter Ball." [49]

The proprietor of Mount Vernon, whose innate dignity has been translated in terms of dull stuffiness for so many generations of schoolboys, quite evidently preferred the wines more generally served at colonial assemblies to the pallid refreshment of weak coffee. But the dancing itself was the lure that drew him even to bread-and-butter balls. One wonders, recalling the marked contrast in his attitude toward social pleasures to that of the man who was to be so closely associated with him in later years, at what point John Adams may have finally admitted that there might be a good dancer who was also good for something else.

Another Virginia planter who thoroughly enjoyed the various aspects of the South's recreational life was Thomas Jefferson. "From the circumstances of my position," he once wrote, "I was often thrown into the society of horse-racers, card-players, fox hunters...." It was not said in disparagement. He thoroughly enjoyed the victory of a favorite horse and being in at the death of a fox. Even greater was his fondness for music—"the favorite passion of my soul"—and there were few more zealous dancers at the fashionable balls in the Raleigh Tavern at Williamsburg. In his young days Jefferson once wrote a friend of his conception of the ideal life: "Get a pole chair and a pair of keen horses, practice the law in the same courts, and drive about to all the dances in the country together." [50]

The colonial South had another amusement in the theatre. It was there the Hallams had first landed, and nowhere did the American Company of Comedians find more appreciative audiences. It was a part of the English tradition this aristocratic society encouraged. Plays were staged not only at Williamsburg, Annapolis, and Charleston, but at Hobb's Hole, Port Tobacco, Upper Marlborough, and other little villages where the near-by planters could congregate. As the players moved on from town to town, many of the audience followed them. In the season of 1771-72 we find Washington attending the play four times at Annapolis and four times at Williamsburg during the fall, and then seven times at Williamsburg and four times at Annapolis in the spring. The total cost of his tickets for these performances of the Hallams (as well as a waxworks exhibition and a puppet-show) came to £17.[51]

Amateur theatricals are recorded in Virginia as early as 1665, when a play "commonly called Ye Bare and Ye Cubb" was put on; Williamsburg had a theatre in 1716, perhaps the first in America, and there is notice of a performance of Otway's *Orphan* in Charleston, South Carolina, in 1735. The Murray and Kean troupe toured the South after playing in Philadelphia and New York. But it was the Hallams, giving their first American performance at Williamsburg on September 15, 1752, that introduced the theatre to the South, as well as to the North, on something like a permanent basis.[52]

Advance notices in the *Virginia Gazette* told of the Hallams' pending performances. Scenes, costumes, and decorations were entirely new, giving every assurance that the audience could count "on being entertained in as polite a Manner as at the Theatre in London." *The Merchant of Venice* was played first, and a few days later *Othello*. Governor Dinwiddie took the royal family of the Cherokee Nation to the latter performance. So convincing was the players' acting that the chieftain's consort could hardly be restrained from ordering "some about her to go and prevent their killing one another." [53]

Possibly the most brilliant dramatic season of the American Company was that at Charleston, the social and cultural capital of the South, in 1773-74. "All seems at present to be trade, riches, magnificence and great state in everything; much gaiety and dissipation," a northern visitor, Josiah Quincy, Jr., wrote that year.[54] And well he might. The visiting players gave over a hundred performances, their repertoire including no less than fifty-eight different offerings. Eleven of Shakespeare's plays were staged, eight of Garrick's, and almost all the popular ballad-operas of the day.[55]

→»«←

THE CENTERS of society—Boston, New York, Philadelphia, Williamsburg, and Charleston—were so widely separated that there was little contact among the aristocracy of the different colonies. The lack of roads, and the miserable condition of such roads as there were, constituted a barrier to pleasure travel which even wealth could not easily overcome. One might journey by boat, at considerable expense, but by coach or stage it was an experience not many people willingly undertook. In few respects have conditions of life so greatly changed as in the broadening of our horizons through modern means of transportation.

Nevertheless there were occasional instances of touring the colonies, and for such hardy travelers, with the proper letters of introduction, an entrée into society was provided through the various social and sporting clubs found in every city. In the next century Alexis de Tocqueville was to note an unusual peculiarity of Americans whenever public pleasure was concerned: an association would be formed "to give more splendor and regularity to the entertainment." [56] This tendency already had expression in the colonies through the social clubs which met at the taverns and coffee-houses for conversation and drinking.

On a trip north in 1744, Dr. Alexander Hamilton of Maryland

was entertained at the Physical Club and Withered's in Boston; in the Philosophical Club at Newport (where he was unduly surprised "to find that no matters of philosophy were brought upon the carpet"); and at the Hungarian Club in New York— "after supper they set in for drinking, to which I was averse, and therefore sat upon nettles." [57] On visiting Philadelphia, Andrew Burnaby wrote of the "Colony in Schuylkill" whose members "divert themselves with walking, fishing, going up the water, dancing, singing, conversing, or just as they please." [58] In Annapolis the Tuesday Club met every week, serving at its dinner only one dish of "vittles" and no liquor after eleven. Charleston had its well-known Jockey Club (as did Annapolis) and a Monday Night Club, while Savannah enjoyed a Quoits Club. [59]

Another meeting-ground for colonial society was Newport, Rhode Island. "It is made the resort every summer," Robert Melville, the governor of Granada, wrote in 1765, "of numerous wealthy inhabitants of the Southern Colonies, and the West Indies, seeking health and pleasure." In the eight years from 1767 to 1775, indeed, the pioneer society column of the *Newport Mercury* listed some four hundred summer visitors. [60]

The amusements of these vacationists included the assemblies, card parties, and concerts that characterized their social activities at home. The *Mercury* carried notices of the availability of Mrs. Cowley's long room for dancing, with a "separate genteel Apartment with card-tables and a good Fire," and of an "Entertainment of Musick every Monday, Tuesday, Wednesday and Thursday, to be given by Mr. Henry Hymes." Newport also offered outdoor dances and evening promenades, driving in chaises, beach races of the famous Narragansett pacers, turtle dinners on Goat Island, and excursions on "the new pleasure-boat, Liberty." [61]

David Douglass even brought the American Company to Newport in a daring theatrical invasion of New England. No more sympathetic audience was likely to be found in all America, but there remained the fact that geographically at least Newport was within the precincts of Puritanism. A performance to be given at the King's Arms Tavern on June 10, 1762, was therefore announced as a moral dialogue. The sole object of the entertainment, it was carefully explained, was to depict "the evil effects of jealousy and other bad passions.... Proving that happiness can only spring from the pursuit of Virtue." Mr. Douglass himself would represent "a noble and magnanimous Moor," Mr. Hallam take the part of a "young and thoughtless officer," while Mrs. Morris would be cast as a "young and virtuous wife, who, being wrongfully suspected, gets smothered (in an adjoining room) by her husband." The dialogue was to conclude at ten-thirty "in order that every spectator may go home at a sober hour, and reflect upon what he has seen, before he retires to rest." [62]

What could be more conducive to morals? What could offer less offense to the puritan conscience? But there were Calvinists in Rhode Island who had heard of *Othello*, who had heard of Shakespeare. They knew the theatre for the Devil's handiwork which it really was. A few performances were given in Newport, the company even ventured to Providence, but the Rhode Island Assembly soon took decisive action. There would be no more theatrical performances, on penalty of £100 fine for every actor.[63] Newport continued to flourish as a summer resort, but it had to get along without its theatre.

->>><<<-

ON THE EVE of the Revolution the Continental Congress proposed to curtail the amusements of the colonial aristocracy. One of the articles of the "Association" of 1774 called upon the several colonies to "discountenance and discourage every Species of Extravagance and Dissipation, especially all Horse Racing, and all Kinds of Gaming, Cock Fighting, Exhibitions of Shows, Plays, and other expensive Diversions and Entertainments...." [64]

It is interesting that these amusements should have had a sufficiently wide vogue to warrant such action; it is interesting to speculate upon the possible motives behind this drastic ban. Was it an expression of popular discontent with an extravagant way of life which contrasted too sharply with the simple, frugal, hard-working life of the colonial yeomanry? Was it the sign of an inherent Puritanism in the attitude of the New England delegates at the Continental Congress which was outraged by the frivolity of the rich planters of the South? The Revolution had its social as well as its political aspects. It was an attack upon economic privilege at home as well as upon political control from abroad. This resolution voiced a protest which may well have reflected the stirrings of a new class consciousness in colonial America.

In any event, the local committees of correspondence and the Sons of Liberty, representing the masses rather than the classes, took it upon themselves to enforce the resolution. Horse-races were effectively prohibited, the American Company of Comedians compelled to leave for the West Indies, and balls and assemblies were on occasion broken up by radical agitators. The recreation of merchant and planter was rudely interrupted even before war broke out, and not until well after the Revolution could a restored society again enjoy a social life in any way comparable to that of the middle of the eighteenth century.

Chapter IV

THE FRONTIER

Apart from the main stream of American recreation, fitting into no general pattern, were the amusements of the frontier. They maintained their place in our national life for almost a century after the establishment of the Republic. New developments affecting other phases of social activity did not touch them. But the frontier during these years was being pushed farther and farther westward, changing in place if not in spirit. And once civilization had caught up with it—on the slopes of the Alleghenies, in the valley of the Mississippi, on the Great Plains —the natural restraints of a more conventional way of life quickly spelled the decline of many of the pioneers' rough and boisterous diversions.

At the opening of the nineteenth century, travelers in Ohio brought home vivid accounts of the "dram-drinking, jockeying, and gambling" that characterized the frontier. They told tall tales of barbecues and backwoods balls where home-distilled whisky stood ready at hand in an open tub, a drinking-gourd beside it. The women sometimes drank toddies; the men took theirs straight:

> Hail Columbia, happy land,
> If you ain't drunk, I'll be damned.

Some three decades later, when this pioneer country had become a state proudly boasting close upon a million inhabitants, Frances Trollope was visiting Cincinnati. "The only rural amusement in which we ever saw the natives engaged," she wrote, "was eating strawberries and cream in a pretty garden about three miles from town." [1] So rapidly did the new West progress from its tumultuous beginnings.

The story was a similar one everywhere. The Federalist period found the western pioneers enjoying very much the same diversions from the backwoods of New York to those of Georgia. Twenty years pass, and the environment has so changed that the life of these early days is almost legend, but the same scenes are being reënacted on the new frontier in the Ohio Valley. Two more decades, and this western border is pushed beyond the Great River; soon the trails to Oregon and California will be opened up. And finally the latter half of the nineteenth century will witness settlement of the prairie states, the establishment of the cow-towns of Kansas and Wyoming, the mining-camps of Colorado and Nevada. Here again the exuberant spirit of the early frontier, with even more riotous emphasis on its drinking and gambling, will flare up and then die away against the colorful background of Abilene or Virginia City.

In this new western country a nation was being born. Its settlers were not transplanted Englishmen, but largely men born on American soil and imbued with American ideals. They poured forth from the older states in successive waves, these pioneers whose restless steps led them continually toward the setting sun. Hunters and trappers, carrying lightly their long rifles, blazed the forest trails; land-hungry settlers followed in their wake with ax and plow to clear the land and build their log-cabin homes; and at last the artisans and mechanics and tradespeople drove over the widening trails in lumbering Conestoga wagons to transform the scattered frontier outposts into thriving towns.

Life in this virgin territory was on a more generous scale than life had been on the shores of the Atlantic at a similar stage of development. Distances were greater, the vast forest lands more impenetrable, the rivers longer and deeper. With land trails more difficult of passage than ocean routes, the first settlers in trans-Appalachia were actually more cut off from civilization than the founders of America had been from their homeland. They were freer from restraining influences; circumstances compelled them to be more independent and self-sufficient. With no overseas trading companies sending them supplies, buying their products, exercising control over their activities, the western pioneers recognized no authority except of their own choosing.

They came from all ranks of contemporary society: there were the amiable and the virtuous, in the approving phrase of Timothy Flint (hopefully distributing copies of "The Swearer's Prayer" to Pennsylvania teamsters), and the scoundrels and wastrels singled out by Timothy Dwight. The pioneers of the new West, that is, comprised a cross-section of society in the older states just as the colonial settlers had represented all social elements of seventeenth-century England. But experience in America had given them a new approach to life. They were tougher and more adaptable. They were not the men to starve when fish and game were plentiful. They had expansive theories of democracy and a strong belief in the equality of man. They had an individualism which would not permit them to settle together in close little towns comparable to those of New England in the early days of settlement. Each man was prepared to hew his own way through the world.

Their recreations reflected their environment. They had no more leisure than the first settlers in America; they had less opportunity for social gatherings. The frontier offered a lonely and hard life. But when the craving for companionship could no longer be ignored, when the need for amusement had to be satisfied, there were no artificial constraints or polite conventions about the pioneer celebrations. Here were no self-constituted magistrates attempting to regulate manners and morals or to enforce rules against the "mispense of time." In so far as earlier traditions affected the pioneer attitude, the liberal influence of the early French settlers in the Mississippi Valley outweighed that of Puritan New England. In a spirit of full democracy, the frontiersmen intended to enjoy themselves when they met at their log-rollings and barbecues and camp-meetings. The repressive influence of the more civilized East would soon reach them, but for a time the pioneers lived their own life.

They drank the raw, stinging whisky of the country with even more gusto than their colonial forebears; they gambled with greater abandon over horses and cards. The sports and games that marked their infrequent social gatherings were always rough, and sometimes brutal. When they met on some festive occasion, they danced through the whole night. They had no thought of observing Sunday quiet and decorum. As the frontier stretched ever farther westward, they boasted that the Sabbath would never cross the Mississippi.

->>)<<-

IN THE FIRST DAYS of settlement the frontiersman was seldom seen without his rifle, generally a long and heavy single-barreled flintlock; his otter-skin bullet pouch, with its string of patches; his powder-horn; and his "iron hook to tote squirrels." Often a pack of mongrel dogs crowded his moccasined heels. The colonial settler with his Old World background had hardly known how to handle his gun; the ways of the forest were entirely strange to him. These later pioneers were thoroughly at home on its narrow, winding trails; they were hunters before everything else.

The wealth of game along this new frontier was even greater than that of the Atlantic seaboard. In his *Memorable Days in America,* William Faux relates that there were times when the flocks of wild pigeons roosting on the trees sent them crashing to the ground amid "a scene of confusion and destruction, too strange to describe, and too dangerous to be approached by either man or beast." [2] The dead pigeons would be gathered up by the cartload—which is recorded as an illustration of the game available rather than of the sport of hunting.

Competitive squirrel hunts are often mentioned in travel accounts. On one occasion two competing teams of four men each returned at nightfall, the one with 152 squirrels and the other

with 141. Another time two thousand tails were brought home
as trophies. The record was perhaps that announced by the
Kentucky Gazette in May, 1796. It reported that a party of
hunters "rendezvoused at Irvine's Lick and produced seven
thousand nine hundred and forty-one Squirrels killed by them
in one day." The frontiersmen were such crack shots, as Audubon and many others have testified, that they could kill a squirrel
by barking it—firing so close to it that the squirrel would fall to
the ground stunned by the concussion, without actually being
touched by the bullet.[3]

Wolf drives and ring hunts were also features of pioneer life.
An army of men and boys from near-by settlements would form
a vast encircling line of huntsmen around an area of perhaps forty
square miles. Gradually they would close in the circle, driving
ahead of them all the game they could scare up. When at last
the ring was so small that the harried animals began to try to
break through, the signal of a huntsman's horn would start a
wholesale slaughter. Guns would be used as long as this was reasonably safe, and then clubs, pitchforks, any available weapon.
At one such hunt, some sixty bear, twenty-five deer, one hundred
turkeys, and even larger numbers of smaller animals and game-
birds were reported to have fallen before the enthusiastic
hunters.

Pride in marksmanship made shooting matches of all kinds
even more popular than they had been in the colonies. They
were an institution along the entire border at the close of the
Revolution, and they followed the frontier westward, bequeath-
ing to more settled communities in the East rifle clubs and trap-
shooting. It was no longer customary to shoot at a live mark, a
staked fowl or animal, and take it off as the trophy. Targets were
more generally used, and a "beeve" or a barrel of whisky was
often the prize.

Entrants in one of these contests would pay twenty-five cents
for each shot, each man supplying his own target, a cross marking the bull's-eye or a center nail. Rules of procedure would be

carefully agreed upon (such as the allowance for an offhand shot as opposed to shooting with a rest) and an impartial board of judges selected. To the marksman who most often hit the bull's-eye, or drove his center nail in farthest, custom decreed award of the hide and tallow of the beef animal for which they were shooting; to the second highest scorer went choice of the animal's hindquarters; third, the remaining hindquarter; fourth, choice of the forequarters; fifth, the remaining forequarter; while the man in sixth place would be entitled to the lead in the tree on which the targets had been set up.

"This is one of our homely amusements," wrote Colonel Davy Crockett. "Each man takes a part, if he pleases, and no one is excepted." Side bets generally enlivened the match, Davy Crockett declaring that he would "never bet anything beyond a quart of whisky upon a rifle shot—which I considered a legal bet, and a gentlemanly and rational amusement." [4]

A more hazardous type of shooting match, which John Bernard mentions as popular in the western parts of the Carolinas early in the century, was "shooting the tin cup." [5] We are told that it meant literally shooting a tin cup off a man's head at thirty paces for a prize of a quart of whisky. Mike Fink, the legendary hero of the Ohio keel-boat men, was to become the great champion at this sport. The redoubtable Mike is said never to have missed until the sad occasion when "corned too heavy...he elevated too low." He shot his man through the head, and it was the resentment of the victim's friends at such inexcusable carelessness that finally brought to a violent end the last of the great rivermen.

Racing was almost as universal an amusement as shooting matches, a characteristic feature of every pioneer celebration. Every owner of a horse was confident of its prowess and eager to match it against all comers. And for the entire community the race offered a chance to bet. America has always had its race meets, from colonial days to the present, but the informal, spontaneous quarter-racing of the countryside was for long a far

Shooting for the Beef

Painting by George Caleb Bingham, 1850. Garvan Collection. Courtesy
of the Metropolitan Museum of Art.

Joys of the Camp-Meeting

Lithograph by Kennedy and Lucas after a painting by A. Rider. Courtesy of Harry T. Peters.

more general sport. It followed the frontier from the Atlantic seaboard to Wyoming and Arizona. In the early days of settlement in the valley of the Ohio, there were races of every kind. Lively accounts tell of all Pittsburgh turning out in that city: the local course lined with an excited crowd; the betting, drinking, and occasional fisticuffs; the sudden rush to the rails as the cry rang out, "To horse, to horse!" [6]

The importance of physical strength in pioneer life gave a fresh interest to other traditional colonial sports, and also accounted for new variations of the older events. Throwing the long bullet, hurling the tomahawk, and flinging the rail were added to the usual foot-races, jumping contests, and wrestling matches. In place of the old sport of quoits—at which Chief Justice Marshall had been a club champion—the homely pastime of pitching horseshoes became a favorite game. It was to remain one for the next century, a typically American amusement.

Andrew Jackson was reputed to be a champion at throwing the long bullet—a sport which involved throwing, or slinging from a leather strap, an iron ball of several pounds weight in such a way as to make it roll through a marked goal. Abraham Lincoln won wide fame for his weight-lifting and wrestling prowess. Reminiscences of the latter's contemporaries recall that the awkward country boy, so strong that he could pick up a whisky barrel and drink out of the bung-hole, was among the most active in the sports of the little town of New Salem, Illinois. His friends were always ready to back him against all comers. One time he failed them. He was matched against a local wrestling champion, and for all their efforts neither man could get a fall. Lincoln recognized his equal: "Jack, let's quit. I can't throw you—you can't throw me." [7]

Mark Twain has written of a rough-and-tumble fighter of the western country somewhat more confident of himself. "Whoo-oop! I'm the old original iron-jawed, brass-mounted, copper-bellied corpse-maker from the wilds of Arkansaw!" this shrinking violet announced as he challenged all comers. "Look at me! I'm the man they call Sudden Death and General Desolation! Sired by a hurricane, dam'd by an earthquake, half-brother to the cholera, nearly related to the small-pox on the mother's side! Look at me! I take nineteen alligators and a bar'l of whiskey for breakfast when I'm in robust health, and a bushel of rattlesnakes and a dead body when I'm ailing. I split the everlasting rocks with my glance, and I squench the thunder when I speak! Stand back and give me room according to my strength! Blood's my natural drink, and the wails of the dying is music to my ear! Cast your eye on me, gentlemen, and lay low and hold your breath, for I'm 'bout to turn myself loose." [8]

Sometimes these frontier bouts ended very close to Sudden Death. All holds were allowed, and kicking, biting, punching, and gouging freely permitted. "I saw more than one man, who wanted an eye," one traveler reported as he crossed the border into Kentucky, "and ascertained that I was now in the region of 'gouging.'" [9] Another judged the respectability of the inns at which he was forced to put up by whether mine host still had his ears.

"Very few rounds had taken place," runs a vivid account of one fight, "before the Virginian contracted his whole form, drew up his arms to his face, with his hands closed in a concave, by the fingers being bent to the full extension of the flexors, and summoning up all his energy for one act of desperation, pitched himself into the bosom of his opponent.... The shock received by the Kentuckian and the want of breath brought him instantly to the ground. The Virginian never lost his hold; fixing his claws in his hair and his thumbs in his eyes, he gave them an instantaneous start from their sockets. The sufferer roared aloud, but uttered no complaint. The Kentuckian not being able to disentangle his adversary from his face, adopted a new mode of warfare. He extended his arms around the Virginian, and hugged him into closer contact with his huge body. The latter, disliking this, made one further effort and fastening the under lip of his mutilator tore it over the chin. The Kentuckian at length gave out, on which the people carried off the victor, and he preferring a triumph to a doctor ... suffered himself to be chaired round the grounds as the first rough and tumbler." [10]

While this record bears the mark of a lively imagination, the brutality reflected in such fighting was perhaps only natural in a frontier community. It was also shown in the popularity of cock-fighting and gander-pulling. Lincoln attended cock-fights, as had George Washington before him, and William Herndon has left a fragmentary description of one such affair. "They formed a ring, and the time having arrived, Lincoln, with one hand on each hip and in a squatting position, cried, 'Ready.' Into the ring they toss their fowls, Bap's red rooster along with the rest. But no sooner had the little beauty discovered what was to be done than he dropped his tail and ran." [11]

Whether Lincoln had a wager on Bap's disappointing game-cock is not revealed, but if the story had been told of Andrew Jackson, we could have been sure of the betting. As a young man in North Carolina, he was known as "the most roaring, rollicking, game-cocking, horse-racing, card-playing, mischievous fellow, that ever lived in Salisbury." The earliest document found among his personal papers is a memorandum: "How to feed a Cock before you him fight Take and give him some Pickle Beef cut fine...." [12]

More surprising to find in these early years are the occasional instances of cricket-playing reported by some travelers. Wherever settlements were made by English immigrants in the nineteenth century, this sport was introduced. They played it on the open fields of the settled East; they played it on the little clearings of this new western country. William Faux noted it in Kentucky in 1818, and both John Woods and Richard Flower report it as a sport in Illinois a year later. [13] The Chicago of 1840, where foot-races, boating, and quoits were also general diversions, had three cricket teams. Here was fertile ground for the introduction of baseball in the middle of the century. [14]

➤➤➤⫷⫷⫷

BEES and frolics, which had become so universal a feature of American folk life, were often the occasion for sports and games, for informal horse-races, and for frontier dances. One English visitor came to the conclusion that Americans could not do anything without a frolic. "They have husking, reaping, rolling frolics, &," he wrote; "among the females, they have picking, sewing and quilting frolics." [15] Their most general characteristic appears to have been their enthusiastic drinking. They had changed from colonial days in only one respect, the substitution of whisky for rum.

The log-rolling was perhaps the most typical of these gatherings. A settler taking up land in the West had a hard task clearing his ground. He would first girdle the trees on the plot he expected to plant, cutting a wide circle in the bark to kill them, but when he finally cut them down, he had to have help to roll the huge logs into piles for burning. Neighbors from miles around came to aid in this work, and the log-rolling was made a holiday spree in which whole families—wives and children—took part.

Dinner was a gargantuan feast: a barbecued beef or hog, roasted in a deep hole lined with hot stones; quantities of buffalo steaks, venison, baked 'possum or wild turkey; and always hominy, corn dodgers, and wheatcakes fried in bear's oil. After dinner and general sports, the climax of every gathering was a dance. The men and women of the frontier loved to dance. It was a favorite amusement everywhere, singled out by traveler after traveler surprised to find such rollicking gaiety in the gloomy shadows of the deep western forests.

There were no formal rules of etiquette for the backwoods ball, no costumes in the latest mode of London or Paris. Deerskin hunting-jackets, leggings, and moccasins for the men; for the women, homespun dresses of linsey-woolsey and worn shoes which they had perhaps carried in their hands on the long walk along forest trails. As for the dances themselves, "None of your straddling, mincing, sadying," wrote Davy Crockett, "but a regu-

lar sifter, cut-the-buckle, chicken flutter set-to. It is a good wholesome exercise; and when one of our boys puts his arm around
his partner, it's a good hug, and no harm in it." [16]

Virginia reels, country jigs, shakedowns, were the order of the
day, danced on the forest floor as the fiddler made the catgut
screech through the night air and the pine knots flared against a
full moon. Some one called the numbers:

> First lady to the right, cheat and swing,
> Ladies do so do, and gents you know.
>
> Gents hands in your pockets, backs to the wall,
> Take a chaw of tabacker and balance all.

Well into the morning the backwoodsmen danced: every now
and then a halt for a "bite and a swig," but the violins always
called them back to their wooded ball-room.

"Every countenance beamed with joy," wrote Audubon, lyrically describing a Kentucky barbecue in 1834, "every heart
leaped with gladness; no pride, no pomp, no affectation were
there; their spirits brightened as they continued their exhilarating exercise, and care and sorrow were flung to the winds. During each interval of rest, refreshments of all sorts were handed
round, and while the fair one cooled her lips with the grateful
juice of the melon, the hunter of Kentucky quenched his thirst
with ample draughts of well-tempered punch." [17] He too describes the racing and shooting at a mark, the tables heaped
with food and the ready barrels of Old Monongahela.

On the sod-house frontier soon to be opened up beyond the
Mississippi, dancing became as popular as it had been in the
Ohio Valley. There was always a great scarcity of women for
the holiday balls, and the young men would scour the prairies
looking for partners. They would ride in to the dance with
young girls or grandmothers, it little mattered, perched on the
saddle behind them, calico dresses neatly tucked in, sunbonnets
swinging in the wind. On one mid-century occasion no less than
two thousand people gathered at Brownsville, Nebraska, for a

Fourth of July barbecue and dance. The buffalo, venison, oxen, sheep, hogs, and pigs slaughtered were said to have been "enough to have fed the whole territory." Another time a New Year's dance at Lecompton, Kansas, found the ladies dancing on the open prairie in mackinaws and overshoes. Dinner, brought in by hunters, was served in tents pitched by a roaring fire. For a frolic at Blue Springs, Nebraska, a special committee caught one thousand pounds of catfish.[18]

They danced the scamperdown, double shuffle, western swing, and half-moon:

> Grab your honies, don't let 'em fall,
> Shake your hoofs and balance all.

A deep pull from the little brown jug; the men would swing their partners until they kicked the ceiling—if there was any ceiling. Faster, faster, the old fiddler would sway over his precious instrument, and heavy boots stamp on the hard ground floor. Receptions, and assemblies, and cotillions were just over the horizon. This was still the frontier. Another swig from the little brown jug; call out the numbers:

> Ringtailed coons in the trees at play:
> Grab your pardners and all run away.

Weddings and infares provided other bright spots in pioneer life. On the occasion of the former, the day usually started with the groom's friends escorting him to the bride's house, on horseback, in solemn procession. But the moment the party came in sight of their destination, they would be off on a mad race to be the first to arrive. For custom decreed a prize for the winner—a whisky bottle affectionately known as Black Betty. Once the ceremony itself was performed, this bottle circulated briskly, and the party took care of itself.

The wedding guests had a friendly obligation, however. They put the newly married couple to bed, with the crude jokes and good-natured ribaldry typical of the frontier. Then, as the evening grew gayer and the whisky flowed more freely—"Where is Black Betty, I want to kiss her sweet lips"—they would thoughtfully send up drinks with uproarious shouted toasts: "Here's to the bride, thumping luck and big children."

The horse-play was sometimes rough. Uninvited guests might try to cut off the manes and tails of the wedding party's horses; they sometimes attempted to set up a pair of horns on a pole near the house as a subtle reflection on the bride's chastity. To interrupt the ceremony just as the minister started to read the service by letting loose so noisy a serenade that he could not be heard, or even to try kidnapping the groom, was a popular sport. The charivari or "shivaree," that noisy concert in which no instrument was more effective than a horseshoe and a sugar-kettle, in time became so regular a feature of frontier wedding celebrations that the bride's family had always to stand ready to buy obstreperous serenaders off with more liquor.[19]

The story is told that Lincoln once almost broke up a wedding party. He was not invited, perhaps as the result of some earlier feud, to a double ceremony in the Grigsby family, and he arranged with a confederate for a sensational revenge. When the grooms were escorted to their respective bridal chambers, they found themselves with the wrong brides. Lincoln then went on to add insult to injury by writing a scandalous version of the whole affair—"The Chronicle of Reuben." The consequences are obscure: a renewed feud, a general fight, and Lincoln waving a triumphant whisky bottle over his head and shouting that he was "the big buck of the lick." [20]

The accounts of this incident may be embroidered, for nothing was more typical of the frontier than the telling of tall tales. At every frolic, as well as at trading-posts, about camp-fires, on the decks of flatboats, and at the village taverns, the pioneers whiled away hours with story and anecdote. In no other part of the country has talk played a larger rôle in popular diversion. There grew up in the West a wealth of legend and folklore, at once realistic and wildly exaggerated, which was American to the core. Stories of Daniel Boone, Kit Carson, Davy Crockett, or some even more mythical figure as Mike Fink, Paul Bunyan, or Jim Henry, are still a delight to an age far removed from that which gave birth to them.

There were the traditional tales of mighty hunters, of wonderful marksmanship, of the great feats of the rivermen. A host of popular legends developed about "the ugly man" (Lincoln himself could have filled this rôle) who became a western folk hero. It was related of Davy Crockett that his grin had such a paralyzing effect that he could bring down raccoons without either powder or shot: he merely grinned at the 'coon and it would fall at his feet. One day his grin failed to work. The raccoon appeared glued to the tree. But Davy finally discovered that it was his eyes rather than his ugliness that had failed him. There was no raccoon, merely an unusual knot in the oak-tree . . . and he had grinned all the bark off it!

A story of the western plains, not of the forest, describes a part of the country where the atmosphere was so rarefied that the sound of one's voice would be thrown back from a mountain several hundred miles off. It took six hours for the echo to return. Making camp for the night, Jim Bridger would turn toward the mountain and shout at the top of his voice, "Time to turn out!" He could then roll up in his blankets, confident that the echo would awaken him at daybreak.[21]

➤➤✕◄◄

ANOTHER OUTLET valve for men and women who had so few chances to escape their loneliness was the camp-meeting. Its primary purpose was to work a spiritual regeneration among those who attended it, to point the path of salvation from the ungodly ways fostered by the rough life of the pioneer country. The Methodist circuit-riders warned of fire and brimstone for all those who indulged in the frontier amusements of dancing, card-playing, horse-racing, gambling, and drinking. But at the same time the camp-meeting was an occasion which often provided exciting entertainment. The crowds, the intoxication of revivalist oratory, the hymn-singing, all contributed to an emotional release from the cares of everyday life which had every aspect of hearty recreation.

"Vast numbers are there from curiosity and merely to enjoy the spectacle," wrote one observant visitor. "The young and the beautiful are there with mixed motives, which it were not best severely to scrutinize." [22]

When a meeting was announced, the people would gather from miles around, many of them undertaking a several-days journey. The countryside would present the appearance of a general migration. From the more settled communities heavy ox carts carrying whole families would bump over the rough plank roads. Lonely men and women from isolated cabins in the depths of the forest threaded their way along trails seldom pierced by the light of the sun. At the appointed place, usually some clearing on the edge of the woods, near water, they would make camp. Tents were pitched, a platform built for the preachers, and sometimes benches set up for the huge audience which would crowd the enclosure. The meeting would last perhaps a week, with continual services. It was a gigantic community picnic.

"Large fires of timber were kindled," reads the description of one such meeting, "which cast a new lustre on every object. The white tents gleamed in the glare. Over them the dusky woods formed a most romantic gloom, only the tall trunks of the first rank were distinctly visible, and these seemed so many members of a lofty charade. The illuminated camp lay on a declivity, and exposed a scene that suggested to my mind the moonlit gambols of beings known to us only through the fictions of credulous eyes. The greatest turmoil prevailed within the fence, where the inmates were leaping and holding together with upward looks and extended arms. Around this busy mass, the crowd formed a thicker ring than the famous Macedonian phalanx; and among them a mixture of the exercised were interspersed. . . . The sublimity of the music served to give an enchanting effect to the whole.... It had been thought proper to place sentinels without the camp. Females were not allowed to pass into the woods after dark." [23]

The manifestations of the Holy Spirit were strange and wondrous as the shouting, gesticulating, hair-tearing revivalists warmed to their vehement attacks on the Devil and all his ways. "It was supposed that no less than three hundred fell like dead men in a mighty battle," Peter Cartwright, a Methodist circuit-rider of wide fame, reports of one meeting in his autobiography; "and there was no calling of mourners, for they were strewed all over the camp ground: loud wailing went up to Heaven from sinners for mercy, and a general shout from the Christians, so that the noise was heard afar off." [24] Another witness tells of "twenty thousand persons tossed to and fro like the tumultuous waves of the sea in a storm, or swept down like trees of the forest under the blast of a wild tornado." [25]

Nor was falling beneath the power of God the only hysterical response to the flaming oratory of the camp-meeting. Other accounts tell of the Holy Laugh and the Holy Dance, of people barking like a flock of spaniels, of great crowds uncontrollably seized by the jerks. "No matter whether they were saints or sinners," Cartwright wrote another time, "they would be taken under a warm song or sermon, and seized with convulsive jerking all over, which they could not by any possibility avoid, and the more they resisted the more they jerked.... I have seen more than five hundred persons jerking at one time in my large congregations." [26]

In bringing men and women together, especially young people, under such circumstances, the camp-meeting had its dangerous aspects because of the intense emotionalism it stirred up. The placing of sentinels about the ring of camp-fires was a common practice, but with all precautions there were many camp-meeting babies. William Herndon has a story of a young couple at a camp-meeting in the Lincoln country. "Slowly and gracefully they worked their way towards the centre," he writes, "singing, shouting, hugging and kissing, generally their own sex, until at last nearer and nearer they came. The centre of the altar was reached, and the two closed, with their arms around each other, the man singing and shouting at the top of his voice

> "I have my Jesus in my arms
> Sweet as honey, strong as bacon ham." [27]

Whether an active participant or an interested spectator, it is not difficult to understand why the frontiersman found the camp-meeting an exciting experience. A drunken spree at barbecue or log-rolling could hardly rival taking one's place on the "anxious bench," mingling one's hallelujahs with those of a thousand other frenzied converts, or joining in the Holy Dance as some inspired preacher called the tune. A revival was something for the pioneer to look forward to as he swung his heavy ax to clear another half-acre or hoed at his stubborn cornpatch. Conversion might of course limit his other amusements, but it was not necessary, as he must often have thought on his exhausted journey home, to stay saved for very long.

CHAPTER V

A CHANGING SOCIETY

IN THE OPENING DECADES OF THE NINETEENTH CENTURY, THE American people throughout the eastern parts of the country were enjoying very much the same recreations as they had in colonial days. The Revolution had marked a distinct break in many customs, especially for the wealthier classes, but old threads of activity were quickly picked up. Writing about 1821, Timothy Dwight singled out the principle amusements as "visiting, dancing, music, conversation, walking, riding, sailing, shooting at a mark, draughts, chess, and unhappily in some of the larger towns, cards and dramatic exhibitions."[1] Social life had a relative simplicity, and popular diversions conformed to familiar patterns.

But new winds were blowing. The turbulent, expansive years of the first half of the century were to usher in changes in recreation as far-reaching as those in any other department of the national life. The country was going through the first phase of its transformation from a simple agricultural community into a highly complex urban society. New means of amusement had to be found to replace those from which increasingly large numbers of persons were cut off by the very circumstance of city life. The rise of a working class imbued with the pervasive ideals of Jacksonian democracy created a demand for popular entertainment which had hardly been felt in colonial days.

The trend toward urbanization and the growth of a factory population were to continue in later years at a greatly accelerated pace. It was the novelty of these developments, crowding people together in living conditions entirely new to America, that gave them their importance in this period. Between 1800 and 1850 the proportion of the population living in urban communities of more than 8,000 tripled, representing in the latter year twelve per cent of the total. Some of the little colonial towns had become real cities. In mid-century New York had a population of more than 500,000, Philadelphia of over 300,000, and there were six other cities with more than 100,000 each.[2] Still small by to-day's standards, they nevertheless gave rise to a serious problem. What was to be the recreation of the new urban democracy which could no longer look to rural sports and informal country pastimes for relaxation? Some substitute had to be found to meet a demand growing greater every year because of the indoor confinement and monotonous routine of so much city work.

"Democracy is too new a comer upon the earth," wrote a shrewd foreign observer, Michael Chevalier, in 1833, "to have been able as yet to organize its pleasures and amusements. In Europe, our pleasures are essentially exclusive, they are aristocratic like Europe itself. In this matter, then, as in politics, the American democracy has yet to create every thing fresh."[3]

The answer to this challenge was the gradual growth of commercial amusements, the beginnings of what has now become a vast entertainment industry. But for many years during this difficult period of transition, recreation appears to have been more limited than at any other time in our history. The general shift from active to passive diversion did not make for a normal, healthy adjustment, and not until after the Civil War was this balance redressed by the rise of organized sports. New forms of recreation, moreover, found all the moral forces of the age arrayed against them. Whatever their actual value as a relief from the tedium of everyday life, they generally stood condemned.

A renewed emphasis upon the importance of work was one of the most telling repressive influences. The spirit of the times was expressed in the preamble of a New Hampshire law: "All young countries have much more occasion to encourage a spirit of industry and application to business, than to countenance schemes of pleasure and amusement." And this attitude was strengthened and intensified by a revived Puritanism which again provided a moral sanction for the disapproval of recreation. It was in 1839, however reminiscent of 1639 it may seem, that public speakers everywhere were preaching the doctrine upheld by one prominent lecturer who sententiously declared, "We tolerate no drones in our hive.... The sweat-drops on the brow of honest toil are more precious than the jewels of a ducal coronet." [4]

The intolerance of the seventeenth century, rather than the liberalism of the eighteenth, swayed public opinion. It was the dark period of Victorian repression. For the recreational scene actually to broaden under these circumstances, as it eventually did, was proof of an underlying need on the part of the American democracy which could not permanently be left unanswered. It was the expression of an unconscious determination in the pursuit of pleasure which had even stronger roots than Puritan tradition.

->>><<<-

THE OPPORTUNITY to develop the boundless resources of a continent, the need to build up trade and industry in order to assert our economic as well as our political independence, afforded very real justification for a return to the gospel of work. Without our national response to this opportunity the material development of the country would have been substantially slowed up. But it was equally true that continual application to business, with increasing concern over its profits, greatly narrowed the horizon of the average American. He became obsessed with a mania for making money. "In no country are the faces of the people furrowed with harder lines of care," wrote one sympathetic observer. "In no country that I know is there so much hard, toilsome, unremitting labor: in none so little of the recreation and enjoyment of life. Work and worry eat out the heart of the people, and they die before their time.... It is seldom that an

"Light May the Boat Row"

Lithographed cover of a music sheet of 1836. Courtesy of the New York Historical Society.

Dr. Rich's Institute for Physical Education

About 1850. J. Clarence Davies Collection, Museum of the City of New York.

A Picnic on the Wissahickon

Engraving by Rawdon, Wright and Hatch after a drawing by William Croome. *Graham's American Monthly Magazine*, 1844.

American retires from business to enjoy his fortune in comfort. Money-making becomes a habit. He works because he has always worked, and knows no other way." [5]

The Almighty Dollar cast its long shadow over the land. With depressing unanimity the host of English travelers who examined American democracy in the 1830's and 1840's found us too absorbed in work's daily routine to recognize any other phase of life. Never has criticism on this score been more general or persistent. Frances Trollope, Basil Hall, Thomas Hamilton, Frances Wright, and Charles Dickens—they all rang the changes on the same tune. Our only pleasure was business, our only amusement making money. Arriving at New Orleans at the time of that city's colorful Mardi Gras, Sir Charles Lyell breathed a sigh of relief to find at last some signs of gaiety in the United States. "From the time we landed in New England to this hour," he wrote, "we seemed to have been in a country where all, whether rich or poor, were laboring from morning till night, without ever indulging in a holiday." [6]

Frances Trollope's observations were colored by her snobbish scorn of the crudities of American life, but with all proper allowance for prejudice her repeated complaints of how dull she found this country carry conviction. "We are by no means as gay as our lively neighbors on the other side of the Channel," she wrote, "but compared with Americans, we are whirligigs and teetotums; every day is a holiday and every night a festival." She concluded that Americans must somehow not have the same need of being amused as other people—"they may be the wiser for this, perhaps, but it makes them less agreeable to a looker-on." [7]

Dickens was greatly depressed by a point of view which not only left no time for normal recreation, but gave a businesslike efficiency to activity outside the counting-house as well as within it. Among the people he encountered at boarding-houses and hotels, in stage-coaches and on steamboats, there were always the same rush and hurry. We may look back upon life a century ago as having had infinite leisure, but it was already marked by quick drinks and quick lunches. The American meal-hour horrified Dickens: "No conversation, no laughter, no cheerfulness; no sociality, except in spitting; and that is done in silent fellowship round the stove, when the meal is over. Every man sits down, dull and languid; swallows his fare as if breakfasts, dinners, and suppers, were necessities of nature never to be coupled with recreation or enjoyment; and having bolted his food in a gloomy silence bolts himself, in the same state." [8]

Our English visitor wandered forth from his hotel to observe the habits of the frenetic dollar-chasers of New York. "But how quiet the streets are! Are there no itinerant bands; no wind or stringed instruments? No, not one. By day are there no Punches, Fantocinne, Dancing Dogs, Jugglers, Conjurers, Orchestrinas, or even Barrel-organs? No, not one. Yes, I remember one, one barrel-organ and a dancing monkey, sportive by nature, but fast fading into a dull, lumpish monkey of the Utilitarian school. Beyond that, nothing lively; no, not so much as a white mouse in a twirling cage.

"Are there no amusements? Yes, there is a lecture room across the way, from which that glare of light proceeds, and there may be evening service for the ladies there thrice a week, or oftener. For the young gentlemen, there is the counting-house, the store, the bar-room...." [9]

→»«←

THE MORAL APPROVAL given this attitude served the same end as had Puritanism's support of the early colonial laws in detestation of idleness. The reawakening that succeeded the skepticism and apathy of the close of the eighteenth century made the period one of intense religious interest, and nowhere was it more strongly manifest than in its influence on recreation. A new generation of spiritual leaders took up arms against any broadening whatsoever of the field of amusements. They preached the sinfulness of idle pleasure with a fierce intolerance. Their prohibitions were most effective among those who actually had little chance to enjoy many diversions, again demonstrating the close relationship between reform and economic environment; but they affected all classes. The influence of the church largely determined the public attitude.

The full force of religious disapproval was thrown against the struggling theatre. President Dwight of Yale flatly declared that "to indulge a taste for playgoing means nothing more nor less than the loss of that most valuable treasure the immortal soul." [10] The church generally condemned commercial amusement, whatever its form, as "the door to all the sinks of iniquity," an attitude clearly revealing its complete failure to realize that a people growing further away from the simpler pastimes of an agricultural civilization had to have some substitute for them. As late as 1844 Henry Ward Beecher singled out for attack, with a vitriolic bitterness reminiscent of Cotton Mather, the stage, the concert-hall, and the circus. He made no distinctions. Any one who pandered to the new taste for entertainment was a moral assassin. The fate awaiting this enemy of society was certain: "As borne on the blast thy guilty spirit whistles towards the gates of hell, the hideous shrieks of those whom thy hand hath destroyed, shall pierce thee—hell's first welcome." [11]

The pulpit's wholesale denouncement of pleasure was more typical of New England, but other parts of the country also felt the heavy hand of puritan repression. The evangelical churches everywhere banned the race-course and all games of chance, forbade card-playing in whatever guise, and disapproved severely of dancing. Nineteenth-century Presbyterians, Baptists, and Methodists, gathering thousands of converts into their folds as they went south along the mountain ridges and then spread westward into the Mississippi Valley, reimposed many of the prohibitions of seventeenth-century Calvinists. In some sections the Middle West was to become more New England than New England itself.

In these circumstances another phenomenon of seventeenth-century life was repeated in the growing towns and cities of nineteenth-century America. The saloon and grog-shop became more than ever the workingman's club as urban life cut him off from other emotional outlets. Heavy drinking was a widely prevalent habit. It played a rôle fully as important as it had in colonial days, and had more serious consequences. It was the common belief of English visitors that a man could get drunk twice in America for sixpence—and usually did.[12]

In their efforts to suppress intemperance the reformers made no attempt to find a substitute for the saloon. Anne Royall once argued that establishment of theatres might be the means of saving the people "from the effects of an evil which seems to threaten their morals with a total overthrow," [13] but no one listened. The church easily fell in with the attitude of the merchant-manufacturer class, whose sole objective was to get as much work as possible out of its employees. The theory here was that drinking was the result of idleness, and consequently long hours of labor should be maintained for the sake of the wage-earners' moral welfare. They should not be allowed time for anything else. Spokesmen of religion turned a deaf ear to labor's contention that the intolerable burden of a twelve- or fourteen-hour day compelled some "excitement fully proportioned to the depression," which under existing circumstances could be found only in drinking. They gave full support to the new order of industrialists in upholding "the wholesome discipline of factory life." [14]

Nor was there any toleration of recreation on the one day in the week on which workers were free. The old issue of Sabbath observance was revived. At the close of the eighteenth century a marked weakening of Puritan restrictions had taken place. Even in Boston travelers reported that the townspeople had in great measure lost "that rigidity of manners and vigilant way of keeping Sunday" which had formerly characterized New England.[15] But as the nineteenth century progressed, many of the old bans were reapplied. No sports or games were allowed on the Lord's

Day, let alone public amusements. Travel was no longer permitted. In many states even the Government mails were stopped.
Public opinion, if not actual laws, decreed church attendance as
the only permissible Sunday activity.

"In 1800," Emerson Davis wrote in mid-century, "good men
slumbered over the desecration of the Sabbath. They have since
awoke." [16] This simply meant that on this count the harsh rule of
the Puritans was firmly refastened upon the country—"all was
solemn and drear. Laughter was considered irreverent." [17] It has
taken almost a century for Sunday bonds to become sufficiently
relaxed to sanction normal recreation.

Deprived of support from the more responsible elements of
society because of the church's attitude, public entertainment
often fell into the hands of those who on occasion did not hesi-
tate to pander to the lowest order of popular taste. This in turn
aroused further opposition to commercial amusements. The vicious circle continued until social leaders began to recognize the
importance of recreation in the national life, accepting the fact
that in what was becoming an urban society, it necessarily had to
be organized, and often placed on a commercial basis.

->>)((<-

ANOTHER FACTOR serving at times to discourage the growth of
amusements as such was a nation-wide cultural reawakening
which affected all classes. The 1830's and 1840's were an age of
intense activity along many lines. American thought was going
through a period of ferment which was expressed by a keen and
active interest in things of the mind and spirit. New concepts
of democracy, of humanitarianism, of the brotherhood of man,
were in the air. Among the factory workers there was often
strong disapproval of the recreational use of even such little
leisure as they commanded because of an unusual sense of civic
responsibility.

When labor urged the reduction of the working-day from the
prevailing twelve and fourteen hours to ten, it did not assert any

claim for time to play. "All men have a just right, derived from their creator," a resolution of the Journeymen Carpenters of Philadelphia stated in 1827, "to have a sufficient time in each day for the cultivation of their mind and for self-improvement; Therefore, resolved, that we think ten hours industriously employed are sufficient for a day's labor." "Let the mechanic's labour be over when he has wrought ten or twelve hours in the long days of summer," reads another piece of propaganda, "and he will be able to return to his family in season, and with sufficient vigour, to pass some hours in the instruction of his children, or in the improvement of his own mind." [18]

With this strong feeling of the importance of self-education and widespread interest in intellectual matters, a great vogue developed for public lectures. The lyceum movement, bringing public speakers to every town throughout the country, spread rapidly. It was started in 1826. Five years later a national organization was formed with some nine hundred local lyceums.[19] They provided a platform for speakers on every conceivable topic—history, philosophy, and geology; women's rights, prison reform, insane asylums; temperance and abolition. Sir Charles Lyell was astounded in the 1840's to find the general public rushing to the lecture as they might formerly have done to a play; Philip Hone observed with amazement that in New York the craze had left the theatres flat on their backs.[20]

Many of our foreign visitors spoke of the workingmen audiences at these lectures. They were especially noted in New England, and one of the most striking instances of cultural enthusiasm was found at the cotton-mills of Lowell, Massachusetts. Its atmosphere was far from typical of most manufacturing towns, and even here the roseate picture drawn by foreigners was greatly exaggerated. Nevertheless, the great majority of the workers were self-respecting country girls, serious and intelligent. Their attitude may be taken as a symbol of the zest for knowledge.

"In Lowell reading is the only recreation," wrote Michael

Chevalier; [21] Professor Peabody of Harvard found his lecture-room crowded with factory operatives who laid aside their books only to take notes on his talk; [22] and Dickens, visiting the city in 1842, was impressed by three facts: "Firstly, there is a joint stock piano in a great many of the boarding houses. Secondly, nearly all the young people subscribe to circulating libraries. Thirdly, they have got among themselves a periodical called The Lowell Offering." [23] This publication exuded the factory town's lofty spirit. There was the story of Abby's first year in the mills: "She gratified no feeling but a newly awakened desire for mental improvement, and spent her leisure hours in reading useful books." [24]

In many instances the public crowded the lecture-hall with less elevated motives than self-education. George Combe, lecturing on the popular fad of phrenology, freely admitted that "entertainment and excitement, as much as instruction," drew the crowds that nightly attended his lectures in Boston.[25] And there was even less pretense of culture in the audiences that gathered to hear the ever-popular spiritualists, hypnotists, mesmerists, psychometrists, hydropathists.... A woman speaker advertised a lecture on animal magnetism in which she would painlessly draw the teeth of any person who so desired, and a lecturer on mesmerism promised to operate on the entire audience and produce a variety of results in trance and catalepsy. This was clearly entertainment as much as concert-hall or theatre. Philip Hone considered it of an even lower order, but commented philosophically, "the people will be amused."

Nevertheless the serious purpose that lay behind this vogue for lectures was their important feature. It reflected the idealistic belief that in a democracy all citizens should be able to take an intelligent part in the conduct of government. They should be educated to fulfil their social obligations. Self-improvement was not a selfish goal: it was a responsibility of citizenship. In the awakening desire of democracy to play a full rôle in public affairs, the need for a wide diffusion of knowledge seemed implicit.

Female Calisthenics in the Pantalette Era

The Casket, 1832.

In considering popular lectures, in this or other periods, it is never possible to draw a hard and fast line between education and entertainment. In most cases both elements were present. The lecture craze of the 1840's, however, had the full support of all those who felt it was sinful to use leisure solely for enjoyment. For that reason it was an important phenomenon both in itself and because of its retarding influence on the growth of amusements which could make no cultural claims.

→>>‹‹‹-

THE STATUS of women in the social life of the nineteenth century also had a very definite bearing on recreation. Prevailing concepts of the proper relationship to be maintained between the sexes were a barrier which, apart from all other considerations, prevented the natural development of many forms of diversion. They gave an atmosphere of artificial restraint to ordinary social functions. For long they made it almost impossible for men and women to enjoy together any outdoor activities. And it was not only that there was less freedom in social intercourse than there is to-day. Popular ideas on the delicacy of females—a basic canon of the mid-nineteenth century—and an almost morbid prudery meant a more restricted life for women than in the eighteenth century. In colonial days they had been able to enter far more fully into both the work and the recreation of men. They took part in the farm festivals and holiday celebrations; they enjoyed as spectators if not as actual participants whatever amusements were available. But now women were more and more condemned to a life separate and apart.

It was a man's world, with its tremendous emphasis on work and getting ahead. Young people were allowed great liberty. "They dance, sing, walk and run in sleighs together, by sunshine and moonshine," wrote Frances Wright, "without the occurrence or even the apprehension of any impropriety." [26] But this dispensation was short-lived. "Once married," another contemporary observer reported, "the young lady entirely changes her habits. Farewell gaiety and frivolity." [27] Whatever their position in society, women were expected to devote themselves wholly to the duties of domestic life. Visitors from abroad often singled this out as a bizarre and unexpected aspect of the American scene. The sparkling Fanny Kemble found it impossible to conform to such a narrow tradition after her own American marriage. Frances Trollope was incensed at an attitude which so closely restrained those of her sex.

If they had any leisure, the ladies took up embroidery, painting on glass or china, and waxwork—with commendable perseverance and devastating results. But they kept indoors, and everything else, including health, was sacrificed to incredible standards of proper female decorum. Viewing the results, Thomas Hamilton mourned that "at one or two-and-twenty, the bloom of an American lady is gone, and the more substantial materials of beauty follow soon after. At thirty the whole fabric is in decay, and nothing remains but the tradition of former conquests." [28] Delicacy became the hall-mark of gentility, the sign and symbol (as the Chinese mandarin's long finger-nails) of freedom from manual labor. It was not, indeed, a general characteristic. By far the larger number of women could not afford delicacy: their household work would not permit it. But it was the goal toward which they all aspired, and the dominant male encouraged it. It contributed to his own sense of importance and established social status.

The few attempts that were made to persuade women to take outdoor recreation illustrate this general attitude even more pointedly. In mid-century there was a revival of skating which brought out thousands to country ponds and city rinks. During twenty-seven days of good ice in one season, over two hundred thousand skaters were estimated to have visited the lakes of New York's new Central Park; excursion trains daily carried from a thousand to fifteen hundred Boston enthusiasts to Jamaica Pond.[29] It was urged as a suitable sport for both sexes. But the female skater was advised in one such appeal to take fast hold

A Family Party Playing at Fox and Geese

Drawing by Winslow Homer. *Ballou's Pictorial Drawing-Room Companion*, 1857.

The Dance after the Husking

Harper's Weekly. 1858.

Skating in Central Park, New York

of the coat tails of her gentleman partner, for then, "if he was a dextrous glider, and she maintained a firm position, a gay time she could have of it enjoying all the pleasure without incurring any of the fatigue of the exercise." [30]

One English visitor who greatly missed feminine society as he traveled about America, Captain Basil Hall, reported sadly that he had positively never once seen "anything approaching within many degrees to what we should call a flirtation." His lively wife confirmed his impression that there was "a great separation between the ladies and gentlemen in society here." They found few women at the theatre in New York or at the race-track in Charleston; even at dances, hardly possible without some recognition of females, the two sexes "appeared to be entire strangers to each other." At a country fair at Brighton, Massachusetts, only nine women were counted in a crowd of several thousand. Captain Hall heard some music and rushed excitedly to the spot. "What was there?—four men dancing a reel." [31]

He was taken to task, however, by a dissenting English observer for the conclusions he drew from this incident. James Stuart explained the absence of women at the Brighton Fair. "For very obvious reasons," he pointed out quietly, "it would be reckoned a breach of delicacy in Britain for ladies to attend cattle-shows." [32]

The prudery of the period to which Queen Victoria has lent her unblemished name may be interpreted as both cause and consequence of this failure of men and women to associate more naturally in their everyday life. When modesty and decorum were carried to such lengths that an English book of etiquette adapted for publication in the United States could state "that, in America, female delicacy has become morbid," [33] one could hardly expect society to be as lively and gay as it had once been. It is not necessary to take overseriously such tales as Captain Marryat's account of his visit to the home of Edward Everett, where he found a statue of the Apollo Belvidere carefully draped and the legs of the piano "in modest little trousers, with frills at the bottom of them." [34] One may largely discount Mrs. Trollope's amazing stories of flounces painted on immodest sign-post milk-maids, the ostracism of a man who used the word "corset" in mixed company, and the consternation of the young girl in a boarding-house who, unexpectedly encountering a member of the other sex, ran from the room screaming "A man! A man! A man [35] !" Nevertheless the artificial restraints growing out of such prudishness had a depressing effect. Men could not help feeling more at ease when alone with other men. Recreation lost something which only the participation of women could give it.

>>><<<

THESE WERE the influences which served to make the American scene so dull in the first half of the nineteenth century. Serious-ness of purpose was heightened by strong religious feeling; the average man locked himself in his office and his wife in his home. But the forces let loose by the growth of cities and the rise of a new working class could not be withstood. The demand of the urban democracy for amusements to take the place of the rural pastimes they could no longer enjoy was too insistent. Mrs. Trollope notwithstanding, the American people had the same need for being amused as the people of any other nation. The development of new forms of entertainment could not be per-manently stayed for all the prejudice and opposition of those social forces which disapproved of them.

So it was that this period of repression was actually marked by the beginning and gradual expansion of popular amusements which have ever since played an increasingly important part in our recreational life. The first half of the nineteenth century witnessed the growth of the theatre as entertainment reaching out to all classes of people. It saw the beginnings of variety, minstrel shows, and the circus; the establishment of amusement parks, public dance-halls, concert-saloons and beer-gardens; a revival of horse-racing and the rise of other spectator sports. By the Civil War the nation was in the midst of those far-reaching changes in the recreational scene which were a natural corollary of the broader social changes through which it was passing.

The new amusements may not have been as healthful and innocent as those they replaced. They were generally something to be watched rather than enjoyed through active participation. But in opposing them so indiscriminately the confused reformers of the day were combating something essential for a society shaped by nineteenth-century industrialism. Despite prejudice and opposition from so many quarters, a new America, a fumbling, often inept democracy, was feeling its way toward a fuller, more satisfying life for the masses of its people.

CHAPTER VI

THE THEATRE COMES OF AGE

IN SPITE OF THE DISAPPROVAL OF THE STRONG RELIGIOUS FORCES of the day, the theatre was forging steadily ahead after 1800. It was attempting to establish itself by pleasing all classes, and with this end in view the playhouses of the period welcomed everything on their hospitable stages with delightful indiscrimination. A century ago the same house might advertise Junius Brutus Booth in *Hamlet* on one night, the "Original, Aboriginal, Erratic, Operatic, Semi-Civilized and Demi-Savage Extravaganza of Pocohontas" on the next, and on the third an equestrian melodrama with a cast of circus performers playing on horseback. A single evening often produced almost as varied theatrical fare, *Macbeth*, a daring French ballet, and perhaps such a popular and rowdy farce as *My Young Wife and the Old Umbrella*, making up the program. The theatre, that is, was a democratic institution, playing a rôle which in later years it largely surrendered, first to the vaudeville stage and then to the moving picture.

The trend was steadily away from Shakespeare and toward more farce and variety. But the function of the theatre before the days of vaudeville, let alone those of the movies, made this natural. "The rapid increase in population in newly formed cities," wrote an observant visiting actor, William Davidge, "produces a style of patrons whose habits and associations afford no opportunity for the cultivation of the arts." [1] When the craze for lectures in the 1840's drew off the theatre's more sophisticated patrons, there was even greater need to meet the populace's demand for undiluted entertainment. "Opera and burlesque, the melodrama and the ballet," sighed one critic, "have literally swallowed up the

100

legitimate drama....We are not a theatrical people." [2] But this was a prejudiced view. In its growth and development in these years the theatre was merely reflecting those diverse and contradictory impulses which animated American democracy in its awkward age.

-»»«««-

Upon their return from exile after the Revolution, the English actors who had introduced the theatre to America struggled against heavy odds. There was always puritanic prejudice, but for a time colonial traditions also led to the theatre's being vigorously attacked as an aristocratic, un-American institution. It was declared an enemy of true republican principles, a foe to democracy. The giddy ideas of the stage could not be reconciled with the virtue which was the true basis of the freedom so lately won on revolutionary battlefields. And it undermined public morals. "At present," shouted an irate speaker in the Pennsylvania legislature, "play-writers are held at liberty, when they wish to throw their audiences into fits of laughter, to make a smutty joke, throw the ladies into confusion, and give the jessamies a chance of tittering to show their teeth." [3]

Nevertheless the theatre quickly gained a foothold. It could not hope to win full popular approval with the church thundering against it as the Devil's workshop, but before the close of the eighteenth century it had at least broken through official prohibitions which might have completely barred it. After long debate the battle may fairly be said to have been won when the newly built Chestnut Street Theatre opened in Philadelphia in 1794 with the legend carved over its door, "The Eagle Suffers Little Birds to Sing." In the meantime the old John Street Theatre, soon to be replaced by the first Park Theatre, had won a popular following in New York, and after furtive ventures into the dangerous territory of Boston under the guise of moral lectures, the theatre was even admitted within the sacred precincts of Puritanism.[4]

For some two decades these three cities were almost the only ones supporting the stage, and in each instance a single playhouse dominated the scene. Only gradually was the theatre able to extend its scope and become a national institution.

Albany had a surprisingly long theatrical tradition, John Bernard managing the company there at the opening of the nineteenth century. Near-by Rochester was hardly as hospitable. "It is really astonishing to think that the trustees of so respectable a village," its newspaper declared in 1828, "should permit such a disorderly place as the theatre." In New England we find a troupe of Boston players visiting Salem in 1792, but its theatre languished and died, for the townspeople "found it a much more profitable mode of spending their time and money, to hear lectures on interesting and useful subjects." James Silk Buckingham reported a theatre as far afield as Bangor, Maine, in 1840, commenting, however, that as in all provincial towns it was not attended by the better class of people.[5]

The South was far more receptive, as it had been in colonial days. Before there were any real playhouses in New England outside of Boston, theatres had been established in all the principal southern cities from Baltimore to Savannah. The West too was cordial. Soon after the War of 1812 a company of players brought together by Samuel Drake, an English actor who had been playing with Bernard's company in Albany, made its adventurous way to Kentucky by wagon and flatboat. Soon what was still the pioneer country of trans-Appalachia was dotted with theatre towns.[6]

The theatrical circuit by the fourth decade of the century is illustrated by the tour of Tyrone Power, the Irish comedian. From his first engagement at the Park in New York, now the country's amusement capital with half a dozen playhouses, he went to Philadelphia, where he played at the Chestnut Street and the Walnut Street. Then he went to the Tremont in Boston. Starting on a southern tour, he visited Baltimore, Washington, Alexandria, Charleston, Savannah, and Columbus. There were engagements also at New Orleans, Mobile, and Natchez, and back again in the North somewhat later, at Albany.[7] These were the more accessible theatres. Those in St. Louis and Cincinnati were also important, and before mid-century the roster included cities as far west as Dubuque, Iowa. In all, more than fifty established stock companies scattered throughout the country marked the theatre's half-century advance.[8]

·An outstanding characteristic of the playhouses of this period, in contrast to theatres of the legitimate stage in the twentieth century, was their immense size. The second Park Theatre in New York, opening in 1821, provided accommodations in its great yawning pit, three tiers of boxes, and top gallery for 2,500 persons; the Bowery, bursting upon a startled world a few years later with all the magnificence of gas-lights, held 3,500; and in another decade the Broadway advertised seats for 4,000. Theatres in other cities were not quite as big as these New York houses, but they too were far larger than the average to-day.[9]

They were large because of the theatre's appeal to the masses, and, once built, their very size forced them to cater more and more to the general public. The amusement business acted on the principle of volume production at a low cost. When the first Park Theatre opened at the close of the eighteenth century, admission prices were $2.00 in the boxes, $1.50 in the pit, and $1.00 in the gallery. Before the second Park closed its doors fifty years later, these prices had been reduced to 75 cents, 50 cents, and 37½ cents. The more general scale in the 1840's was a 50-cent top and gallery seats for 12½ cents.[10]

Under these conditions the theatre could not in any sense constitute the comparatively select entertainment it had been in colonial days and has subsequently become again through the growth of other forms of commercial amusement. It was taken over by "our sovereigns"—as the conservatives now fearfully designated those whom they had formerly complacently dismissed as "the people of no importance"—in a spirit of militant democracy. Writing of the theatres even in conservative Philadelphia, an English traveler pointedly observed that they were "not much frequented by the more opulent and intelligent classes, but sustained by the middle and humbler ranks." [11] Society might remain ensconced in the boxes, where "elegant and well-dressed females" could look disdainfully down on the crowd below, but it was the common man who ruled the show. At Mitchell's Olympic in New York the pit was exclusively reserved every Saturday afternoon for newsboys and butcher-boys.[12]

The theatre's democratic appeal is further illustrated by the popular interest shown in favorite actors, especially by the excitement occasioned when some player offended the public. The most sensational instance of this was the famous Astor Place riot in 1849, which grew out of the bitter feud between Charles Macready, the English tragedian, and Edwin Forrest, favorite of the American stage. The populace translated a professional quarrel in terms of English aristocracy versus American democracy, rallying to Forrest's defense in behalf of their "almighty independence." New York was plastered with posters calling upon workingmen to decide the issue: "We advocate no violence, but lawful rights." Influenced by such appeals, a Bowery mob stormed the theatre where Macready was playing; the troops were called out to restore order, and before the affair ended, twenty-two persons had been killed and a large number wounded.[13]

The size of the buildings and the character of the audiences combined to make the early nineteenth-century theatre a somewhat appalling place according to modern standards. It had few of the comforts to which the polite audiences of to-day are accustomed. Women stayed away quite as much on these grounds as from moral prejudice. Nor could one always be certain that the performance would be allowed to proceed in peace. Although Astor Place riots might be exceptional, special police had always to be on hand to preserve order. Theatre-going a century ago had about it certain adventurous aspects which are now lost.

The cold was a great discomfort in winter. Wood-burning stoves in foyers could not adequately heat such huge, barnlike structures, and though box-holders still brought their own charcoal foot-warmers and the entire audience kept on coats and hats, there was no really satisfactory way of keeping comfortable. The audience slowly congealed, and the actors almost literally froze. The various lighting systems were also a hazard. Candles dripped and sputtered; oil lamps hung in immense chandeliers smoked unmercifully; and when gas-lights were introduced, it was long before they became anywhere nearly satisfactory. Curtains and scenery were constantly catching on fire, and theatres burned down with distressing regularity—thirty-three were wholly or partially destroyed by fire, including the Park and the Chestnut Street, between 1798 and 1852. The old Bowery burned down no less than four times in seventeen years. The worst conflagration of the period was the burning of the theatre in Richmond, Virginia, in 1811 with the loss of some seventy lives—a catastrophe interpreted by the pious as a judgment of God.[14]

There were no really comfortable seats anywhere in the house. The boxes were "like pens for beasts," reads a contemporary description of the Park.[15] The benches with which they were fitted were no more than scantily upholstered boards with narrow, shoulder-high backs, and they were so closely crowded together that their occupants could hardly move. Mrs. Trollope has a lively description of the gentlemen trying to get comfortable. Their postures were "perfectly indescribable," she wrote; and then added somewhat cryptically, "heels higher than the head, the entire rear of the person presented to the audience." It was also this observant visitor who noted a lady in a box at the Chatham in New York, "performing the most maternal office possible." [16]

The pit was far worse than the boxes, with its backless benches set in serried rows on the rough, unswept floor. Women were not generally allowed in this section. What is now considered the choice part of the theatre would be crowded with a conglomerate mass of men who left on their hats, took off their coats, and made themselves at home with complete disregard of the more polite amenities. The habit of standing on the benches and spitting into the boxes or on the stage was deprecated, a writer in the *New York Herald* satirically approving the custom at Niblo's, where a gentleman could place his hat on the floor and have it serve "as a spittoon for three men behind him, who ingeniously spit over each other's shoulders." [17] The audience moved about freely, there was a constant cracking and crunching of peanuts, and a rank odor of onions and whisky rose like a miasmic cloud. "The place was pervaded by evil smells," the description of the Park states, "and not uncommonly in the midst of a performance, rats ran out of the holes in the floor and across into the orchestra." [18]

The top gallery was shared by toughs, Negroes, and prostitutes. Their sections were railed off, and to add to the congeniality of the surroundings there was usually an adjacent bar. Approval or disapproval of the play was most vociferously expressed in these upper reaches of the theatre. In his letters to the *Morning Chronicle* at the opening of the century, Washington Irving commented feelingly on the gallery barrage of apples, nuts, and gingerbread, and its continual stamping, roaring, hissing, and whistling. [19] The police kept what order they could, but in the more popular houses it was a difficult task—especially when some insulted actor broke off his lines to step to the front of the stage and tell "the dirty blackguards" just what he thought of them. [20]

Conditions in what was commonly called the "third tier" were in part responsible for the continued opposition of church-goers to the stage. They were no less condemned by the better managers. William Dunlap—actor, manager, playwright, historian—vehemently protested when the Federal Street Theatre in Boston allotted this special section of the theatre to "the unfortunate females," as he gallantly characterized them, "who have been the victims of seduction." [21] With almost puritan restraint Noah Miller Ludlow strictly barred both liquor and prostitutes from

A Society Audience at the Park Theatre, New York

Water-color by John Searle, November, 1822. Courtesy of the New York Historical Society.

Scenes from "Uncle Tom's Cabin"

Lithographed poster with manuscript alterations. Courtesy of the New York Historical Society.

his theatre in St. Louis.[22] Edmund Simpson made the same experiment in New York but lost so considerable a part of his clientele that he had to restore to the third tier its privileges.

The newspapers often took occasion to condemn these customs, but their disapproval was aimed at the ladies' display of "their meretricious attractions, before the very faces of the chaste part of the audience," rather than at their presence in the theatre. In an editorial on September 19, 1838, the *New York Herald* reported that eighty-three of "the most profligate and abandoned women that ever disgraced humanity" had been freely mingling the night before with the virtuous and respectable at the Park. It urged the citizens of New York not to take their wives and daughters to this theatre. It was a disgrace to society. The management could hope to win back popular favor only "by constructing a separate entrance for the abandoned of the sex." [23]

In the smaller towns, conditions differed very markedly from those in the large cities. Their theatres could not expect patronage comparable to that in the more sophisticated urban communities, and circumstances often compelled the staging of performances with crude, makeshift scenery which made heroic demands upon the ingenuity and imagination of both cast and audience. An old warehouse or barn might be temporarily converted into a theatre by the erection of a stage, installation of some benches, and provision of a few makeshift properties and an improvised curtain. Often a shop or a tavern dining-room served even more informally for strolling players. Joseph Jefferson, barnstorming through Illinois in its pioneer days, described one performance in an old barn where moonlight and candles provided a dramatic atmosphere for the production of *The Spectre Bridegroom*. Another time his company built its own theatre—a shaky structure with "the appearance of a large dry-goods box with a roof." A young lawyer named Abraham Lincoln defended the players on this occasion against the town's attempt to impose an exorbitant license fee.[24]

Traveling players on the western circuit experienced one of

their greatest difficulties in finding the supers necessary for a chorus. Ludlow tells of an early performance of Sheridan's *Pizarro* before an audience of four hundred keel-boat men and foundry workers in Pittsburgh at which the ceremony of the Virgins of the Sun presented an acute problem. Pittsburgh offered no virgins—Ludlow carefully explains that of course he means theatrical virgins—and it finally became necessary to fall back on an old Irish cleaning woman and the property man. They came on the stage draped in cotton gowns and gauze veils, and they were doing very well indeed until a piteous groan came from the audience, "Oh! what virgins!" There was an immediate outburst. The play could not go on until the manager stepped to the front of the stage and rebuked the audience for insulting actors who had come so many miles to entertain them.[25]

Further brilliant inspiration in providing supers is related by Sol Smith, another pioneer of the western circuit who formed a partnership with Ludlow. Again it was *Pizarro,* and twenty-four Creek Indians were engaged to play the parts of the Peruvian soldiery. They were given 50 cents apiece and a glass of whisky —unfortunately, paid in advance. When their cue was given, the Indians broke into a war-dance with the greatest enthusiasm. As they leapt about the stage brandishing tomahawks and yelling at the top of their voices, the frightened virgins of the cast fled precipitantly to their dressing-room. The Indians had driven every one off the stage and demolished the Temple of the Sun before they could be quieted down.[26]

->>>-<<<-

EXCEPT in a few of the houses in the larger cities, the stock companies making up the American theatre were for the most part composed of casual collections of actors and actresses whose histrionic deficiencies appear to have been monumental. They seldom knew their parts completely, although the frequent changes of plays and scant rehearsals provided some excuse for this; they were as apt as not to disregard all stage business; and in keeping with a memorable tradition of the dramatic profession they often came on quite drunk. The diverting journal of Harry Watkins, a strolling player of the 1850's, reports that after reading his part over three or four times, he often went on stage knowing as much as any one in the cast. Another journal entry speaks of "winging a part," or going on in complete ignorance of it. Drunkenness often led to dramatic quarrels. There was the occasion in Louisville, also related by Watkins, when the leading lady chased one of the actors off the stage with a spear. When he tried to return, she renewed the attack with a screw-driver, dramatically screaming, "You son of a bitch, die!" [27]

The theatre was really sustained by a handful of stars who played engagements of varying lengths in the eastern cities and then took to the road. They completely dominated the stage. Often there was barely time for a rehearsal with the local stock companies which supported them, and the star went blithely ahead almost regardless of other members of the cast. "I'm not much of a judge," commented one member of a Philadelphia audience at a performance of *King Lear* by James Wallack, "but I should think he was a damned fine actor for he played this piece all by himself." [28]

In the first decades of the century these stars were primarily English actors: George Frederick Cooke, Edmund Kean, the elder Charles Mathews, Charles Kemble and the delightful Fanny Kemble, William Charles Macready, and Junius Brutus Booth. Only very slowly did American actors begin to rival them. But by mid-century native talent had won enthusiastic recognition. The melodramatic genius of Edwin Forrest made him the country's foremost tragedian, James H. Hackett swung into popular favor with his comic Yankee rôles, and the American-born Edwin Booth was starting on his memorable career. The entire country was immensely proud of Charlotte Cushman, an actress whose emotional power carried her to dramatic heights unscaled by her contemporaries. There were others: Henry Placide, John Gilbert, E. L. Davenport, William Warren, Jr., James E. Murdoch, the young Joseph Jefferson. . . . A theatrical tradition was being firmly established.

The temperamental eccentricities of many of the stars, their arrogance, their frequent drinking, their disregard of conventions, clothed them with a fatal fascination for the theatre-going public. But these habits also brought down on their heads the horrified attacks of all custodians of public morals. The stars gave the theatre its artistic standing, but they also made far more difficult the slow process of winning approval for the theatre in the country at large.

Cooke was an unregenerate drunkard; Kean was involved in scandals which finally led to his being hissed off the stage; the records of Forrest's unsavory divorce case were spread over the pages of the country's newspapers; and the drunken brawls of Junius Brutus Booth, the preludes to his repeated fits of insanity, won him nationwide notoriety.

Booth's managers were at times compelled to resort to every possible stratagem to get him on the stage in a reasonably sober condition. They would take him out for long carriage drives just before a performance, lock him in his hotel room, or dose him with vinegar. When he escaped their vigilance, there was no telling what might happen. Sometimes he would stagger through his part, his voice hardly audible; at other times he would give a brilliant performance which would bring down the house. On one occasion he could not be found. A thorough search of the city's bars finally led to his discovery, very drunk, a good half-hour after the curtain should have gone up. The audience was going wild. Booth rushed on the stage, shaking an infuriated fist at the galleries. "Shut up!" he yelled. "You shut up out there and in ten minutes I'll give you the god-damnedest King Lear you ever saw in your life!" The story is that he did, and a delighted audience was with him from his opening line.[29]

The plays necessarily conformed to the taste of a democratic audience. Shakespeare was the favorite vehicle of the stars—they would condescend to play few other parts—and the theatre-going public appears to have hugely enjoyed the dramatic and fervid oratory, "the rant and cant," which marked their acting of the great tragedies. It was an age of oratory, of theatricalism. The actors were the rivals of Clay, Calhoun, and Webster, and they had to outdo them at their own trade. It must have been an experience to see and hear Forrest as King Lear. "Played it, Sir? Played it?" this redoubtable actor exclaimed when complimented on how he had acted the rôle. "By God, I *am* King Lear." [30] But while Shakespeare was a great drawing-card among all classes, the public demanded above all else change and variety. Programs were shifted so frequently, and so many different plays were given, that when an entire season's repertoire is considered, Shakespearean drama did not actually fill a very large place.

A single theatre might present more than a hundred different plays in one season (the St. Louis theatre gave no less than one hundred and fifty-seven in the season of 1839), and few of them would have as many as three or four performances. The bill changed almost every night. Under such circumstances sixty-five performances of Shakespeare in Philadelphia's three theatres during the season of 1835 far exceeded performances of plays by any other single dramatist. Eighty-three productions of *Richard III* over an eight-year period made it the most frequently presented of all dramas. When Forrest actually played *Macbeth* for twenty consecutive nights at a New York theatre in 1853, he set up a phenomenal record. [31]

The public enjoyed the stars in these rôles, but the domination of the individual actor is responsible for the overemphasis always placed on the Shakespearean tradition. The more general run of plays provides a clearer indication of popular taste. Hundreds of thoroughly second-rate comedies, farces, and melodramas, now happily forgotten, innumerable musical shows, extravaganzas, and burlesques, were the theatre's real stock in trade. There were plays hastily adapted from novel or story, crudely concocted by managers or actors for a single perform-

ance. Watkins tells of writing a five-act drama in eight days—
"the last two days I suffered a great deal of pain." [32]

Even when Shakespeare was presented, the principal play did
not stand alone. Other entertainment was interpolated between
the acts—specialty dances, popular music, jugglers, acrobats, or
even trained animals. And the whole performance invariably
concluded with a farce. As the Prince of Denmark wandered off
the stage, the clown came on; the echo of Othello's threats was
a comic song; and Lady Macbeth washed her frenzied hands
only to provide the cue for a French danseuse. When the Hallams had invaded New England almost a century earlier, their
Shakespearean performance had concluded at ten-thirty so that
"every spectator may go home at a sober hour, and reflect upon
what he has seen." Not so these audiences of the new democracy. They did not want to be kept awake pondering over Hamlet's soliloquies or Desdemona's wrongs. They couldn't take their
Shakespeare straight; they demanded a chaser.

Booth played *Hamlet* at the Boston Museum in a program also
including Miss Avila and Master Phillipa in a Pas Hongrois and
the new farce *Village Gossip*. A performance of *Much Ado about
Nothing* with Clare Fisher was followed by a musical farce in
which the leading lady returned to sing "Oh! Brave Rub a Dub."
Romeo and Juliet, with a comic clog-dance as an entr'acte, was
followed on occasion by the double bill of *Oh! Hush* and *The
Good Looking Fellow*. A performance of *Richelieu* with Edwin
Forrest was enlivened by a "grand pas de deux" and a "national
descriptive melange" between acts, the performance then closing
with *The Double Bedded Room*.[33] The early nineteenth-century
audience got its full money's worth at the theatre—a good fifty
cents' worth of lively entertainment. The program of main
feature, several shorts, and a comedy pointed the way to the
modern movie program. So did the occasional double feature.
The theatre of the 1840's reached out to very much the same type
of audience.

Apart from Shakespeare, few of the plays constituting the theatre's principal offerings have survived even in memory. They were largely English in origin, or adapted from the German of such a popular playwright as Kotzebue. American dramas were a long time in coming, and those written in this period hardly deserved to last. For the excellent plays with which the colonial theatre had supplemented Shakespeare, there was substituted a miscellany of largely worthless trash. *The Lady of Lyons* and *Richelieu,* both by Bulwer-Lytton, were popular; Sheridan Knowles' *The Hunchback* was a favorite; and a number of plays specially written for Forrest—*The Gladiator* and *Metamora, The Last of the Wamponoags*—had a wide vogue. Mrs. Anna Cora Mowatt struck a new note with her comedy of manners *Fashion;* Dion Boucicault started the long list of his popular dramas with *London Assurance,* and in mid-century came *Our American Cousin,* which Lincoln was seeing on the fatal night of his assassination. Even more typical of this day were such plays as the historical romance *The Green Mountain Boys of 1776;* the French adaptation *Adeline, or The Victim of Seduction;* the old farce of *High Life below Stairs;* and the exciting melodrama *Nick of the Woods:*

Hold, murdering villain! Richard Braxley, forbear!
Now, Rowland Forester, I defy thee!
Monster, hold. . . .
Behold thy promised bride. Consent to make her mine or down yon boiling cataract I'll hurl her to destruction. . . .

Shakespeare's greatest rival, however, was probably John Baldwin Buckingstone, the prolific author (one hundred and fifty plays) of *The Pet of the Petticoats* and *A Kiss in the Dark.*

No one of these plays ever had a run comparable to those achieved to-day by scores of modern productions. It was *The Drunkard, or The Fallen Saved,* with a record of some one hundred and thirty performances at the Boston Museum in 1844, that inaugurated the more modern custom of an unchanging bill over any considerable period.[34] Its highly moral treatment of the universal topic of temperance (Watkins almost killed himself with his realistic interpretation of delirium tremens), made a tremendous appeal to those pious elements of society who usually condemned the theatre as a subversive influence undermining morals.

Even more important in winning new converts to the theatre, a landmark in the gradual breaking down of religious prejudice against the stage, was *Uncle Tom's Cabin.* Its dramatic version —its many dramatic versions—toured the country with phenomenal success in the 1850's. Performances were given by troupes of Tommers in villages and hamlets where a play had never before been seen. Its exploitation of antislavery sentiment brought thousands of persons to the theatre who justified their attendance by devotion to what the *Herald,* assailing the play as a firebrand, called the "pestilent principles of abolitionism." [35] After the Civil War there was a revival of *Uncle Tom's Cabin.* It became a classic of the stage, performed more times than any other American play; and Uncle Tom, Little Eva, Simon Legree, became a part of our national folklore.

-»>«<-

As THE CENTURY advanced and theatre audiences became more and more plebeian, various specialty performances with an even wider popular appeal increasingly overshadowed serious drama. The hodgepodge of entertainment in which acrobatic acts and farces lightened Shakespearean tragedy gave way to a new differentiation in programs. The legitimate stage and wholly popular entertainment were at last divorced. There was a franker appeal to "the blood and thunder taste of the lower half million" by producers whose sole goal was to chalk up large box-office receipts.

One such type of performance coming down from an early day was the equestrian drama. It was soon to merge with traveling menageries and country road shows to form the modern circus, but throughout the first half of the century there were many heroic spectacles in which troops of horses clattered noisily on and off stage at even the most aristocratic houses. The great size of the stage made this easily possible, and there was continuous rivalry among the managers in presenting more and more elaborate spectacles. They crowded the background with precipices, waterfalls, forest groves, lakes, terraces, palaces, and castle walls. The scenery was always advertised as being of the most gorgeous description, the dresses extraordinarily costly, and the stage machinery the most complicated and expensive yet devised.

Consider the stage directions of the prologue of *Putnam, or The Iron Son of '76:*

THE VISION

Slow music. Three quarters dark. Ethereal firmament filled with silver stars. Eagle flying in the air, to ascend, looking down upon a lion couchant, on trap to descend. The goddesses discovered in various groups bearing blue wands with silver stars. God of War on small Roman chariot, to descend. Goddess of Liberty on trap in small Roman chariot, to descend.

In the more serious business of the play, Putnam is continually dashing about the stage on horseback, guns and drums keeping up a terrific uproar in the wings. Finally he leaps a gate, falls on the stage covered with blood:

CLARA. Dear Uncle, you are wounded!
PUTNAM. A mere flea bite! Arm boys, arm; the white skins and red skins are upon us! The war kettle boils! Three cheers, and upon them! [36]

In 1803 the grand pantomime of *La Fille Hussar* was performed in New York with real horses—"never before attempted in America." A few years later Philadelphia went wild over *Timour the Tartar*, an exciting drama in which the heroine, mounted on her splendid white charger, "ran up the stupendous cataract to the very height of the stage." During the depression year of 1837 the immensely popular *Mazeppa, or The Wild*

Horse, was playing to standing-room only in New York with "Mr. Cook's unrivalled stud of horses, amounting to fifty in number." [37]

Even Shakespeare was put on horseback with a neat blending of classic drama and the circus. *Henry IV* was staged as a mammoth spectacle, *Richard III* performed with the principal characters mounted. Toward the close of its long career the Park attempted to remain loyal to its traditions and at the same time profit from a broader appeal by staging what it called a Tribute to Shakespeare. Neither Forrest nor Macready nor Booth was the star attraction, but the famous southern equestrian C. J. Rogers, assisted by twenty-one riders in correct and superb costumes. To the delight of his audience Mr. Rogers impersonated on horseback, among a number of other less distinguished horsemen, both Falstaff and Shylock. [38]

Quite a different and surprisingly popular show was the ballet. The first arrival of a troupe of French dancers in the 1820's caused a sensation. Many contemporary accounts bear witness to the consternation of even veteran theatre-goers. "I was at the first presentation," Achille Murat wrote. "The appearance of the dancers in short dresses, created an astonishment I know not how to describe. But at the first pirouette when the short petticoats, with lead at the extremities began to mount and assume a horizontal position, it was quite another matter; the women screamed aloud and the greater part left the theatre; the men remained, for the most part roaring and sobbing with ecstasy, the sole idea which struck them being that of the ridiculous." [39]

Audiences quickly became more sophisticated. Even in Boston the ballet was a great success, a contemporary reporting that "the more outré the dancing, the more applause." When the divine Fanny Elssler arrived in the 1840's, her triumph was a milestone in theatrical history. Her sensational dancing of La Cracovienne and La Tarentule became "all the rage—all the mania—all the talk." "The grace, the beauty, the purity, the hue of innocence and virtue which surrounded the highest and most

MAD.lle FANNY ELSSLER,

IN

La Tarentule

Pr. 50 cts

Fleetwood's Lithog.!

NEW YORK Published by FIRTH & HALL, No 1 Franklin Sq.

Lithographed cover of a music sheet of 1840. Courtesy of the American
Antiquarian Society.

Wonders of Barnum's Museum

Wood engraving by Waters and Son after a drawing by Edward A. Hall. Courtesy of Harry T. Peters.

classical order of dancing," rhapsodized the *New York Herald,*
"was never presented here in so marked and distinct style." [40]

The lamentations of outraged prudes did not stay for a moment
her triumphal tour about the country or prevent her from being
invited to sit in the chair of the Speaker of the House of Representatives.[41] "The good newspapers rail dreadfully at the bad
people who will go to see her," Philip Hone noted in his diary,
"... but the more they rail the more people won't mind them.
Nothing is more ridiculous than these abortive attempts to stem
the current of public opinion in relation to the people's amusement." [42]

The 1840's also saw the growth of a new type of burlesque
and musical travesty, the forerunners of to-day's topical revues,
which delighted both the newsboys at Mitchell's Olympic Theatre and the more fashionable audience at Brougham's Lyceum.
Everything was burlesqued: Shakespeare in *Much Ado about
a Merchant of Venice,* the dancing of Fanny Elssler in *La
Mosquito,* and grand opera in *Lucy Did Lamm Her Moor.*
Elaborate extravaganzas were staged, such as *Pocahontas* with
its lusty chorus:

> Well roared, indeed, my jolly Tuscaroras
> Most loyal corps, your King encores your chorus.

A revue centered upon the marital customs of the Mormons had
an even greater success. The Bowery Amphitheatre made a sensation with *The Revolt of the Harem.* Over the horizon was *The
Black Crook* (it was to run at Niblo's for sixteen months when
first staged in 1866 and was thereafter revived again and again
until the close of the century) and the rage for what were already being called leg shows.[43]

This trend in theatrical entertainment inevitably awoke new
opposition to the stage and served in some part to offset the approval it was winning among former foes by the production of
such plays as *The Drunkard* and *Uncle Tom's Cabin.* When some
of the managers went a step further still and staged a series of

tableaux vivants in which appeared "living men and women in almost the same state in which Gabriel saw them in the Garden of Eden," the godly were still more convinced that the stage was the Devil's workshop.

Advertisements of the Living Models assured the public that nothing would be shown that could bring a blush to the most chaste cheek, but with this concession to prevailing morals they went unashamedly ahead to stress the "beautiful symmetry" of the artists who would appear in "Psyche Going to the Bath" and "Venus Rising from the Sea." [44] Crowds flocked to the new attractions. The *Tribune* forcefully declared that "the majority go because of depraved taste rather than pure love of art"; the *Herald* stigmatized the audiences as "fashionable old rakes and ineffable scoundrels about town"; [45] but the fact remained that the classes as well as the masses found their senses agreeably titillated. Nothing could better illustrate the curious blend of prudery and prurience which characterized the period.

Finally the police were goaded into action and descended on one of the shows. There ensued a "scene of stirring interest" in the dressing-rooms, again to quote the *Herald*, "where some five or six well formed females were in the act of preparing for the next tableau. In one corner was seen a very fleshly lady dressed as Bacchus, studying her position on a barrel. Another beautifully formed creature, just drawing on her tights for the Greek Slave, and some of the others, were so dreadfully alarmed at the sight of the police with their clubs in hand that they seized up a portion of their garments in order to hide their faces, forgetting their lower extremities, thus making a scene mixed up with the sublime and the ridiculous." [46]

The girls were duly escorted to the police station (where a supper of roast turkey and wine was served to "cheer their souls"), and measures taken to prevent any further performances. Eventually they proved successful. In the *Sunday Mercury* in May, 1848, we find a plaintive correspondent sorrowfully asking what has happened to

Those nice tableaux vivants
Of beautiful young ladies, sans
Both petticoats and pants,
Who, scorning fashion's shifts and whims
Did nightly crowds delight
By showing up their handsome limbs
At fifty cents a sight. . . .[47]

A more important development was the production of variety
shows clearly foreshadowing modern vaudeville. By the middle
of the century every city had playhouses presenting varied programs of specialty acts designed solely for the entertainment of
the democracy. The theatrical advertising columns fairly bristled
with announcements of such performances. At Niblo's a program
featuring the celebrated Ravels, a band of pantomimists, acrobats, and dancers, was even advertised as "French Vaudeville."
Another playhouse was renamed the New Theatre of Mirth and
Variety. Its shows included "Elboleros, Cachuchas, Scotch flings
and Strathspeys," a selection of "the most astonishing feats of
Gymnastics and Contortions ever presented in this country," and
an act billed as "the Flying Cord by the unequalled Mr. Ruggles."
The whole performance, admission from 6¼ to 25 cents, was enlivened with music by the New York Brass Band.[48]

The program at the Franklin Theatre on one occasion included
Chemistry, French plays, Magic, Mesmeric Clairvoyance, beautiful and admired Astronomical Diagrams, and Diaphanous
Tableaux—a selection clearly designed to meet all tastes, including the educational. The popularity of infant prodigies was reflected on the variety stage, a featured act being the Bateman
children, aged six and eleven, who played in *Romeo and Juliet*
and *The Merchant of Venice*. Other shows paid less attention
to the vogue for culture. Ballad-singers, strong men (breaking
eighty-pound stones with their bare fists), burlesque dancers,
and companies of female minstrels were widely advertised. A
new costume suggested for women at this time was responsible
for the Bloomer Troupe, while a mysterious act sandwiched in

between the bloomer girls and the juvenile Shakespeareans was titled "Spirituall Nekings." As the variety theatre worked its way down through the free-and-easy concert-halls, the entertainment became more and more questionable. Free Sunday performances were given at the Melodeon, advertising "prettiest female attendants, best wines and segars and liquors." [49]

➼〉〉《〈

LEGITIMATE DRAMA was not entirely given up even though the theatres devoted to circus stunts and variety multiplied much faster than the more conservative houses. But mid-century critics gave the impression that it was forever doomed by such unashamed catering to a debased public taste through "senseless, absurd, inconsistent, tinselled, vulgar and immodest spectacles." None of them was more alarmed than the future poet of democracy. "Of all 'low' places," Walt Whitman stormily wrote in the *Brooklyn Eagle* of February 8, 1847, "where vulgarity (not only on the stage, but in front of it) is in the ascendant, and bad taste carries the day with hardly a pleasant point to mitigate its coarseness, the New York theatres—except the Park—may be put down . . . at the top of the heap." [50]

In so far as these attacks were justified, the reason could largely be found in the failure of the better elements of the population to give the theatre decent support. In a day when the stage was "indiscriminately voted immoral, irreligious, and what is much worse, unfashionable," as Philip Hone sharply declared, [51] there was very little the managers could do other than give the general public what it wanted. The survival of the theatre during the hard times that followed the panic of 1837, its success in riding out that financial storm, was largely due to this broadening of its popular appeal. It could not afford to be artistic or too fastidious.

It was really more firmly established, however, than the contemporary critics thought. Looking back upon the age that saw the great acting of Edmund Kean, Edwin Forrest, and Junius

Brutus Booth, of Fanny Kemble and Charlotte Cushman, as well
as the equestrian melodrama, living models, and variety shows
of the cheaper houses, writers on the theatre now declare that the
second quarter of the nineteenth century ushered in a golden
era in the history of the American stage.[52]

"Still does the Drama sit with the mob; still is Pegasus yoked
with the ox," a contributor to the *Dial* declared in 1860.[53] Entertainment for the democracy was the theatre's primary function
at a time when it was the only public diversion, as the *Southern
Literary Messenger* stated, to furnish "entertainment to all
classes." [54]

Chapter VII

MR. BARNUM SHOWS THE WAY

WHILE THE THEATRE CONTINUED TO BROADEN ITS POPULAR appeal, it faced the increasing competition of other forms of commercial entertainment. By the 1850's almost every city had a museum with a jumbled collection of curiosities, dead and alive, and a program of concerts and variety acts which could be seen for twenty-five or fifty cents. At scores of music-halls bands of black-faced comedians broke happily into the "Lucy Long Walk Around" or plaintively sang "Old Black Joe" as a phenomenal rage for minstrelsy swept the land. And into towns and villages from Maine to Georgia, westward to the Mississippi, rolled the red and gold wagons housing the properties of what was to become one of America's great institutions—the circus.

Phineas T. Barnum stands out as the leading figure of this period in amusing the populace. No struggle between dramatic standards and popular taste ever troubled the master showman of them all. He was not one whit interested in art; he was interested in entertainment. He recognized the potential market in the restless urban masses. With uncanny prescience he sensed what they wanted, or could be made to want, and gave it to them. He gave it enthusiastically, generously, lavishly—whether Jenny Lind, the country's pioneer baby show, or his Grand Colossal Museum and Menagerie. Nor did Mr. Barnum ever wait for his public to become bored; he believed in infinite variety. The Feejee mermaid gave way to General Tom Thumb, General Tom Thumb to the Bearded Lady, the Bearded Lady to Campagnolian Bell Ringers. His American Museum took in everything from trained fleas to panoramas of the Holy Land. James Gordon Bennett called him the Napoleon of Public Caterers:[1] he always provided a good show, and the eager, unsophisticated, amusement-hungry public of his day loved it.

Barnum represented democracy in public entertainment much as Andrew Jackson had represented it in politics. Government in the interests of the common man, amusements in the interests of the common man. No one did more to promote the leveling influence of popular recreation. The theatre had tried to compromise. It staged its equestrian dramas, its burlesques, its extravaganzas, but it was always trying to get back to Shakespeare, looking a little down its nose at the raucous taste of the lower half-million. Mr. Barnum was out to take the lower half-million into camp, and he succeeded because his methods were direct and simple. The democratic masses followed his lead as docilely as the Irish visitors at his Museum followed the sign "to the Egress"—and found themselves in the street. For though sometimes he outrageously fooled his public, put over elaborate hoaxes, they enjoyed it hugely.

It was all highly educational and strictly moral—the exhibitions in his museum, the strange curiosities touring the country under his sponsorship, the variety acts staged in his sumptuous lecture-room. When the old lady from Dubuque asked him when the service began, the great showman soberly told her that the congregation were already taking their seats. Spellbound country folk who delighted in his presentations of *The Drunkard* and *Uncle Tom's Cabin* would have been horrified at the suggestion that they had attended the theatre.

This skilful exploitation of the prejudices of his day was one of the secrets of Barnum's success. The gospel of work, the urge for self-education, religious disapproval of amusements, never hampered his activities. The theatre struggled against the spirit of the times. Barnum capitalized it. The "chaste scenic entertainments" of his lecture-room were generously staged for "all those who disapprove of the dissipations, debaucheries, pro-

fanity, vulgarity, and other abominations, which characterize ou
modern theatres." [2] Not a thought would be breathed in hi
museum, let alone act performed or word uttered, that coul
bring a blush to the cheek of modesty. The Puritan in entertain
ment, Barnum proudly recorded that "even Shakespeare's drama
were shorn of their objectionable features when placed upo
my stage." [3] He saw sermons in circus elephants and preache
them to the discomfiture of rival managers. No one better under
stood the temper of the Victorian era.

→»)«←

BARNUM's American Museum—it was in New York, but it had it
counterpart in other cities and its features were widely copied-
became a national institution in the 1840's. No out-of-towner eve
missed it; it was the delight of country visitors. They might occa
sionally have seen giants and dwarfs, jugglers and rope-dancers
pantomimes and acrobats, but here under one roof was a wealth
of amusements (six hundred thousand curiosities) such as im
agination could hardly picture. The visitor bored by the nationa
portrait gallery could watch the three living serpents of enor
mous size being given their noonday meal. When he had ex
hausted the wonders of the model of Niagara Falls (with rea
water from the new Croton Reservoir), he could have his fortune
told by the mysterious Madame Rockwell. There were statues o
scriptural characters and waxwork figures depicting the horror
of intemperance; models of new machines and an anatomica
Venus; an ever-changing selection of panoramas, dioramas, cy
cloramas, and georamas. [4]

Urban workers and country farmers were not the only visitors
When a Canadian giant was exhibited, the aristocratic Philip
Hone, one-time mayor, made careful measurements of thi
natural phenomenon, reporting in his diary that the 619-pound
monstrosity had ankles three feet five inches around. He wen
repeatedly to see General Tom Thumb. Upon the midget's re
turn from his triumphal foreign tour ("kissed by a million pair

of the sweetest lips in Europe"), Mr. Hone proudly noted that
Tom Thumb spoke to him by name.[5]

From the portals of the Museum went out scores of traveling
exhibitions which gave Barnum his nation-wide fame. Some of
them were authentic, some of them cleverly faked. There was no
denying the genuineness of the giants and midgets. Possibly the
bearded lady was a border-line case, although her whiskers were
guaranteed "to put at a single glance all incredulity at defiance."
But there were also Joice Heth, whom Barnum blandly claimed
to have been the nurse of George Washington; the notorious
Woolly Horse, supposedly captured by John C. Frémont; and in
later years the famous white elephants of Siam.[6] Few people
really cared whether the elephants owed their color to art rather
than nature, even when the whitewash began to fade. No one
minded being taken in by the Prince of Humbugs.

When exhibitions began to pall, Barnum experimented with
melodrama and variety acts in his sumptuous Lecture Room.
He was prepared to stage anything—so long as it was highly
moral—and he gradually evolved a program with two and three
performances a day which won his show-place still greater popularity. In midsummer of 1843 we find him advertising Chang
Fong, the Chinese juggler; the inimitable Winchell, famous for
"Droll, quizzical, mirth-provoking impersonations"; a knitting-
machine run by a dog; and the Ethiopian Serenaders, with "six
performers, each one of whom is a professor of music." [7]

The most spectacular triumph of Barnum's career—more notable than the European tour with General Tom Thumb—was his
mid-century presentation of Jenny Lind. The country had never
known anything comparable to the excitement evoked by the
tour of the Swedish Nightingale. Fanny Kemble had won the
heart of America in the 1830's, Fanny Elssler had swept all before
her in the 1840's. Jenny Lind became the idol of millions who
would not have anything to do with the stage. New York, Boston, Philadelphia, the South and the West, worshiped at her
shrine.

"Not a day passes," wrote a contemporary diarist just before her appearance at Castle Garden, "without some article lauding her talents until Jenny Lind is in every mouth; Jenny Lind hats, Jenny Lind coats, cigars, oysters, etc., in short, everything is Jenny Lind. When she arrived on Sunday from England, thousands of people swarmed the wharf eager to glimpse the 'Divine Creature.' Her carriage to the hotel could hardly make its way through the dense crowds. At night she was serenaded, and by day the Irving House was besieged by men, women and children anxious to peek at her." [8]

The newspapers estimated these crowds milling about her hotel at thirty thousand. They reported a street fight growing out of a struggle to recover a peach-stone which she had supposedly dropped from the balcony; the enterprise of a speculator who had secured what was declared to be one of her gloves, charging twenty-five cents to kiss the outside of it, fifty cents the inside. A competition for a Jenny Lind prize song, won by Bayard Taylor, attracted seven hundred and fifty entries. "New York is conquered," the press agreed, "a hostile army or fleet could not effect a conquest so complete." "The excitement is of the hottest temperature," one paper declared. "It is universally conceded that Jenny Lind is the greatest woman, Barnum is the greatest man . . . in the world." Tickets for the first concert were auctioned off at $225. Boston showed a supercilious scorn for such emotionalism on the part of New York—and was soon paying $625 for the first ticket at its own auction. [9]

It was inspired showmanship. Barnum knew his public and played upon its emotions with a sure touch. America had not seen Jenny Lind (no more had Barnum before she landed in New York), had not heard her, knew nothing of her. He publicized her beauty, her generosity, her goodness, so eloquently that he made her a heroine whom all America could take to its sentimental heart. The popularity of twentieth-century movie stars can hardly be compared with it. Accounts of Lindomania reaching the staid office of the London *Times* aroused deep con-

First Appearance of Jenny Lind in America

Castle Garden, New York, September 11, 1850. Lithograph by N. Currier.
J. Clarence Davies Collection, Museum of the City of New York.

...m Crow

...as D. Rice
... fifty-seventh
... of his sensa-
... success at the
...ican Theatre,
...York, Novem-
..., 1833. Con-
...rary painting
...ssession of the
...m of the
...f New York.

Christy's Minstrels

Lithograph by Sarony and Major after a drawing by N. Sarony, 1847.
J. Clarence Davies Collection, Museum of the City of New York.

cern. If the American people could be so easily swayed by an appeal to their emotions, they would be at the mercy of the first political adventurer who attempted to exploit them.[10]

Accounts of her first appearance at Castle Garden state that seven thousand persons crowded the auditorium, and when Jenny Lind appeared on the stage, demurely dressed in white, the audience rose as one man to greet her with such prolonged cheering, handkerchief-waving, and clapping that it appeared doubtful if the performance could ever get under way. She sang "Casta Diva," Rossini's "I Turchi in Italia," the "Herdsman's Song," and the prize-winning "Greeting to America." Her success could not have been greater. "To Castle Garden," commented the *Tribune's* critic, "is reserved the sublime spectacle of a whole people, as it were, worshiping at the shrine of art. . . . Jenny Lind is evidently most herself and most inspired when she sings most *for all.*" [11]

That was the symbol of her triumph. Barnum knew very well what he was about. He was not concerned with Jenny Lind's contribution to American music (although she paved the way for successful tours by many other singers and musicians) or with any other phase of her artistic career. He had sensed the new market for entertainment, a market which took in the masses of citizenry, and he supplied a popular product. He dressed it up in the sort of package that he knew would please American taste, and as he traveled about the country with his prima donna, he lectured alternate nights on temperance.

During her nine months' tour, visiting every major city in the United States, Jenny Lind gave ninety-five concerts. The gross receipts were $712,161, affording Jenny Lind $176,675 and Barnum (including expenses) $535,486.[12] Popular amusement paid; it was becoming big business. Nor did the American people criticize Barnum for his financial success. That he could make money out of offering them entertainment—whatever it was— endeared him even more to them.

->>><<<-

THE MINSTREL SHOWS which were so popular in the 1840's and 1850's were something far more than an amusing act incorporated in the program of a variety bill or occasionally presented at Barnum's Museum. They were a unique form of entertainment, thoroughly American in their inspiration, whose appeal was universal. The gay, rollicking walk-arounds, the sad, sweet notes of the sentimental ballads, the grotesque exaggerations and tall stories, the incessant cross-fire of shrewd jokes, were so native to the soil that the democracy crowded to hear them. The minstrels won instant popularity in New England, spread throughout the Middle West, and went to California with the gold-rush. Every city had several bands of black-faced comedians. Road companies playing in local halls or under canvas toured back and forth throughout the country. The most eminent in comedy or tragedy toiled with but slight reward, mourned an English actor, while "fantazias upon the bones, or banjo, have called forth the plaudits of admiring thousands." [13]

Minstrelsy made its formal bow before an unsuspecting public when Dan Emmett's "novel, grotesque, original and surpassingly melodious Ethiopian band, entitled the Virginia Minstrels," opened at the Chatham Theatre, in New York, early in 1843.[14] But it had had predecessors. The most popular (for the first black-face performer on the American stage is not known) was the Jim Crow act of the comedian Thomas D. Rice. From the first time it was given (the records variously stating it was at Louisville, Cincinnati, and Pittsburgh about 1829)[15] thunderous applause greeted the shuffling steps danced to the plaintive little song:

> Wheel about, turn about,
> Do jis so,
> An' ebery time I wheel about
> I jump Jim Crow.

It was as popular in New York and Boston as in the cities of the Mississippi Valley; it was a success in London. Joseph Jefferson was introduced to the stage by way of Jim Crow. Rice brought him on, aged four, in a bag and dumped him on the floor:

> Ladies and gentlemen,
> I'd have for you to know,
> I'se got a little darky here
> To jump Jim Crow.[16]

The vogue for this act had prepared the way for the real minstrel shows. Their success, one magazine declared, was "unparalleled by any popular exhibition that has ever been offered in New York."[17] Barnum early jumped aboard the bandwagon with his own Ethiopian Serenaders, but the most famous minstrel band was Christy's. Established at Mechanics Hall in New York in 1846, it gave its "unique and chaste" performance almost nightly for a period of ten years, drawing crowds which were always enthusiastic over the performers' tuneful songs, clever dancing, and engaging humor. At one time there were some ten minstrel shows playing simultaneously in New York; Boston had several companies; and Cincinnati was the minstrelsy center of the West. The Kentucky Minstrels, Bryant's Minstrels, the Nightingale Serenaders, the Washington Utopians, the Sable Brothers, Ordway's Aeolians. . . . Throughout the country—traveling "a world of belated railway trains, steamboat explosions and collisions, and runaway stage horses"—these blackface comedians sang and danced.[18]

From the moment the interlocutor gave his stentorian command, "Gentlemen, be seated," and the end-men, resplendent in gaudy full-dress suits, wide white collars setting off their heavily blackened faces, took their places, happy audiences sank back to revel in a show whose spontaneity removed it far from the artificialities of so much of the contemporary theatre. Mistah Tambo and Mistah Bones spoke the language of the people—for all their exaggerated dialect. Their jokes, timely and topical, were meant to be understood and laughed at by the man in the street. When they sang, it was a song all the world knew and could sing. Delighted audiences stamped and cheered when the min-

strels swung into "The Essence of Old Virginnv" or "Old Dan
Tucker":

> Old Dan Tucker was a fine old man,
> Washed his face in a frying pan,
> Combed his hair with a wagon wheel,
> Died with the toothache in his heel.

There were many other favorites: "Stop dat Knockin' at My
Door," "Dandy Jim of Caroline," "Hard Times Come Again No
More," "Big Sunflower," "Root, Hog, or Die":

> I'se de happiest darkee on de top ob de earth,
> I get fat as possum in de time ob de dearth,
> Like pig in a tater patch, dar let me lie,
> Way down in old Virginny, where it's
> Root, hog, or die. . . .[19]

The humor of the old-time minstrel show was rough and
ready, although the essentially clean and moral atmosphere of
the performance was one of its greatest assets. The jigs and fancy
steps danced to tambourine and castanets were lively and amusing. But in its songs, minstrelsy had something genuine and
enduring. While everything else about it was ephemeral, its
music won a hold which it has never lost. It was for these black-
face comedians, these knights of the burnt cork, that Stephen
C. Foster wrote "My Old Kentucky Home," "Old Black Joe,"
"The Old Folks at Home," and "O Susanna." It was as a minstrel-
show walk-around that "Dixie," written by Dan Emmett, won
its popular vogue. Lincoln heard it at a performance in 1860.
"Let's have it again!" he shouted from his box. "Let's have it
again!" Within the year Lincoln was President and "Dixie" the
battle-song of the Confederacy.[20]

Through its songs the minstrel show has won immortality, but
in the form in which the nineteenth century so enjoyed it, it
has almost completely faded away. The other types of popular
entertainment developing in this period gradually expanded, or
took on new shapes, but Mistah Tambo and Mistah Bones are

to-day seldom seen. The limitations of minstrelsy were too marked. There was no room for the change and diversification that the public in time demanded. There were no women in the cast. As interest began to decline in the decade after the Civil War, the minstrels drew further and further away from the carefree, homely atmosphere of the plantation life they had tried to depict. It had always been fanciful rather than realistic— who can say to what extent the popular conception of Negro character was framed by minstrelsy, how influential it was in winning northern sympathy for the slave?—but the minstrels of the latter part of the century bore no relation whatsoever to the plantation blacks. When the slender thread that bound their performances to real life was snapped, their shows were doomed.

-->>><<<-

THE CIRCUS was another form of popular entertainment now gradually evolving. It did not spring full-panoplied upon the world, this dazzling combination of animal exhibits, equestrian performances, band music, and crude comedy. Nor was it a revival of those elaborate spectacles, marked by the cruelty of the gladiatorial contest, whereby the rulers of Rome had sought to quell the restlessness of the populace. The American circus, with all its distinctive features, was a native product. It was a combination of the little menageries and bands of itinerant acrobats which had put on their performances at the colonial taverns and the more sophisticated equestrian circuses which had been staged in city amphitheatres (the pit easily converted into a ring) since the close of the eighteenth century. It became primarily a traveling tent show, providing the rural population with an equivalent for the popular theatre and the variety-hall. It was one answer to the need for diversion of country people who found themselves isolated from the multiplying attractions of city life.

Among the traveling animal exhibits early in the century, the most ambitious was that of Hackaliah Bailey, of Somers, New

York. Soon after the War of 1812 he toured New England with the famous elephant Old Bet. She created a tremendous sensation; everywhere crowds flocked to see her. To avoid giving a free show en route, Bailey had to travel by night. But learning that the elephant was coming the farmers lined the road with huge bonfires, and Old Bet literally traveled in a blaze of glory. Until she met her tragic end—shot by an irate Maine farmer whose bigotry could not condone even the exhibition of an elephant—she had a spectacular success.[21]

It inspired other managers of traveling menageries. They began to make more extensive tours, aided by the slow improvement of roads, and animal exhibits became a feature of village entertainment. Barn shows were given, with admission usually 12½ cents, at which the farmers gaped wonderingly at strange apparitions from another world. Contemporary notices tell of one in Salem, Massachusetts, in 1816 at which a tiger, buffalo, and dancing dogs were exhibited; of another in Lawrenceville, Pennsylvania, twelve years later with a bear, a wolf, a camel, and a monkey.[22]

In this same period acrobats also began to join forces to travel about the country together. These little groups of entertainers would send a clown ahead to announce their coming with a few antics on the village green (precursor of the circus parade), and the performance would be given at night. Not in a tent. A piece of canvas would be stretched about a small platform, the troupe's wagons drawn up to serve as box seats at twenty-five cents apiece; and tight-rope dancer, juggler, or sword-swallower would go through his fascinating routine on a stage lit by flaring pine torches.[23]

For long the menageries and the acrobatic troupes maintained a separate identity. Sometimes they traveled together, the one staging its performance in the afternoon and the other in the evening; but there were two distinct shows. Gradually they began to join forces. The proprietors of the menageries added a few acrobatic performers; managers of the acrobats included ani-

Barnum Enters the Circus Field

Lithographed poster, about 1840. Courtesy of the American Antiquarian
Society.

Circus Day in Chicago

Parade passing the Sherman House at Clark and Randolph Streets, about 1866. Lithograph by Jevene and Almini. Courtesy of the New York Historical Society.

mal exhibits. A more ambitious joint entertainment developed which was usually staged under canvas.

The country about Somers, New York, where Old Bet had had her start, became the headquarters for a number of these new rolling shows. They toured New England, worked their way south where warm weather gave them longer playing seasons, and gradually crept westward toward the frontier. But these pioneers of the circus had to be both enterprising and daring. Traveling conditions were still difficult, and in the rural districts the popular attitude was often severely disapproving. They had to perform miracles in meeting the problem of transportation, and they could combat prejudice only by continually stressing the supposed cultural features of their entertainment. It was long before a circus dared call itself a circus. It clung to the name menagerie which the pious approved, invariably advertising the performance as "a great moral and educational exhibition." It was perhaps from their early association with such shows that James Fisk and Daniel Drew, both circus men in their young days, learned the technique which stood them in such good stead in their later exploitation of a gullible investing public.

By the 1830's some thirty rolling shows were regularly touring the country. Buckley and Wick had eight wagons, forty horses, thirty-five performers, and a tent holding eight hundred people. Soon the Zoölogical Institute advertised forty-seven carriages and wagons, one hundred and twenty matched gray horses, fourteen musicians, and sixty performers. The parade had by now been introduced; the performers came to town to the blare of a brass band. Still it was not the real circus. There was no ring; there were no riding acts.[24]

The final step in the evolution of this institution, its merger with the equestrian shows of urban amphitheatres, took place just before mid-century. The popular appeal of riding and tumbling acts (President Washington had been an impressed spectator at John Bill Ricketts' indoor circus in the 1790's) naturally suggested an addition to the program of the traveling tent shows.[25] The more enterprising managers introduced a ring beneath the big top; the country as well as the city was treated to bareback riding and trick horsemanship. The thrills of equestrianism supplemented the lure of wild animals, and the circus as we know it to-day at last emerged in all its spangled glory.[26]

The Mammoth Circus of Howe and Mabie—"Greatest Establishment of its Kind in the World"—ventured as far west as Chicago in the 1850's, and there faced the unexpected competition of the Grand Olympic Arena and United States Circus. Van Amburg and Company's Menagerie—still advertising itself as "the only moral and instructive exhibition in America"—carried east and west its African ostriches nine feet high, its polar bears, and Hannibal, the world's largest elephant. Dan Rice, King of American Clowns, was earning $1,000 a week with his acrobatic nonsense; the famous Herr Driesbach was nonchalantly having his supper "at a table set in the den of his animals." Finally, in 1856, the Spaulding and Roger's Circus announced it would travel by railroad, nine special cars: "team horses and wagons won't do in this age of steam."[27]

Nothing could have been more democratic than the circus. Traveling what was still pioneer country, Edmund Flagg found the little village of Carkinsville, Illinois, "absolutely reeling under the excitement of the 'Grand Menagerie.' From all points of the compass men, women and children, emerging from the forest, came pouring into the place, some upon horses, some in farm wagons, and troops of others on foot."[28] Seeing a performance at Newport, Belle Brittan wrote: "Everybody went—all classes, ages, colors and conditions. There were as many as five thousand people there, all mixed up with the most democratic indiscrimination—Fifth Avenue belles sitting on narrow boards with their dresses under their arms, alongside of Irish chambermaids and colored persons of all sizes and sexes."[29]

Barnum now entered the circus field. It was not yet the Greatest Show on Earth, only a Grand Colossal Museum and

Menagerie, but nothing in the 1850's could rival it. General Tom Thumb was a first drawing-card; there was choice of all the freaks and curiosities of the American Museum, and a menagerie drawn from the four quarters of the earth. Barnum had chartered a ship, sent abroad for his own animals. It was an epochal day in circus history when his ten elephants, fresh from Ceylon, paraded up Broadway harnessed in pairs to a gilded chariot and amid the cheers of an immense crowd were reviewed by Jenny Lind from the balcony of the Irving House.[30]

Chapter VIII

THE BEGINNING OF SPECTATOR SPORTS

THE SAME PEOPLE WHO CROWDED PIT AND GALLERY AT THE
country's early theatres, who made up the vast audience so
cleverly exploited by Mr. Barnum, were also responsible for the
beginnings of what are termed spectator sports. City crowds early
developed that habit of watching others perform in the field of
sport which has so often given rise to the charge that Americans
are a nation of onlookers. It was a complaint more justified a
century ago than it is to-day. "Society would drop a man who
should run around the Common in five minutes," declared Oliver
Wendell Holmes,[1] but thousands flocked to watch some one else
run—to witness a horse-race, a boat-race, or a professional foot-
race.

The failure of the increasing mass of urban dwellers, of whatever class, to get outdoors themselves did not mean that the
American people had lost the Anglo-Saxon love for sports. The
rise of cities had broken the traditional pattern of recreational
life. Restrictions of time and space, the limitations imposed upon
people crowded into small living areas without parks or open
spaces, did not permit the familiar games and athletic contests of
village life. And organized sports to replace these informal pastimes were a long time in developing, discouraged by those social
influences which in every direction were holding up the normal
expansion of recreation.

Nevertheless, the commercial amusements whose rise we have
traced could not wholly satisfy the needs of men who unconsciously missed the wrestling match, the shooting contest, the
foot-race, in which they themselves might have taken part or at

least watched their friends and neighbors. Theatrical entertainment did not offer the excitement of competition, of taking sides, of betting; it did not get one out of doors and into the open. A people whose attitude was greatly influenced by the traditions of a pioneering frontier life were restless under city restraints. Until they found the escape-valve of new sports for themselves, they eagerly took up the next best thing. If they could not play or compete, they could at least get the thrill of vicarious participation by cheering on their favorites from a grand stand.

Crowds ranging from twenty to fifty thousand, made up of all members of society, were consequently turning out as early as the 1820's for widely heralded horse-races, for the regattas held at cities along the Atlantic seaboard, and for the grueling five- and ten-mile races of professional runners. The available stands would be packed, the overflow spreading to every point of vantage. A contemporary newspaper reporting on a foot-race in 1835 declared that "it would have required the amphitheatre of Titus to have accommodated all." [2]

The eagerness for such amusements was a striking manifestation of changing times. "Every new attraction gathers its countless throng," an Englishman commented on visiting New York in 1842, "as if the people had no other occupation than sight-seeing, though it is well known that they are among the most constantly occupied and busiest people in the world." [3]

How explain this apparent paradox? The city crowd was composed of many elements quite unknown in that earlier period when virtually the entire population lived in the country. If a majority of all classes were employed in various mercantile and manufacturing pursuits, there were always large numbers unemployed or at least temporarily not working. Periods of depression threw men out of jobs; every city had its influx of immigrants and country boys looking for work which took some time to materialize even under the best conditions; and the seasonal nature of much employment accounted for a good deal of leisure despite the long hours of labor generally prevailing. Also, city life inevitably created a class of ne'er-do-well floaters and professional sport followers who swelled the ranks of the temporarily idle.

All this was new. It gave rise to many problems. These restless crowds, with so few opportunities for healthy recreation, made up the mobs through which democracy often attempted to assert its rights. The rougher elements hung around the bar-rooms. They frequented the so-called sporting-halls where cock-fights were staged, dogs pitted against each other, and "rat worries" held. They supplied the recruits for a sporting fraternity known as "the fancy" (from which the word *fan* is derived), as ready to bet on a yacht-race as on a back-room game of faro or chuck-a-luck. They furnished material for the city's notorious gangs. They populated the underworld. And while commercial sports were a far from adequate answer to problems created by the new conditions of urban life, they were at least better than saloons and pool-rooms for the army of discontented ready for anything that promised to satisfy their thirst for amusement.

In general, the sporting events of the period were professional affairs, put on, like any other form of public amusement, for profit. Proprietors of the resorts beginning to spring up on the outskirts of the new cities and owners of transportation facilities —stage-coaches, ferries, and, later, the railroads—were the pioneer sports promoters. Even before they erected grand stands and collected admission charges, they could make money by bringing large numbers of people together for any sort of race. There were the fares collected for ferry or omnibus service, and the profits from drinks and refreshments. The new sports were promoted much as the tavern sports of an earlier day had been, with the further aid of professional gamblers who would put up money purses for the chance to bet.

Barnum never applied his talents to this field, but he tells of one venture which reveals the indirect profits, entirely apart from possible admission charges, to be made from staging such outdoor performances. Happening to pick up a herd of about

fifteen calf buffalo in the summer of 1843, he organized a great
buffalo-hunt and western-sports spectacle which was to be held
in New Jersey "on the extensive grounds and race course of the
Messrs. Stevens, within a few rods of the Hoboken Ferry." It
was widely advertised that no admission would be charged, and
in enthusiastic response to such an exceptional opportunity for
a free show some twenty-four thousand persons crossed the Hudson to watch the sport. The buffaloes, as it turned out, were sick
and frightened; they could hardly be goaded into any action at
all. But the twenty-four thousand enjoyed their excursion nevertheless. Profits? "I had engaged all the ferry boats to Hoboken,"
Barnum wrote in his autobiography, "at a stipulated price, and
all the receipts on the day specified were to be mine." [4]

->>><<<-

HORSE-RACING, with its traditions going back to early colonial
days, was the first of the popular spectator sports. Widely prohibited in the early years of the century, it gradually came back
into favor, and city crowds naturally turned to the highly organized meets which replaced the more informal rural races.
New courses were established throughout the country, with
enlarged grand stands for paying customers. The early impetus
for racing had largely come from the desire of breeders to improve their stock, but a broader popular interest caused *The Spirit
of the Times*, the most important journal devoted to the sport,
to declare in mid-century that racing was now mainly, if not
exclusively, intended for the public amusement.[5]

Every one went to the races, from the President (John Quincy
Adams as well as Andrew Jackson) to newsboys. There was the
gambling fraternity, referred to by *Frank Leslie's Illustrated
Newspaper* as "this racing world—this huge agglomeration of
gambling and fraud, of weakness and wickedness"; the fashionable race-track followers— "galaxies of beauty and booty"; and in
addition thousands of everyday working people. The more strait-
laced could never countenance racing: it was damned forever by

the betting. But at the new Fashion Course things were so well managed that *Leslie's* stated in 1856 "that families can visit the races with propriety and have no fear of their sensibilities being shocked by improper exhibitions." [6]

The crowds that attended the Union Course on Long Island were the largest at any track. A series of North-South matches held there aroused a nation-wide excitement which drew visitors from all over the country. In 1823 a crowd variously estimated at from fifty to one hundred thousand, including some twenty thousand out-of-town visitors, turned out to see the famous race between Eclipse and Sir Henry which has come down in sporting annals as one of the great events of the century. It was for a purse of $20,000 a side, to be decided by two out of three four-mile heats. When the northern horse, Eclipse, won the final heat, the huge crowd went wild. "The air was now rent with shouts of extacy from the New Yorkers, and the press around the judges' stand for a short time was so great that nothing could overcome it." [7]

Later races drew almost as many spectators. When Fashion and Peytona met in 1845, a wide-eyed reporter from the *Herald* (which brought out extras between the heats) informed his paper that fifty thousand persons had crossed the East River by noon, while the roads were still so densely packed with omnibuses and hacks that many of the spectators would never get near the course. [8] Another time transportation facilities appear to have been even more seriously overtaxed. "The tens of thousands of the sovereign people who wished to see this race," a spectator wrote, "made their arrangements to go by railroad from the South Ferry, but the numbers were so great that the locomotives refused to draw. They balked and would not go ahead; the mob who had provided themselves with tickets, finding it was 'no go' became riotous, upset the cars, placed obstructions in the rails, and induced all sorts of violence." [9]

Racing flourished in all parts of the country except New England. The South and West were great centers for the sport.

Peytona and Fashion's Great Match

For $20,000, Union Course, Long Island, May 13, 1845, Peytona of Alabama winning in two four-mile heats. Lithograph by H. R. Robinson after a drawing by C. Severin. Courtesy of Harry T. Peters.

Lady Suffolk and O'Blennis

"The Old Gray Mare of Long Island" at St. Louis, 1851, in her nineteenth year still doing the mile in 2:33 to sulky. Painting by R. S. Hillman in the collection of Harry T. Peters.

And if the best-known courses after those of New York were at Washington, Louisville, Cincinnati, and New Orleans, other widely scattered tracks held race meets which became a distinctive feature of community life. Those at Nashville, Tennessee, drew immense crowds from all the western country. When Andrew Jackson's Truxton beat out Captain Joseph Erwin's Ploughboy, the future President declared there was on hand "the largest concourse of people I ever saw assembled, unless in an army." [10] The races of even the small towns beyond the Mississippi were drawing considerable crowds by the 1850's. The Wichita *Eagle* reported one at which over a thousand men were present—"besides some five carriage loads of soiled doves." [11]

Even more popular than running races was the distinctively American sport of trotting matches. In addition to their place on the schedules of all regular tracks, they had become by mid-century almost the most important feature of country fairs. Even New England welcomed this sport. At a trotting carnival and horse show held in Massachusetts in 1856 there was a daily attendance of thirty thousand, including "the very cream of the Boston population." [12] Thousands upon thousands who cared not a whit for running horses were eager spectators. Among others, such famous trotters of the period as Tacona, Lady Suffolk, and Flora Temple were known the length and breadth of the land; the most famous of sulky-drivers, Hiram Woodruff, was a national hero. As the record for the mile was progressively lowered to under 2:20 minutes, an English expert simply refused to believe it had been done. "I apprehend no horse ever did, or could trot over the measured English mile in that short space of time," he scornfully wrote. "From the extensive rapidity of his trot his feet would be apt to strike fire and set him ablaze." [13]

-»»«««-

Rowing and sailing regattas had a very unusual place in the life of the times. While many of the boat-races were for sweepstakes and involved heavy betting on the merits of the rival craft as well as rival crews, amateur contests brought out tremendous crowds which found them a thrilling spectacle. Members of the clubs that staged these events were of the wealthy class. The Castle Garden Amateur Boat Club Association was restricted, in the 1830's and 1840's, to "young men of the highest respectability, who were determined to combine with pleasure the utmost propriety of conduct." [14] Membership in the yacht clubs even more inevitably meant social position. But tradespeople and mechanics who could never expect to pull an oar in a racing-barge or hold the tiller of a sailing-yacht were perfectly free to watch their regattas. A race in Boston, calling out eighty-odd entries; a match between two lap-streak gigs from among Philadelphia's forty rowing clubs; the races of oarsmen in Baltimore, Charleston, New Orleans; a long-heralded contest between one of New York's eight-oared barges and a boat from St. John's, Newfoundland—all these events meant crowded water-fronts.[15]

In 1824 a boat-race in New York harbor for a $1,000 purse attracted a throng estimated by the *Evening Post* at fifty thousand. The victory of the winning *Whitehall* boat was acclaimed as a baseball world's championship might have been a century later, its crew appearing at the Park Theatre to receive a tremendous ovation.[16] Some years later a regatta of the New York Yacht Club, which was organized in 1844, found the harbor filled with excursion steamers and other craft, all with "densely packed masses of pleasure seekers," while the piers of lower New York, Jersey City, and Staten Island were crowded with "multitudinous and vociferous citizens." [17] In mid-century the fever spread to inland cities—Chicago, Pittsburgh, St. Louis— and regattas at such widely separated points as Portland, Maine, and Milwaukee, Wisconsin, were watched by twenty thousand to thirty-five thousand spectators.[18]

"The beauty and the fashion of the city were there," reads the description of a regatta at Louisville on July 4, 1839; "ladies and gentlemen, loafers and laborers, white folks and 'niggers,' steam-

boat cooks, scullions, cabin boys, mates, passengers, and captains, and all the paraphernalia of a city life on an Independence
Day, formed the constituent parts of the heterogeneous mass that
stood jammed and crowded upon the levee." [19] And that same
year a spectator at the annual regatta at Newburgh, New York,
wrote of how "the innumerable windows of the Warehouses and
Factories were crowded with ladies... every piazza and house-
top was stirring with animated beauty—the locks and steamboats,
and the rigging of sloops and schooners, were all crowded with an
indescribable mass of men, women and children of all ranks
and all ages." [20]

→»«←

THE FOOT-RACES were wholly professional events, and the runners
of the day (*pedestrians* as they were called) had large numbers
of followers who gambled heavily on their prowess. The races
were at first run through city streets, men on horseback riding
ahead to open lanes through the dense crowds of onlookers, but
their popularity soon led to their being moved to race-courses
where admission could be charged. Great excitement was aroused
in New York in 1835 by the offer of a $1,000 purse for any man
who could run a ten-mile course in under an hour. "Without
intending it by any means," wrote Philip Hone, "when I arose
this morning I found myself with Robert in the barouche, en-
veloped in clouds of dust... on the road to the race course,
jostled by every description of vehicle, conveying every description of people." He thought the total attendance approached
that at the race between Eclipse and Sir Henry, although it was
probably nearer twenty or thirty thousand. When one of the
nine starters completed the course in just under the stipulated
hour, the crowd went wild, while the winner jumped on a horse
and rode triumphantly around the track.[21]

Individual match races, growing out of challenges flying back
and forth among the professional runners, were most common.
"Thomas Wood, of East Cambridge," reads a typical announce-

ment in the new sporting journal, the *New York Clipper*, in 1856, "will run Joe Travis, three or five miles for $250 a side. Man and money ready at Adams Billiard Hall." There were scores of popular champions: Henry Stannard, the man who had run the ten-mile event in under an hour; William Jackson, the American Deer, who was disastrously defeated by the English runner John Barlow; the Welsh Bantam, the Worcester Pet, the Boston Buck, the Bunker Hill Boy.... Each "ped" had his own colors—a gaily hued shirt, and in one case red shoes tipped with blue.[22]

→»)«←

PRIZE-FIGHTING was not really a spectator sport in this period: "We are not yet fashionable enough," *Niles' Weekly Register* commented sarcastically, "for such things in the United States." [23] But despite the brutality which everywhere placed it under official ban, fights surreptitiously staged by "the fancy" were beginning to attract ever-widening notice. The champions were winning a popular following for all the disapproval voiced by the more respectable elements of society.

"The amusement of prize fighting," again to quote Philip Hone, that estimable diarist of so many phases of New York life, "has become one of the most fashionable abominations of our loafer ridden city. Several matches have been made lately. The parties, their backers, betters, and abettors, with thousands and tens of thousands of degraded amateurs of this noble science, conveyed by steamboats chartered for the purpose, have been following the champions to Staten Island, Westchester, and up the North River, out of the jurisdiction (as was supposed) of the authorities of New York; and the horrid details, with all their disgusting technicalities and vulgar slang, have been regularly presented in the *New York Herald* to gratify the vitiated palates of its readers, whilst the orderly citizens have wept for the shame which they could not prevent." [24]

There was no denying the brutality of old-style bare-knuckle fighting. It was as cruel as the gouging match of the frontier,

Boat-Race on the Charles River, Boston
Ballou's Pictorial Drawing-Room Companion, 1857.

A Great Foot-Race at Hoboken
Illustrated London News, 1845.

THE GREAT FIGHT FOR THE CHAMPIONSHIP,

PUBLISHED BY CURRIER & IVES.

Entered according to Act of Congress in the Year 1860, by Currier & Ives, in the Clerks Office at the District Court for the Southern District of N.Y.

152 NASSAU ST. NEW YORK.

sometimes quite literally being a fight to the death. A con-temporary account tells of one bout in which for almost three hours two bruisers "thumped and battered each other for the gratification of a brutal gang of spectators," until after being knocked down eighty-one times, one of them fell dead in the ring.[25] There was no science in this fighting: a pugilist's greatest asset was his ability to take punishment. With little thought of self-defense, his one object was to pummel the other fellow into unconsciousness.

Police regulations forced secrecy upon the promoters, and actual attendance at the bouts was consequently small. It was not until some time after gloves were substituted for bare fists and the Marquis of Queensberry rules had been adopted that prize-fighting was legally approved. When Yankee Sullivan and Tom Hyer fought their championship bout in 1849, they had to hold it in the woods on Maryland's Western Shore, having been driven away from the chosen site, Peel Island, by a boatload of militia. A few years later the fight in which Hyer lost the championship to John Morrissey was held under equally furtive circumstances, while the latter's successful defense of his title against John C. Heenan, "Benicia Boy," took place before two thousand spec-tators who had sailed over from Buffalo in three steamers to a point on the Canadian border.[26]

The growing attraction of prize-fighting, with its primitive appeal even for those who were shocked by its brutality, was graphically displayed on the eve of the Civil War in the universal interest aroused by Heenan's challenge of the English champion, Tom Sayers. Although he had not beaten John Morrissey, the latter's retirement from the ring left "Benicia Boy" undisputed champion, and the good wishes of all America followed him to England. His name was on everybody's lips—Concord philos-opher and Nevada miner, New York newsboy and Ohio farmer. What were his chances? Could he stand up against Sayers? "Benicia Boy" himself was confident. *Vanity Fair* published his farewell:

I'll wind our colors 'round my loins—
The blue and crimson bars—
And if Tom does not feel the stripes,
I'll make him see the stars! [27]

The country breathlessly awaited the outcome. It was inde-
cisive. Historians of the prize-ring still quarrel over who might
have won if the crowd had not broken up the fight in the forty-
third round. But "Benicia Boy" was the hero of the day. *The
Spirit of the Times,* getting out an extra edition of one hundred
thousand copies with the first report of the fight, hailed him as
the world champion.[28]

Upon his return to this country Heenan began giving boxing
exhibitions. They drew the crowds that prize-fighting itself could
not command because of its illegality. In Boston some twelve
thousand persons turned out to see the champion, while a boxing
festival he staged at Jones Woods, outside of New York, attracted
thirty thousand.[29]

→>>«<←

THESE spectator sports of the first half of the nineteenth century,
harbingers of the tremendous development of this type of amusement in later years, were at best but a poor substitute for games
or athletic contests in which the spectators themselves might
have actively participated. But again it must be remembered
that city crowds a century ago had no ready means for getting
out into the country—either by street-car or automobile. Our
whole modern organization of sports, together with parks and
public playing-fields, was completely unknown. The idle city
worker who did not spend the afternoon at the race-track, watching a boat-race, or cheering his favorite "ped" was driven to some
indoor amusement. The habit of watching professional athletes
fastened itself upon the city dweller a century ago because he
had almost no other alternative for daytime recreation.

These spectator events nevertheless helped to make possible
the rise of modern organized athletics and the public participa-

tion of later decades. The interest in professional running in the 1840's provided the impetus for the growth of amateur athletic organizations in the 1870's. The crowds drawn to regattas created an ever-widening interest in rowing and sailing. The immense vogue for trotting matches inspired every horse-owner to see if he could not develop a champion; it crowded the roads, town and country, with drivers always ready for a "brush" with friend or neighbor. Even pugilism led in time to the development of boxing as a popular pastime for young men and boys. These activities of a century ago promoted the audience habit, but they also played their part in maintaining an interest in sports for themselves which was soon to have a phenomenal flowering.

Chapter IX

MID-CENTURY

B<small>Y</small> MID-CENTURY GREATER WEALTH AND MORE LEISURE MEANT broader opportunities for recreation among the well-to-do. They began to give increasingly elaborate balls and entertainments. When Charles Dickens landed in New York, the great Boz Ball—"the tallest compliment ever paid a little man, the fullest libation ever poured upon the altar of the muses," as Philip Hone described it—was attended by twenty-five hundred persons representing the world of society. The decorations were scenes from *Pickwick Papers,* and *tableaux vivants* were presented of *Nicholas Nickleby, Oliver Twist,* and *The Old Curiosity Shop.* Supper was enlivened with quantities of champagne. It was an occasion typifying a new measure of sumptuous display in American social life.[1]

There was also a growing enthusiasm for yachting, inspired by the memorable victory of the *America* in the first international cup race; an increasing vogue for driving in summer and sleighing in winter; and greater interest in field sports. Game hunting had always been popular in the South. It had long been commended in Baltimore for drawing the young gentlemen of the town into the open fields "where no man ever contracted dyspepsia, or imbibed an ignoble passion." Wealthy eastern sportsmen—and visiting Englishmen—now went to the Far West to shoot elk and buffalo.[2]

More significant was the beginning of pleasure travel and the growth of summer resorts. New turnpikes and canals, the steamboat and the railroad, were working revolutionary changes in American life which affected recreation as well as business and

ndustry. In 1825 the appearance of a little booklet called "The
Fashionable Tour" had signalized the new trend, and Timothy
Flint declared that the better classes were carrying their desire
or travel "to a passion and a fever." [3] It was soon possible for
even the less well-to-do to undertake trips of which an earlier
generation would hardly have dreamed. "There is scarcely an
individual in so reduced circumstances," marveled one foreign
visitor, "as to be unable to afford his 'dollar or so,' to travel a
couple of hundred miles from home, in order to see the country
and the improvements which are going on." [4]

The establishment of summer resorts came as a direct result
of these improved means of transportation, and the fashionable
world rapidly made them popular. It flocked to the new watering-
places, turning what had been quiet little havens for invalids
into bustling social centers. Nahant, near Boston, began to advertise "its sports and fare" for vacation visitors. Newport re-
sumed its rôle of colonial days, attracting a larger and larger
summer population until in mid-century the *New York Herald*
disagreeably declared that "fashion, handmaid of vice, has set
her seal upon the escutcheon of this town." New Jersey offered
Cape May and Long Branch. New York had the most fashionable
of all resorts of this period in Saratoga Springs, where

> Hotels of vast Extent at length arose,
> In whose capacious bosoms were receiv'd
> Of guests the copious streams, that hither flow'd
> From various regions. . . . [5]

Easterners were naturally in a majority among the visitors at
these resorts, but every westerner with social aspirations labored
under the necessity of staying for a time at one of them, and the
wealthy plantation-owners of the South made a virtual hegira
north every summer. Until the bitterness aroused over the slavery
issue caused them to stay at home, at some such southern resort
as White Sulphur Springs, some fifty thousand southerners were
said to visit the northern states annually. [6]

Many of these visitors were not so much seeking rest or amusement as the establishment of their position in the social world.
Resort life reflected the confused gropings of society toward a
new order, and itself contributed to the decline of former distinctions. The elegant hotels at Saratoga or Newport attracted
people who formerly would have vacationed in the country only
at exclusive house-parties, and the socially ambitious saw their
opportunity. "Hundreds, who, in their own towns could not find
admittance into the circles of fashionable society," James Silk
Buckingham observed in 1838, "...come to Saratoga where...
they may be seated at the same table, and often side by side
with the first families of the country."[7]

On the deep verandahs of the huge, sprawling Congress House
or United States Hotel (accommodations for two thousand), on
the neat gravel walks cutting across Saratoga's well-mowed
lawns, might be seen "the fairest sample of the better class
throughout the United States.... What bustle, and display, and
expense, and frivolity!"[8] The frock-coated Washington politician tipped his tall silk hat to modish ladies in billowing hoop-
skirts; the smart New Yorker in tight-fitting trousers and flowery
waistcoat, inordinately proud of his curled whiskers, bowed to
blushing southern belles in beribboned satin bonnets. "All the
world is here," marveled Philip Hone on visiting Saratoga in
1839; "politicians and dandies; cabinet ministers and ministers
of the gospel; officeholders and office seekers; humbuggers and
humbugged; fortune hunters and hunters of woodcock; anxious
mothers and lovely daughters; the ruddy cheek mantling with
saucy health, and the flickering lamp almost extinguished beneath the rude breath of dissipation."[9]

Flirtation was a major amusement. The Courting Yard was
an institution at Saratoga; White Sulphur Springs had its "Billing,
Wooing and Cooing Society." There was not much else to do.
Cards and backgammon, bowling and billiards were possible,
but none of the outdoor sports to-day associated with the summer resort. Exercise was still unfashionable. There was not even

A Yachting Club on Lake Erie

Painting by an unknown artist, about 1870, owned by A. Hyatt Mayor.
Courtesy of the Metropolitan Museum of Art.

the horse-racing of a later day. The gentlemen whiled away long hours in smoke-filled bar-rooms over their gin slings, sangarees, sherry cobblers, and mint juleps. The ladies were relegated to the piazza, or possibly allowed an afternoon carriage drive. Nowhere were the restraints of the Victorian era, the respect for female delicacy, more rigidly observed. "Our amusements were simple and distinctly ladylike," Eliza Ripley recalled of resort life at Pass Christian, on the Gulf of Mexico. "There was no golf or tennis, not even the innocent croquet, to tempt the demoiselles to athletics." [10]

Two French visitors found this life unutterably dull. "People rise early," Achille Murat wrote of Saratoga, "go and drink, or make believe drink, of the water at the fountain; return to breakfast in common; the papas and mamas are ready to die with ennui all the day; the young ladies play music, the young gentlemen make love to them; from time to time some excursion is made in the neighborhood; in the evening comes dancing. People are very soon tired of this sort of life.[11] Michael Chevalier even more devastatingly summarized a day's program at Bedford Springs. He wondered how its visitors could get any possible satisfaction out "of gaping on a chair in the piazza the whole day; of going arms in hand (I mean the knife and fork) to secure their share of a wretched dinner; of being stifled in the crowd of the ball-room during the evening, and of sleeping, if it is possible, upon a miserable pallet in a cell echoing one's tread from its own floor of pine boards." [12]

The evening hop or Saturday-night ball nevertheless made up for a good deal of the day's deficiencies. The introduction of such exciting new dances as the waltz and the polka had given the ball-room a new popularity. Although there was shocked criticism from those who clung to puritanic traditions, the pulpit holding forth bitterly "against the abomination of permitting a man who was neither your lover nor your husband to encircle you with his arms, and slightly press the contour of your waist," [13] these importations won their way into society. The *New York*

Herald might rave about "the indecency of the polka as danced at Saratoga and Newport. . . . It even outstrips the most disgraceful exhibitions of the lowest haunts of Paris and London," [14] but the floor would be crowded on a Saturday night. The company whirled away the evening in grand style until it settled down to its midnight supper of champagne, ice-cream, and blancmange.

At the shore resorts there was one diversion that such watering-places as Saratoga lacked. This was sea bathing. Occasional references to it may be found in earlier days. A Mr. Bailey planned to institute "bathing machines, and several species of entertainment" at his resort on Long Island in 1794. [15] A few years later a hotel proprietor at Nahant advertised "a machine of peculiar construction for bathing in the open sea." [16] But not until much later were the first daring steps taken toward popularizing it as a sport for mixed company.

An early record of this is found in a description of Long Branch written by James Stuart in 1829. "Because of the swell," wrote the circumspect Mr. Stuart, "females are often afraid to venture into the sea with a female bathing woman, and on that account prefer the assistance of a man. This custom, which is very far from being general, has given rise to ill-founded stories of want of delicacy on the part of American females. The fact is, I believe, exactly as I have stated it, and the parties always go into the water completely dressed." [17]

A few years later a correspondent of *Frank Leslie's Illustrated Newspaper* described the costumes that accounted for Stuart's phrase, "completely dressed." "Some wear Bloomers, buckled nattily about the waists, with cunning little blue-veined feet twinkling in the shallow water," he wrote; "some are wrapped in crimson Turkish dressing gowns, and flounder through the water like long-legged flamingoes; and others in old pantaloons and worn-out jackets." Bathing-suits, it would appear, had not yet been invented, and after lunch there was a gentleman's hour, as our correspondent phrased it, "sans costume." [18]

Prejudice against mixed bathing gave way slowly. But soon visitors to Newport told of parties of ladies and gentlemen dashing out "hand in hand, sometimes forty of them together, into the surf upon the beach." They described with engaging enthusiasm how the men "handed about their pretty partners as if they were dancing water quadrilles." [19] "I do not believe," a writer in the *New York Herald* lyrically reported in 1853, "that Franconi's Hippodrome ever presents a gayer, more grotesque and animated scene than I witnessed. Hundreds of bathers, clad in garments of every shape and color—green, blue, orange and white—were gaily disporting before me, and within a few yards of my window. The blooming girl, the matronized yet blushing maiden, the dignified mamma, were all playing, dancing, romping, and shouting together, as if they were alive with one feeling. I noticed several ladies of admirable shapes. . . . Oh! ye happy waves, what a blissful destiny is yours, when you can enclasp and kiss such lovely forms." [20]

->>><<<-

IN THE MISSISSIPPI VALLEY the flush times of mid-century were marked by a spirit of boisterous gaiety which held its ground firmly against the pressure of those civilizing influences curbing the old sports and diversions of the frontier.[21] The Great River was an artery for amusements as well as commerce. Palatial steamers made their perilous way back and forth between St. Louis and New Orleans, their passengers gaily dancing on the hurricane-deck and gambling in the saloon; gaudy show-boats— the *Snow Queen* or the *Fanny Elssler*—tied up every night at village landings, with uniformed bands announcing their coming, and traveling entertainers of every kind brought to the river towns dazzling visions of the outside world. Farce and melo-drama, musical extravaganza, elaborate minstrel shows, were staged in the gilded concert-saloons. Less ambitious entertainers went from town to town by smaller steamer. Aboard one of them Thackeray saw a bearded lady who in shipboard life delicately concealed her hirsute growth beneath a red silk hand-kerchief.[22]

In the 1850's some two thousand professional gamblers were operating on the river boats.[23] There has always been a great deal of gambling in American life, from colonial lotteries to the present-day policy-game, but never has this major diversion flourished so mightily as in those booming days of the Mississippi Valley. Faro, monte, and chuck-a-luck were the favorite card games. Poker had been introduced by way of New Orleans and was soon to make its way still farther west. For those who wanted to lose their money with even less effort, the steamers had their full quota of three-card monte-throwers, dice-coggers, and thimble-riggers. The Mississippi River travelers do not seem to have ever caught on to the old shell-game.

"They'd just flutter them up like a flock of quail," one traveler wrote of the skilful way the gamblers handled their cards, "and get the aces, kings, queens, jacks and tens all together as easy as pie. A sucker had no more chance against those fellows than a snow-ball in a red-hot oven."[24] But it was not entirely skill. The professional gentlemen of chance freely availed themselves of the wares advertised by a certain Monsieur Grandine: "Advantage and Marked-Back Playing Cards ... an exact imitation of the fair Playing Cards in use, and are adapted for bluff or poker, Seven-Up, Forty-Five, Euchre, Cribbage, Vingt-et-un, or Twenty-One, Loo. ..." Monsieur Grandine was also obligingly ready to provide "sleeve machines" which held the cards in a most natural manner and allowed them to slip out perfectly noiselessly.[25]

The gamblers had a well recognized costume—black slouch hat, broadcloth coat, flowing tie, black high-heeled boots, white shirt elegantly frilled and ruffled, gaudy vest, and invariably a large diamond in the shirt-front and a massive gold watch and chain. They were the aristocrats of the river, making fortunes in fleecing the innocent, and then as promptly losing them at faro establishments in New Orleans. One of the best-known of them, George H. Devol, has left in his *Forty Years a Gambler on the*

Mississippi an engaging record of adventures which often involved hasty dives overboard when his victims discovered they
had been tricked. Usually he was ready to defend himself. "I
was always very stubborn," he admits, "about giving up money if
any one wanted to compel me to do it." On one occasion his
victim tried to call his bluff: "He took off his coat, and after he
got it off he weakened, and picked up a big iron poker that lay
by the stove. I pulled out old 'Betsy Jane,' one of the best
tarantula pistols in the Southern country...." And so Mr. Devol
kept his winnings.

Three-card monte always got them, ministers and all, this
hardened soul declared. "I caught a preacher once for all his
money, his gold spectacles, and his sermons. Then I had some
of those queer feelings come over me...so I gave him his
sermons and specs back." [26]

Away from the river there were other amusements—political
rallies, horse-races, dancing assemblies, the theatre, and traveling
shows from eastern cities.[27] The local paper of one small Ohio
town recorded the visit of Swiss bell-ringers, an exhibition of dis-
solving views by the aid of a magic lantern, "the inimitable
Winchell," a panorama of the Mississippi Valley half a mile long
and twelve feet high, "J. H. Green, Reformed Gambler, with
card tricks," Joe Ginger's Minstrels, and "Moxon & Kemp's Great
Eastern Circus, Five Nations, and a Steam Calliope drawn by
forty horses." [28]

The moving panorama, exhibited not only in western towns
but in eastern cities, was almost the equivalent of the later-day
moving picture. The Mississippi Valley exhibition just noted
toured the entire country, was advertised in New York as one of
the great attractions of the age, and disappeared from the American scene only when it was taken abroad, to Europe and the
Far East, for still further conquests. Many others were widely
known: the "Classical Panorama of Roman History," the "Sacred
Panorama of Pilgrim's Progress," the "Moving Mirror of the
Overland Route to California." The long rolls of painted canvas

were slowly unwound before admiring audiences as a lecturer
described the background for the scene depicted. In the dioramas
these scenes were made to change and dissolve into each other
by means of cloth transparencies and complicated overhead lighting effects.[29]

On the sod-house frontier, opening up in Kansas and Nebraska,
life was incredibly hard—bitter winters with sweeping snow-
storms, summers of searing drought, devastating plagues of
locusts, and always the terrible isolation of the prairies. Strong-
willed settlers struggled against immense odds to build a familiar
life against an unfamiliar background. But they early had their
amusements. Lawrence, Kansas, had a bowling-alley within a
few months of its being sacked in the free-soil struggle; the
People's Press of Nebraska City declared a few years later that
"the fever is now for billiards." [30] There was a theatre of sorts
at Leavenworth in 1858 which welcomed to its boards a minstrel
show, the New England Bards, a troupe of saxhorn players, and
a circus.

Marked differences, of course, still existed between East and
West, between the long-settled communities on the Atlantic seaboard and these rapidly growing states of the Mississippi Valley.
But improved means of transportation and closer communications
gradually promoted a uniformity in modes and manners which
was directly reflected in amusements. Whatever was in vogue
in commercial entertainment in New York or Philadelphia
eventually made its way west; social life in western cities and
towns aped that of eastern cities as much as it could; and as
other forms of recreation developed on the seaboard, they were
rapidly transferred to the Mississippi Valley and beyond.

⊢≫≪⊣

THE SOCIAL LIFE of the South throughout the first half of the
nineteenth century, and until the outbreak of the Civil War, is
generally viewed through a haze of romantic glamour. The pattern is all too familiar: gay young couples dancing on the

Sleighing in New York

Lithograph by Nagel and Lewis, composed and lithographed by Theodore Benecke, 1855. Courtesy of Harry T. Peters.

A Home on the Mississippi

Painting by an unknown artist, about 1850, owned by Mrs. Alice T. McLean. Courtesy of the Metropolitan Museum of Art.

The Turk Shoot

Painting by Cl Deas, about Rutherford S vesant Colle Courtesy of Metropolitan seum of A colonnaded porches of the "big house" as moonlight floods through the magnolia trees; race meets and fox-hunts; barbecues and oyster suppers; the cool tinkle of mint juleps . . . and carefree, happy slaves singing spirituals as they picked the cotton that made possible this leisured, luxurious way of life.

With what acute nostalgia did Thomas Nelson Page, only one of a host of reminiscent southern writers, look back upon such scenes. Here is a gay picnic, carriages laden with "precious loads of lily-fingered, pink-faced, laughing girls with teeth like pearls and eyes like stars," and gallant riders bursting with southern chivalry "who would have thrown not only their cloaks but their hearts into the mud to keep these dainty feet from being soiled." The social life of Dixie? "It made men noble, gentle and brave, and women tender and pure and true. . . . It has passed from the earth, but it left its benignant influence behind it to sweeten and sustain its children. The ivory palaces have been destroyed, but myrrh, aloes and cassia still breathe amid their dismantled ruins." [31]

It is true that there were a grace and dignity, and at the same time a gay spirit, about life in the ante-bellum South which were swept away in the cataclysm of civil war. The comfortable mode of living and easy acceptance of everything that contributed to amusement had continued over from colonial days on the great plantations. "Leisure and ease are inmates of his roof," one northern visitor wrote of the southern aristocrat. "He takes no note of time. Your Yankee will take time by the forelock, and push business through. But a Southerner never heard of the 'old man with a scythe.' " And he went on to note that under these circumstances, so foreign to the bustling life of the North, recreation played a different rôle. Where life had a more definite pursuit, it was perhaps not so necessary—"but here, where one finds golden leisure, amusements are indispensable." [32]

Other records tell of these amusements. Henry Barnard, a young northerner visiting in a southern family, wrote home enthusiastically of the lavish hospitality at "Shirley," the plantation of Hill Carter on the James River.[33] Susan Dabney Smedes has depicted in glowing colors the life at "Burleigh," in Mississippi, with its music and dancing, charades and cards, riding and driving.[34] Herbert Ravenel Sass recalls the house-parties, the deer-hunts, the chivalric tournaments (costumed knights jousting with their ladies' colors on their sleeves), which enlivened the long, languorous days on South Carolina's rice plantations.[35] For the wealthy planters in all parts of the South, and especially in those states newly carved out of the western wilderness to grow the cotton which brought them such dazzling prosperity, life had a flavor in mid-century known to no other part of the country.

But it concerned only that small group at the apex of the pyramid that made up southern society. It was no more typical of Dixie than the crowded ball-rooms of Saratoga were representative of recreation in the North. What of the great mass of southern yeomanry, small farmers still working their own land? What of the poor whites, that pitiful class of "vagrom-men, idlers, and squatters, useless to themselves and the rest of mankind"? And what of the slaves? The majority of people in the South had little direct contact with the life of the great plantations. Nowhere were class lines drawn more rigidly; nowhere was there a greater gulf between the different strata of society.

The statistics of that "peculiar institution" on which southern life was based rudely shatter many legends. At the close of the ante-bellum period, some three-fourths of the white population had no proprietary interest in slavery whatsoever. They were humble folk, largely engaged in grubbing out a living on their own small farms, in bitter competition with the slave labor they could not themselves command. There were in all only some fifty thousand estates on which there were as many as twenty slaves. The entire planter class totaled but a quarter of a million among the South's eight million white population.[36]

The slaves and the poor whites—it is difficult to say which class should be considered as the lowest order of society—could enjoy only such amusements as their owners or abject poverty permitted them. In the case of the former, conditions greatly varied. They often went out with their masters on moonlight 'possum- and 'coon-hunts; they were among the spectators at horse-races and cock-fights. On many of the plantations they were given free rein on such festive occasions as holidays or weddings to enjoy themselves with music and dancing, with contests in clogging, cakewalks, and Charlestons. "To see a group of them on the floor," wrote an entranced northerner, "or on the lawn, beneath the shade of the China-trees, when

> Hornpipes, jigs, strathspeys and reels
> Put life and mettle in their heels

whirling in the giddy mazes of the dance with their buxom dulcineas, each seeming to vie with the other in dancing the most; it is one of the finest specimens of animated nature I ever gazed upon.... No restraint of the etiquettish ball-room... whew! They'd burst like steamers.... What luxury of motion, what looks—breathing and sighs! what oglings, exclamations and enjoyment! This is *dancing*. It knocks the spangles off your light fantastic tripping, and sends it whirling out of the ball-room." [37]

Sometimes a Baptist revival would induce the Negroes to forswear dancing and music—"I done buss' my fiddle an' my banjo, and done fling 'em away"—but there was no restraining them for very long. God could not blame them for such simple amusements. The Negro preacher explained it in his Christmas prayer:

> Des dance bekase dey's happy—like de birds hop in de trees,
> De pine-top fiddle soundin' to be blowin' ob de breeze. [38]

Wherever the master did not approve, however, there would be no dancing and no banjo-playing in the slave quarters, no time for hunting or fishing. In many instances the slaves were harshly or cruelly treated, deprived of much more than the opportunity to play. That is the other side of the picture of plantation life in old Dixie. But even where they were well taken care of and allowed such amusements as did not interfere with their work, there could be no real freedom for enjoyment. The pleasures of the slave were always wholly dependent on the will of his owner.

The poor whites had the leisure and freedom that the blacks so often lacked, but their leisure was born of complete poverty and unwillingness to work. They were the forgotten men in this thriving Kingdom of Cotton, isolated in the pine-barrens or the back-country mountain areas. The chronic disease that made them so lazy and apathetic, that drove them to become clay-eaters, was not then recognized as hookworm. Fanny Kemble sorrowfully characterized them as "the most degraded race of human beings claiming Anglo-Saxon origin that can be found on the face of the earth." [39] "Even their motions are slow, and their speech is a sickening drawl," wrote D. R. Hundley, a good Alabaman, "... while their thoughts and ideas seem likewise to creep along at a snail's pace. All they seem to care for is to live from hand to mouth; to get drunk ... to shoot for beef; to attend gander pullings; to vote at elections; to eat and sleep; to lounge in the sunshine of a bright summer's day, and to bask in the warmth of a roaring fire, when summer days are over." [40]

Here were amusements, perhaps, but the amusements of idleness and debility. They did not awaken in the dulled minds of the poor whites any zest for living. Among the slum outcasts of the industrial North might be found men and women for whom life offered as little as it did for these unfortunates. But there was this marked difference: the North was slowly awakening to the needs of its depressed classes; the South was blind to the degraded status of the poor whites.

Between the wealthy planter and the Mississippi hillbilly or Florida clay-eater there was an impassable gulf. The self-respecting southern yeoman, sometimes working in the fields side by side with a Negro slave whom he either owned or hired, had at least some opportunity. He might conceivably make his way into the planter class. But in his own life he had little contact with his social superiors. Susan Dabney Smedes recalled that the Christmas egg-nog party that was always given at "Burleigh" for the overseer and "other plain neighbors" was one of the few occasions when plantation life and that of the small farmers overlapped.[41]

For these people, bound to the soil and hard pressed to earn a livelihood, hunting and fishing were still the most universal recreation. They also had their occasional farm festivals—corn-shuckings and cotton-pickings enlivened by persimmon beer or jugs of whisky—and annual country fairs and militia musters. There were horse-races and cock-fights, sometimes a circus or other traveling entertainment. The latter were rare. In the little town of Tarboro, North Carolina, there was but one such show in 1832, and twenty years later only five—three concerts, an ex-hibition of curiosities, and a circus. Many of the frontier customs lingered on in the back country. Rough sports and heavy drink-ing vied with the camp-meeting.[42]

One pastime peculiar to this part of the country was gander-pulling. The Dutch settlers in New York had practised this sport, and there was to be a later variation of it on the western prairies, but here it had a much stronger hold among the common people. A well greased gander was strung head down from the over-hanging bough of a tree. One by one the contestants, mounted on horseback, would ride full speed under the struggling bird, trying to seize it by its slippery neck as they tore by. The man who made off with the goose's head was declared the winner. A contemporary record describing gander-pulling in North Carolina declares that it was "anticipated with rapture by all bruisers either at fist or grog, all heavy bottomed, well balanced riders, all women who wanted a holiday and had the curiosity to see the weight and prowess of their sweethearts tried in open field."[43]

Augustus Baldwin Longstreet singles out dancing as a fa-vorite amusement. In his *Georgia Scenes* he describes the dinner out under the trees, the old Negro sawing on his fiddle, the awkward farm boys and fresh-cheeked girls. It was all simple and wholesome. The women "used no artificial means of spreading their frock-tails to an interesting extent from their ankles. They had no boards laced to their breasts." As for the dances themselves, "none of your immodest waltzes; none of your detestable, disgusting gallopades." [44]

Sometimes there were plank dances. "You stand face to face with your partner on a plank and keep on dancing," a countryman explained to one visiting northerner. "Put the plank up on two barrel heads, so it'll kind of spring. At some of our parties— that's among common kind o' people, you know, it's great fun. They dance as fast as they can, and the folks all stand around and holler, 'Keep it up, John!' 'Go it, Nance!' 'Don't give it up so!' 'Old Virginny never tire!' ''Eel and toe, ketch a-fire!' and such kind of observation, and clop and stamp 'em." [45]

Diversions of this character represented the recreation of the people of the South more faithfully than the formal balls, the fashionable picnics, the chivalric tournaments of the planters. But the opportunities to enjoy them were few and far between. The common man had a hard time. For him the slavery that brought wealth and leisure to the aristocracy meant a more narrowly circumscribed life, greater toil, and even less chance than had the small farmers of the North and West for real amusement. Not for him the frosted julep on a shaded porch; he was busy picking cotton.

-»>«<-

THROUGHOUT the land, holidays were a great occasion in the mid-century years. In town and country, east and west, these infrequent breaks in a life which for the workingman might still mean twelve hours' daily labor for six full days a week were seized upon with a zest that this age can hardly appreciate. They meant far more than they do in a day when every weekend is free for recreation, and they were enjoyed in great crowd activities.

A parade almost invariably led off the day's festivities. Every one turned out—the militia companies in their handsome uniforms, the patriotic societies and political clubs, the volunteer firemen in glistening helmets and flaming red shirts. The generation of the 1850's was fascinated by parades; a band stirred urban crowds even more than it does to-day. At election time— and there was no more exciting holiday—the streets of every town and city would be filled with rival marchers. Torch-light parades added a new zest to the absorbing game of politics which neither young nor old could resist. On other occasions the crowds gathered to watch and cheer military parades with a fervor which was the essence of the period's intense nationalism. There was no artificiality, no regimentation, about the public demonstrations of the young democracy.

In the cities the parade was often followed by a mass-meeting or public banquet; in the rural areas there were picnics and barbecues to which the entire countryside flocked. Scores of aspiring Daniel Websters orated eloquently to the great crowds gathered on New England village greens; innumerable Davy Crocketts attempted to spellbind their audiences as the oxen roasted at frontier barbecues. Hogsheads of punch or rum or whisky were consumed in toasts to the Universal Yankee Nation. Horse-races, impromptu sports, dancing to patriotic airs, were throughout the entire country a prelude to the night's fireworks displays.

The urban dweller also had his amusement park. The social world was being forced to share its near-by country retreats with working people. On a visit to Hoboken's Elysian Fields, Fanny Kemble was amazed to find the resort crowded with people from a quite different stratum of society from that of her own party. "Journeymen, labourers, handicraftsmen, tradespeople, with their families, bearing all in their dress and looks evident signs of well-being and contentment," she wrote, "were all flocking from their confined avocations into the pure air, the bright sunshine and beautiful shade of this lovely place." [46] There was no parallel in England to such a scene. It went far toward reconciling Miss Kemble to the crudities of American democracy. Children played on the swings, visited the bear dens, and enjoyed Punch and Judy shows as their parents picnicked and listened to the band music. The fastidious Samuel Dexter Ward noted "that there were a great many people here, male and female, but in my opinion few respectable ones." [47] The exclusiveness of an earlier day was gone.

Steamboat excursions enjoyed an immense popularity. Sir Charles Lyell noted that the passengers on Hudson River boats, on week-days as well as holidays, were very largely shopkeepers, artisans, and mechanics taking pleasure trips.[48] Horace Greeley, worrying over the $10 weekly budget of a New York workingman, wondered where he could get the money for his Sunday trip up and down the river to get some fresh air. Here was a new means of recreation, and the common man was taking full advantage of it.[49]

The *New York Herald* advertised dozens of holiday excursions for which the fare was never more than $1.00. One could cruise to Coney Island, already starting on its career as a popular resort, for fifty cents, visit the Lower Bay and Staten Island for twenty-five cents, and sail up river from the Battery to Harlem for twelve and one-half cents. Sometimes the excursions were organized by special groups. The Shamrock Benevolent Society and the Laborers' Union Benevolent Society had annual Independence Day outings. On one occasion the Thistle Benevolent Society gave a Grand Excursion and Cotillion Party aboard the steamboat *Robert L. Stevens* and an accompanying barge. The moonlight return down the river from West Point, the barge's deck cleared for dancing and the band playing gaily, rockets cutting their flaring paths of light across the sky, was a fitting climax to a day of enthusiastic festivities.[50]

Balloon ascensions drew great crowds. They may be traced back to the close of the eighteenth century, when President Washington was an eager spectator at Blanchard's stirring flights.

The Fashionable Singing Class

Leslie's Gazette of Fashions, 1862.

The Dance

Lithograph by E. B. and E. C. Kellogg, about 1852. Courtesy of
Harry T. Peters.

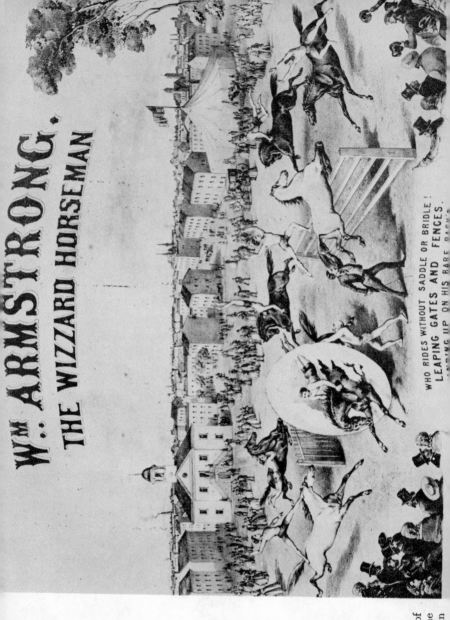

WM ARMSTRONG.
THE WIZZARD HORSEMAN

WHO RIDES WITHOUT SADDLE OR BRIDLE!
LEAPING GATES AND FENCES.

*Enter the Trick
Horseman*

Lithographed poster of
1856. Courtesy of the
American Antiquarian

In the 1830's Charles F. Durant was charging fifty cents admission for "the inspiring spectacle" of his embarkation. As the band played, he distributed copies of an appropriate poetical address, stepped into the cage of his balloon, and, waving an American flag, started aloft to the booming of guns. Some years later John Wise had become the popular aeronaut. He provided twenty thousand seats at the scene of ascension, including in the price of admission souvenir watches and jewelry.[51]

Every place of entertainment in the cities would be filled on holidays. People crowded the open-air gardens to hear band music and watch the fireworks. In New York's City Hall Park scores of booths would be set up to cater to holiday needs. Here were roast pig and spruce beer, lemonade and boiled eggs, lobsters and mint juleps, myriads of pies and cakes. The band played, and again there were free fireworks.[52]

Public balls, the populace's equivalent for the assemblies and cotillions of society, were coming into favor. The popular clubs vied with each other in staging entertainments for which general admission might range from twenty-five cents to $1.00, the latter price usually including a gentleman and two ladies. Mr. Parker's ball at Tammany Hall, the Third Ward American Republican Ball at the Minerva Assembly Rooms, the Native American Ball at the Park Theatre, were New York affairs, but they had their counterpart in every town and city throughout the country.[53]

Less respectable were the dance-halls—"branches of Satan's den," the puritans termed them; the cheap variety shows, twelve cents admission with refreshments; the free and easy concert-saloons, which became especially popular in Philadelphia; and the beer-gardens where the growing German population was giving the country a taste for lager beer. These were the amusements already beginning to shock rural communities—the dreadful lure of the wicked city; but they were a part of the recreation of great masses of the people.[54]

Of all the holidays, democracy took over especially for its own the Fourth of July. On this day of all others it paraded with riotous enthusiasm, cheered itself hoarse, drank a thousand patriotic toasts; listened eagerly at banquets, barbecues, and picnics to the flamboyant oratory of an age which could get drunk almost as easily on words as on whisky; crowded the circus tent, museum, minstrel show, and popular theatre; overran the amusement parks and packed the holiday steamboat excursions; watched horse-races, sailing regattas, and pedestrian races; danced on the open prairie, at country taverns, and in crowded city dance-halls; fired off cannon and watched the sky redden with the fireworks of a nation still young enough, careless enough, exuberant enough, to take the keenest joy in this fervid expression of patriotism and high spirits.

The American people never indulge in a holiday? Too absorbed in money-making to let themselves go? The caustic English critics of the first half of the nineteenth century must have shut themselves into ivory towers on the Fourth of July. The crowd of ladies and gentlemen, loafers and laborers, white folks and "niggers," who jammed the Louisville levee to watch an Independence Day regatta; the two thousand people who gathered on the Nebraska plains for a barbecue and night-long dance, feasting on enough buffalo, venison, sheep, hogs, and pigs to have fed the whole territory; the holiday seekers overrunning the swings, flying deer, bowling-alleys, and target ranges of city amusement parks—were they too dull-spirited and depressed ever to enjoy themselves?

"It was remarkable for the general turn out of all classes, ages, sexes, and conditions," the *New York Herald* ecstatically reported of one Fourth of July celebration; "it was remarkable for the most splendid pageant ever displayed in this city since the war; it was remarkable for the extraordinary amusements and recreations of the day, not the least of which was the exhibition of the tall, the graceful, the majestic, the beautiful giraffes; and for the elegant display of beautiful women that grouped within the pleasure gardens of Niblo, at Vauxhall, at Castle Garden, at the Museums, at the Theatres, or at the Cotillion parties, in the numerous aquatic excursions in the evening." [55]

Not enjoy themselves? The American people were gradually breaking down the one-time exclusive barriers in the world of amusements. Michael Chevalier had declared democracy to be "too new a comer upon the earth to have been able as yet to organize its pleasures and amusements." It was doing so now, as he had advised, without regard to the aristocratic precedents of Europe. The gospel of work still gave a popular sanction to long hours of labor. Holidays were few and far between. Nineteenth-century puritanism continued to disapprove the theatre, dancing, card-playing, and many other amusements. But the common man's need for recreation was asserting itself.

CHAPTER X

COW-TOWNS AND MINING-CAMPS

NO ACCOUNT OF THE AMUSEMENTS OF THE AMERICAN PEOPLE would be complete without some record of the rough-and-ready life in that new West which was growing up during the troubled years that saw the rest of the country convulsed by civil war and then largely absorbed in the problems of Reconstruction. Its vivid story has often been told in western dime novel, melodrama, and moving picture. They have portrayed in lurid colors the roaring, wide-open days when drunken cowboys rode their horses into the saloons and shot out the lights, suave professional gamblers dealt out poker hands with guns on the table, and pistol-shots punctuated the dance music as flannel-shirted miners sported at hurdy-gurdy or honky-tonk.

It is true that the whisky-mill, the gambling-palace, and the dance-hall dominated recreation. There was little to amuse the solitary miner prospecting among the ravines and gulches of the Sierras, the cowboy riding the range or driving cattle north from the Texas plains. Their pleasures were almost entirely centered on their occasional visits to civilization. For six months or longer they worked hard, lived in the open, and never saw a woman. "When they hit the bright lights of some little town that looked like gay Paree to them, they just went crazy." [1] With silver dollars jingling in their pockets, crying to be spent, they needed only a haircut and shave, a new outfit of clothing, and a few drinks to be ready to go.

> Whoopee! drink that rotgut, drink that red nose,
> Whenever you get to town;
> Drink it straight and swig it mighty,
> Till the world goes round and round. [2]

168

Cowboy or prospector, they were all alike. "It is he that bucks at Monte; plays draw-poker; fights the tiger; patronizes the Hurdies; sings like a 'Washoe canary,'" Dan De Quille wrote of the western miner; "it is he who first sees the peep of dawn—through the bottom of a tumbler—through the same cocks his eye on the last smile of evening."[3]

->>><<<-

LIFE in the gold-fields of California during the feverish days that followed Forty-Nine has been graphically portrayed (discounting their sentimentality) in "The Luck of Roaring Camp" and "The Outcasts of Poker Flat." A few years later similar scenes were being enacted in the camps that sprang up in Nevada, Montana, Idaho, and Colorado.[4] At the same time the larger mining-towns which grew up around the more important gold and silver deposits offered entertainment even more typical of this violent era.

The most fantastically extravagant of them all during the entire period from 1860 through 1880 was Virginia City, Nevada. The Comstock Lode yielded in these two decades treasure estimated at $300,000,000, and some twenty-five thousand people, almost entirely men, worked and played on that barren mountainside with an intensity hardly paralleled in any other community of the West.[5] The narrow streets were always crowded with quartz wagons taking the mines' daily output to the reducing mills, and freight teams laden with supplies which had been brought over the long mountain road from California. Stage-coaches were setting off or arriving almost hourly in front of the hotels; riders of the Pony Express dashed madly through the tangled traffic; and sometimes a string of camels might be seen laboriously packing salt up the steep trails.

Mark Twain was in Virginia City during the height of its boom as a reporter on the *Territorial Enterprise*. He found it "the livest town, for its age and population, that America had ever produced." He was fascinated by its carefree, gambling spirit, by all its color and movement. "There were military companies," he wrote, "fire companies, brass bands, hotels, theatres, 'hurdy-gurdy houses,' wide-open gambling palaces, political pow-wows, civic processions, street fights, murders, inquests, riots, a whisky mill every fifteen steps . . . and some talk of building a church!" [6]

The miners who thronged every thoroughfare had only one objective when their long, back-breaking shift was over—entertainment. Over a hundred saloons were ready to aid them. The more pretentious "two-bit" houses (every kind of drink cost a quarter) were the most sumptuous establishments in town—long mahogany bars, glistening chandeliers, a bright façade of mirrors, showy pictures in heavy gilded frames. No expense was spared to enable the miners to drink and gamble in as garish an atmosphere as the easy money of Virginia City could provide.

Faro, roulette, monte, and poker had their devotees. Another game was keno. "Fline glame," was the Chinaman's reputed comment. "Velly slimple. Dlealer slay 'Kleno,' and ellybolly ellse slay 'O Hlell!'" [7] After one house had experimented by having on hand "a real living, pretty, modest-looking young girl, in a close-fitting black silk dress," the custom spread of having female croupiers and dealers, through whom thousands of dollars changed hands nightly without causing comment.[8] Gambling was so much a part of the life of the mining-town that everything about it was taken for granted.

The hurdy-gurdy houses were a favorite resort. In a community where women were so scarce, their popularity may well be imagined. An eastern visitor reports that they were not all given over entirely to the usual personnel of such establishments. Such respectable women as the town might boast frequented some of the dance-halls, and they were invariably treated with deep respect. But more generally standards were not maintained on such a high level. "Four girls, about fifty men, an Irish fiddler, a bar-keeper and a bar, constituted the outfit," reads the description of one cheap house. "The gents were charged fifty cents each for a dance with the fair damsels, and after the dance were required to pay a like sum at the bar for drinks for themselves and their partners. . . . Gambling, prostitution, dancing and drinking were sometimes combined." [9] As in the case of saloons, the more expensive hurdy-gurdies had the most luxurious fittings. The dance-floors were highly polished, the music was provided by a full orchestra of skilled musicians, and the assorted collection of available ladies rivaled that of any eastern dance-hall.

Amusement of another kind was provided in Virginia City by prize-fights. The keen interest they aroused among the miners, supplemented by the betting and drinking, sometimes led to critical situations. But though a disputed decision often found the patrons hauling out their guns, the *Territorial Enterprise* (was it Mark Twain's phrase?) could usually report that the referee "failed to be killed." [10]

"A rush was made into the ring to break up the fight in a general row so that the bets might be declared off," an alarmed easterner wrote of one disputed prize-fight, "and instantly fifty pistols clicked and were drawn. . . . Colonel Beidler at once sprang into the ring, drew his revolvers, and declared that he would kill the first man who attempted to interfere with the fight. All well understood that when Beidler's pistol was drawn it meant business; and the ring was almost instantly cleared, leaving him standing alone in the center. 'Boys,' said he, 'this must be a fair fight. Go on with the show!' and time was promptly called again." [11]

There were occasionally other sports. Many of the miners were Cornishmen (it was a mixed population of all nationalities), and their canvas-jacketed wrestling matches were a popular spectacle. Sunday horse-races were held on the one level spot on the mountainside; rifle- and pistol-shooting contests sometimes took place; and members of the Virginia Alkali and Sagebrush Sporting Club chased coyotes with greyhounds on Forty-Mile Desert. But sooner or later every one came back to gamble at the Eldorado, dance at the Melodeon, and drink at the Sazerac, the Delta, or the Howling Wilderness. [12]

"The Comstock is an improving place to live on," declared the *Gold Hill News* of December 7, 1876. "Both Gold Hill and Virginia are well supplied with schools, and there is no lack of churches. We have more saloons than any place in the country. Every Sunday when there is a show in town we have a matinee and an evening performance. On the Sabbath, also, we are entertained with a horse-race or a fight between a bulldog and a wildcat. Every month or so the prize-fighters favor us with a mill, which we all go to see and then indict the fighters, as a sort of concession to the Puritanical element.... Every Saturday night small boys parade up and down the principal street of Virginia, carrying transparencies which inform our sport-loving people where cockfighting may be enjoyed. Faro, keno, chuck-a-luck and roulette may be found in every second saloon, and a special policeman, wearing his star, frequently conducts the game. Taking everything into consideration, there are few pleasanter places to live than on the Comstock." [13]

➤➤»«««

THEATRICAL entertainment had had an unusual popularity in the mining-camps, indeed throughout the West, since the California gold-rush. It brought the miners glimpses of a world from which they were otherwise completely cut off. Nowhere did strolling players, minstrel bands, variety shows, and straight dramatic companies win a more enthusiastic reception. In no other part of the country had the theatre come "into such unchastened, free and abundant life." [14] The miners showered gold-dust with equal abandon upon the quavering soprano who touched their sentimental hearts with her rendering of "When the Swallows Homeward Fly," and upon Edwin Booth (he was listed in the San Francisco directory of the 1850's as "comedian and ranchero" [15]) in his early performances of *Hamlet*. They cheered themselves hoarse when the beautiful heroine was finally rescued in a Broadway melodrama, and brushed away the tears as they watched a juvenile troupe of Fairy Minstrels.

San Francisco had its first real theatre when the Jenny Lind was opened in 1850, some two thousand miners packing pit and gallery for a performance of *Macbeth*. Many stars of the eastern stage trod its boards: Junius Brutus Booth as well as the young Edwin Booth, Laura Keene, Catherine Sinclair (the divorced wife of Edwin Forrest), Lola Montez, the glamorous Countess of Landsfeldt who had been mistress of the King of Bavaria.... A favorite of the western stage was California's own star, Lotta Crabtree. She first played as a child actress in mining-camp bar-rooms, wandering through the mountains with her mother in a wagon drawn by tasseled mules. "La Petite Lotta," singing "Young Ladies, Won't You Marry?" and dancing her famed Spider Dance, early won her way into the miners' hearts.[16]

In Virginia City's flush days there were five legitimate theatres and six variety houses running at the same time. At Maguire's, and later at Piper's Opera House, the plays were representative of everything being staged in the East. Here were seen Shakespearean revivals and other serious dramas; Irish farces, Italian light operas, and sentimental comedies; Victoria Loftus' British Blondes; Haverly's Mastodon Minstrels; Tom shows with double quartettes of educated hounds; and French dancers in the wicked can-can. Also lectures—Horace Greeley talking on the state of the nation, Artemus Ward on "Babes in the Wood."[17]

The sensational Adah Isaacs Menken won a triumph in 1863 which is reserved for few actresses. The miners went mad over her beauty, her incomparable voice, her daring. When she appeared in *Mazeppa, or The Wild Horse*, an excited audience cheered and applauded to the echo. The climax of this stirring melodrama is reached when the heroine is strapped to the side of the wild horse to be driven off into the mountains. The Menken, wearing only a slight gauze chiton, played the part with an abandon which had the miners standing on their chairs. When the horse dashed up the rocky mountain trail with her beautiful, almost naked body lashed to its flank, pandemonium broke loose.

Virginia City had never been so thrilled. It christened a new mining district The Menken and organized a Menken Shaft and Tunnel Company. When their dazzling heroine finally left, she was laden down with the bars of bullion, silver ingots, certificates of mining stock, with which the admiring miners had expressed their homage.[18]

>>>✄<<<

IN THE COW COUNTRY of the 1870's and 1880's the men who rode the range often got to town only once or twice a year. Their periodic binges were far less frequent than those of the miners who worked and lived at Virginia City, or those of the gold prospectors in the Sierras. They had a great deal of time on their hands. But as one of them phrased it, they were "merely folks, just plain, every-day, bow-legged humans," [19] and they sought every possible means of whiling away the tedium of long days in the saddle and empty evenings at camp or ranch-house.

The pride they developed in their horses made them eager to meet any challenge as to their speed, and the impromptu horse-race was as popular a sport on the range as in any other phase of frontier life. The cowboy was ready to bet anything he owned (except perhaps his saddle) on such races. He seldom had money, but he would put up his bridle, his rope, his quirt, sometimes the horse itself. Rival outfits would stake everything they could collectively raise on a match between two favorite horses. When a cowboy met a friendly Indian, there was invariably a race, sometimes leaving one or the other to go his way on foot.

The range-rider always had his six-shooter with him, and he amused himself by taking pot-shots at the jack-rabbits, prairie-dogs, or occasional coyotes that crossed his trail. Sometimes he gave chase to game with a swinging lariat. Cowboys would attempt to rope anything that came their way. They tried their skill on buffalo calves, went after antelopes, and sometimes even roped bears. There is the tale of one cowpuncher who made the

The Hurdy-Gurdy House at Virginia City, Montana

Albert D. Richardson, *Beyond the Mississippi*, 1867.

Cow-Town Vaudeville

Cheyenne, Wyoming. *Frank Leslie's Illustrated Newspaper*, 1877.

Bucking the Tige

Faro in a Cheyen
gambling saloon. *Fra
Leslie's Illustrated Neu
paper, 1877.*

Cowboys in Town for Christmas

Drawing by Frederic Remington. *Harper's Weekly,* 1889.

experiment of throwing his rope over the smokestack of a locomotive—and was almost jerked to eternity. When wolves were
discovered attacking the cattle, a hunt would be organized with
the pack of greyhounds that many ranches kept on hand for
just such occasions. All hands would turn out for what was
exciting sport, as well as a necessary measure for protection of
the stock.[20]

The cowboy played no competitive games. He never wrestled
or boxed. They appeared futile sports when any physical encounter was generally settled by the sharp crack of a revolver.
But foot-races were sometimes held. Although the object of the
race was to reach a certain spot in the shortest possible time,
this did not mean following a straight line when run on the
western prairie. To offset the handicap of the bow-leggedness
which revealed the real horseman, the course would be plotted
over the most difficult terrain. Cunning in avoiding the hazards
of sage-brush and gopher-holes, rather than mere speed, was
the real test.

The cowboy sang a great deal to mitigate his loneliness while
riding the range or to soothe and quiet the cattle on the drive.
In his collection of cowboy songs, John A. Lomax has told of
their part in the social life of the ranch. Whenever a puncher
from another outfit drifted into camp, he was expected to sing
any new song he knew or additional stanzas for an old one.[21]
Plaintive love songs, sentimental ditties, and sorrowful dirges
grew into a balladry of the plains which has taken its place as
one of the most distinctive forms of American folk-song. With
incredible pathos the cowboy sang "The Home I Ne'er Will Live
to See," "Oh, Bury Me Not on the Lone Prai-rie," and "I'm a
Poor, Lonesome Cowboy."

Sometimes the tune was livelier:

> Whoopee ti yi yo, git along, little dogies;
>   It's your misfortune and none of my own.
> Whoopee ti yi yo, git along, little dogies;
>   For you know Wyoming will be your new home.

At night about the camp-fire there was always some one in the outfit with a banjo, mouth-organ, or jew's-harp. They would sing "The Old Chisholm Trail," "Ten Thousand God-Damn Cattle," "The Gal I Left Behind Me," or "The Little Black Bull":

> The little black bull came down from the mount-tain
> (Hoorah Johnny and a hoo-rah Johnny)
> The little black bull came down from the mount-tain
> Long time ago, a long time ago, a long time ago
> And he run his horn in a white oak sap-ling
> Long time ago. . . .[22]

Apart from singing, evenings afforded little entertainment. Night after night, for weeks and months on end, the same little group of men sat about trying to kill time. They knew each other far too well—every idea, every trick of language, every irritating peculiarity—to get much pleasure from their own company. Men without women became touchy and quarrelsome. Long hard hours in the saddle, a monotonous diet of miserably cooked canned goods, made for frayed nerves and a readiness to take offense which often left the atmosphere electric.

The scene was seldom the gay, roistering one of fiction. Drinking was very rare, for the simple reason that the cowboys had no liquor. When some one did bring whisky into camp, it would not last long. Nor was there much gambling. The ranch hands generally spent all their money on their periodic trips to town and had nothing with which to bet. Dreary and apparently endless games of poker or seven-up nevertheless went on, with packs of cards so greasy from use that only those who knew them personally could guess what they were. More exciting were the occasional fights in which tarantulas were matched against each other much as favorite cocks had been on the earlier frontier. A champion spider was a much-prized possession, carefully tended.

How far monotony ruled the ranch-house is illustrated by the popularity of those contests in which the cowboys recited the manufacturers' labels on their tins of canned goods. They read very little (a few magazines, seldom books) but would carefully memorize the advertisements for condensed milk or baked beans. The eastern tenderfoot was sometimes amazed to hear the ranch-house suddenly break into a rapid singsong recital whose mysterious significance it often took him some time to discover.

A visitor could always be sure of a warm welcome among men so starved for society. The cowboys would dig up whatever cash or mobile possessions they could find in a happy attempt to take in the newcomer at whatever game he chose. Should punchers ride in from some rival outfit, the visit would be celebrated as freely as all available resources in the matter of liquor would permit. When an innocent easterner happened upon that restless company, he was greeted with a cordiality which lost nothing from the fact that the cowboys were hoping to have as much fun as possible at his expense. They hazed not because of any inherent cruelty in their nature, but because they were bored.[23]

The wild excitement of a day in town can be understood only against this background and in comparison with the almost unrelieved monotony of ranch-house leisure. It was little wonder that when the end of the round-up or drive gave the outfit a holiday, everything but the desire to have a good time was completely forgotten. The cowboy was out to enjoy himself, to make up for those long weeks whose amusements were so rare and unsatisfying. What if all his pay did disappear in a single night? He might not get to town for another six months. To gamble and drink away his money the one time he had the chance to spend it freely was unquestioned logic.

The cow-town was created by the extension of the railroad across the western plains, becoming a central point for the shipment of cattle to eastern markets. It was often no more than a string of frame houses which had little excuse for existence except as an entertainment center for all those varied elements which went into the floating population of the plains—cowboys, ranchers, freighters, teamsters, hunters, storekeepers, government officials, half-breeds, gamblers, and professional bad men. Every one went armed. Brawls and shooting affrays were common. "The town was simply an eddy in the troubled stream of Western immigration," wrote Emerson Hough, "and it caught the odd bits of driftwood and wreck—the flotsam and jetsam of a chaotic flood." [24]

To cowpunchers and ranchmen who had seen nothing but the prairie and the members of their own outfit for seemingly endless months, it was nevertheless full of high promise. They rode in booted and spurred, sometimes without fanfare but often with the wild yipping of the western thriller, and headed straight for the nearest saloon. "Buying the town" was in order if the outfit was really in money. A stack of silver dollars was planked down on the bar—"Gents, it's on us. She's opened up. The town is yours." Until it was gone, drinks were free for anybody whatsoever. There were instances of as much as $1,000 being spent on opening up a town, the saloon-keepers prorating the money until it had all been consumed in hard liquor. [25]

Many stories are told. One cowman walked into a restaurant and with a lordly gesture ordered a hundred dollars' worth of ham and eggs. Another had a champagne bath in the town's rickety little hotel. It drained the entire supply of every saloon, at five dollars a bottle, but the rancher's theory was a simple one. He wanted a bath, nothing was too good for him, and champagne was the most costly liquid of which he knew. [26]

Gambling drew the cowboy as surely as it did the miner. Any game, any time, but poker was the great sport of the cow country. Professional gamblers were always on hand, but there was not much cheating. The bad man caught with an ace up his sleeve got short shrift, as western thrillers have shown an admiring world, in a society where trigger fingers were so well exercised. "The click of a six-shooter is music to my ears, and a bowie-knife is my looking glass," was a favorite boast of the frontier. There came a time when the punchers were required to check their guns when they came into town, and the sheriff promptly took the bad man into custody, but in the early days little differences of opinion were decided in favor of whoever was quickest on the draw.

If the possible favors of the fancy ladies were largely responsible for the popularity of the dance-hall, the cowboy often made a straight course for it just for sociability and a good time. "Three of us was in the parlor of Maggie Burn's house giving a song number called 'The Texas Ranger,'" Teddy Blue wrote in We Pointed Them North, "John Bowen was playing the piano and he couldn't play the piano, and Johnny Stringfellow was there sawing on a fiddle and he couldn't play the fiddle, and I was singing, and between the three of us we was raising the roof. And Maggie—the redheaded, fighting son of a gun—got hopping mad and says: 'If you leather-legged sons of bitches want to give a concert, why don't you hire a hall? You're ruining my piano.'" [27] It is also Teddy Blue who tells of Connie the Cowboy Queen and her $250 dress: "They said there wasn't an outfit from the Yellowstone down to the Platte, and over in the Dakotas too, that couldn't find its brand on that dress." [28]

For the few respectable women who found their way to the Far West the cowboy had an idolatrous respect. Their rarity set them so far apart that one old-timer declared fervently that there were only two things a cowpuncher was afraid of, a decent woman and being set afoot.[29] When an occasional ball was held, young and old, beautiful and plain, were treated with awed chivalry. Such functions were popular, and the cowboys gathered in full war-paint—silk handkerchief and fancy vest, chaps and spurs—from a neighborhood of two hundred miles. Owen Wister has described such a dance in his story of how the Virginian mixed up the sleeping babies which had been parked for the evening in the woodshed. If there were not enough women to go around, which was usually the case, some of the cowboys would let themselves be "heifer-branded" with a handkerchief tied about the arm.[30]

At the end of the trail along which the cattle were driven

north from Texas was Dodge City—the Beautiful, Bibulous Babylon of the Frontier. There were other cow-towns—Abilene, Newtown, Ogalalla, Julesburg, Cheyenne—where it took several generations of orderly living to blot out the unsavory reputation of the early days, but Dodge City was reputedly the most wicked of them all. "Her incorporated limits," a local historian wrote, "are the rendezvous of all the unemployed scallawagism in seven states." [31] There might be seventy-five thousand head of cattle grazing in the surrounding meadows as they waited shipment east, and the Texas buckaroos who had driven them north packed the saloons and dance-halls which alternated with every business house on the town's crowded streets:

> It was hot July when we got to Dodge,
> That wickedest little town;
> And we started in to have some fun
> Just as the sun went down.
>
> We killed a few of the worst bad men
> For the pleasure of seeing them kick;
> We rode right into a billiard hall,
> And I guessed we raised Old Nick.
> The bartender left in a wonderful haste
> On that hot and sultry day;
> He never came back to get his hat
> Until we were miles away.
>
> We went from Dodge to the town Caldwell,
> As we wished to prolong the fun;
> When the marshal there caught sight of us,
> You ought to have seen him run.
> We rode right into a big dance hall
> That opened upon the street;
> The music and dancing both were fine,
> And the girlies sure looked sweet.
>
> We drank all the Caldwell whisky,
> We ate everything in sight;
> We took in all the dances,
> And they say we had a fight. [32]

THE LIBERTY and license of cow-towns and mining-camps did not last for very long. Once the civilization of the East had caught up with it, the colorful excitement of the Far West quickly faded. More orderly government led to the regulation of its wide-open entertainment palaces, and the refining influence of women toned down the freedom of a man's world. But the West's exuberant spirit of fun, its refusal to allow itself to be cramped by traditional tabus, the spirit typified by the comment that while the church might be tolerated, the saloon and the dance-hall were regarded as necessities, had its influence on the attitude of the country as a whole toward work and play. It served to undermine still further the Puritan tradition and gave a new impetus to the expansion of recreation.

Chapter XI

THE RISE OF SPORTS

WHILE THE WEST WAS GOING THROUGH ITS GORGEOUS EPOCH OF gambling, drinking, and gun-play, a series of athletic crazes were sweeping through the states of the East. Baseball developed from its humble beginnings in the days before the Civil War to its recognized status as America's national game. The rapid spread of croquet caused the startled editors of *The Nation* to describe it as the swiftest and most infectious epidemic the country had ever experienced.[1] Lawn tennis was introduced to polite society by enthusiasts who had seen it played in England, and the old sport of archery was revived as still another fashionable lawn game. Roller-skating attained a popularity which extended to all parts of the country. What the sewing-machine is to our industrial wants and the telegraph to our commercial pursuits, one devotee wrote rapturously, this new system of exercise had become to society's physical and social wants.[2]

Track and field events were also promoted with the widespread organization of amateur athletic clubs; gymnastic games were sponsored both by the German Turnverein and the Y.M.C.A.; and in the colleges a spectacular sports phenomenon loomed over the horizon with the development of intercollegiate football. Society welcomed polo as an importation from abroad, took up the English sport of coaching. And finally a craze for bicycling arose to supersede all other outdoor activities as city streets and country roads became crowded with nattily dressed cyclists out on their club runs.

All this took place in the late 1860's and the 1870's. Previously the country had had virtually no organized sports as we know them to-day. Neither men nor women played outdoor games. Alarmed observers in mid-century had found the national health deteriorating because of a general lack of exercise more widespread than among the people of any other nation. Ralph Waldo Emerson had written despairingly of "the invalid habits of this country,"[3] and from abroad the London *Times* had issued grave warnings of possibly dire consequences for our national well-being.[4] No transformation in the recreational scene has been more startling than this sudden burgeoning of an interest in sports which almost overnight introduced millions of Americans to a phase of life shortly destined to become a major preoccupation among all classes.

It was a phenomenon somewhat difficult to explain, but the first faint stirrings of popular interest may be traced to the decade before the Civil War. The decline of the informal sports associated with country festivals and frontier frolics, a consequence of the breaking-up of old forms of village association as the nation became more urbanized and of changes in farm economy which brought about the disappearance of such work-play occasions as the barn-raising and the husking-bee, had drawn attention to a parlous state of affairs. Many observers suddenly realized that the spectator sports of the period were a sorry substitute for what was being lost. This was not so important for the rural population, but it affected the townsman very seriously. "Who in this community really takes exercise?" Thomas Wentworth Higginson asked in the first issue of the *Atlantic Monthly*, in 1858. "Even the mechanic confines himself to one set of muscles; the blacksmith acquires strength in his right arm, and the dancing teacher in his left leg. But the professional or business man, what muscles has he at all?"[5]

A campaign was started to break down the prejudice against sports as an idle diversion and to encourage more active participation in outdoor games. "The Americans as a people—at least the professional and mercantile classes," Edward Everett declared, "have too little considered the importance of healthful, generous recreation.... Noble, athletic sports, manly outdoor exercises ... which strengthen the mind by strengthening the body, and bring man into a generous and exhilarating communion with nature ... are too little cultivated in town or country." [6] With far greater emphasis but on very much the same grounds the editor of *Harper's Monthly Magazine* and Dr. Oliver Wendell Holmes lent the weight of their authority to the new cause. The former held the want of sports responsible for turning young America into "a pale, pasty-faced, narrow chested, spindled-shanked, dwarfed race—a mere walking mannikin to advertise the latest cut of the fashionable tailor." [7] The Autocrat of the Breakfast-Table declared himself satisfied "that such a set of black-coated, stiff-jointed, soft-muscled, paste-complexioned youth as we can boast in our Atlantic cities never before sprang from the loins of Anglo-Saxon lineage." [8]

These diatribes bore some fruit in the 1850's. Skating was taken up so widely that the vogue for it became known as Higginson's Revival. Rowing grew so popular (Charles W. Eliot was on the Harvard crew) that the *New York Herald* declared that if the boating era should continue another five years, "the coming generation will relieve America from the odium of physical decline." [9] Nevertheless the flowering of sports awaited the post-war period, when they were given a primary impetus through being adopted by the world of fashion. The early rowing clubs had been composed of "young men of the highest respectability," but as the new games of the 1870's were introduced from England, for the rise of sports in the United States owed a very considerable debt to the sports revival in the mother country, it was more than ever society's leaders who first played them. [10] The attempt was even made to monopolize them. Again and again the complacent statement may be found in contemporary articles in the better magazines that such and such a sport— whether tennis, polo, or bicycling—does not "offer any attractions to the more vulgar elements of society." [11] But the real significance of fashionable approval of sports lay in the fact that it awoke the interest of democracy. The common man eagerly followed where the aristocrat led. He could not be kept from any diversion within his means. "We may turn up our noses generally at those who in this country profess to lead fashions," Caspar Whitney, an early sports writer, declared some years later, "but in the matter of showing the way to healthy, vigorous outdoor play they have set a fine example and one that has taken a firm hold upon the people." [12]

A basic need for outdoor exercise to conserve national health and the sponsorship of social leaders thus served in large measure to break down the barriers that had formerly stood in the way of the development of organized sports. Games which could appeal to every one had at last been invented or developed. And a post-war atmosphere, in which the instinct for pleasure is naturally intensified, provided fertile ground for the growth of these new forms of recreation. It is perhaps not so surprising after all that within a short quarter-century of the day when one English visitor declared that "to roll balls in a ten pin alley by gas-light or to drive a fast trotting horse in a light wagon along a very bad and dusty road, seems the Alpha and Omega of sport in the United States," [13] almost every one of our modern games was being played by a rapidly growing army of enthusiasts.

-->>><<<-

THE PIONEER of them all, baseball, had evolved from the various bat-and-ball games that the early settlers had brought with them from England. A children's game actually known as base-ball had been played in the eighteenth century. It is noted in *A Pretty Little Pocket Book, Intended for the Amusement of Little Master Tommy and Pretty Miss Polly*, which was first published in England in 1744 and soon after reprinted in this country. Jane Austen refers to it in *Northanger Abbey*.[14] Four-old-cat, rounders, and town-ball, each of which contributed something to baseball, were also being played in the early nineteenth century by young men and boys throughout the country. Samuel Woodruff, writing on amusements in 1833, speaks of New Englanders as being experts in such games of ball as "cricket, base, cat, football, trap-ball." [15]

But there was no formality about these early games—no regular teams, no accepted rules of play, no scheduled contests. Cricket was the only one at all organized. New arrivals from England almost invariably formed cricket teams. It was an occasional diversion in all parts of the country, played north and south and on the western prairies. It was most general in and about Philadelphia, where groups of English factory-workers played weekly games.[16] But cricket never really took hold in America. Its leisurely pace could not be reconciled with a frontier-nourished love for speed, excitement, action. It was steadily driven to the wall as the far more lively game of baseball, slowly taking its modern form and shape, made a more universal bid for popularity.

The date of baseball's emergence as a game definitely different from rounders or town-ball has been patriotically determined by a national commission which set out in 1907 to establish its American origins. But there is no recorded evidence to justify its conclusion that modern baseball stems from Abner Doubleday's supposed adoption of the diamond at Cooperstown, New York, in 1839.[17] Although town-ball as it was generally played at that time had four bases at the corners of a square and there were no foul balls (one hit the ball in any direction and ran), the diamond and other attributes of the modern game had already been adopted in both rounders and children's base-ball. The beginnings of the organized sport may perhaps be more accurately traced to a group of New York business and professional men who about 1842 began playing it at the Elysian Fields in Hoboken. They formally organized the Knickerbocker Club and under the lead of Alexander J. Cartwright adopted a code of rules which was printed in 1845. There were to be nine players

A Great Game for the Baseball Championship

Return match between the Athletic Base Ball Club of Philadelphia and the Atlantics of Brooklyn, Philadelphia, October 22, 1866, won by the Athletics, 31 to 12. Lithograph drawn and published by J. L. Magee. Courtesy of Harry T. Peters.

The Game of Croquet

Drawing by C. G. Bush. *Harper's Weekly, 1866.*

A Spring Meeting of the New York Archery Club

Drawing by T. de Thulstrup. *Frank Leslie's Illustrated Newspaper, 1880.*

on each side, three men out constituted an inning, and the game was won by the first team to make twenty-one runs, or "aces" as they were then called.[18] The first match game on record was played a year later with a picked team which called itself the New York Baseball Club, the "all-stars" winning 23 to 4 in four innings.

In keeping with their social status, the members of the Knickerbocker Club played in neat uniforms of blue trousers, white shirts, and straw hats. As important as the game was the formal dinner which followed it. For some time, indeed, every effort was made to keep baseball an exclusive sport, and not until the 1850's were more democratic clubs organized and the Knickerbockers compelled to recognize that workers as well as gentlemen could play the game. For there was no need in baseball to undergo the expense of maintaining a boat club or keeping up a stable of riding-horses. It wanted only an open field, a bat, and a ball. "The great mass, who are in a subordinate capacity," a contemporary pointed out succinctly, "can participate in this health giving and noble pastime."[19]

One of the first clubs that brought a more democratic spirit into the baseball world was the Eckford Club of Brooklyn, formed in 1855. By this year the Knickerbockers had many rivals in and about New York. Games were being placed regularly among such teams as the Gothams, the Putnams, the Harlems, the Excelsiors, and the Eagles. But the Eckford Club had this distinction: its members were shipwrights and mechanics. They suffered the disadvantage in comparison with other clubs of not having very much time to practise, but they soon proved their worth by defeating the Excelsior Club, made up of merchants and clerks.[20] The Newark Mechanics Club was among other organizations composed of workingmen, while one of the best teams playing on the Boston Common, where games were often scheduled at five in the morning so as not to interfere with the players' work, was made up of truckmen.[21] And then in 1856 a young man named Henry Wright, employed in a jewelry manufactory and also a professional bowler with the St. George Cricket Club, joined the Knickerbockers. Social barriers were breaking down completely. The ball clubs wanted to win their games. Here also was a hint of the professionalism toward which they were headed. Another decade and Wright will have gone to Cincinnati to organize the Red Stockings as the country's first admittedly professional team.[22]

Baseball slowly spread north, south, east, and west. It drove out town-ball in New England and cricket in Philadelphia, made its way to the Mississippi Valley (Chicago had four clubs in 1858), crossed the trans-Mississippi frontier, reached out to the Pacific Coast. Everywhere it was bringing men and boys into active outdoor play. It was also becoming highly organized. The National Association of Base Ball Players was formed in 1858, with twenty-five clubs applying for charter membership, and two years later delegates from fifty organizations attended its annual meeting. New York and New Jersey led in the number of clubs (New England had a separate association for teams still playing town-ball), but Philadelphia, Washington, Detroit, Chicago, and New Orleans were but a few among the cities where baseball was now established.[23]

The game was attracting spectators as well as players, and a wider public interest was growing out of the reports carried in the newspaper of the interclub matches. It still had features strange to modern times. A man was out on a ball caught on the first bounce; pitching was an underhand throw. Even though there were players who "sent the ball with exceeding velocity," the scales were more heavily weighted in favor of the batter than they are to-day. No gloves were worn. We find *The Spirit of the Times* praising Mr. Wadsworth of the Knickerbockers for his fearlessness "in the dangerous position of catcher." Contemporary prints portray the umpire sitting out in the field somewhere near first base under an umbrella, in frock-coat and stove-pipe hat.[24]

But baseball was exciting. In 1858 some two thousand persons actually paid fifty cents admission for a match at the Fashion Race Course, the first recorded game with gate receipts.[25] Two years later the champion Excelsiors, of Brooklyn, went on tour and defeated challenging clubs in cities throughout New York, Pennsylvania, Delaware, and Maryland. Returning for a match with another Brooklyn team, the Atlantics, they played a game which drew fifteen thousand spectators.[26] Baseball was on its way.

The Civil War interrupted this forward march, but it brought an even larger popular following. The game was everywhere played behind the lines and in base camps, almost on the battle-field. Country boys and factory-workers were introduced to the new sport, and with the end of the war they took it back to their home communities. One result of wartime playing is seen in the attendance of clubs at the first post-war meetings of the National Association. The total jumped to ninety-one in 1865. A year later the membership, representing seventeen states and the District of Columbia, totaled 202. "Since the war, it has run like wildfire," the *Galaxy* declared editorially. Charles A. Peverelly believed it to be beyond question "the leading feature in the outdoor sports of the United States." And by 1872 the magazine *Sports and Games* categorically stated that it had become "the national game of the United States." [27]

The American genius for organization was outdoing itself in the growth of the National Association, however, and the keen rivalry among member clubs was promoting professionalism. The practice developed of engaging expert players for a local club through offering them better-paid jobs in the community than they could normally expect to obtain. On occasion players were directly paid for their services in important games. A confusing quasi-professionalism invaded the ranks of what had formerly been a wholly amateur sport. The next step was inevitable. In 1869 the Cincinnati Red Stockings were definitely hired as a professional team for a country-wide tour. They did not lose a game that summer, and the practical advantage of salaried players was recognized by all those sports followers primarily interested in championship teams.

These moves toward professional baseball were both cause and consequence of the heavy betting that began to be made on interclub games. For the gambling fraternity quickly became interested in the new sport. It was taken up as professional foot-races and prize-fighting had been. Charges also began to be made that the gamblers were not only beginning to control the ball players, but were operating pools and arranging for games to be won or lost on a strictly business basis.[28] Amateur members of the National Association bitterly contested the increasing influence of these new elements in the game, but their organization was losing its control. In 1871 its place was taken by a new association frankly composed of professional players.

For a time this association did not function very effectively. It was either unwilling or unable to suppress gambling, and base-ball fell under a cloud of popular disapproval. Efforts at reform were finally crowned when five years later William A. Hulbert undertook the organization of the National League of Professional Baseball Clubs. Rules and regulations were now adopted which set up strict standards for inter-club competition.[29] With an original membership made up of teams from New York, Philadelphia, Hartford, Boston, Chicago, Louisville, Cincinnati, and St. Louis, baseball had a controlling body. Through its ministrations there grew up the immensely complicated system of franchises, major and minor leagues, player contracts, and other business controls that now characterize the professional game. The National League gave baseball a new stability, restored public confidence in the contests among league teams, and put the sport really on its feet.

Amateur playing had naturally suffered from the conflict with professionalism and the disrepute into which the game had been brought by gambling. But it quickly responded to these new developments. Completely divorced from the professional game so far as organization was concerned but following its lead on all

playing rules, it flourished as it never had before. Baseball became the favorite game in the colleges. It was played by every
high school and was encouraged by Y.M.C.A.'s. Ball clubs became a feature of every American community.

The game had many qualities that appealed to the average
young American. It met his newly felt need for healthful outdoor exercise. It offered him competitive team play. But perhaps Mark Twain had an even more suggestive explanation of
its popularity. "Baseball is the very symbol," he wrote, "the out-
ward and visible expression of the drive and push and rush and
struggle of the raging, tearing, booming nineteenth century." [30]

->>><<<-

CROQUET had in the meantime performed the miracle of getting
both men and women out-of-doors for an activity they could enjoy
together. The first of the post-war games to be introduced from
England, it reached an even broader public than baseball. Croquet was more than a game; it was a social function. Contemporary writers were soon pointing out what an unmixed blessing
it was for the American damsel, and warning bachelors to beware.[31]

" 'Charming' is the universal exclamation of all who play or
who watch the playing of Croquet...," an early rules book
stated. "Hitherto, while men and boys have had their healthy
means of recreation in the open air, the women and girls have
been restricted to the less exhilarating sports of indoor life....
Grace in holding and using the mallet, easy and pleasing atti-
tudes in playing, promptness in taking your turn, and gentlemanly and ladylike manners generally throughout the game, are
points which it is unnecessary for us to enlarge on.... Young
ladies are proverbially fond of cheating at this game; but they
only do so because they think that men like it." [32]

George Makepeace Towle has an idyllic picture of people
playing croquet: "The sunshine glimmering through the branches
—the soft velvety grass—the cool, pure country air—the quiet

broken only by the twittering of the birds, and now and then a passing footstep." [33] Only occasionally did some controversial issue arise to mar the sweet felicity of the croquet court. There was the problem of "spooning." This was not a mode of behavior, but the practice of hitting the croquet-ball by what is now called the pendulum stroke. Obviously women in hooped-skirts were at a disadvantage. *The Nation* gave its considered opinion: "We agree that spooning is perfectly fair in a match of gentlemen, but it is decidedly ungenerous when played with ladies, unless those ladies are bloomers." [34]

Croquet was by no means confined to the fashionable lawns of the effete East, however. It went west with the homesteaders. Many accounts tell of its popularity in the small towns of the prairie states. So great was the vogue in the 1870's that manufacturers put out playing sets with candle-sockets on the wickets for night playing.

Archery and lawn tennis, the former the revival of an old sport and the latter newly introduced from England about 1874, had also been taken up widely by this time. They too were sports, gentle and genteel, which could be played by both sexes. "The contestants were ladies and gentlemen from the cultured circles of society," *Harper's Weekly* reported of an archery tournament in the White Stocking Park at Chicago in 1879, "and while the rivalry among the shooters was keen to the last degree, an air of such refinement and courteous dignity as is not often witnessed by observers of public games characterized every one connected with the contest." [35] Writing on tennis in 1881, the magazine *Outing*, whose establishment reflected the rising interest in sports, assured its feminine readers that this was far too refined a game to offer any attractions for the lower orders of society. A lady who took part in a tennis match would find herself "in the company of persons in whose society she is accustomed to move." [36]

At this stage of its development, lawn tennis as played in the United States did not involve hard, overhand serves, back-court drives, or smashes at the net. Women players suffered only the slightest handicap in having to hold up the trains of their long, dragging skirts; they were not expected actually to run for the ball. It was patted gently back and forth over a high net stretched across any level space of lawn. Competition gradually led to changed methods of play, and with the organization of the United States National Lawn Tennis Association (there were forty member clubs in 1883) and the institution of annual tournaments at Newport, men began to take the game more seriously. The active features of play that now characterize it were developed. A group of players whose names are still remembered emerged from the ranks—R. D. Sears, James Dwight, Robert D. Wrenn, William A. Larned, Dwight F. Davis. . . . Finally in 1900 the establishment of the International Davis Cup matches definitely marked the transformation of tennis from a pastime to a sport.[37]

—»»)«««—

ROLLER-SKATING had been introduced by James L. Plimpton in 1863, and New York's social leaders, hoping it could be restricted to "the educated and refined classes," quickly made it fashionable. Their Roller Skating Association leased the Atlantic House in Newport and made over its dining-hall and piazza into a skating-rink. It held weekly assemblies where such distinguished guests as General Sherman and Chief Justice Bigelow watched "tastefully dressed young men and girls, sailing, swimming, floating through the mazes of the march, as if impelled by magic power."[38]

But Newport soon had to surrender to the democracy. Rinks were built in every town and immense ones established in the cities, with a general admission of fifty or twenty-five cents, which welcomed all comers. In Chicago the Casino accommodated four thousand persons—three thousand spectators and one thousand skaters. There were not only dancing and racing. Professor A. E. Smith introduced special fancy skating—the Richmond Roll, the Picket Fence, the Philadelphia Twist ("rolling his limbs far apart and laying his head sideways on one of them"), and the Dude on Wheels. Night after night the band played, the new Siemens lights shone down on the hard-maple floor, and a vast attendance crowded the Casino's spacious and elegant rink.[39]

Going further west, skating was even more popular. The Olympian Club Roller Skating Rink in San Francisco advertised five thousand pairs of skates and 69,000 square feet of hard-maple floor. It was holding races, roller-skating polo, and "tall hat and high collar" parties.[40]

Young and old skated—men, women, and children. For a time no other sport seemed able to match its popularity. A writer in *Harper's Weekly* cited a gravestone inscription:

> Our Jane has climbed the golden stair
> And passed the jasper gates;
> Henceforth she will have wings to wear,
> Instead of roller skates.[41]

-»»«(-

But it remained for bicycling to become the most spectacular craze of all. While it had had a brief vogue in the 1860's (the first velocipedes—the French "dandy horses"—were known as early as the opening of the century), it was the introduction about 1876 of the high-wheeled bicycles, supplanting the old wooden bone-shakers, that first made it a popular sport. Within half a dozen years of the first manufacture of the new wheels, there were some twenty thousand confirmed cyclists in the country; in 1886 the total had swelled to some fifty thousand, and a year later it was over a hundred thousand. Clubs were organized in almost every town and city throughout the land, and to bring together organizations of like interest and promote cycling as a sport, they banded together, in 1881, to form the League of American Wheelmen.[42]

"There has been heretofore in our American life, crowded to excess as it has been with the harassing cares and anxieties of business," a writer in *Harper's Monthly Magazine* stated in July, 1881, "so little attention paid to the organized practice of health-giving outdoor exercise, to which bicycling is peculiarly adopted, that the organization of this League of American Wheelmen can not fail to be recognized as an important subject for public congratulation." [43]

The safety bicycle and the drop frame for women were still almost a decade away. This was the first enthusiasm of the high-wheeled pioneers, those daring riders who went forth perched on a postage-stamp saddle athwart a sixty-inch wheel. A header from that dizzy eminence meant broken bones, if not a broken head. But forth the wheelmen rode—high-necked jackets, close-fitting knee-pants, and little round hats (later, ventilated duck helmets and imported English hose)—prepared to defy all the hazards of the road. They generally went in company. Club runs were the fashion. The cyclists mounted to the bugle call of "Boots and Saddles," and sober pedestrians watched in awe as they wheeled past in military formation.

It was also the era of impressive bicycle parades, competitive club drills, hill-climbing contests, and race meetings. On July 4, 1884, news of the bicycle world included a meet on the Boston Common drawing thousands of spectators; a parade of seventy cyclists at Portsmouth, New Hampshire; the first club run of the Kishwaukee Bicycle Club at Syracuse, Illinois; races for the Georgia championship at Columbus; and medal runs at Salt Lake City. Thomas Stevens was off on his famous bicycle trip round the world, and in New York a bicycle school with thirty uniformed instructors was teaching Wall Street bankers to wheel to band music.[44]

The rôle of women in this bright dawn of the bicycle age was limited but none the less well recognized. The high-wheeled machine was too much for them, but they were given the tricycle. Here was recreation on "a higher plane than the ball-field or the walking rink," an outdoor activity which marked "a step towards the emancipation of woman from her usually too inactive indoor life." [45] In this vigorous propaganda to promote female cycling, *The Wheelman* also called upon the support of ministers and physicians. Bicycling was both godly and healthy. One word of warning, from A Family Physician: "Do not think of sitting down to table until you have changed your underclothing, and, after a delightful wash and rub-down, quietly and leisurely dressed again." [46]

Tricycles were not scorned by men. They were sometimes as fast as the bicycle (the mile record was 2:33 minutes for the tricycle, 2:29 minutes for the bicycle in 1890), [47] and a day's run in the country could be managed with a good deal more ease. Professor Hoffman's *Tips to Tricyclists* was written for both the sexes. It was an all-inclusive guide, with advice on the wearing of celluloid collars and on management of breath, on cleaning the machine and on the desirability of lady cyclists' carrying menthol cones for emergencies. [48]

There were all types of tricycles—the Surprise Tricycle, the Quadrant Tricycle, the Coventry Rotary Tricycle. Another vehicle was the Sociable. It was in effect a small self-wheeled carriage, the cyclists happily sitting beside each other. It was widely advertised for honeymoons. Other machines completely defy description—the Coventry Convertible Four in Hand and the Rudge Triplet Quadricycle. [49]

The social consequences of bicycling, to be so much more apparent in the next decade, were already becoming evident in the 1880's. Although the price of machines ($100 to $125 for an ordinary and $180 for a tricycle) still made them an expensive luxury, the number of cyclists was increasing year by year. The rediscovery of the outdoors had received its greatest encouragement, and the League of American Wheelmen was performing heroic services in demanding improved roads. "Bicycling is a fraternity of more permanent organization," *Outing* declared in 1882, "than ever characterized any sport since the world began." [50]

→»«←

The First National Tennis Tournament at New Brighton
Drawing by H. A. Ogden. *Frank Leslie's Illustrated Newspaper*, 1880.

Washington Meet of the League of American Wheelmen
Frank Leslie's Illustrated Newspaper, 1884.

Yale Meets Princeton in Football

Their fifth match, at St. George's Cricket Club, Hoboken, Thanksgiving
Day, November 27, 1879, a scoreless tie. Drawing by A. B. Frost.
Harper's Weekly, 1879.

THE RÔLE of the colleges in the rise of sports was not one of leadership. It was not their example that first set people playing games, bicycling, or generally getting outdoors for recreation. The epidemics sweeping the country did not pass them by,[51] but undergraduates neither introduced nor popularized any one of the games that have so far been described. The only sport they developed was intercollegiate football.

It descended from a game played in England at least as early as the days of Edward II. "For as much as there is great noise in the city," reads a decree of 1314, "caused by hustling over large balls from which many evils arise which God forbid; we forbid such game to be used in the city in the future." [52] And again and again in later years England's sovereigns fruitlessly legislated against a sport which the common people insisted on playing. The early colonists brought it to this country, and throughout the eighteenth and the first half of the nineteenth centuries it was popular in the colleges. The game generally played in this period was something like association football, or soccer, but it was completely unorganized, and any number of players was usually allowed on each side. The first recorded intercollegiate contests (there is notice of an earlier game between two groups of Boston schoolboys),[53] took place in 1869 between Princeton and Rutgers. They played three games with twenty-five men on each team.[54]

A revival of football at Harvard and Yale about 1872 (it had been prohibited for some years because of increasing roughness) [55] was the first real step in its emergence as an organized sport. The English variant known as Rugby, rather than association football, was played, and at a conference among representatives of Harvard, Yale, Princeton, and Columbia a set of rules derived from those of the English Rugby Union was formally adopted. If the game was still far removed from the intercollegiate football we know to-day, its development from that date, 1876, followed a steady and persistent course.

Among the early changes which transformed Rugby into our

modern game were the reduction of the number of players from fifteen to eleven; their assignment to specific positions in line and backfield; new provisions for running with the ball, kicking and passing; and the substitution of the modern "scrimmage" for the old "scrummage"—that confused huddle of the original game in which, instead of being passed back, the ball was indiscriminately kicked out after being put in play. When the new Intercollegiate Football Association gave its sanction to these new rules in 1881, there was little left of English Rugby in American colleges.[56]

Football aroused spectator interest from the start, and the Big Three of the eastern colleges—Harvard, Yale and Princeton—at first completely overshadowed all other teams. It was long before comparable elevens were in the field. The Thanksgiving Day games of these universities were consequently the great events of the fall season. Some four thousand spectators turned out for the first Princeton-Yale game in 1878; little more than a decade later, attendance was almost forty thousand.[57]

Few adults found themselves able or willing to play football. Although teams made up of former college players were for a time quite active, the game was primarily for boys. But many were glad to watch so exciting a sport. Its dependence upon brute force satisfied atavistic instincts as could no other modern spectacle except the prize-fight. Baseball had become the national game because so many people played it as well as watched it. Football was destined from the first to be primarily a spectator sport.

->>><<<-

This phenomenal expansion in the field of sports was the most significant development in the nation's recreational life that had yet taken place. Apart from all the considerations already mentioned, athletics provided an outlet for surplus energy and suppressed emotions which the American people greatly needed. The traditions of pioneer life had influenced them along very definite lines, and the restrictions of urban living warred against a feeling for the outdoors which was in their blood. With the gradual passing of so much of what the frontier had always stood for, sports provided a new outlet for an inherently restless people.[58]

In subsequent years they were to become far more general. Outdoor recreation was to develop into a much more marked feature of American life as new opportunities opened up for ever larger numbers of people to play games. The democracy was to take over sport to an extent which its limited leisure and lack of resources still made impossible in these decades after the Civil War. But the path had been cleared. America had discovered a new world.

A Six-day Walk for the Pedestrian Championship

The O'Leary-Hughes match at Gilmore's Garden, New York.

CHAPTER XII

THE NEW ORDER

WITH THE RISE OF SPORTS SUPPLEMENTING THE CONTINUED growth of commercial amusements, there was a steadily broadening interest in recreation in the 1880's and 1890's. The doldrums of half a century earlier had been left far behind. The gospel of work still held good, but it was tempered by a new realization of the need for play. The decline of puritan influence resulted in wider popular sanction for many diversions which had once been generally disapproved. And the new sports themselves, as a writer in *Outing* declared, had made a breach in the walls "which that awful personage Mrs. Grundy had raised up to separate the sexes in outdoor games." [1] The era of Victorian repression was drawing to a close.

Newspapers and magazines all reflected this. During the summer of 1886 the *New York Tribune* devoted no less than five hundred columns to sports, also issuing its *Book of Open-Air Sports*, and a decade later William Randolph Hearst started a custom which the entire press quickly adopted. He began publishing daily in the *New York Journal* a page headed "In the World of Professional and Amateur Sports." [2] Magazines devoted to these new activities were also started. *Outing* had shown the way. It was followed by a wide choice of weeklies and monthlies ranging from the *American Canoeist* to the *Bicycling World,* from the *Ball Players' Chronicle* to *Archery and Tennis News.*

It could still be said that many more people watched sports than took part in them. James F. Muirhead, a sympathetic but critical English observer of the new movement, reported that games were widely played in the East but in the Middle West "baseball and other sports, like dancing in China, are almost wholly in the hands of paid performers." [3] Nevertheless, hundreds of thousands were being recruited annually to fill the ranks of a growing army of sportsmen and sportswomen. The outdoor movement was gathering increasing momentum. There was a vogue for walking and mountain-climbing, fishing and hunting, camping in the woods. A craze for canoeing is attested by notices of railroad excursions into the country with freight-cars equipped with special canoe racks and also with accommodations for folding boats. Steamship lines advertised outings for amateur photographers—"Up the river the artists sailed, popping away with their cameras." [4]

There were summer resorts. It was no longer only Saratoga, Newport, Long Branch, and a relatively small number of fashionable watering-places that represented this phase of recreation. The number of resorts, especially in what was becoming the vacationland of New England mountain and seashore, was legion. In May, 1890, the *New York Tribune* was running some eight columns of summer-hotel advertisements, appealing directly to the middle class rather than to the more exclusive ranks of society. The popular *Summer Tourist and Excursion Guide*, listing moderate-priced hotels and cheap railroad excursions, represented a far departure from "The Fashionable Tour" of half a century earlier.

The attractions the resorts offered also mirrored the changing scene. One hotel, inordinately proud of its gas-lights and electric bells, glowingly advertised extensive grounds for lawn tennis, croquet, and archery. Another singled out as its most popular feature its facilities for fishing, boating, driving, tennis, and croquet. [5] Every seashore resort stressed the bathing. There were no longer any reservations as to its propriety. The prudent female still went into the water fully clothed. *Godey's Lady's Book* advertised a costume of Turkey red "consisting of a yoke polonaise and full drawers," to be worn with a sash around the waist, long black stockings, and a straw hat. [6] But the old prejudices

Camping Out

Lithograph by N. Currier after a painting by Louis Maurer, 1856. Courtesy of Harry T. Peters.

against men and women going into the surf together had completely disappeared.

Visitors from abroad in the 1890's were as much struck by the
way Americans were now seeking out opportunities for play as
those who had come to this country in the 1840's had been impressed by our apparent lack of interest in amusements. The
United States was still the Land of the Dollar. We were a nation
absorbed in money-making. But there was a new appreciation of
the rôle of recreation "as a leaven to the toilsome year of the
world." [7] Among others, James Bryce, as keen an interpreter of
the American scene as any European who has ever visited the
United States, found a remarkable faculty for enjoyment among
Americans, a power to draw happiness from simple and innocent
pleasures which was seldom found in overburdened Europe.
"The sadness of Puritanism," he wrote, "seems to have been shed
off." [8] Two French travelers made reports which contrasted even
more sharply with those of their mid-century predecessors. Paul
de Rousiers was specially impressed with what he considered the
general air of honesty and decency about our recreation; [9] Paul
Blouet by the freedom and gaiety with which American men and
women took part in so many activities together. "They have not
the English tendency," the latter told his countrymen, "to convert
their pleasures into funeral services." [10]

-»»«←-

THESE GAINS had been made gradually. Americans generally had
not suddenly thrown off that psychological restraint which one
writer termed "the doom of work." [11] Many of the generation
of the 1890's had had much too deeply imprinted on their
minds the moral lessons taught by the little homilies they
had read as children in the famous McGuffey readers. In one of
them, "The Idle Boy Reformed," a little lad who unaccountably
disliked work asked several animal friends to play with him. The
invariable answer was, "No, I must not be idle." The story con-
cludes: " 'What? is nobody idle? Then little boys must not be

idle.' So he made haste and went to school and learned his lesson very well, and the master said he was a good boy." [12]

Even when decreasing hours of labor (the twelve-hour day had now largely given way to the ten-hour day) and such revolutionary changes as Saturday half-holidays and two-week summer vacations afforded a new measure of justified leisure, there was still the old prejudice against any frivolous "mispense" of time. It was particularly strong in rural sections and primarily directed against commercial entertainment. The pleasures of the city stood condemned, as partaking of the Devil, by those who did not have the opportunity to enjoy them. It was the cry of the Lollards against the pernicious amusements of the fourteenth century; of the early middle-class Puritans against the diversions of the English aristocracy; of the humble followers of the New England way against the fashionable pleasures of the rich merchants; of the frontier converts to Methodism against urban dancing, card-playing, and theatre-going.

The metropolis stood for vice and wickedness. Religious journals painted its traps and pitfalls in lurid colors, vividly revealed its pleasures as sinister invitations to evil. New York was the outstanding symbol of "all the abominations which curse humanity," but readers of the more exciting exposures were warned that "the giddy voluptuaries who find pleasure in guilty abandon and corrupt morals are not indigenous to New York, but flourish to a lesser degree in all great cities." In *Metropolitan Life Unveiled, or Mysteries and Miseries of America's Great Cities,* the author was careful to point out that he was not prompted by "pessimistical reflections," but unmasked the sins of the cities solely that the beauties of refinement and purity might appear nobler by contrast.[13] Yet naturally enough the warnings of the godly only heightened the discontent of country youths with a life which so signally lacked these dangers and excitements. Bright lights were made all the more alluring.

Vitriolic attacks which would have had the admiring approval of Cotton Mather were still being launched against the theatre.

As a leader of the die-hards, the Reverend Josiah W. Leeds was profoundly shocked that playhouses should be looked upon with more tolerance than during the early days of the Republic, although they were probably "as low in character and proportionally as great in number as they were in Paris when that city was under the sway of the God-denying, blood-seeking, and depraved leaders of the French Revolution." He would tolerate nothing that had to do with the theatre. "If avowed Christians of 're-spectability' would have the vile variety theatres of the poorer classes removed from our cities," he warned, "such persons cannot consistently give countenance to the playhouses of the so-styled 'better sort'; and if they would have the low music-halls, with their tawdry and lewd accessories abolished, they, on their part, should have naught to do with the elegant opera, its alluring ballet and unsavory plot." [14]

But while the heirs of the Puritan tradition might still rail again all urban entertainments, clinging tenaciously to outmoded ideals of conduct, they could not possibly prevent developments which were an inevitable consequence of changing social and economic conditions. The church as a whole adopted a more realistic attitude. It listened to the people, realizing it had lost the power to impose arbitrary prohibitions. When it disapproved of certain types of commercial amusements, it sought to substitute its own entertainments. "The church must not attempt to take away the theatre, the dance, the card party," stated William D. Hyde, "unless it can give in its place not merely a religious or intellectual substitute, like a prayer meeting or a literary society, but a genuine social equivalent." [15] "If amusing young people aids to save them," the *Northwestern Christian Advocate,* an organ of the Methodist Episcopal Church unequivocally stated in one issue, "then the work is fully and gloriously worthy of the church." [16]

Provision was made in the new institutional or socialized churches of the 1880's and 1890's for libraries, gymnasiums, and assemblies; for games, concerts, and amusements. One of them

built a $400,000 People's Palace to meet the community's needs
for "sanctified amusement and recreation." [17] The Y.M.C.A. had
already become a leader in the promotion of sports (it had some
261 gymnasiums in cities throughout the country [18]), and other
religious organizations vied with the churches themselves in
providing social activities of all kinds. It was the era of sociables,
fairs, suppers, and strawberry festivals. In mild and innocent
form, these affairs could reproduce through raffles, grab-bags,
charades, games, and refreshments the sophisticated pleasures of
more worldly society.[19]

But again it would be misleading to imply that this revolutionary change in the attitude of the church was accomplished
without strong opposition from within the ranks. Religion was
combating the rivalry of entertainment over its hold upon the
public, but not all churchmen realized what was happening. "We
are not informed," Dr. William Bayard Hale caustically wrote
in *The Forum*, ". . . that the Church at Ephesus or Philippi ever
advertised a bazaar, a clam-bake, or a strawberry social. We have
no information that St. Paul was accustomed to give stereopticon
lectures, Barnabas operating the lantern. It is not clearly established that St. Athanasius ever arranged a kirmess, a broom-drill,
or a pink tea." [20] He cited flagrant examples of churches seeking
at one and the same time to raise money and entertain their
members. It was his forthright conclusion that "the world does
not need the church as a purveyor of vaudeville."

The crusading Mr. Leeds sprang joyfully into the fray. He
was as strongly opposed to church socials as to the lowest music-
hall performances. He had no tolerance whatsoever for the idea
that the church should in any way recognize the popular craving
for amusement—"It used to be held that Jesus and His work
furnished ample resources to meet the loftiest aspirations of a
saved soul." He condemned with equal vigor dramas, comedies,
farces, suppers, fairs, and entertainments of any conceivable sort.
A strawberry festival was a step which led straight to the variety
show or public dance-hall:

And fairs and shows in the halls were held,
And the world and her children were there,
And laughter and music and feasts prevailed
In the Place that was meant for prayer.[21]

Observance of the Lord's Day also brought about another clash
with conservative religion. Its dedication to rest and meditation
had broken down somewhat in the late eighteenth century, and
then, as we have seen, been vigorously revived early in the nineteenth. Now the doctrine was again being undermined. The great
influx of foreign immigrants, bringing with them wholly different
ideas of how Sunday should be spent, had a great influence in the
cities. The Germans particularly followed the customs of the
Continental Sabbath, so completely at variance with those of the
Puritan Sabbath, and their picnics and beer-garden entertainments became a Sunday feature wherever they had settled in
large numbers. Industrious, sober, hard-working, they set an example which was widely followed. The popularity of Sunday
excursions and the practice of making the day primarily an occasion for recreation spread rapidly after mid-century among
working people.[22]

In the running fight against this trend, rural America stub-
bornly maintained its old-fashioned ways. South Carolina continued to make church attendance compulsory as late as 1885, and
the rock-ribbed state of Vermont attempted to enforce the old-
time bans on its statute-books that forbade all Sunday diversions.
Wherever the evangelical religions had a popular following, there
the Sabbath was rigidly observed. Even in the cities the more
conservative ministers preached innumerable sermons against
profaning the Lord's Day, promising dire punishment for whoever dared to depart from the straight and narrow path. Excursions to the country, picnics and ball games, Sunday concerts,
came under as severe a ban as theatre-going, dancing, or card-
playing. "You cannot serve God and skylark on a bicycle," one
minister told his abashed congregation. Such militant organizations as the American Sabbath Union, the Sunday League of

America, the Lord's Day Alliance, were startling proof of the vitality of the strong forces still arrayed in support of this phase of Puritan doctrine.[23]

In one part of their campaign these religious forces had powerful allies. When they urged legislation to maintain the Sabbath that forbade all work on that day, they could count upon the support of the Knights of Labor and the American Federation of Labor. But on the issue of recreation on the Lord's Day there was a definite parting of the ways. Labor was as much in favor of complete Sunday freedom in this respect as the religious reformers were opposed to it. Times had greatly changed, but the forces of labor could ask their religious friends, as King James had asked the leaders of Puritan reform, "For when shall the common people have leave to exercise if not upon the Sundayes and Holydays, seeing they must apply their labour, and winne their living in all working dayes?"

The fight to maintain the sanctity of the Lord's Day was inevitably foredoomed in the light of changing social conditions. "Where is the city in which the Sabbath is not losing ground?" one discouraged reformer asked in 1887. "To the mass of the workingmen Sunday is no more than a holiday . . . it is a day for labor meetings, for excursions, for saloons, beer-gardens, baseball games and carousels." [24]

In the West, if not in the East, even the theatres were opening on the Sabbath. Sunday notices in such a paper as the *Chicago Tribune* advertised special attractions for the day—a spectacular melodrama at one theatre and a comic-opera company at another. All the variety houses and music-halls were open.[25] There was no question that the city had broken the shackles imposed upon Sunday amusements by religious dogma. And the freedom once won would not be surrendered. Judged by modern standards, great numbers of Americans still observed the Sabbath religiously, but for many others the day had become by the 1890's one for play and enjoyment which presented a striking contrast to conditions in mid-century. It was the most important single development of the late nineteenth century increasing the opportunities of the common man for recreation.

->>)<<-

ON A VISIT to this country during these years, the English sociologist Herbert Spencer recognized the changes that had come over the recreational scene. He also drew attention to another aspect of the popular attitude toward amusement. "Old Froissart, who said of the English of his day 'that they take their pleasures sadly after their fashion,'" Spencer wrote, "would doubtless, if he lived now, say of the Americans that they take their pleasures hurriedly after their fashion. In large measure with us, and still more with you, there is not that abandonment to the moment which is requisite for full enjoyment, and this abandonment is prevented by the ever-present sense of multitudinous responsibilities." [26]

It was natural that Americans should not entirely escape the shadow of work in their play, should carry into it something of the competitive spirit which characterized their other activities. In the best of circumstances there was likely to be that residue from old traditions. Horace Greeley had noted the tendency to make play a business rather than a diversion from business as early as 1876. He complained that with teachers for every art, science, and "ology," there should be no room for professors of play. "Who will teach us incessant workers," he asked plaintively, "how to achieve leisure and enjoy it?" [27]

And in 1880 James A. Garfield, in an address at Lake Chautauqua, had made a striking characterization of the age on whose threshold America now stood which both emphasized and carried one step further the ideas expressed by Horace Greeley. "We may divide the whole struggle of the human race into two chapters," Garfield declared; "first, the fight to get leisure; and then the second fight of civilization—what shall we do with our leisure when we get it." [28]

In going on to discover what Americans were now doing with

their increasing leisure, it must be realized that the pattern of recreation had become inconceivably complex. Every year new strands were being woven into it. At no point is it possible to draw a complete picture of America at play. The scene in the 1880's and 1890's can only be traced in broadest outline through a general account of the principal diversions of the various groups that made up contemporary society.

CHAPTER XIII

METROPOLIS

W HAT WAS TYPICAL OF URBAN AMUSEMENTS AT THE CLOSE OF the past century? Everything, and nothing. But the great mass of city dwellers sought out as they had throughout the century the most lively and exciting popular entertainment. In the 1840's spokesmen of labor had declared that the intolerable burden of working conditions in the city demanded "excitement fully proportioned to the depression." It was even truer half a century later. Imperial Rome had sought to appease the restlessness of its laboring masses by providing the free spectacles of the circus and gladiatorial combat. Imperial America had its amusement palaces, its prize-fights, its concert-saloons, for which the modern workingman had to pay.

These phases of recreation now bulked larger than ever on the national horizon. The tremendous growth of cities made them of great importance. In 1850 there had been but eighty-five urban communities with a population of more than 8,000; there were almost seven times as many by the end of the century. Between 1880 and 1900 alone the urban population had more than doubled, rising from fourteen to thirty million. New York and Brooklyn accounted for over two million in 1890; Chicago and Philadelphia for over a million each; Boston, Baltimore, and Washington for about half a million apiece. There were in all twenty-eight cities with more than 100,000 inhabitants.[1]

These great masses of people were made up of all types and all nationalities. In Chicago the foreign-born numbered nearly as many in 1890 as the entire population ten years earlier. Germans, Swedes, Norwegians, Bohemians, Irish, Italians, Poles, thronged its busy streets. New York presented an even more polyglot population. It had as many Italians as Naples, as many Germans as Hamburg, twice as many Irish as Dublin, and two and a half times as many Jews as Warsaw. It had thickly settled districts taken over in their entirety by Hungarians, Greeks, Syrians, Chinese.[2] In large part the foreign elements carried on the humbler tasks of society, but they also began to crowd and push the native Americans in this bustling, thriving urban world. Competition was intense. Yet every year more people were irresistibly drawn to metropolis from rural America. In some parts of the country there was actual depopulation. New England villages were abandoned as their inhabitants fled to the great eastern manufacturing centers; even in Missouri, eastern Iowa, southeastern Indiana, and western Illinois the countryside was depleted in favor of the young and vigorous cities of the Middle West.[3]

These swarms of newcomers from the country and from abroad went into all trades and occupations. They became day laborers, street-car conductors, mechanics, factory-hands, teamsters, hod-carriers, clerks, grocers, haberdashers, restaurant keepers, carpenters, policemen ... and also domestic servants, garment-workers, salesgirls, typists, telephone operators. ... New occupations were opening up every day as the city and the machine more and more dominated the changing economy.

Despite long hours of work and the economic precariousness of their lives, or all the more because of such conditions, these wage-earners were eager for amusement of any kind. Little attention was paid to their social welfare. The cities had not yet developed their present park systems; there were no municipal recreation programs. It was difficult if not impossible to escape crowded streets and noisome tenements. The sports and outdoor activities being so widely taken up by the country at large were not yet within the realm of practical possibility for the majority of urban workers. Their entertainment was necessarily passive, commercialized, and cheap.

Sunday "Social Freedom" in the Bowery

A religious paper's view. *Illustrated Christian Weekly*, 1874. Courtesy of the New York Historical Society.

A Chicago Pool-Room on Sunday
Drawing by T. de Thulstrup. *Harper's Weekly*, 1892.

Barnum had pioneered in meeting such limitations of taste and pocket-book. He had had innumerable imitators. Public amusements—tawdry though they might often be, sometimes vicious—had expanded with the growth of cities at a rate never before known. The American metropolis far surpassed that of Europe in the wealth and variety of entertainment it offered to its surging population.

->>|<<-

THE MID-CENTURY THEATRE had played a leading rôle in satisfying urban needs. We have seen the great playhouses of the period packed with "all classes of fraternized humanity." But now the separation of different types of theatrical entertainment just starting in the 1850's had been carried through to its logical conclusion. The circus, the variety show, and burlesque were completely divorced from the legitimate stage. There was a new popular theatre of farce and melodrama quite distinct from the serious drama and polite comedy produced for the world of culture and education.

The old stock companies had also largely given way to a further variant of the star system. Managers staged what they hoped would be a successful play, in the main built up about a single actor or actress, and kept it on the boards as long as they possibly could. Its welcome exhausted in the city, it was then sent to the provinces. The "traveling combination" typified the theatre of the 1890's, and there was a phenomenal growth in the quantity, if not the quality, of companies on the road. They brought to many smaller cities whatever had first pleased metropolitan audiences, both popular entertainment and the more sophisticated plays. Throughout the country "temples of amusement" with the people's own prices (ten, twenty, and thirty cents) blatantly defied the "temples of art" given over to classic revivals and contemporary problem plays.

The new Bowery in New York, opening on the eve of the Civil War, had been one of the first of the truly popular theatres. A reporter of the *Herald* found the house on its first night "jammed with the democracy, unwashed and unterrified, to the number of a couple of thousand." In a smoke-laden atmosphere redolent of beer and sweat, this boisterous audience watched the play with an enthusiasm untempered by any polite conventions. A sergeant-at-arms with a rattan cane did what he could to keep the Bowery "bhoys" in order, but woe betide the player who did not please that shirt-sleeved gallery. Catcalls and hisses might still be emphasized, as they had been in an earlier day, by a barrage of eggs and rotten fruit.[4]

Many of this theatre's old customs survived at the Bowery of the 1890's. It was a house which combined melodrama and variety for the delectation of as rough-and-ready an audience as ever crowded its predecessor. Admission to a box was seventy-five cents, but the gallery cost only a dime. House policemen endeavored to maintain order. The officer assigned to the parquet was accustomed to stand throughout the performance with his back to the orchestra leader, a formidable figure with long black mustaches, wearing a derby. Any one who became too noisy would feel the sharp rap of his cane and the hissed warning, "Cheese it!" The theatre had a convenient bar. Throughout the show waiters hurried about, and glasses of foaming beer were continually being passed back and forth.[5]

The People's, the Windsor, the Third Avenue, the National, the London, were other popular New York houses largely given over to melodrama at ten to thirty cents.[6] Chicago had a bloc of what were called provincial theatres, presenting "entertainment of the more democratic type." The Alhambra and the Madison Street Opera House had a wide fame. At the Park the actresses were glad to join members of the audience for a casual drink, and boys sold rotten cabbages—even an occasional dead cat—to the gallery gods.[7] An air of somewhat greater respectability hovered over Boston's Grand Opera House and the People's Theatre in Philadelphia (it was advertised as "the largest and handsomest popular price theatre in America"), but standards of decorum were not unduly high. The playhouses of San Francisco and other western cities granted nothing to those of the East in their air of democratic informality.

The dime-novel influence dominated this popular theatre. Melodrama was all the rage, staged with extravagant elaboration. Four acts with twenty-odd scenes were the rule for a good sizzling play of death and destruction. Harbor-fronts with lapping waves of real water were ingeniously constructed, and rugged papier-maché mountains erected with rock faces and fearsome precipices. Horses raced on treadmills, railroad trains were wrecked, and violent explosions sent the property houses crashing. Through these exciting scenes strode scowling, heavy-mustached villains who treacherously bound lovely girls on the railroad tracks before approaching locomotives, or locked them in gloomy subterranean dungeons while the river slowly rose to the only window. But the handsome hero was always in time for a dramatic last-minute rescue. Murder, arson, burglary were vividly depicted—everything but rape and seduction. The theme often involved the pitfalls that beset the innocent country girl lured to the big city, but she was invariably saved from that fate worse than death.

There were five main characters in this popular drama, and the audience came to know exactly what to expect of each of them— the hero and heroine, the light-comedy boy, the soubrette, and the heavy man. Owen Davis, accustomed at this period to turn out ten to twenty melodramas a year reaching an audience of seven million (he had a good plot, he explained), once tried to have the comedy boy fall in love with some one other than the soubrette. He had to revise his play: the audience was too bewildered.[8]

The melodramas were written by the ream—*Under the Gaslight* (one of the earliest and most popular), *Only a Working Girl, The Limited Mail, Dangers of a Great City, The Turf Digger's Doom, The Power of Gold, Wilful Murder,* and *Nellie, the Beautiful Cloak Model.* In *On the Bowery* Steve Brodie himself jumped off a shaky Brooklyn Bridge and plunged through the trap amid a shower of rock salt thrown up by stage-hands. *The Naval Cadet* found James J. Corbett heroically saving the heroine from a foul cellar dive: "So you've come for the gal," sneered the villain, gliding stealthily forward, an ugly knife clenched between his gleaming teeth. Gentleman Jim would calmly take off his white gloves, lay them carefully beside his silk hat, and step forward.[9] How the audience stamped and shouted as evil was vanquished by honor in the person of the new champion prizefighter!

Virtue always won in the last round of melodrama. Poverty was honorable and innocence unassailable. Currency was given to the most noble sentiments. "An honest shop girl is as far above a fashionable idler as heaven is above earth," the honest shop girl sententiously declaimed. Sympathetic audiences at *The White Slave* learned for all time that "rags are royal raiment when worn for virtue's sake."

Most popular of all the melodramas were the westerns, reflecting the romantic glamour that clung to the passing frontier. Its wild and woolly heroes appeared in person—"Texas Jack" Omohundro, "Wild Bill" Hickok, and "Buffalo Bill" Cody. They reënacted for cheering audiences saloon brawls, stage-coach hold-ups, and blood-curdling Indian attacks. Trusty rifles and murderous six-shooters barked continuously in *The Gambler of the West,* and at every bark another redskin bit the dust. Between the acts Jack Dalton threw bowie-knives at Baby Bess, the Pet of the Gulch, and Rattle Snake Oil was sold at a dime a bottle in the lobby.[10]

After his success in such plays as *The Scouts of the Plains* and *The Red Right Hand; or The First Scalp for Custer*—their thrilling scenes sometimes interpolated (shades of Mr. Barnum!) with a temperance lecture—Buffalo Bill launched his Wild West, Rocky Mountain and Prairie Exhibition. It went from triumph to triumph, playing to over a million people in one five-months season: Indians, cowboys, Mexicans; wild Texas steers and buffaloes; the Deadwood Coach and Sitting Bull; Annie Oakley and Buffalo Bill himself in his broad white sombrero.[11]

Almost as popular as the melodrama, greatly favored by the lone male in the big city, were the burlesque shows. They had come in shortly after the Civil War, in those wicked days when the cancan was all the rage and English burlesque queens first offered up their "fatted calves at the shrine of a prodigal New York audience." [12] There had been outraged protests against this type of show. Critics almost wept at the public's "porcine taste for indelicate buffoonery," but the managers of the popular theatres knew a good thing, from a strictly commercial point of view, when they saw it. If reformers chose to describe a production as a "disgraceful spectacle of padded legs jigging and wriggling in the insensate follies and indecencies of the hour," it seldom hurt box-office receipts.[13]

The modern version of burlesque soon omitted entirely the gaily extravagant satire which had distinguished the early performances of the Black Crook Company, the British Blondes, the Red Stocking Blondes. The advertisements of the 1890's told the whole story: "50—Pairs of Rounded Limbs, Ruby Lips, Tantalizing Torsos—50." Many theatres in the large cities were given over entirely to this entertainment; traveling companies took it on the road. In 1895 Sam T. Jack, "King of Burlesque," was proprietor of Lily Clay's Colossal Gaiety Company, the Ada Richmond Folly Company, the Creole Burlesque Company.... The rounded limbs and dazzling torsos of these merry maidens were clothed in "close-fitting, flesh colored silk tights," but the Madison Street Opera House in Chicago happily advertised that this was really far more attractive than no costume at all.[14]

Variety also had come into its own in this popular theatre; it was taking form and shape as modern vaudeville. The transition was an important one. While the acts did not differ greatly from those at Niblo's, the American Museum, or the mid-century Theatre of Mirth and Variety, they marked a distinct improvement over the music-hall show that had flourished in the 1860's and 1870's. Recognizing that there was a far larger audience for this type of entertainment if it were reasonably decent, a new generation of producers was determined to rescue variety from the ill repute into which it had fallen and elevate it to "a high plane of respectability and moral cleanliness." [15]

Tony Pastor had initiated refined vaudeville, entertainment for the whole family, in New York, and his famous theatre was soon rivaled by the Globe, the Olympic, and the Theatre Comique. Other cities gave it a no less enthusiastic welcome. By the 1880's there were six vaudeville houses in Philadelphia, two in Baltimore, two in Chicago, three in St. Louis, and three in San Francisco.[16] As in the case of melodrama and burlesque, traveling companies took it on the road. Among the more popular troupes listed by M. N. Leavitt, who controlled six companies himself, were Tony Pastor's Combination, Harry Minor's Comedy Four, Tillotson's Varieties, The All Star Specialty Company, and Charlie Shay's Quincuplexals. Here was a new departure in entertainment —"natural offspring of the old-time minstrel, circus and variety sketch stage." [17]

There were acrobats and trained animals, sentimental ballads and comic songs, bicycle-riders and fancy roller-skaters, jugglers and magicians, innumerable dancing acts—all the tricks and stunts that have always been a lowly adjunct of the legitimate stage. Often one-act farces or comedies were given—*Lost in New York* or *The Mud Town Rubes*. Sometimes there were prudent borrowings from burlesque.

Among the head-liners in the 1890's were Weber and Fields, Montgomery and Stone, Maggie Cline singing "Throw Him Down, McCloskey," and Lillian Russell "Kiss Me Mother, Ere I Die"; Carmencita in her Spanish dances; Sandow, the Strong Man; the Russell Brothers in short skirts ("Maggie, have you put fresh water in the goldfish bowl?" "No, they ain't drunk up what I give 'em yesterday."); Pat Rooney dancing his famous jig; and the Cohan family with Master George in *The Lively Bootblack* and *Peck's Bad Boy*.[18]

The entry into this profitable field of entertainment of B. F. Keith and F. F. Proctor brought about still further expansion of vaudeville. The former introduced the continuous performance at his Boston theatre in 1883 (Barnum had offered it for holidays half a century earlier at his American Museum), and a decade later Proctor adopted it at his New York Pleasure Palace. At the Ladies' Club Theatre still another forward step was taken—the show began at 11 A.M. and ran for twelve hours.[19]

As vaudeville spread to the provinces, theatres were organized in chains, and a nation-wide system for booking individual acts was developed. The two-a-day circuit came into being. One group of theatres alone was estimated to provide entertainment for five million every year. Refined vaudeville, observed one commentator at the close of the century, belonged to the era of the short story and the department store: "It may be a kind of lunch counter art, but then art is so vague and lunch is so real." [20]

There were performances at the popular theatres other than melodrama, burlesque, and vaudeville. Farces, musical shows, comedies, and serious drama were sometimes produced. The better houses warmly welcomed the stars of the legitimate stage; there was still a taste for good theatre. Even the People's and the Windsor, on New York's notorious Bowery, interrupted their usual programs to stage *Macbeth, King Lear,* and *Hamlet.*[21] But in comparison with an earlier day, the general public was far more interested in shows which pretended to be nothing more than entertainment. It unreservedly approved "the cheap and coarse sensationalism" decried by the critics. It thoroughly enjoyed "the silly buffoonery and vulgar nonsense" which offended the purists. When Keith and Proctor joined forces early in the twentieth century to establish their well-known circuit, the number of houses under their control alone soon grew to four hundred.[22] Vaudeville, spiced with melodrama and burlesque, had become the principal commercial amusement of America's urban democracy.

DIME MUSEUMS, dance-halls, shooting-galleries, beer-gardens, bowling-alleys, billiard-parlors, saloons, and other more questionable resorts made up another whole world of entertainment whose glaring gas-lights symbolized the lure of the wicked city. And in the 1890's it often was wicked. It was an age of notoriously corrupt municipal governments. The line between virtue and vice was hard to distinguish; perfectly respectable places of entertainment shaded off imperceptibly into notorious dives. There were plenty of dance-halls that found "the young mechanics and dressmakers in their glory," but as many where the floor was crowded with prostitutes. Every large city had its red-light district given over to saloons and sporting-houses. Drinking, gambling, and prostitution had become tremendous social problems as the size of the constantly growing cities made control more and more difficult, particularly when politics formed its profitable alliance with vice.

The dime museums, which preyed upon the gullibility of their patrons rather than upon any less innocent tastes, had taken over the curiosities and freaks which had always had a peculiar attraction for the populace. Again Mr. Barnum had pointed the way. Here could be seen the fat woman and the sword-swallower, the bearded lady and the ossified girl, the tattooed man and the iron-jawed lady. There were always a stuffed mermaid, a wild man from Borneo, and a snake-charmer. What passer-by could resist the feverish ballyhoo of the museum barker when he offered them—frankly—such a show as the world had never seen? "The greatest, the most astounding aggregation of marvels and monstrosities ever gathered together in one edifice! From the ends of the earth, the wilds of darkest Africa, the miasmic jungles of Brazil, the mystic waters of the Yang-tse-Kiang, the cannibal isles of the Antipodes, the frosty slopes of the Himalayas and barren steppes of the Caucasus; sparing no expense, every town, every village, every hamlet, every nook and cranny of the globe has been searched with a fine-tooth comb to provide a feast for the eye and mind.... No waiting, no delays. Step up, ladies and gentlemen, and avoid the rush. Tickets now selling in the doorway." [23]

Sometimes a special performance would be given in the basement with such celebrities as Jo-Jo, the Dog-faced Boy, or Peerless Corinne, the Circassian Princess and Sword Swallower. And an extra dime was often drawn from the unwary by the promise of a chance to see "the unclad female form in all its loveliness"— generally a dim view of a show-window dummy.

Music-halls, free-and-easies, concert-saloons, provided an opportunity to drink in the garish atmosphere created by music, scantily dressed girl waitresses, and beautiful entertainers. Chicago, which liked to call itself the Paris of America, had scores of these places,[24] but New York really held unchallenged leadership. In 1898 the police of Gotham listed ninety-nine amusement resorts, including saloons with music and entertainment, on the Bowery alone. They classed only fourteen of them as respectable.[25] It was at one of these places that a singing waiter named Izzy Baline, crooning to delighted audiences such songs as "Just Break the News to Mother" and "You Made Me What I Am Today," started on a career which led to fame and fortune on Tin Pan Alley under the name of Irving Berlin.

At dance-halls and other establishments, local social clubs held balls and assemblies as they had since mid-century, generously inviting the public at the usual admission charge (lady included) of one dollar. The Zig Zag Club social was an event in San Francisco; Chicago went in for masquerade balls; and a fixture of the New York social calendar was the annual ball at Tammany Hall of the Chuck Connors Association. The latter was a democratic assemblage. Members of the Racquet Club and the New York Athletic Club came down town to mingle with representatives of the Knickerbocker Icemen, the East Side Democratic and Pleasure Association, the Lee Hung Fat Club, and the Lady Truck Drivers.

Toward the close of the century the electric trolley began to provide a Sunday or holiday substitute for these amusements.

Steamboat and even railroad excursions had long been possible, but here was a far easier and cheaper means of getting away from the city. The trolley ride was an outstanding feature of week-end recreation: the amusement parks to which the pleasure-seekers were carried became the holiday Mecca of thousands upon thousands of workers.[26] A writer in *Harper's Weekly*, impressed by the immense crowds that throughout the summer took advantage of these excursions, described the parks as "the great breathing-places for the millions of people in the city who get little fresh air at home." [27] And another observer declared that their pastimes yielded more enjoyment "than all the courtly balls and fashionable dissipation indulged in by fortune's favorites." [28]

The new rapid-transit companies not only offered reduced rates for daytime trips into the country, but advertised special trolley carnivals in the evening—the cars gaily illuminated with multicolored lights and boasting even a number of musicians to provide popular band music. They established their own amusement resorts in the outskirts of cities from Claremont, New Hampshire, to San Antonio, Texas. Some of these parks had little more than a pavilion or dance-hall; others had all possible attractions—roller coasters, merry-go-rounds, circle swings, bump-the-bumps, and shoot-the-chutes. In 1893 the Ferris Wheel crowned the attractions of the Midway at Chicago's World Fair, and soon thereafter it was the star feature of hundreds of trolley parks throughout the country.

Chicago had its Cheltenham Beach, popular for barbecues and clam-bakes, and later its famous White City. There were Paragon Park near Boston, the Chutes at San Francisco, and Forest Park Highlands at St. Louis. Crowds listened to band concerts, watched balloon ascensions and parachute jumps, cheered at professional bicycle races. At Manhattan Beach near Denver there was an ostrich farm and two open-air theatres. Willow Grove at Philadelphia had an auditorium seating ten thousand people.[29]

Winter Amateur Athletic Meet at the Boston Athletic Club

Drawing by Henry Sandham. *Harper's Weekly*, 1890.

The Bathing Hour on the Beach at Atlantic City
Drawing by Frank H. Schell. *Harper's Weekly, 1890.*

A Double Play to Open the League Season
Boston at New York. Drawing by W. P. Snyder. *Harper's Weekly, 1886.*

Coney Island also had by this time those varied entertainments which continue to draw throngs of New Yorkers every summer day. Bathing-houses lined the beach, minstrel bands played on the boardwalk, and everywhere the shrill cry of barkers advertised carrousels, freak shows, shooting-galleries, and dance-halls. In 1897 George C. Tilyou opened his famed Steeplechase Park with a fantastic array of his own inventions—the Bounding Billows, Blow Hole, Barrel of Love, Human Roulette Wheel, Electric Seat, and Razzle Dazzle.[30] There was "a spurious toboggan slide of mammoth proportions," one observer noted, and on the boardwalk was being sold something new and strange which proved a more practical mobile form of nourishment than the clam chowder which had formerly ruled supreme. This new concoction was "a weird-looking sausage muffled up in two halves of a roll."

-->>X<<-

ONE of the most popular acts on the vaudeville stage in these days was De Wolf Hopper's rendering of a famous poem:

Oh! somewhere in this favored land the sun is shining bright;
The band is playing somewhere, and somewhere hearts are light.
And somewhere men are laughing, and somewhere children shout;
But there is no joy in Mudville—mighty Casey has struck out.[31]

It was sign and symbol of the immense interest and enthusiasm baseball everywhere aroused. The fans crowded the grand stands and packed the bleachers almost every summer afternoon to watch the professional teams. "The fascination of the game," Harper's Weekly commented, "has seized upon the American people, irrespective of age, sex or other condition." [32] It was estimated that daily attendance at the games of clubs organized under the National Agreement was some sixty thousand, with the annual total amounting to almost eight million.[33] When the matches of small-town clubs and semiprofessional leagues were included, it was many times this figure. Baseball had come a long way from those early beginnings traced in mid-century. It was

far and away the leading spectator sport, a boon to bank clerk
and factory-worker, shopkeeper and mechanic, the business exec-
utive and his office-boy.

Together with the growth in popular interest, there had been a
number of changes in the game itself since the National League
was organized in 1876. The umpire had been empowered to call
four balls and three strikes; a ball had to be caught on the fly
for the batsman to be out—in his hands and not in his cap, as
the practice had been; restrictions on pitching had been removed
to make possible new refinements in curves and fade-aways;
gloves were being worn; and the risks of the catcher's position
had been reduced by arming him with mask, breastpad, and mitt.
There had been difficulty over the best type of ball. It was at
first too fast. Among the immense scores rolled up in this period
was one of 201 to 11 at a game in Buffalo. Then the substitute
ball had proved too dead. A twenty-four inning game between
Harvard and Manchester ended in a scoreless tie. Finally a better
balanced ball made more reasonable scores the rule. The game
became generally faster, and with much improved playing, it was
more exciting than ever.[34]

The National League had a friendly rival in the American
Association, with which it held an annual championship series,
but in 1889-90 a serious threat developed to its dominance over
the professional game. The players themselves, in protest over
what they considered unfair practices, attempted to win control
through organization of the National Brotherhood of Baseball
Players. Big-league ball was thrown into chaos; attendance
dwindled away alarmingly. But the revolt was short-lived. The
Brotherhood collapsed after a single season, dragging the American Association down in its fall, and the National League
emerged from the conflict stronger than ever. It was left alone
in the field with twelve member clubs, six in the East and six
in the West, and it did not again have a major rival (although
there were many minor associations) until the formation of the
American League in 1899.[35] After a brief struggle for supremacy,

these two associations amicably divided the field represented by the larger cities, and their establishment of an official World Series in 1903 added still more to popular interest.

Professional baseball had become at once big business, entertainment for the masses, and the guide and mentor of the thousands of amateur players throughout the country. Every city followed closely the fortunes of its own team, with the newspapers giving tremendous publicity to all league games. The genius of the sporting page had already arrived half a century ago, and he was enriching the American language with the expressive, pungent vocabulary of sport. On May 4, 1891, Chicago won a notable victory over Pittsburgh under the inspired leadership of "Pop" Anson. On the following morning Leonard Dana Washburn started his account of the affray in the Chicago *Inter-Ocean* in a new style of reporting:

You can write home that Grandpa won yesterday.

And say in the postscript that Willie Hutchinson did it. The sweet child stood out in the middle of the big diamond of pompadour grass and slammed balls down the path that looked like the biscuits of a bride. The day was dark, and when Mr. Hutchinson shook out the coils of his right arm, rubbed his left toe meditatively in the soil he loves so well, and let go, there was a blinding streak through the air like the tail of a skyrocket against a black sky. There would follow the ball a hopeless shriek, the shrill, whistling noise of a bat grippling with the wind, and a dull, stifled squash like a portly gentleman sitting down on a ripe tomato. . . .

There were ten of the visiting delegation who walked jauntily to the plate and argued with the cold, moist air. Mr. Field lacerated the ethereal microbes three times out of four opportunities to get solid with the ball, and Brer Lewis Robinson Browning walked away from the plate with a pained expression twice in succession. The Gastown folks found the ball six times. Two of their runs were earned.

Mr. Staley, who pitches for the strangers, did not have enough speed to pass a street car going in an opposite direction. His balls wandered down toward the plate like a boy on his way to school. If our zealous and public-spirited townsmen did not baste them all over that voting precinct it was because they grew weary and faint waiting for them to arrive. . . .[36]

The entire country was proud of the Chicago White Sox and the All-American team that A. G. Spalding took on a world tour in 1888-89, playing in Ceylon, in the shadow of the pyramids, and before the Prince of Wales in England.[37] Baseball had its national heroes, worshiped by small boys from Maine to California. There was not an American who did not recognize the fame of "Pop" Anson, "Iron Man" Joe McGinnity, and Honus Wagner, or know the significance of "Slide, Kelly, Slide." It was the national game beyond possible dispute.

"Let me say," declared Cardinal Gibbons in a speech made in 1896, "that I favor Base Ball as an amusement for the greatest pleasure-loving people in the world. . . . It is a healthy sport, and since the people of the country generally demand some sporting event for their amusement, I should single this out as the one best to be patronized and heartily approve of it as a popular pastime." [38]

->>)(<<-

THERE WERE other spectator sports, though none really compared with baseball in popular appeal, during this period at the close of the past century. Racing and trotting matches were flourishing, drawing large crowds to the rapidly multiplying city tracks. Chicago had three, and four clustered about New York. It was the day of Salvator's reign as the horse of the century. His sensational victory over Tenny at Sheepshead Bay was cheered by an excited mob of many thousands.[39] Professional rowing matches —from single sculls to six-oared lap-streak gigs—created more excitement than they ever have since. In the days of the memorable duel between Edward Hanlan, Canada's Boy in Blue, and Charles E. Courtney, later coach at Cornell, they were a major sport.[40] Intercollegiate football, of course, had its followers, but we shall trace its further development in a later chapter—it was still more a sport of society than of the masses.

If there was a rival to the national game in sustained popular interest, it was prize-fighting, not wholly out from under the

cloud of disapproval but nevertheless arousing a nation-wide excitement which official bans on championship bouts in no way
diminished. The fortunes of favorite bruisers were followed
avidly, and although it was still true that comparatively few
people actually saw the fights, the reports of them were read by
millions. An English visitor was somewhat shocked that his
newspaper one morning in 1892 gave twelve prominent columns
to a championship bout while the death of John Greenleaf Whit-
tier rated only a single inside column.[41] But it was a correct
appraisal of public interest.

The great event of the prize-fight world was the emergence of
a champion of champions who dominated the ring from 1882 to
1892. America has perhaps never had a sports hero comparable
to John L. Sullivan, the Strong Boy of Boston. He climbed to
eminence over the prone body of Paddy Ryan, but it was when
he knocked out Jake Kilrain in a fierce, grueling, seventy-five-
round battle at New Orleans, the last of the bare-knuckle championship fights, that the great John L. was acknowledged lord
of all he surveyed. His fame resounded throughout the world
after this epic encounter, from which he won a purse of $20,000
and a diamond-studded championship belt presented by *The
Police Gazette*.[42]

Boston's hero—the city once turned out *en masse* to honor
him at a ceremony which found the Boston Theatre packed: the
aldermen and mayor in the boxes, Beacon Street in the orchestra,
and the gallery overflowing with the Irish [43]—owed his tremendous popularity to an aggressive pugnacity which made him
always eager for a fight. He toured the country, first offering $50,
and then raising the ante to $1,000, to any one who would stay
with him four rounds. Mobs fought their way to see him whenever he appeared. On one occasion New York's new Madison
Square Garden was crowded to the doors with a motley throng
which embraced every element in the city's diverse population
from Fifth Avenue to the Bowery. His only losing fight was with
that insistent enemy John Barleycorn. Once when the great

John L. was scheduled to fight Charlie Mitchell, the English boxer, liquor won the preliminary round. When the gong rang, the Strong Boy staggered into the ring, not in his usual green trunks encircled by an American flag, but in full evening dress with a shirt-front flashing with diamonds. He was ready to fight —he was always ready, drunk or sober—but to the bitter disappointment of an excited audience the referee called off the bout.[44]

When Sullivan finally went down to defeat at the Olympic Club in New Orleans before Gentleman Jim Corbett, fighting under the Marquis of Queensberry rules, with five-ounce gloves, the world appeared to totter. An incredulous public refused to believe the dire news which appeared in bold-face headlines from coast to coast. The Strong Boy of Boston knocked out? It was not believed possible. A sorrowing poet sang of his downfall. To the tune of "Throw Him Down, McCloskey" the entire country joined in the chorus:

> John L. has been knocked out! the people all did cry
> Corbett is the champion! how the news did fly.
> And future generations, with wonder and delight,
> Will read in hist'ry's pages of the Sullivan-Corbett fight.[45]

Corbett reigned for five years, another popular champion, and then on St. Patrick's Day, 1897, was knocked out by the flying fists of Robert Prometheus Fitzsimmons, inventor of the solar-plexus punch. The bout was held in Carson City, went to fourteen rounds, and was fought for a $15,000 purse.

->>><<<-

"THE SOCIAL CIVILIZATION of a people," Lord Lytton has written, "is always and infallibly indicated by the intellectual character of its amusements." [46] On the basis of those most widely enjoyed by the urban democracy of the nineteenth century, American civilization would not appear to have attained a very high level. Living and working conditions in the large city were primarily responsible for this. "When there is a lack of nourishing food and of the tonic of pure air," a thoughtful contemporary observed, "debilitated nerves crave excitement; hence the large number of saloons, gambling hells, dance halls, and theatres in the most crowded portions of the city." [47]

It is easy to overemphasize these more lurid aspects of urban recreation. Any account of public amusements forces far into the background the simpler pleasures of home and family life. Nevertheless it does remain true that the concentration of such large numbers of people in very small areas, working with the intensity enforced by the new industrialism, made them demand in their leisure hours stimulation that could relieve the strain of their long day in factory, store, or office. The simplicity and spontaneity of community life in the country or small town could not be preserved in the city. Mass entertainment was an inevitable development. Excursions into the country, the opportunity to enjoy sports for themselves, other active types of amusement were developing, but at a discouragingly slow rate. The democracy had asserted in ever-stronger terms its right to play. America had become a pleasure-loving nation, but the character of its amusements, in so far as the urban population was concerned, could not but cause serious misgivings.

The new century was to witness many changes. Living and working conditions were to be improved, stricter and more honest supervision was adopted for places of amusement that were definitely undesirable, and the growth of city park systems soon held out the promise of greater opportunities for outdoor activities. Recreation became a primary concern of the twentieth-century social movement to reform the evils of urban life, and there was already impending a revolution in the field of commercial amusements which was to have incalculable effects. Although it could hardly be recognized at the time, the 1890's represented the culminating stage in the development of many of those popular forms of entertainment which were the past century's answer to the needs of metropolis.

Chapter XIV

WORLD OF FASHION

THE WAYS IN WHICH SOCIETY MAY AMUSE ITSELF AFFORD, IN any country and at any time, an exceptional opportunity for the display of wealth and the assertion of social importance. Thorstein Veblen has graphically demonstrated this conscious or unconscious motivation in many forms of recreation. It is clearly evident throughout American social history. The worthy citizens of eighteenth-century Philadelphia vied with each other in the magnificence of their banquets, loading their tables with massive silver plate and serving such a choice selection of imported wines that the visiting John Adams stood amazed at the "sinful feasts." The planters of Virginia rode to hounds in close imitation of the English country squires whose social status they sought to emulate in every possible way. Merchants of New York and Boston were already aspiring to yachts in the 1850's, their sons to membership in the exclusive boating clubs, while all the fashionable world sought out Saratoga or Newport as a step upward on the social ladder.

It was in the latter half of the past century, however, the Gilded Age of American civilization, that society most flagrantly bent its pleasures to display. The newly rich born of industry's great advance since the Civil War—owners of railways, copper-mines, textile-mills, steel-plants, packing-houses, and cattle ranches—sought to establish social leadership through their extravagance in entertainments and amusements. A little band of idle rich held the final redoubt in the fashionable world of the 1880's and 1890's, and the families of the new plutocracy felt it essential to prove beyond shadow of doubt that they too were idle and rich. It was not in the American tradition, which esteemed riches and abhorred idleness, but urban society was running after strange gods. And, in any event, the new plutocrats generally supplied the riches and left it to willing wives and a younger generation to demonstrate the idleness.

With the first post-war boom in the 1860's, observers began to note that New York society was becoming entirely based upon wealth, social prestige being won by those who had the most splendid carriages, drawing-rooms, and opera boxes. George Makepeace Towle has described the balls and assemblies—ladies in sparkling tiaras, suppers of oysters and champagne, fountains gushing wine or sprays of perfume. He was somewhat horrified by "so unceasing a round of glittering gaiety and dissipation." [1] The advance of the new millionaires was picturesquely described as "the Gold Rush" by representatives of older social traditions. "From an unofficial oligarchy of aristocrats," Mrs. John King Van Rensselaer sadly wrote, "society was transformed into an extravagant body that set increasing store by fashion and display." [2]

Nor was New York alone in this competitive rage for showy display. A sycophant press might boast that its ornate fancy-dress balls and ten-thousand-dollar dinner parties were the most expensive ever known, but the world of fashion throughout the land was closely following its lead. There was an epidemic of gaudy magnificence in the amusements of what went for society. One Chicago magnate brought an entire theatrical company from New York to entertain a group of his friends, and a wealthy woman in another city engaged a large orchestra to serenade her new-born child.[3] San Francisco was notorious for its "terribly fast so-called society set, engrossed by the emptiest and most trivial pleasures." [4] A fortunate miner who had struck it rich in Virginia City drove a coach and four with silver harness; another had champagne running from the taps at his wedding party.[5]

The famous ball with which Mrs. William K. Vanderbilt crashed the gates of society in 1883 was admitted by the press to have been more magnificent than the entertainments of Alexander, Cleopatra, or Louis XIV.[6] It was soon outshown by other affairs of New York's Four Hundred. In his *Society as I Have Found It*, Ward McAllister describes dinner parties with squadrons of butlers and footmen in light plush livery, silk stockings, and powdered hair; orchestras concealed behind flowered screens; and every out-of-season fruit and vegetable served on golden plates. At society's fancy-dress balls, men weighed down in suits of medieval armor tripped over their swords as they attempted to dance quadrilles; the women wore wreaths of electric lights in their hair to add a new luster to their diamonds.[7]

"Everything that skill and art could suggest," McAllister notes at one point, "was added to make the dinners not a vulgar display, but a great gastronomic effort, evidencing the possession by the host of both money and taste."[8] But always taste was secondary, and Crœsus was crowned society's Lord of Misrule. A marveling correspondent of the London *Spectator* found America's newly rich pouring out money on festal occasions as from a purse of Fortunatus, making feasts as of the Great King Belshazzar.[9]

For one ball the host built a special addition to his house providing a magnificent Louis XIV ball-room which would accommodate twelve hundred. Another time a restaurant was entirely made over with a plum-shaded conservatory, a Japanese room, and a medieval hall hung with Gobelin tapestries especially imported from Paris. At a reception given at the Metropolitan Opera House, twelve hundred guests danced the Sir Roger de Coverley on a floor built over stage and auditorium, and were then served supper at small tables by three hundred liveried servants. It was a world of jewels and satins, of terrapin and canvasbacks, of Château Lafite and imported champagne—"luxurious in adornment . . . epicurean in its feasting."[10]

In the cities of the West, where the golden stream flowed so freely in these thriving days and those who would scale society's heights often had so much to forget, even greater extravagances were sometimes recorded. It took many diamonds and much

Trotting Cracks of Philadelphia Returning from the Races

Having a brush past Turner's Hotel, Rope Ferry Road. Lithograph by
H. Pharazyn, 1870. Courtesy of the New York Historical Society.

ashionable
urnouts in
entral Park

ograph by Cur-
and Ives after
ches from life
Thomas Worth,
. J. Clarence
ies Collection,
eum of the
of New York.

Baltimore Society Dances for Charity

Grand ball at the Academy of Music for the benefit of the Nursery and Child's Hospital. *Frank Leslie's Illustrated Newspaper*, 1880.

wine for some of the new dowagers to erase entirely the mark of the laundry tub or kitchen sink. Only money could do it, and the sensational inspired most newspaper copy. The new plutocracy gave dinners at which cigarettes were wrapped in hundred-dollar bills or the guests found fine black pearls in their oysters. For one gala occasion the room was filled with cages of rare song-birds and dwarf fruit-trees, while half a dozen graceful swans swam in a miniature lake. There was a famous horseback dinner. "The guests were attired in riding habits," wrote Frederick Townsend Martin; "the handsomely groomed horses pranced and clattered about the magnificent dining-room, each bearing, besides its rider, a miniature table. The hoofs of the animals were covered with soft rubber pads to save the waxed floor from destruction." [11]

The Bradley Martin ball in 1897 created the greatest sensation of the Gilded Age. The ball-room of the Waldorf-Astoria Hotel was converted into a replica of Versailles and sumptuously decorated with rare tapestries and beautiful flowers. Mrs. Bradley Martin, as Mary Queen of Scots, wore a necklace of Marie Antoinette's and a cluster of diamond grapes once owned by Louis XIV. The suit of gold-inlaid armor worn by Mr. Belmont was valued at ten thousand dollars. The publicity given this affair was incredible. The *New York Times* and the *Herald* virtually gave over their front pages to descriptions of it, and the London papers all carried cabled dispatches. On the morning after the affair, the London *Daily Mail*, with allowance for the difference in time, reported: "Mrs. Bradley Martin, we have every reason to believe, is dressed at this very moment in a train of black velvet lined with cerise satin, and a petticoat, if it is not indiscreet to say so, of white satin, embroidered with flowers and arabesques of silver." The London *Chronicle* congratulated New York society on its triumph—"It has cut out Belshazzar's feast and Wardour Street and Mme. Tussaud's and the Bank of England. There is no doubt about that."

But there were limits to which even the American public

would go in condoning such heartless extravagance in a year when there was widespread distress among the poor. The storm of disapproval that followed in the train of this ball drove the Bradley Martins out of the country. Depressed by their unexpected notoriety, they settled permanently in England.[12]

->>><<-

FOR ALL the lavish prodigality of these affairs, and despite the widespread publicity they obtained, they were not important. They directly touched the lives of only a very small coterie in the upper brackets of the fashionable world. Society in a broader sense, members of the community in which wealth was allied with culture, had many other forms of recreation where their patronage had some real significance. One of these was the legitimate stage, as contrasted with the more popular theatrical entertainment of the urban democracy.

The small, luxuriously appointed theatres where reserved seats ranged in price from one to three dollars had become the home of a relatively exclusive amusement. Every city had its fashionable playhouses. Writing of New York, Henry Collins Brown speaks of the friendly social atmosphere of Wallack's, Daly's Fifth Avenue Theatre, the Madison Square ("most exquisite theatre in all the world"), and the Union Square. In Chicago there were McVicker's and Hooley's; Boston offered the Museum and the old Boston Theatre. These houses appealed to the carriage trade. Here, in a new elegance of surroundings—the pit had become the parquet with sloping floor; upholstered plush seats were furnished throughout; steam heat (the Lyceum also had "medicated air, charged with ozone") had replaced the foyer stove; and the new electric lights were being installed—the world of fashion could enjoy the play in a quiet and comfortable atmosphere far removed from the democratic hurly-burly of mid-century.[13]

The productions at these theatres generally centered about some starred actor or actress, although a few able stock companies still survived, and they often achieved long-sustained runs comparable to those of to-day's popular plays. With the great expansion of popular entertainment for the masses, it had become not only possible but also necessary for managers of the better theatres to pay more attention to the cultural standards of their comparatively limited and sophisticated audience. There were revivals of Shakespeare and other classic writers; well-staged productions of serious contemporary drama, both American and foreign; and comedies and light operas which bore little resemblance to the blood-and-thunder melodrama and questionable burlesque that ruled at the people's theatres.

Contemporary critics often failed to realize that the divorcing of popular entertainment from the legitimate stage rivaled development of the star system as the outstanding feature of theatrical history in the second half of the century. Forgetting the slapstick and circus stunts with which it had been so heavily cluttered, they looked back nostalgically to the theatre of an earlier day and remembered only Shakespeare. They could not understand how a public which had once seemed to enjoy the drama so much had shifted its allegiance to vaudeville and burlesque. Deciding it had degenerated into "vulgarians," they damned the producers for their "practical, shopkeeping cultivation of this popular appetite." They often seemed totally unaware that vaudeville's assumption of the task of entertaining the million, which the theatre itself had once borne, was actually affording the legitimate stage far greater opportunity for the development of the drama than it had ever had before in the democratic society of America.[14]

In time they looked back upon this period, as dramatic critics are so wont to do, with entirely different eyes. In retrospect the actors and actresses who supported the legitimate stage, even the plays produced at the more fashionable playhouses, took on Olympian stature. The years between 1870 and 1890 were said in many critical memoirs to stand out as the theatre's golden age.[15] The last decade of the century fell under something of a cloud. The rise of a theatrical trust, dominated by a group of managers who appeared to be deserting the ways of Wallack and Daly, threatened to impose a monopolistic control which considered only the box-office.[16] But even in those days there could be no real question that dramatic standards were far higher than in mid-century.

If one chose one's theatre, it was not necessary to see an equestrian exhibition or sensational melodrama, as had so often been the case in the first half of the century. There was no need, as there once had been, to sit through cheap variety acts to enjoy *Romeo and Juliet,* or listen to a series of comic songs as entr'actes in a performance of *Hamlet.* And in response to a more intelligent audience, contemporary playwrights were beginning to write with a little more perception and sense of reality than had inspired *Putnam, the Iron Son of '76, The Lady of Lyons,* or *The Drunkard.*

Bronson Howard had written *Young Mrs. Winthrop* and *Shenandoah,* William Gillette his *Held by the Enemy* and *Secret Service.* There were *The County Fair* by Charles Barnard and Neil Burgess, and Steele Mackaye's phenomenally successful *Hazel Kirk.* A serious attempt to introduce realism to the stage was made by James A. Herne with *Shore Acres* and *Margaret Fleming.* Still more important, perhaps, were the plays of European dramatists. Ibsen, Pinero, Oscar Wilde, and Shaw all had a wide and friendly reception on the American stage.

In this golden age of the theatre, Mrs. Fiske was adding to her laurels in *Becky Sharp* and *A Doll's House;* Clara Morris played in *Camille* and Fanny Davenport in *Tosca;* Richard Mansfield introduced *Cyrano de Bergerac;* E. H. Sothern was starring in *The Prisoner of Zenda,* James O'Neill, the father of Eugene O'Neill, in *The Count of Monte Cristo* (in which he acted almost five thousand times), and William Gillette in *Sherlock Holmes.* Until he left the stage, Edwin Booth was the greatest of Shakespearean stars; his tour of the country with Lawrence Barrett in 1890 was a continuous triumph. There was none really to take his place. But Mansfield, Barrett, McCullough, and Mantell carried on the Shakespearean tradition among the actors, while Julia Marlowe was a lovely Rosalind in *As You Like It,* and Mary Anderson made an incomparable Juliet. Many other names —producers, dramatists, and actors—might be mentioned: Charles Frohman and David Belasco; Augustus Thomas and Clyde Fitch; the Barrymores, John Drew, Otis Skinner, Mrs. Leslie Carter, Margaret Anglin. . . . There were also such foreign stars as Henry Irving and Tommaso Salvini, Helena Modjeska, Sarah Bernhardt, and Eleanora Duse.

Among the light operas, *Pinafore,* first of the delightful concoctions of Gilbert and Sullivan to cross the Atlantic, was a sensation. It was first played at the Boston Museum, on November 25, 1878, then in San Francisco and Philadelphia, and finally in New York. There it was produced simultaneously in half a dozen theatres. There were children's companies, church-choir companies, and colored opera companies playing *Pinafore.* The fish exhibition had to be removed from the Aquarium for an engagement in what had been Castle Garden.[17] All New York, all America, sang and whistled "Little Buttercup."

Still another triumph was won by English operetta in the 1880's when *Erminie* had a phenomenal run of 1,256 performances at the New York Casino. Soon thereafter the Boston Ideals presented in Chicago the most popular of all American light operas, Reginald De Koven's *Robin Hood.* It was followed by other De Koven scores, and at the close of the century John Philip Sousa and Victor Herbert were further embellishing this type of polite musical entertainment with *El Capitan* and *The Wizard of the Nile.*

Concert singing, visits by foreign musicians, and orchestral playing also revealed a growing taste among the sophisticated for more serious music. Jenny Lind had paved the way for the tours of European artists in the middle of the century, and Ole Bull had made two memorable visits. In the 1890's Ysaye, Paderewski, Fritz Kreisler, Adelina Patti, Melba, Calvé, and Madame

Schumann-Heink were all on tour. Symphonic music had had its start with the organization of the New York Philharmonic as early as 1842, but it was not until 1878 that this orchestra had any real rival. In that year the New York Symphony Orchestra was established, to be followed in another three years by the Boston Symphony, and in 1891 by the Chicago Orchestra. Walter Damrosch and Theodore Thomas were adding a new interest to the musical scene.

Grand opera also had become firmly established. It had long been a distinctive feature of the social life of New Orleans, and there had been various attempts to introduce it in New York and other cities. Troupes of Italian singers had come and gone; elaborate opera houses had been opened—usually to fail after one or two seasons. "Will this splendid and refined amusement be supported in New York?" we find Philip Hone asking in 1833. "I am doubtful." And for almost half a century his doubts were largely justified. It was in 1883 that the Metropolitan Opera House, costing nearly $2,000,000, provided grand opera with its first really permanent home in America.[18]

The opening of the Metropolitan, for all its importance in the world of music and drama, illustrated even more vividly than any formal dinner or fancy-dress ball society's irresistible impulse to make its amusements an occasion to flaunt its wealth. For true music-lovers of the 1880's the operas currently being given at the Academy of Music fully met all artistic standards. The sole difficulty was that while there was plenty of available room at these performances in orchestra and galleries, every box at the Academy was taken for the season. And society had made an opera box one of the hall-marks of social success. The Metropolitan was built not in response to a demand for music, but to meet this need for fashionable display.[19]

It was financed by a group of social aspirants stung into action by the refusal of an offer of $30,000 for one of the boxes at the Academy of Music.[20] They would have their own opera house. Naturally enough its predominant feature became its two ornate

When Wallack's Theatre Was New

Harper's Weekly, 1882.

Defense of the "America's" Cup

Winner *Magic* leading. Painting by James E. Buttersworth, 1870. Courtesy of the Metropolitan Museum of Art.

New York's First Coach

Colonel De Lancey Kane's "The Tally-Ho" on its first run, May 1, 1876. Lithograph after a painting by H. C. Bispham. Courtesy of Harry T. Peters.

tiers of boxes. At the formal opening it was toward the Golden Horseshoe rather than the stage that all eyes turned. "The Goulds and the Vanderbilts and people of that ilk," the *New York Dramatic Mirror* reported with forthright candor on that memorable occasion, "perfumed the air with the odor of crisp greenbacks. The tiers of boxes looked like cages in a menagerie of monopolists." [21]

This did not mean that the Metropolitan did not uphold the highest standards of operatic art. It did. Italian operas were staged during its first season, and musical history was made when German music and the Wagnerian operas were given the Metropolitan's formal approval in 1884.[22] The company made an annual post-season tour, visiting Boston, Chicago, Cincinnati, St. Louis, Baltimore, Washington. . . . The world of society in these cities had its opportunity to emulate that of New York. Grand opera took its place, despite a sprinkling of more humble music-lovers in the upper galleries, as one of the most exclusive and fashionable of all diversions.

->>><<<-

SOCIETY had been the pioneer in the promotion of sports. We have seen that in the middle of the century the more wealthy had been almost the only people with the leisure and means to enjoy them. As the opportunity to play games became available for a wider public in the 1890's, the world of fashion tended more and more to favor those activities of which the expense definitely excluded the common man. The same impulse that motivated the rivalry over elaborate entertainment and opera boxes was responsible for an attitude toward sport in which conspicuous waste rather than simple enjoyment became the general rule. James Gordon Bennett, Jr., determined to win the position in society denied his father, made sport his means of entrée into that exclusive world. He sailed yachts and fought his way to the proud post of commodore of the New York Yacht Club; he took up coaching and drove his four-in-hand in the

Newport parade; he introduced polo and founded the West-chester Polo Club.[23]

The days were indeed far distant when society, in the person of members of the old Knickerbocker Club, had taken up base-ball and endeavored to keep it an exclusive pastime. "Naturally," wrote a correspondent of *Outing* in 1894, describing the sporting life of fashionable Philadelphia, "since baseball is so much of a professional game, it can hardly come under the head of what we recognize as out-of-door recreation." [24] But society could still approve archery and tennis. Tournaments in these lawn games remained social functions. When the clubs of archers, merry bowmen, or toxophilites that made up the National Archery Association had their annual meeting in 1897 on the grounds of the Chicago White Sox, band music and refreshments still con-tributed to the enjoyment of a select gathering.[25] The tennis matches at Newport, despite increasing interest in a sport which had become so much more active and competitive, were also a festival of the fashionable world. As late as 1886 the *Tribune Book of Open-Air Sports* complacently stated that lawn tennis remained "the game of polite society, essentially one for ladies and gentlemen.[26]

Yachts and horses were expensive enough to be proof against any alarming tendency toward democratization, and society was enthusiastic over these aristocratic pastimes. There was a great revival of yachting, marked by renewal of the America's Cup races. The wealthy engaged in lively competition both in the regattas for smaller boats (the one-design classes had been introduced) sponsored by such organizations as the New York Yacht Club, and in the purchase of expensive and elaborate ocean-going yachts. In the same way, ownership of a stable of thoroughbreds became highly fashionable, and the very rich ex-tended their patronage as never before to the turf. The exclusive American Jockey Club was founded, an ultrafashionable course laid out at Jerome Park, and the Kentucky Derby became an annual feature of an invigorated racing calendar.[27] The common man could watch the races, and the gambling fraternity made a profitable living from betting on them, but only the very wealthy could support a stable.

The horse was glorified in other ways. Fox-hunting in the English manner was taken up by clubs on Long Island, in the suburbs of Philadelphia, and in Virginia and Maryland. In 1885 the National Horse Show was instituted, to become one of the outstanding social events of the year. There was a beginning of polo, introduced in 1876, at Westchester and Newport. Coaching was imported from England, a further refinement of the fashionable driving that already crowded the roads of such resorts as Tuxedo and Lenox with expensively turned out dog-carts, buckboards, landaus, and phaetons.[28]

The annual coaching parade in New York was one of the city's most colorful shows. Four-in-hand drags and tally-hos bowled down Fifth Avenue in the crisp autumn air, the guards gaily winding their horns, while crowds lined the street to watch their triumphant progress. The coaches were painted pink, blue, or dark-green with under-carriages of some sharply contrasting shade, and the beautifully matched and carefully groomed horses wore artificial flowers on their throat-latches. Society rode proudly atop these splendid equipages, the men in striped waistcoats and silk toppers, the ladies holding gay parasols over their immense picture hats.[29]

For the fullest enjoyment of these varied sports, a new institution sprang into being in the 1880's—the country club. The first of the genus is believed to have been the Brookline Country Club, near Boston, but it was soon followed by the Westchester Country Club, the Essex Country Club, the Tuxedo Club, the Philadelphia Country Club, the Meadowbrook Hunt Club, and the Country Club of Chicago. Those near the shore promoted yachting and sailing; others were a center for hunting, pony-races, and polo. Coaching parties drove out from the city for sports events, dances, teas, and the annual hunt ball.[30]

Together with such pastimes as lawn tennis, archery, and trap-shooting, some of these clubs began also to provide facilities for a game new to America. It was far more important than yachting, coaching, or polo. It was not for very long to remain, as *Harper's Weekly* termed it in 1895, "pre-eminently a game of good society." It was soon to give rise to a tremendous growth in country clubs which were to become the special prerogative of the great middle class in cities and towns throughout the country. This sport, of course, was golf.

It did not really take hold in this country, despite its hoary antiquity in Scotland and occasional attempts to introduce it on this side of the Atlantic ever since colonial days, until after 1888. The organization in that year of the St. Andrews Club, near New York, may well be taken as the first important date in golf's history in the United States.[31] Other courses were built—whatever number of holes was most convenient—after St. Andrews had showed the way. Soon a great number of the country clubs about Boston, New York, and Philadelphia had their links. By 1892 golf was spreading westward. It took Chicago by storm and moved on to St. Louis, Milwaukee, Denver, and the Pacific Coast. In 1894 the United States Golf Association was formed.[32]

No other game has evoked such scorn among the uninitiated. The democracy still considered tennis a rather feminine game, a chance to sport white flannels and gay-colored blazers rather than exercise. It simply did not know what to make of the absurd spectacle of enthusiastic gentlemen in scarlet coats furiously digging up the turf in frenzied—and wholly serious—efforts to drive a little white ball into a little round hole some hundreds of yards away. Nor were the red coats of these pioneer golfers the only article of costume that seemed singularly inappropriate on the rolling fairways of the new courses. They wore elaborate leg-wrappings to protect themselves from the gorse indigenous to Scottish hills but quite foreign to this country, and they pulled down over their foreheads visored caps in the best Sherlock Holmes tradition. Women had not yet taken up the game, although it was already being urged upon them as an admirable

compromise between "the tediousness of croquet and the hurly-
burly of lawn tennis," but together with wondering little boys
who had been pressed into service as caddies, they often accompanied their lords and masters about the links. The public guf-
fawed, little dreaming of golf's popularity in another two decades or of the public courses of to-day.[33]

->>><<<-

IN THE FIELD of spectator sports, which we have seen becoming
more and more important toward the close of the century, the
world of fashion also showed a lively interest. If it paid little
attention to baseball, it rubbed shoulders with the roughest
elements of the sporting world at horse-races and prize-fights.
But above all else it turned out *en masse* for intercollegiate
football. The games of the Big Three, which still provided the
grand climax of the football season, were fully as much social
as sporting events in the 1890's. In New York a parade of
coaches would make its stately way to the playing-field. No small
part of the crowd, after lunching on chicken sandwiches and
champagne, watched the game from atop tally-hos.

"The air was tinged with the blue and the orange and the
black as the great throngs poured through the city over the
bridges, invaded Brooklyn and swept like a rising tide into
Eastern Park," the *New York Tribune* reported after one Yale-
Princeton game. "They came by the railroads, horsecars, drags
and coaches and afoot. Coaches, drags and tally-hos decorated
with the blue or the orange and black wound through the thor-
oughfares and quiet side streets in a glittering procession,
freighted with jubilant college boys and pretty girls, who woke
the echoes of the church bells with the cheers and tooting of
horns. In an almost endless procession they inundated the big
enclosure, and when it was 2 p.m. the sight was that of a coli-
seum of the nineteenth century, reflecting the changes and tints
of a panoramic spectacle." [34]

The great crowds attracted by football—totaling thirty and

forty thousand [35]—were naturally not entirely made up of those in the higher social brackets. The game had a wider appeal, as the tremendous publicity given it clearly proves. At the time of the Yale-Princeton game in 1895, the *New York Journal* published a full two and a half pages of news and sketches—running accounts of the game, a full page of technical descriptive comment by James J. Corbett, signed stories by the captains of the teams, and a feature article entitled "The Journal's Woman Reporter Trains with the Little Boys in Blue." [36] But despite this furor of publicity, football was a sport for the classes rather than the masses. It largely reflected the interests of the college world.

It was dominated by the eastern universities. In one season Yale had a championship team—with such great players as Heffelfinger and Hinkey—which won thirteen games and piled up a season's score of 488 while its own goal-line was uncrossed. But colleges throughout the country were now taking it up and playing increasingly better football. By the late 1890's the Army-Navy game had become an established annual feature; among southern colleges, Virginia, Vanderbilt, Washington and Lee, had well-known teams; in the Middle West there was already fierce competition among such colleges as Michigan, Minnesota, Wisconsin, Ohio State, and the new University of Chicago; Leland Stanford stood out among Pacific Coast teams.[37] Even though Walter Camp might not have to look much beyond the Big Three for his famous All-American teams, there were signs that the East's supremacy would soon be challenged. Intercollegiate football had become a nation-wide sport.

Bitter criticism had marked its progress. The attacks made upon football overemphasis in the 1890's make comparable comments in the 1920's and 1930's appear mild and innocuous. The preference accorded football-players in their college work, undue absorption in the game through long training-seasons, the prevalent spirit of winning at any cost, and the open hiring of star players awoke a resentment which echoed throughout the country. *The Nation* was foremost in these early onslaughts: it saw

Polo at Jerome Park

James Gordon Bennett on the white pony, center. Painting by H. C. Bispham, 1877. Courtesy of the Piping Rock Club.

A Corner of the Grand Stand

Discussing "pitchers" in the Princeton Inn Grill

"My big brother"

Going to the Game

The Social Side of Intercollegiate Baseball

Drawing by A. I. Keller. *Harper's Weekly,* 1896.

all the worst elements of American character reflected in the game. "The spirit of the American youth, as of the American man, is to win, to 'get there,' by fair means or foul," it declared caustically, "and the lack of moral scruple which pervades the business world meets with temptations equally irresistible in the miniature contests of the football field." [38] Although far more sympathetic, the special sports writer of *Harper's Weekly* was fully as outspoken against the rising tide of professionalism. It was prevalent among the eastern colleges, but even worse in other parts of the country. No one could have any conception, Caspar Whitney wrote in 1895, "of the rottenness of the whole structure through the middle and far West. Men are bought and sold like cattle to play this autumn on 'strictly amateur' elevens." [39]

The brutality of the game awoke even fiercer attacks. It was the day of flying wedges, tackle-back tandems, and other mass plays. And the injuries these tactics inevitably caused were supplemented by casualties arising from the frequent slugging and free-for-all fights which the referees were powerless to control. A fair-minded English observer was horrified at the roughness of the games. And his impressions of it were amply confirmed in a report he quoted from *The Nation* on the Harvard-Yale game of 1894. It declared that one-third of the original combatants had had to be carried off the field. "Brewer was so badly injured that he had to be taken off crying with mortification. Wright, captain of the Yale men, jumped on him with both knees, breaking his collar bone. Beard was next turned over to the doctors. Hallowell had his nose broken. Murphy was soon badly injured and taken off the field in a stretcher unconscious, with concussion of the brain. Butterworth, who is said merely to have lost an eye, soon followed...." [40]

The New York *World* expressed a growing conviction that reform was absolutely imperative "if ruffianism and brutality and sneaking cowardice are not to be bred into our youth as a part of their training." [41] Writing in *Harper's Weekly*, Theodore Roosevelt (apostle of the strenuous life) defended the game as best he could, but he also declared in forthright terms that roughness and professionalism must cease if football was to be preserved.[42]

This chorus of disapproval compelled action. Under the leadership of Walter Camp, efforts were made to bring about reforms. The block game was done away with through the adoption of the rule requiring surrender of the ball after the fourth down unless a gain of ten yards had been made; massed rushes were discouraged by providing for more open play; and referees were empowered to deal drastically with slugging or any unnecessary roughness. The attempt was made to prevent professionalism and enforce stricter rules of eligibility.[43] Nothing could be done to suppress the instinct to win by almost any means (that had become a part of football, and spectator interest already demanded a fierce and bitter struggle), but the game was saved from this threat of suppression for the further triumphs which awaited it in the twentieth century.

->>><<<-

THE SOCIAL WORLD as represented by the little coterie of the very wealthy who gave elaborate fancy-dress balls, had their boxes at the opera, and hunted or played polo at the new country clubs was insignificant in numbers. That larger group of the privileged who less ostentatiously supported the legitimate stage, had the leisure to enjoy such sports as tennis and golf, and made up the college-bred crowd at football games was considerably larger, but still it did not bulk very large in a total population which had grown by the 1890's to more than sixty-three millions. Nevertheless this world of society in the broader sense had a tremendous influence in the development of recreation, for it set the standards that the democracy tried to follow as best it could.

Social activities received immense publicity in the Gilded Age. The extravagant balls of New York and Chicago millionaires, the yacht-races and the polo matches, the coaching parade at

Newport, were written up with great gusto and vivid detail in the nation's press. All the world knew what was happening in these circles, and very often it wanted to go out and do likewise. The middle class was ambitious to take up every activity on which society had set the stamp of fashionable approval.

While this too often meant that a premium was placed on ostentation, it also encouraged the healthy growth of many forms of amusement. It can at least be said that society's sponsorship of the theatre and opera, of sports and outdoor activities, partly counteracted in its social effects the example it set in luxury and extravagance.

Chapter XV

MAIN STREET

THE SMALL TOWN WAS THE BACKBONE OF THE NATION IN THE closing decades of the past century. It was more typically American than the city. The people who lived and worked and played in its familiar environment largely made up the middle class which carried forward the traditions and ideals of democracy. The quarterly town dances of the Middle West were attended by banker and mill-hand, lawyer and grocery boy, their wives and their sweethearts. Every one gathered at the ball park of a Saturday afternoon to watch the local team in action and listened that evening to the amateur band concert in the public square. The town might have its "old whist crowd" and "young dancing crowd," as William Allen White wrote of Kansas in the 1890's, its "lodge crowd," its "church social crowd," and its "surprise party crowd,"[1] but they primarily represented people of common interests getting together. There was already a right and a wrong side of the railroad tracks, but social distinctions were not as rigid as they were to become in a later day.

This neighborliness made for a pleasant informality, but it also imposed its restraints. The Victorian era was passing, but the town clung to old ways. The fact that every one knew what every one else was doing enforced a certain conventionality which often made for dullness. There had been no expansion in recreation comparable to that in the city. Conservatism was implicit in the social order, and any departure—the introduction of the two-step at the Pastime Club's annual assembly, a production of *Sappho* at the opera house—led to a storm of criticism.

John Quincy Adams would have known just what to expect at

a small-town party in this period. It would not have differed greatly from an evening at Newburyport a century earlier. He would have known how to play most of the games, including I Love My Love with an A. He would often have found that forfeits still involved that "profanation of one of the most endearing expressions of love" which had once so disturbed him, and thoroughly approved a contemporary game book that suggested substitute forfeits to enable the players to avoid the "childish and absurd kissing of the one you love best." And the performance of the young lady of the house, with guitar accompaniment should there be no piano, might well have been as trying as he had found it in the 1780's.

The church still played a dominant rôle in setting the tone of social life. Its ban on drinking, for example, had the support of all the better elements in the town. Lodge night or the firemen's ball was sometimes a lively occasion, but even where the community was not thoroughly dry through local option, alcoholic drinks were seldom served at the parties of either the surprise-party crowd or the young dancing crowd. Nor did the old whist crowd play cards for money. Church-going folk in the 1890's— and that meant almost every one—did not countenance gambling in even its mildest forms. The Sabbath was generally observed. Whatever might be true of the city, it was not yet a day of recreation for the town.

→→»«←←

To MAKE UP for the restraints it imposed upon more worldly amusements, the church provided its own entertainments. Ladies' Aids, Christian Endeavors, and missionary societies engaged in lively competition over their sociables, fairs, and festivals. The Congregational ladies, the Methodist ladies, the Baptist ladies, were rivals in both good works and good times. The Sunday School picnic was a great occasion. The church had always been a center of social life since those distant colonial days when New England's farmers drove in to Sunday sermons and midweek lectures, gossiping at the horse-sheds after service, but it now recognized a social obligation in sponsoring community recreation.

At the church supper, which became so universal a feature on the small-town social calendar, the entertainment was mild and innocuous by urban standards. Lectures and talks, readings and poetic recitations by the more gifted members of the congregation, instrumental music and singing, occasionally tableaux or charades, made up the usual program. Sometimes lecture courses were definitely arranged to meet the competition of commercial entertainment. The First Church of Chelsea, Massachusetts, at one time advertised in the local paper "a people's course" of ten lectures for fifty cents, with popular speakers, readings, music, and stereopticon views.[2]

At the fairs, bazaars, and strawberry festivals, which had the further goal of raising money, there were usually grab-bags or fish-ponds, fortune-telling, and guessing games. Young men were invited to spend ten cents to see something they would hate, and then were shown a mitten. A cake would be sold piece by piece until some lucky purchaser found the ring that had been cooked with it. At five cents a cup one could draw lemonade out of a miniature well. The popularity of beauty contests (which had come down from colonial fairs) found expression in a vote for the prettiest girl at the festival, the blushing winner then being called upon to sell kisses. A daring innovation was a game in which young men bid for partners hidden behind a curtain raised just high enough to reveal their ankles.

In the attack that Dr. William Bayard Hale made upon the extent to which churches were entering the amusement field, he listed an exhibition of waxworks, a living-picture show, a performance of *The Mikado,* and a song recital in which the Peak sisters sang the ballad, "Do You Know the Mouth of Man?" One church staged the Blackbird Ballet, Sacred Female Minstrels, the performers appearing in burnt cork and bloomers.[3]

These more exciting ventures into the realm of vaudeville were admittedly exceptional. The typical church entertainment mirrored the spirit of an age in which the small town faithfully observed Victorian concepts of propriety. In the *Eighty Pleasant Evenings* issued by the United Society of Christian Endeavor, there was no suggestion of such sprightly entertainment. Take the popular Patriotic Social: "'Uncle Sam' or 'Columbia' in appropriate costume may receive the guests. Flags and bunting should decorate the walls, together with portraits of famous Americans, which may be made an occasion for a guessing contest. Have a 'post-office,' the letters consisting of extracts from patriotic speeches.... The following program has been rendered on one occasion:

> CHORUS. 'Star Spangled Banner.'
> RECITATION. 'Independence Bell.'
> SOLO. 'The Dying Soldier,' or 'The Soldier's Farewell.'
> RECITATION. 'Old Ironsides.'
> CHORUS. 'Red, White and Blue.'

A list of historic battles, with the generals commanding them should be prepared in advance.... These may be passed and matched to arrange partners for refreshments, which may consist of saltines, cheese, and phosphate of wild cherry." [4]

→≫≪←

THERE WERE other "jolly affairs" besides church suppers and Ladies' Aid sociables. Trolley parties, progressive tiddly-winks, taffy-pulls, and surprise parties were popular. "A pleasant surprise was held last night at the elegant residence of Oliver J.... in honor of the fortieth anniversary of the birth of Mrs. Ella...." reads the account of one such party in the 1890's as recorded in *Middletown*. "Every face was beaming with delight, and happiness flowed from heart to heart.... After dinner a season of song and prayer was had, after which the house was made to ring with music.... Mr. McC.... favored us with a song, 'A Thousand Years My Own Columbia!'" [5]

When cards were introduced, this generation usually played, in addition to whist, such games as euchre, five hundred, seven-up, progressive fifty-eight, or Sancho Pedro. And there were always parlor games and conundrums: Dumb Crambo, Fiz Buzz, Wall Street Brokers, the Feejee Islanders at Home, Princess Hugger Mugger, and Hot Cockles. These were in many instances simply new variations of old games, and such favorites as Authors, Twenty Questions, and Going to Jerusalem were still popular.[6] For over a century successive American editions of Hoyle had been setting the established rules of play.

Music not only played an important part in these evening entertainments but entered into the whole life of the town. In addition to local bands, there were many choral societies. Young people often went out of an evening to serenade one another, or gathered at the home of one of their number for "a sing." Every family that prided itself on respectability had a piano. "There is no country," a French writer reported, "where there are so many pianos and players on them." [7] In a few homes an odd contraption known as a talking-machine might be found (Edison had put it on the market about 1878), but with its tin-foil cylinder record, turned by a hand crank, it was still a rather disappointing instrument. Generally people who wanted music had to produce it themselves. Throaty tenors and quavering sopranos lustily sang the songs given popular currency by the minstrel show, the musical-comedy road company, and the circus. The barber-shop quartette was in its heyday; the young lady with a passable voice needed no other charms to be the success of the party.

The songs were sentimental, and old songs were the best songs. The Southern melodies introduced by the minstrels—"Old Black Joe," "Carry Me Back to Ole Virginny," "The Old Folks at Home" —were always favorites. At every party there was some one to sing such Scotch or Irish ballads as "John Anderson, My Jo," "Comin' Through the Rye," and "Annie Laurie." Then there were "Juanita," "Oh, My Darling Clementine," "Wait Till the

Clouds Roll By, Jennie," "In the Gloaming," and "Kiss But Never Tell"—

> A starry night for a ramble,
> In the flowery dell,
> Through the bush and bramble,
> Kiss, but never tell!
> Kiss, but never tell to any—
> Telling breaks the spell.

Sometimes the theme was the dangers of the wicked urban world:

> I've come to the great city
> To find a brother dear,
> And you wouldn't dare insult me, Sir,
> If Jack were only here.

"The Sidewalks of New York," "On the Banks of the Wabash," "Just Tell Them That You Saw Me," "O Promise Me," "The Bowery," "My Gal Is a High-Born Lady," were all of the 1890's. It was in this prolific decade that Charles K. Harris wrote "After the Ball":

> Many a heart is aching
> If you could read them all;
> Many the hopes that have vanished
> After the ball.

Reflecting prevailing standards of decorum was the pretty lament, "What Could the Poor Girl Do," which described the dilemma of the young lady endeavoring to keep her dress off the pavement on a rainy day:

> But what could the poor girl do?
> Boys, what could the poor girl do?
> She'd a pretty little shoe, and she liked to show it too,
> So I couldn't blame the girl, could you?

They were sung, these songs and many others, as they never had been before or have been since. Young and old joined in the chorus. Many were the parties that broke up to "Auld Lang Syne" or "Good Night, Ladies." [8]

Dancing was probably not as general as it had been in the late eighteenth century or as it was to become in the early decades of the twentieth. But various clubs and associations gave annual balls; businessmen and their wives attended dancing-classes which usually terminated in an assembly or German. The program of one dance held in Marion, New York, during this period included the following numbers: lancers (5), waltz (4), polka (3), military march (3), quadrille (2), York (2), Portland Fancy, Caledonia, and Virginia Reel. It opened with a grand march and closed with "Home Sweet Home." [9] In more worldly circles the two-step was coming into vogue. The music of John Philip Sousa, touring the country with his famous band, had introduced a more lively rhythm into dancing. "The Washington Post," so popular that in other countries it gave its name to the two-step, was everywhere played at the more fashionable dances.[10]

->>><<<-

LODGE NIGHT had become a nation-wide institution. Fraternal orders were nothing new. Freemasonry had crossed the Atlantic in colonial days and in the 1820's had been for a time a disturbing political issue. The Independent Order of Odd Fellows also dated from the middle of the eighteenth century, and among other organizations that were either offshoots of the Masons and Odd Fellows or had been newly formed somewhat in imitation of them were the Elks, the Knights of Pythias, and the Ancient Order of United Workmen. But after 1880 there was a phenomenal increase in the number and membership of these orders. No less than five hundred were founded before the close of the century, and the nation-wide enrolment suddenly leaped to over six millions, something like forty per cent of the male population over twenty-one.[11]

The country fairly bristled with temples, camps, clans, castles, conclaves, rulings, hives, and tents. Some of them were limited to workers in certain trades and occupations, others made up their membership from immigrant groups, and there were many Negro orders. To the older organizations were added the Ancient Arabic Order of Nobles of the Mystic Shrine, the Independent Order of Good Templars, the United Order of Druids, the Tribes of Ben Hur, the Independent Order of Gophers, the Prudent Patricians of Pompeii, the Mystic Workers of the World, the Modern Woodmen of America, the Concatenated Order of Hoo-Hoo.... Every town had one or more lodges, their membership embracing every element in its society. Initiation ceremonies, the induction of new members, carnivals, and other fraternal social functions became more and more important.[12]

Many men joined the orders for the sake of the sickness and death benefits they provided, which were the nominal purpose of their being formed; others took out membership because they felt it advisable for business or to make useful social contacts. But such prosaic reasons could not possibly explain the amazing stampede to become a Mason or an Odd Fellow, an Elk or a Gopher, in the last quarter of the nineteenth century. It was the urge to be accepted as one of the crowd—half a century earlier Alexis de Tocqueville had diagnosed America as a nation of joiners—and to be able to slip away for a time from one's humdrum daily routine into a mysterious world of pageantry and make-believe.

The elaborate ceremony and ritual of the lodge, with its secret grips and passwords; the colorful regalia of the officers; the grandiloquent titles and forms of address, provided such a striking contrast to workshop or factory, to the dull level of so much home life, that their appeal could hardly be withstood. There were so few other ways to forget the cares of trade or business—no movies or radio to create an even more fantastic land of never-never. Any one might find himself a Most Illustrious Grand Potentate, Supreme Kahalijah, or Most Worthy and Illustrious Imperial Prince on lodge night. In gorgeous robes of state, jeweled collars, imposing helmets or high-crowned fezzes; carrying the swords, lances, and axes that constituted the impressive symbols of their office, butchers and bakers and candlestick makers strutted for a brief hour before a worshiping audience of Knights and Nobles, Nomads and Rams—sometimes Daughters of Isis or Pythian Sisters—in all the magnificence of the borrowed plumes of mystic imagery. The lodges had become a national vice, a contemporary critic wrote in the *Atlantic Monthly;* a contributor to the *Century* found them the great American safety-valve.[13]

Many other organizations were witness to the national love for joining something. One foreign visitor, touring the country in 1892, was amazed at the number and variety of associations "founded simply to make it easier to procure some pleasure." [14] But most of them had at least originally a practical purpose. Militia companies still held annual musters, and though they may not have been as exciting occasions as the old colonial training days, the whole town would turn out to watch the drills and parades, listen to the band music, and help the militiamen celebrate. More colorful were the musters and carnivals staged by the local volunteer firemen. Sometimes companies from the neighboring towns of half a state would gather, resplendent in red shirts and shiny helmets, for fierce contests with the old hand-pumping engines. The company that sent a stream of water farthest won a championship as important as that of the local baseball league. There were also local posts of the G.A.R., workingmen's clubs, sports clubs, and businessmen's associations pointing the way to Rotary and Kiwanis. The town was honeycombed with such organizations, and everywhere the general pattern of their activities was much the same.

Women were not left out of this movement to organize. They had auxiliaries formed on the lines of the men's fraternal orders— Daughters of Rebekah, Pythian Sisters, Daughters of Isis; associations such as the Women's Relief Corp and Ladies' Aid; and a wide array of social clubs which multiplied in this period as

Knights Templar in Conclave at Chicago

Ball tendered the Grand Encampment by the local commanderies. *Frank Leslie's Illustrated Newspaper,* 1880.

A Chautauqua Tent
Courtesy of H. J. Thornton.

*The Lig
Side
Chauta*

Feichtl's tr
Tyrolese y
Courtesy o
Thorn

never before. There were Shakespeare and Beethoven Circles, Noon-Day Rest Clubs, Old Maids' Socials, and Ladies' High Jinks, to a total, before the century closed, which is only partially indicated by the twelve hundred associations formally banded together in the General Federation of Women's Clubs.[15]

"We have art clubs, book clubs, dramatic clubs, pottery clubs," a contemporary wrote. "We have sewing circles, philanthropic associations, scientific, literary, religious, athletic, musical and decorative art societies." [16] A visiting Frenchwoman declared that the absence of men would make her compatriots feel "as if they were eating bread without butter." [17] The American women appeared to get along very well under these distressing circumstances.

These clubs represented a conscious effort to fill the increasing leisure that the machine age was making available to the middle-class housewife. Her ordinary work was greatly cut down by factory manufacture of things formerly made in the home and by the introduction of innumerable labor-saving devices. "House-keeping is getting to be ready-made, as well as clothing," one magazine writer stated in 1887.[18] While the men generally had as long hours of work as they had had before, their wives found themselves with free afternoons which they could devote to outside activities. A zealous pursuit of culture, rather than pleasure, was the primary goal of the woman's club, but the lectures, reading of members' papers, and discussions over the tea-table fell within that vague territory where the boundaries between instruction and recreation can hardly be defined.

-»»)«((-

AN ENTIRELY different phase of recreational life centered about the local opera house. Here traveling lecturers, road companies, and variety shows periodically appeared to give the townspeople their one taste of urban entertainment. In quick succession they might welcome Russell H. Conway giving his famed talk on "Acres of Diamonds" (this popular version of the idea that there are riches in your own back yard was given over five thousand times); a Merry Maidens burlesque show; Robert Mantell in a repertoire of Shakespearean plays; an Uncle Tom's Cabin company; and a traveling combination presenting the latest Broadway hit.[19] Although the opera house might attempt to book "first class attractions only," it was in much the same position as the mid-century theatre. Its productions had to reach all members of the community. If serious drama and vaudeville acts were not combined in one performance, as they so often had been in the 1850's, popular demand caused them to alternate almost weekly.

The annual session of Chautauqua was for many a small town the grand climax of this entertainment. It was sometimes the sole occasion when outside talent mounted the platform to offer a glimpse of what was happening in the larger world. This institution—for "the Chautauquay" had a nation-wide scope—had developed out of a camp-meeting course for Sunday-School teachers started in 1874. As it grew to embrace the whole field of adult education, other Chautauquas were established throughout the country, the summer courses were supplemented by winter lecture series, and reading groups enrolled in the Literary and Scientific Circle. In the 1890's there were some seventy Chautauquas. When the twentieth century developed its far-flung system of chain organizations, totaling some ten thousand in 1919, the nation-wide audience slowly grew to an estimated forty million.[20]

Chautauqua was cultural and educational. Its lectures, however, were always supplemented by an entertainment program. When a meeting was held, especially in the small towns of the Middle West, it would be attended by hundreds of neighboring farmers as well as townspeople. They would camp on grounds made available near the auditorium or lecture tents, and for a solid week enjoy an astounding succession of learned and inspirational talks interlarded with the performances of xylophone orchestras, Swiss yodelers, jugglers and magicians, college-girl

Who's Who in Chautauqua 1920

First Day

AFTERNOON AND EVENING

The New York Glee Club

Great male quartet direct from remarkable record in eastern cities. Andres Merkel, 1st tenor, George D. Dewey, 2nd tenor, D. Ward Steady, baritone, and Wm. J. Williams, basso. Four soloists with a most unusual ensemble. Song harmony by music's most popular voice combination.

EVENING

Lou J. Beauchamp "Taking the Sunny Side"

Known as "The Laughing Philosopher." Said to cause more laughter in one evening than any man on the platform. Traveled more than million miles in old world and the new. Nineteen ocean trips. Investigated the lives of the underworld in America's large cities, writing for the press. His books selling through two and three editions, and translated into foreign tongues. Poems on child-life part of the folk lore of the land.

Second Day

AFTERNOON AND EVENING

Germanie Mallebay Company

Headed by Mlle. Mallebay, noted opera singer from Paris, and favorite pupil of M. Hettich of the National Conservatory. Three other artists, Miss Helen Carney, violinist, Clyde Matson, tenor, and Miss Margaret Everett, pianist and accompanist. One of the strongest musical companies on the American concert stage.

EVENING

Frank Dixon

"The Indispensable Tools of Democracy"

A keen, constructive satirist. One of America's foremost economists, who for 17 years has used platform to discuss country's vital problems. One of the "platform giants" of this day. Masterful, scholarly, brilliant, eloquent. Loaded with burning facts about democracy, which the people want to know.

Third Day

AFTERNOON

Elwood T. Bailey

"The Call of the Hour"

An intensely human speaker, painter of graphic word pictures, inspirer to action. Close student of men and situations. Was with the "Devil Dog" Marines at Chateau Thierry, wounded and gassed. Fired with the spirit of Americanism, brotherhood and loyalty.

EVENING

"The Elixir of Youth"

The great American farce comedy with New York cast. Concerning the discovery of a substance supposed to transform old age into youth. Funnier than "It Pays to Advertise." Concocted along the lines of the greatest number of laughs. The best joy-tonic, world-brightener, delicious, sparkling cure for the blues on the market. Runs over with witty lines, ludicrous situations, funny characters.

Fourth Day

AFTERNOON AND EVENING

Dixie Girls

Five talented, winsome girls from below the Mason-Dixon line. Dispensing the sunshine and charm of the Southland, telling stories of their own native southern folk, and singing and playing the rich, southern melodies.

EVENING

Robert Bowman

Through years of study, observation, and experience, achieved the front rank among character impersonators. By the aid of stage "make-up" brings the world's most interesting characters to the chautauqua platform. "The Immortal Lincoln," "Shylock," "Our Imported Americans," and "Characters From Life and Literature," some of the high spots in his humor and pathos

Fifth Day

AFTERNOON

"County Fair"

"Hey, Skinnay! C'm On Over!"

Lots, 'n lots, 'n lots of fun! Big County Fair n'everything! Balloon Man, Nigger Baby Rack, Prize Animals, Powerful Katrinka, Sword Swallower, Fire Eater and Fortune Teller,—'n whole shootin' match! Big parade and stunt program at chautauqua.

Prof. Abel Cantu *"Mexico Today"*

Of a fine, Mexican family, educated in the colleges of his own land, followed by graduate work in American universities. Professor at University of Wisconsin, and Crane Technical High School of Chicago. Authoritative information on Mexico at a time when the subject of intervention is momentous.

EVENING

Landis Singing Orchestra

Form a six-piece orchestra, rendering gems from the symphony classics and syncopated rag-time melodies, a male quartet harmonizing on the tunes the people love to hear, and a vocal, mixed sextet, presenting songologues and "pep" stunts new and novel.

Junior Chautauqua 9:00 a.m.   Afternoon Program 2:30 p.m.   Evening Program 8:00 p.m.

Program of a Typical Chautauqua Week

The Redpath-Vawter System offerings at Milford, Iowa, June 2-6, 1920.

259

octettes, boy whistlers, dramatic monologists, and jubilee singers. Sports also were encouraged in the afternoon, with croquet for the ladies and baseball for the men. "The Chautauqua," declared one of its early speakers, "is a cross between a camp meeting and a country fair." [21]

The atmosphere was highly moral. There could be no drinking or smoking; the Sabbath was rigidly observed. A Methodist Dining Tent or Christian Endeavor Ice Cream Tent supplied all refreshments. Since Chautauqua derived its chief support from the churches and ladies'-aid societies, the emphasis was always placed on the importance of "the Work." As entertainment inevitably proved the more potent drawing-card, it had to be given all possible protective coloring. The prominent singer "lectured" on "The Road to Mandalay"; the monologist "gave a reading" rather than a dramatic performance. When in Chautauqua's later days a musical company staged *Carmen,* it was considered necessary to have the heroine work in a dairy rather than in a cigarette factory. [22]

To meet the town's insistent demand for lectures, the Redpath Lyceum Bureau had for long been sending out the most prominent speakers—P. T. Barnum and Horace Greeley, Wendell Phillips and Henry Ward Beecher, Mark Twain, Bill Nye and James Whitcomb Riley, Presidents Grant, Hayes, Garfield, and McKinley, William Jennings Bryan, Viscount Bryce.... [23] Here was a strong force, one of the most powerful in operation in the 1890's, to broaden the lives of the middle class. Chautauqua was a typically American institution whose cultural and recreational aspects were subtly merged in an age which did not yet know the radio.

The more openly avowed entertainment presented at the opera house by the traveling road companies, which between 1880 and 1900 (as listed by the *New York Dramatic Mirror*) increased from some forty-odd to over five hundred, [24] included almost everything that was being staged at city theatres. Among the performances scheduled for the small towns of Indiana during a week in December, 1898, were a repertoire of Shakespearean plays, several comedies from Broadway, a minstrel show, a musical comedy, and several melodramas and variety shows. The Boston Lyric Opera Company was playing at the Grand Opera House in Marion, and the John L. Sullivan Company was booked at Kokomo. Logansport was enjoying Black Patti's Troubadours, and Elkhart a concert series by Sousa's Band. Eldon's Comedians (Pearl White was once a member of this troupe) staged at Dunkirk three plays representing the most distinctive phases of American life—*The Slums of Greater New York, A Country Sweetheart,* and *The Pride of the West.* At the Grand Opera House in Anderson there was a revival of an old favorite by Jerome's Black Crook Extravaganza Company.[25]

At any time during the 1890's at least one opera house somewhere in the land was producing *East Lynne;* Denman Thompson was always on the road in *The Old Homestead* (it earned over $3,000,000); *The Two Orphans* had already had more than twenty-five hundred performances; and Joseph Jefferson, beloved from coast to coast, had become a part of American folklore in the familiar rôle of Rip Van Winkle.

The smaller towns seldom had very much choice as to what they might see. "Doubtless there are worse theatrical companies than those which visit Kansas," William Allen White wrote in the *Atlantic Monthly* in 1897, "but no one has ever described them." [26] In many cases they were poorer than the old stock companies they had so completely displaced. There were not enough actors to meet the growing demand of the local opera houses, and performances were staged that would have embarrassed the hardy troupers who barn-stormed through the Mississippi Valley in pioneer days. Their quality would hardly have been known from the advance notices. Every variety or minstrel show promised something bigger and better than the town had ever seen. The poorest of the little comedy troupes, rushing through the countryside playing one-night stands at villages which were hardly on the map, were billed as star attractions straight from Broadway. One may follow their blazing path—the Bootle's Baby Company, the Hands Across the Sea Company, the She, Him, Her Comedy Company—as they arrived in town of a late afternoon, hopefully staged their show, and either that very night or early the next morning were again on their way. During a single fortnight in December, 1889, one such company played fourteen stands from Creston, Iowa, to Adrian, Michigan; another put on an equal number of performances in a string of eastern towns from Herkimer, New York, to Keene, New Hampshire.[27]

Marie Dressler has recalled in her reminiscences many of the trials and tribulations these second-rate companies experienced on the road. She played in cheap dramatic stock for a weekly wage of $6.00, and, as in an earlier day, the cast often did not know their lines and ad-libbing was a necessary art. At some of their brief stands the excitement of their arrival brought out welcoming crowds, and after the performance the stage door would be blocked with local admirers. In other places their reception would be so frigid that they were forced to play to almost empty houses and perhaps would be left completely stranded. A lingering prejudice against everything connected with the theatre led many a New England boarding-house to refuse to take in actors or actresses. They were ostracized in a world of railroad trains, second-rate rooming-houses, and cheap restaurants.[28]

The musical shows had the most difficult time. For all their glowing advertisements—"breezy dialogue, gorgeous stage settings, dazzling dancing, spirited repartee, superb music, opulent costumes"—their settings were often woefully inadequate, their costumes old and dingy, and their performances uninspired and shabby. It was a practice to recruit new members of the cast while on the road. Marie Dressler tells of the surprising church attendance of the producers, watching the choir for possible additions to their show's chorus.

The Tommers were still playing America's favorite drama in

village and hamlet. Their performances, heralded by street
parades, might be staged at either the local opera house or under
canvas. To make up for possible deficiencies in the cast, and also
for the lack of novelty in the old play, some announced two
Uncle Toms, two Simon Legrees, two Little Evas. One company
added prize-fighters to its cast, having the colored pugilist Peter
Jackson spar a few rounds with Joe Choynski.[29] These expedients
were not always successful. After one performance a Minnesota
newspaper reported laconically: "Thompson's Uncle Tom's
Cabin Company appeared at the opera house last night. The dogs
were poorly supported." [30]

Despite the large number of traveling combinations, there was
another basic disparity in the theatrical entertainments of town
and city entirely apart from the general standards of acting.
This was the relative infrequency of performances at the opera
house in contrast to the wide choice of nightly entertainment
offered by the dozen or more theatres and vaudeville houses in
the larger cities.[31] The small town had more in the way of
commercial amusements than ever before, but this was often
not more than a single show in the week. And sometimes the
opera house would be darkened for months on end.

->>)<<-

OUTDOOR ACTIVITIES represented a more important phase of
recreation. Lawns, back yards, and playing-fields, so totally
lacking in the cities, opened the way to active participation in
the new sports and games that had been introduced by society.
In every part of the United States, on Saturday afternoons and
holidays, even in some localities on Sundays, there were in
progress baseball matches among teams representing the town,
the factory, the athletic club, the high school, or the Y.M.C.A.
This sport was a distinctive feature of New England town life;
it had invaded the rural areas of the South. In the newspaper
of any western town one may read of local games. Under such
names as the Striped Stockings or Blue Belts, teams in Kansas

and Nebraska carried on a lively feud, the Wichita *Eagle* stating as early as 1873 that baseball (closely pressed by croquet, mumble peg, and keno) was the community's favorite game.[32]

A more interesting development was the rapidly growing popularity of the new indoor winter sport of basketball. It has a unique status. It is the only popular American game that is not derived from some sport whose origins may be clearly traced to England. Baseball and football have been thoroughly Americanized by a slow process of evolution, but basketball sprang fully developed on a world which little realized that in time it was to be played by more persons (including boys and girls) and draw larger numbers of spectators than any other sport—not excepting either professional baseball or intercollegiate football.

Working at the Y.M.C.A. training school in Springfield, Massachusetts, in 1891, James A. Naismith became impressed with the very real need for an indoor game that might serve during the winter as a practical substitute for baseball and football. It had to be active and highly competitive, but he hoped to avoid the roughness which in these years was bringing football into such disrepute. Basketball, the result of his thinking along these lines, caught on immediately. Its sponsorship by the Y.M.C.A. provided the means to carry it throughout the country—and also to other parts of the world. It was taken up almost at once by colleges, high schools, and athletic clubs.[33]

So popular did it become that, as in the case of both baseball and football, the problem of professionalism soon arose. Basketball was threatened by all the evils of gambling and fixed games.[34] Strict enforcement of amateur rules, however, was more feasible in the case of basketball than in that of either baseball or football because it was so widely played by Y.M.C.A. and school teams. It was for many years kept on a non-professional basis, and so popular did it prove among boys that a modified form of it was devised for girls.

Among other games, the craze for croquet, which at one time had been so universal that manufacturers could not keep up

with the demand for sets, had somewhat subsided. It remained
a popular pastime, but it no longer aroused the nation-wide
excitement of the days when for the first time it allowed boys
and girls, men and women, to enjoy an outdoor game together.
They were now doing too many things in company for croquet to
have its original novelty. Interest in tennis was increasing, but at
a relatively slow rate. It was still largely a sport for society. The
young college graduates of the 1890's were bringing it back with
them to the home town, but it had to overcome the prejudice
that it was rather a sissy game which no good baseball player
would be seen playing.

In *The Gentleman from Indiana* Booth Tarkington describes
the sensation caused by his hero when he appeared in tennis
flannels. Dim memories were stirred in the minds of the store-
keeping postmaster and his sister over "that there long-tennis
box we bought and put in the window, and the country people
thought it was a seining outfit."

"'It was a game, the catalogue said,' observed Miss Selina.
'Wasn't it?'"

"'It was a mighty pore investment,' the postman answered." [35]

The popularity of roller-skating had also waned. Boys and
girls still skated happily on the period's wooden sidewalks, but
adult skating no longer aroused the enthusiasm of the 1880's.
The cities had their rinks, but in many a provincial town they
had been converted to other uses. A. G. Spalding did not find it
necessary to issue another guide, and the sale of skates fell off
heavily.

The most universal sport of city, town, and country was bicycling. We have seen how it first won popular favor, but the
golden age of the wheel was the 1890's. The invention of the
safety bicycle, equipped with pneumatic tires, and of the drop-
frame for women riders had made it available for every one.
There were something like a million bicycles in the country in
1893, and soon production was running each year as high as
this nation-wide total.[36] Every sizable community had its club,

associated with the League of American Wheelmen, and rising armies of riders sallied forth every week-end. One commentator found cycling rapidly becoming "more popular than all other out-of-door recreations combined";[37] another declared it to be a final answer to those captious critics who "used to call us money-grubbers, and talk about our excessive lust for the almighty dollar." [38]

It met opposition in some quarters. Its effect on other activities and occupations was occasionally viewed with alarm. A writer in *The Forum* declared that the piano trade had been cut in half, and that of the livery-stable reduced to little more than a third, because of the competition of the bicycle. Even the barbers suffered because the young man took his girl out bicycling instead of to the theatre, and therefore did not need to get a shave! Bicycling led to wholesale violation of the Sabbath. The churches were empty while long lines of Sunday cyclists could be seen rolling down hill "to a place where there is no mud on the streets because of its high temperature." [39] And while bicycling for women was generally encouraged, the Women's Rescue League, in Washington, issued a fierce blast against it on both physical and moral grounds. It declared that within ten years all female cyclists would be invalids, and in the meantime the temptations of the road were daily swelling the army of outcast women.[40]

Nevertheless, cycling remained so popular that no question of the day agitated the monthly journals more seriously than bicycle fashions for women. What could be done about the amply-skirted? "Her windage is multiplied, and so is the exertion she needs to bring to bear on her riding," sadly lamented one handbook. "Added to that, her mind is continually on the strain that her skirt may be preserved in a position of seemliness." [41] *Godey's Lady's Book* as usual came to the rescue. It advocated a kilted skirt trimmed with fancy brandenburgs, jacket bodice and vest, cloth cap and leggings. Other arbiters of fashion favored divided skirts and top-boots; there were suggestions that even bloomers ("bifurcated garments extending from the waist to knee") might be worn without offense to female dignity and modesty. Victorian scruples were giving way before the demand for greater freedom in costume. Folded screens to protect the feet and ankles from view when mounting or riding were advertised in the *Scientific American,* but the lady cyclist seldom bothered with them.[42] "A few years ago," one writer commented, "no woman would dare venture on the street with a skirt that stopped above her ankles, and leggings that reached obviously to her knees. . . . [The bicycle] has given to all American womankind the liberty of dress for which the reformers have been sighing for generations."[43] It was a development, this recognition that women too had legs, of very real significance.

Bicycling was exercise and sport. It was the rediscovery of the outdoors. It was romance. What popular song of the 1890's is better remembered than "Daisy Bell":

> . . . you'll look sweet,
> Upon the seat
> Of a bicycle built for two.

Businessmen, housewives, working people, youths and maidens, all took to the wheel.

The League of American Wheelmen had its consuls everywhere to further the interests of cyclists. It gave the stamp of official approval to League hotels and promoted the good-roads movement. With mass production came lower prices and still further popularity. The bicycle had more than fulfilled its early promise. The countryside was transformed under its influence. The editor of *Scribner's* asked in 1896 whether anything had happened since the building of the first locomotive to affect so materially the human race. Four years later an expert of the Census Bureau declared that few articles ever used by man had created so great a revolution in social conditions.[44]

Other outdoor activities of the town might be cited. Among those who owned a carriage, or could afford to patronize the

Puck's Suggestion to His Religious Friends

Frederick B. Opper in *Pickings from Puck*, 1895.

local livery-stable, there was always a great deal of driving and informal trotting matches. Young men still found the buggy ride the most pleasant way of courting. Winter sleighing had lost none of its popularity, and skating always had its enthusiasts. There were many rod and gun clubs, which promoted competitive shoots with neighboring towns as well as hunting and fishing. Athletic clubs, drawing upon both business and working-class membership, occasionally held track and field events. But the outstanding form of outdoor recreation in the American town of the 1890's, for old and young, men and women, was bicycling.

-»>«<-

SMALL-TOWN STUFF! Skim through the pages of the local paper, in New England, the South or the Middle West, at any time during the 1890's, and there is the record of those amusements and entertainments which so largely served to give the American town its distinctive character. Simple and homely, far removed from the glittering gaiety of the urban world, they provided the recreation half a century ago of a people still living in what we nostalgically call the horse-and-buggy era.

In one town during a single week at the close of the century, new officers were formally installed at the Golden Cross Commandery, a Baptist ladies' social was attended by over one hundred ("supper was served and all sorts of games and music helped to make the time pass quickly away"), and the dramatic club staged a performance for the benefit of the Grange. The Fessenden Helping Hand Society gave a supper and social, and a traveling company presented *My Friend from India* at the Opera House. Twelve pairs took part in the Tuesday-night whist tournament, forty couples attended the adult dancing-class, and a number of informal sleighing parties were held. There were announced, among other coming events, a banquet of the Wheel Club, at which the governor of the state and other prominent guests were to be treated to a number of "entertaining musical features"; an old-fashioned dance sponsored by the Oasis Encampment, I.O.O.F.; a lecture under the auspices of the Daughters of the American Revolution; a basketball game with a neighboring town; and a fair and festival of the Universalist Society, dancing from 8:30 to 1 with Leitsinger's orchestra.[45]

Here it all is—a life which had not greatly changed in the course of years and was to continue almost uninterrupted in some parts of the country for another half-century. But the inventions of a new age were soon to alter greatly the underlying pattern, not as much as in the city or in the more completely rural areas, but enough to broaden the town's horizons and to introduce into its simple life a growing sophistication.

Chapter XVI

FARM AND COUNTRYSIDE

CONTEMPORARY OBSERVERS WERE GENERALLY WELL AGREED UPON the lack of amusements in the rural America of the late nineteenth century. Life on the farm varied greatly in different parts of the country, but it could not anywhere offer social or recreational opportunities comparable to those of town or city. A majority of all Americans—two out of every three people still lived in the country despite the increasing exodus to the cities—found themselves largely cut off from both the commercial amusements and the organized sports which had so transformed urban recreation.

In the Middle West, more typical of the agrarian scene than any other part of the country, the isolation which the telephone, the automobile, and the radio have now broken down was especially marked. The farmer was often miles from his nearest neighbor, and even farther away from the town. The incessant labor, the almost unbroken daily routine, and the dreary loneliness of the great farms being opened up on the prairies have been described again and again in sectional novel and autobiography. The lack of amusements played no small part in stirring up the discontent that led to agricultural revolt and to the Populist movement of the 1890's.

An even gloomier picture is sometimes drawn of rural life in the East with its equally back-breaking work and often less favorable rewards. "As for amusements and recreation," Nathaniel Egleston wrote in 1878, "there is next to none, at least that is worthy of the name. It has been said of the New England villagers particularly that their only recreations are their funeral

271

occasions.... Life drags on with an almost unvarying round of toil. There is little to break up its monotony." [1]

There were several factors in the latter half of the century that tended to make the country scene duller than it had ever been before. "In town one can find the swimming school, the gymnasium, the dancing master, the shooting gallery, opera, theatre, and panorama," Emerson had written in mid-century. "In the country he can find solitude and reading, manly labor, cheap living, and his old shoes; moors for game, hills for geology, and groves for devotion." [2] But not all the world was a philosopher, and in the busy life of the 1890's the greater opportunities of the city were increasingly responsible for that drift to metropolis which had its obverse side in rural stagnation.

"Sloven farms alternate with vast areas of territory half forest, half pasturage," wrote one observant traveler in the New England of 1892; "farm buildings, partly in ruins, testify at once to the former prosperity of agricultural industry and to its present collapse." Another traveler was struck by the number of abandoned churches, dismantled academies, and moribund lodges in sections where the greater number of inhabitants had fled "to the manufacturing villages, to the great cities, to the West." [3] The mute evidence of this depopulation still remains in stone fences running through land now completely overgrown, in the crumbling foundations of houses long since deserted. Every present-day resident of New England encounters them in cross-country rambles.

Under such circumstances the young people were oppressed by the growing contrast between their drab lives and the freedom of the city. With the loss of the more active and enterprising members of the community, the stay-at-homes often lacked the initiative to make the most of such opportunities as still remained to them. They resigned themselves to the limited and circumscribed life that the depleted countryside represented. Moreover, where conditions were more favorable, as has already been pointed out, there was no longer the diversity of occupations on the farm which had given so much variety to rural life in earlier days. Without any shortening of the long hours of labor from sunrise to sunset, the farmer had to work on day after day at the same routine jobs—planting and reaping, the endless weeding of crops, and a multitude of daily chores. Nor could he count, as he had in the past, upon many interruptions to this steady grind. There were still hunting and fishing. The latter remained in some parts of the country a favorite diversion, but the good old days were passing for hunting. The farmer had his rifle or shotgun, possibly a pack of dogs, but the growing scarcity of game, and restrictions on such shooting as still remained, greatly limited the scope of what had once been such universal sport.

Something was lost—and for settlers in the Middle West it was within their own experience—as the years rolled on and agriculture became more a demanding business and less a way of life. Fencing the land and driving out the game marked progress. So did improved farm machinery—reapers, self-binding harvesters, engines for threshing grain. They also spelled the end of an era.

Hamlin Garland has described how the West was affected by these changes. "Buoyant, vital, confident," he wrote of his family and their neighbors in their early years of pioneering, "these sons of the border bent to their work of breaking sod and building fences quite in the spirit of sportsmen. ... With them reaping was a game, husking corn a test of endurance and skill, threshing a 'bee'. ... My father's laughing descriptions of the barn-raisings, harvestings and rail-splittings of the valley filled my mind with vivid pictures of manly deeds." But as time went on there were fewer and fewer of "the changing works" which had served to bring people together. "We held no more quilting bees or barn raisings," he wrote of conditions a decade later. "Women visited less often. ... The work on the farms was never ending, and all teams were in constant use during week days. The young people got together on one excuse or another, but their elders met only at public meetings." [4]

For all this evidence of the dreariness of rural life, a picture of the country painted in such somber colors would nevertheless not be wholly true. There were compensations for the passing of old sports and pastimes. The farmer still had an independence and freedom which the clerk and factory worker lacked; he still had the active outdoor life from which the city dweller was cut off. He was never wholly deprived of normal recreation. His opportunities were rare, spaced at long intervals, but for that very reason they meant a great deal to him. He enjoyed them with an intensity which his city cousin, often surfeited with a wealth of easy entertainment, seldom experienced. Frequency alone is no test for the value of amusements. The isolated farm family may well have got a greater sum of enjoyment from its occasional social gathering or informal entertainment than urbanites could possibly derive from all their passive commercialized amusements. The Grange meeting, a social at the local school-house, a country dance, the Fourth of July picnic, the annual county fair, the coming of the circus—here were events looked forward to for months with eager anticipation, and remembered for months afterwards with continuing pleasure.

→>×<<-

THE GRANGE had been founded, as the Patrons of Husbandry, in 1867. A secret fraternal order, somewhat along the lines of the Odd Fellows, its organizers hoped it could do something to aid the farmers through various coöperative activities. Its growth was amazing—as might be expected in a period which was to witness such a rapid multiplication of fraternal orders, women's clubs, and other comparable organizations. Within six years there were fifteen thousand local granges scattered throughout the country, most numerous in the Middle West and South, with a total membership of a million and a half. The Patrons of Husbandry were fully embarked on a broad program of agricultural education, coöperative buying and selling, and political activity.[5]

The Grange meeting, whatever the business under discussion,

A New England Straw Ride

Frank Leslie's Illustrated Newspaper, 1869.

A Grange Meeting in an Illinois School-House

Frank Leslie's Illustrated Newspaper, 1874.

The Day We Celebrate

Engraving by John C. McRae after a painting by F. A. Chapman, 1875.
Courtesy of the New York Historical Society.

soon became the principal social gathering of the farm community. And this aspect of it was emphasized by the presence of women, admitted from the first into full membership. They gave the Grange a vitality it could not otherwise have had. There were sometimes other farm organizations that promoted rural recreation. In Iowa an Anti-Horse Thief Association, having largely succeeded in its goal of affording protection for its members' live stock, concerned itself with the lighter side of life.[6] But the Grange was the social leader. It undertook to organize lectures and concerts, held young people's debates and spelling-bees, promoted singing-schools, and arranged evenings of general entertainment.

The latter were usually held at the school-house; it was the community center. The bleak little building might be bare and unadorned, but swinging oil lamps and the cheerful warmth of its large wood stove quickly transformed it into an attractive meeting-place. The wooden benches or desk seats, initialed by the jack-knives of countless school-boys, were rearranged for the audience, and the chairman or speaker took the proud eminence of the teacher's platform. The farm families would drive in from miles around, often bringing box suppers, and spend a long evening over the simplest amusements. The program would be very much like that of the social in a small town. Recitations were popular, and the singing of old songs. There were sometimes charades or tableaux. If there were refreshments, they were usually coffee and doughnuts.

Sometimes at these entertainments at the school-house, and once in a while at some farmer's house, there would be a country dance. They were family affairs, young and old taking part. Chairs and tables would be pushed back, the fiddler get out his precious instrument, and the company wait expectantly for the shouted signal "Ba-al-ance all" or "A-al-all dance."

"It was a joy to watch him 'start the set,'" reads a description of one country fiddler (also the butcher and horse-doctor) called upon for a farm-house dance. "With a fiddle under his chin he took his seat in a big chair on the kitchen table in order to command the floor. 'Farm on, farm on!' he called disgustedly. 'Lively now!' and then, when all the couples were in position, with one mighty No. 14 boot uplifted, with one bow laid to the strings he snarled, 'Already—*Gelang!*' and with a thundering crash his foot came down. 'Honors *tew* your pardners—right and left Four!' And the dance was on!" [7]

The tunes were "Money Musk," "Fisher's Hornpipe," "The Irish Washerwoman," "Cut the Pigeon Wing," "Turkey in the Straw"—all the old favorites. One very popular was the minstrel song "Old Dan Tucker." It gave rise to a dance, sometimes known as the "tag dance," which foreshadowed a modern custom. At one point the fiddler, or whoever was calling the numbers, shouted out, "Go in Tucker!" and any odd man was allowed to cut in on a temporarily unattached girl. [8]

In the New England village, a barn or shed was sometimes made over into a dance-hall where the young people from near-by farms met on Saturday nights. A description of one such hall relates that it was an unpainted one-story building with open sides—a kerosene lamp swinging from the ceiling, a few American flags as decorations, and a large sign, "Please do not spit on the floor." Buckboards and buggies were hitched to the horse-rails while the dance was on. [9]

There was a prejudice against playing the fiddle or other instrumental music in some rural communities that still did not go so far as to disapprove dancing. This did not greatly matter: the young people sang the dance tunes, and the party went on no less gaily. "Weevily Wheat" was one of the favorite singing tunes:

> Oh, Charley, he's a fine young man,
> Oh, Charley, he's a dandy;
> Charley is a fine young man,
> For he buys the girls some candy.

Another even more gay and lilting air was "Buffalo Gals," sung with many local variations:

Oh, Buffalo gals, ain't you comin' out tonight,
Ain't you comin' out to-night, ain't you comin' out to-night;
Oh, Buffalo gals, ain't you comin' out to-night,
To dance by the light of the moon?

Reminiscing of life in rural Indiana about 1880, Chase S.
Osborn described such dances in a letter incorporated by Mark
Sullivan in *Our Times*. "The violin (fiddle) was taboo, but we
sang songs and danced to them and hugged the girls until they
would often grunt as we swung them clean off the floor or
ground, in the barn or house or on the green:

Higher up the cherry trees the sweeter grows the cherry,
The more ye hug and kiss the gals the sooner they will marry.

And 'Billy Boy'—'She's a young thing and cannot leave her
mother!' It was the time of Captain Jinks of the Horse Marines,
and 'Down in a Coal Mine'.... And ''Round and 'Round the
Mulberry Bush.'" [10]

In the more thickly settled and prosperous areas the simplicity of these evening entertainments and country dances was
already a thing of the past by the end of the century. Here
recreation on the farm followed more nearly that of the town,
and might be closely associated with it. But for a great part of
the Middle West those twin phenomena, lack of opportunity and
narrow religious views, had the restraining influence so often
observed in earlier days. They upheld a prejudice against any
departures from old customs which was intensified for the older
generation by what they heard of urban amusements.

More exciting and colorful than the school-house socials was
the annual Grange picnic. It did not bring together only friends
and neighbors. From a radius of perhaps a hundred miles, as in
earlier pioneer days, the farmers and their families gathered at
the grove that had been selected for the meeting. A few of the
more prosperous might drive in spring-board buggies, but farm
wagons were far more common. Two families would double up,
making a "bowery wagon" out of their wagon-box by means of

a few planks, and hitch up four-horse or six-horse teams. Members of the different lodges formed in line as they drew near the grove, carrying gay banners on which the women had emblazoned the lodge mottoes. "Some of the columns had bands," reads a contemporary description, "and came preceded by far faint streams of music, with marshals in red sashes galloping to and fro in fine assumption of military command." [11]

There were invariably speeches. If the picnic was held on the Fourth of July, the fervid political oratory that the West loved so much might hold the audience of farmers and their wives for hours. Basket lunches of cold fried chicken—a Grange picnic involved wholesale slaughter in the hen-roosts of the community —were next on the program. The band played, the men talked politics, and the women gossiped. There were often sports in the afternoon, and this was the nearest approach to the old rural pastimes of colonial days: races of all kinds, wrestling matches, and that most popular of rural diversions, pitching horseshoes. There was usually a baseball game. "Nothing more picturesque, more delightful, more helpful," Hamlin Garland has recalled, "has ever arisen out of American rural life. Each of these assemblies was a most grateful relief from the sordid loneliness of the farm." [12]

Sometimes the Fourth of July was celebrated by a gathering in the nearest town—however distant it might be. On July 1, 1890, the local paper of one small Illinois town printed its entire issue in red ink to draw the farmers' attention to the attractions it was planning for the Fourth. In response to such a glowing appeal, they came into town in greater numbers than on any previous holiday. A parade headed by a military band started the festivities, and this was followed by the usual patriotic address and an afternoon of sports. The townspeople had set up refreshment stands where the farmers supplemented their basket lunches. In the evening the firemen gave a ball at the city hall. [13]

The Fourth was always a tremendous day for men and women who day after day, week after week, seldom saw even their nearest neighbors. If they went to town, its life and movement, however small the place might actually be, held them enthralled. The games and sports were incidental. The crowd, the incessant activity of a large number of people, provided the real fun of the day at every Grange picnic or holiday celebration.

-»>«<-

THE ANNUAL state or county fair had its reason for being in the familiar exhibits of cows and pigs and chickens; pumpkins, corn, and tomatoes; jellies, pies, and fancywork. Farmers and their wives competed eagerly for the prized blue ribbons. But as time went on, the side-shows gradually overshadowed the main tent. "The people," sighed Josh Billings, "hanker fur pure agrikultural hosstrots." [14]

From colonial days America had enjoyed market fairs, and whether in New England or in the South, horse-races, prize contests, and the exhibitions of traveling showmen had been one of their distinctive features. When Elkanah Watson introduced the modern country fair early in the nineteenth century, he intended something quite different. The Berkshire Agricultural Society was concerned with crop rotation, use of fertilizer, careful seed selection, and intelligent animal-breeding. Its annual meetings were to teach a lesson the farmers could understand. The experiment was successful and quickly copied. In the period immediately following the Civil War there were over twelve hundred state, district, county, and township agricultural societies, and the greater number of them held annual fairs with an attendance from a few hundred to as many as ten thousand farmers.[15]

From the very first, plowing contests and speed trials had been necessary to show the advantages of careful breeding, and it was not long before the horse-race and the trotting match assumed an importance not entirely warranted on scientific grounds. Heavy milk-producers, mammoth sows, and prize pumpkins drew their crowds, but special stands had to be built at the track to hold the throngs that flocked to the harness races. We have seen what was happening in mid-century when even onetime Puritan New England produced crowds of thirty thousand for the trotting matches of the Boston Agricultural Club. After the Civil War the thousand-odd agricultural societies all had their races. A very reasonable economic motive furthered this development: the trotting matches drew so many people that they virtually supported the whole fair. Large purses consequently were put up to draw horses from all over the country and thereby attract still greater crowds. The fastest trotters, and a new professional class of drivers, made the rounds every fall. In the 1870's Goldsmith and American Maid were the bright stars of the Grand Trotting Circuit, and a few years later the famous Maud S lowered the mile record to 2:08¾ minutes. Adoption of the bicycle sulky and improvements in the tracks soon afterwards made the two-minute mile an almost everyday occurrence.[16]

Other commercial amusements now appeared. At first they were not officially permitted, but traveling showmen naturally took advantage of the crowds attracted by the fair. "On the outside of the grounds," stated the report of an Ohio fair in 1858, "there were any number *of outside shows;* learned pigs, fat women, snakes, monkeys, all jumbling together in Biblical confusion, while lager beer saloons and melon stands supplied those in quest of such delicacies." [17] It became obvious that if these amusements were to become associated with the fair, they might as well be within the grounds as without them, making their contribution to the running expenses of the often hard-pressed management.

"The same horse trots, ball-games, bicycle races, livestock exhibits, and trials of draught horses," a contemporary wrote of a New England fair in the 1890's, "the same side-shows, fakirs, freaks and uproarious fun that always go on such occasions." [18] Prizes were given for female equestrianism as well as for hooked rugs and samplers, for velocipedestrianism as well as for superior Guernseys. In 1888 a Rhode Island fair advertised "a grand tournament of bicyclers, a balloon ascension...polo games, steeple chasing, football match, and racing by wheelbarrows, greased poles, sacks and horses." [19]

On the day of the fair the town would be crowded, the grounds densely packed with medicine shows and itinerant peddlers adding to the confusion and excitement. Hamlin Garland has described the tremendous impression made upon him as a small boy by one of these fakirs. He was a tall, lean man with long black hair, wearing a large white hat, and had as his assistants a little fat man and a sad-eyed girl with a guitar. Dr. Lightner's spiel on his magic oil entranced the boy, but the girl was romance incarnate. As they sang

> O Mary had a little lamb,
> Its fleece was black as jet,

"her voice, a childish soprano, mingled with the robust baritone of the doctor and the shouting tenor of the fat man, like a thread of silver in a skein of brass." [20]

After the Chicago World's Fair one exhibition could be counted upon as certainly as a prize sow or a trotting race. "The lady on my right, who I now interduce," the barker might be heard announcing at every fair throughout the country, "is the world-famed Little Egypt." At other tents on hundreds of midways were dancing-girls, lady boxers, baby shows, and graphic reproductions of the Streets of Cairo—a camel, a donkey, and a few ragged Chicago Arabs. [21] There were always freak exhibitions —the three-legged calf and two-headed chicken; candy booths and soft-drink stalls; shooting-galleries and merry-go-rounds. Where the fair was not big enough to support professional trotting races, farmers drove or rode their own horses. A popular feature was the boys' race—a mad, helter-skelter run on ponies or plow-horses.

Again the farmers would bring their basket lunches of cold chicken and stay the entire day, not spending very much but seeing everything. And again what they enjoyed most were the crowds which gave them a fleeting taste of town life.

->>)(((-

WE LEFT the circus in the 1850's with Barnum touring the country with his Grand Colossal Museum and Menagerie. It had greatly expanded since those days; it reached its highest peak in the last quarter of the century. At least forty large shows were on tour, and many more smaller ones. They played cities, towns, and hamlets, pitching the big top wherever they could hope to draw a crowd. Popular everywhere, the circus meant for the farmer the one taste of theatrical entertainment that he might ever have a chance to enjoy. The circus had a glamour about it which nothing else in rural life could equal.

Barnum's name was still one to conjure with in the circus world. Historians point out that it was really William C. Coup who was the prime mover in establishing the Greatest Show on Earth and that James A. Bailey was the real circus king of the 1890's.[22] But it was Barnum's reputation that packed the main tent. Joining forces with Coup in 1871, he had brought together, with an immense fanfare of ballyhoo, the largest collection of wild animals, curiosities, acrobats, equestrian performers, and clowns ever assembled. There were giraffes from Africa and cannibals from the Fiji Islands; Admiral Dot (successor to General Tom Thumb) and Esau the Bearded Boy; more elephants than ever before; and, wonder of wonders, a hippopotamus—"blood-sweating Behemoth of Holy Writ." The big top was the largest tent area the world had ever known; it covered two rings, and then three rings. The entire company, animals and all, toured by rail in sixty-one special cars.[23]

With its accommodations for ten thousand and then twenty thousand people, this circus naturally played only the larger towns. But the farmers somehow got there. The railroads ran special half-rate excursion trains, and they camped out on the circus grounds. It was more than the event of a year; it seemed

The Country Fair

Proof before letters of a lithograph by Currier and Ives after a drawing by
Louis Maurer, 1866. Courtesy of Harry T. Peters.

Jumbo

Lithographed one-sheet poster, about 1882. Courtesy of Strobridge Lithographing Company.

the event of a lifetime. Each season this popular show (it was already firing a man from the mouth of a cannon as one of its great attractions) took in anywhere from one to two million dollars in gross receipts.[24]

When his circus was almost totally destroyed by fire in 1880, Barnum made another merger. Barnum and Bailey's was born— a still bigger and better Greatest Show on Earth. The fire from whose ashes he had, Phœnix-like, arisen in still greater splendor, the irrepressible showman announced, had only served to illuminate his path of duty as the American people's champion amusement provider. Nor had he forgotten his earlier technique. Barnum still lectured on temperance; he still took care to enlist church support. He was not in this circus business merely to make money, he told the country. It was his mission to "provide clean, moral and healthful recreation for the public." [25]

A sensation almost comparable to those he had achieved in mid-century with his famous mermaid, General Tom Thumb, and Jenny Lind awaited him. His purchase of Jumbo, the world's largest elephant, from the Royal Zoölogical Gardens in London created an international furor in 1882 which brought the Greatest Show on Earth an avalanche of publicity. Englishmen were incensed. They were afraid that the loss of Jumbo would be followed by that of Shakespeare's grave or the Tower of London. All possible means were exhausted to prevent the famous pachyderm's departure. Barnum was adamant. Whatever the difficulty or expense, Jumbo was to be brought to America.

On the fateful day set for his removal, the elephant lay down in the middle of a London street. All England cheered. Barnum's agent cabled frantically for instructions. "Let him lie there a week if he wants to," came the quick answer. "It's the best advertisement in the world." When he finally reached this country, Jumbo led a torch-light parade for the opening of the circus at Madison Square Garden, cheered by half a million people.[26] Little wonder that villagers and farmers would travel miles to see him whenever they had an opportunity.

Barnum and Bailey's had many rivals. The Ringling brothers had developed their Classic and Comic Concert Company into one of the world's great circuses; and the Sells Brothers Circus and Menagerie, merging with Hadj Tahara's Wild Moorish Caravan, boasted four rings and fifty-one animal cages. Then there were Forepaugh's Circus and Menagerie, Van Amburgh's, the Irwin Brothers, Whitney's, Williams'....[27]

The smaller road shows copied these larger circuses in every particular, their grandiloquent advertisements making equally fantastic claims. Miles Orton's New York and New Orleans Circus, Menagerie and Wild West Show toured through Illinois making one-night stands, admission twenty-five cents. With fifty star performers and the marvelous racing elephant Lizzie, its posters shouted from a hundred barns that it was the greatest circus of all time.[28] In Nevada, Montgomery Queen's Caravan, Circus and Menagerie advertised its "grand centralization of genius, concentration of merit, monopoly of equestrian stars, avalanche of attractions." [29]

In rural areas and small towns the program for circus day followed time-honored custom.[30] While the small boys were out at dawn to herald its arrival, watching the elephants cautiously test the bridges wherever the approaching road crossed a stream, the farmers gathered from all directions. Every kind of vehicle would be drafted into use. There were great farm wagons, drawn perhaps by a pair of powerful Clydesdales, the grown-up members of the family sitting stiffly in their best Sunday clothes and the excited children sprawled in the straw behind them; buckboards and carry-alls; phaetons and mule teams. Occasionally the son of some rich farmer might whirl by in a side-bar buggy, his best girl beside him, scattering clouds of dust over the plodding wagons. Even before the morning parade officially opened the day's festivities, the town's quiet streets would be a whirl of excitement. Strolling mountebanks, candy and popcorn sellers, vendors of palm-leaf fans and toy balloons, three-card monte men and sly practitioners of the shell game. Everywhere rang out the shrill cry of the vendors of pink lemonade—"Lemo! Lemo! Ice-cole lemo! Five cents, a nickel, a half-a-dime, the twentieth-potofadollah! Lemo! Ice-cole lemo!"

The parade would burst upon these excited crowds with a blast of trumpets which rattled all the windows on Main Street. The band sweated and puffed at their instruments as they rode proudly by in the great circus wagon, with its twenty- or even forty-horse hitch; chariots driven by helmeted Romans rumbled along behind wagon cages between whose bars could be seen chattering monkeys, restless tigers; the equestrienne performers, dazzling visions of grace and loveliness, haughtily sat their plumed and prancing steeds; the elephants swung ponderously by with swaying howdahs; and the clown made his uproarious progress through the crowd in a flashing donkey cart. Above the crack of whips and rumble of wheels floated the steam calliope's shrill rendition of the popular circus songs: [31]

> My love has joined the circus,
> And I don't know what to do,
> She feeds the elephants crackers and cheese,
> And she plays with the kangaroo.

or the rollicking tune of Van Amburg:

> He sticks his head in the lion's mouth,
> And holds it there awhile,
> And when he takes it out again
> He greets you with a smile.

Even more familiar to later generations was another popular song to which the circus gave a nation-wide currency:

> He flew through the air with the greatest of ease,
> The daring young man on the flying trapeze;
> His movements so graceful, all girls he could please
> And my love he purloined away.

A midsummer sun might beat down relentlessly on all this tin-seled display. The dust might swirl in great clouds about the ponderous elephants and rumbling chariots. But none could resist the excited cry, *The circus is coming!*

After basket lunches, the crowd flowed to the flagged and tented circus lot, and soon the familiar call, "Right this way to the big show!" was packing them in close rows on the wooden benches which rose around the sides of the tent. The bands blared forth the signal for the grand opening march. Here it all was—the ring-master cracking his whip, the cry of the popcorn vendors, the white-faced clowns, the dizzying swings on the flying trapeze, the living statues, the pervasive smell of sawdust. . . .

Even after the equestrians had given their last exhibition of trick riding, the tumblers and tight-rope dancers performed their final stunts, the day was not quite over for those whose endurance could stand further excitement. There were still the freaks and wild animals, and the raucous voice of the announcer declared that the minstrel show, all the songs and dances of the big city, was just about to start. As the tired holiday-makers finally jogged homewards in the gathering dusk, the children asleep on the straw-covered floor, it is not surprising that they often felt they had had entertainment enough to last them for many months.

"Each year one came along from the east," Hamlin Garland has written in vivid portrayal of what the circus meant not only for the small boy but for the entire family on the western prairie, "trailing clouds of glorified dust and filling our minds with the color of romance. . . . It brought to our ears the latest band pieces and taught us the popular songs. It furnished us with jokes. It relieved our dullness. It gave us something to talk about." [32]

Chapter XVII

THE GROWTH OF THE MOVIES

THREE EVENTS TOOK PLACE IN THE YEAR 1895 WHICH PASSED almost unnoticed in a world absorbed in affairs of more immediate importance: Two young men who had been following the path pointed out by Edison's invention of the kinetoscope succeeded in throwing moving pictures on a screen at a public performance at the Cotton States Exposition in Atlanta. This country's first motor-vehicle race was held at Chicago on Thanksgiving Day, two of the six entries (gasoline-driven) actually completing the fifty-two-mile course in a little over ten and one-half hours. And, on the other side of the Atlantic, Guglielmo Marconi publicly demonstrated (although the continuing skepticism of the Italian Government sent him the next year to England) the practicality of wireless telegraphy.[1]

The generation of the 1890's could not possibly realize the significance of these milestones in the progress of human invention. But here were dimly foreshadowed developments which were to have the broadest social consequences and affect recreation in this country more profoundly than anything that had ever happened before. There was to be a great expansion in sports and other diversions in the twentieth century, but within a strikingly short time from these inconspicuous events of 1895, moving pictures, the pleasure use of automobiles, and the radio were to become by every criterion the principal amusements of the great majority of American people.

Their popularity was a result of the changing social and economic scene. A century earlier it would not have been possible. The increased leisure and generally higher standard of living of the laboring masses in the first instance made possible the rôle of these diversions in modern life, but equally important was the new attitude toward amusement which was itself born of this economic progress. By the opening of the twentieth century, recreation had become fully accepted in this country as a natural right of people of whatever social status. The concept of democracy coalesced with the profitable economy of mass production to flood the land with moving pictures, automobiles, and radios. It was not by accident that in no other country of the world did any comparable diffusion of these new means of amusement take place among the masses of the people.

It was symbolic of the new industrial era that the machine should at last be harnessed to the amusements of an age which it dominated so completely in every other way. Its more general effect during the nineteenth century had been at one and the same time to intensify the people's need for recreation and to deprive them of many of their traditional diversions. It had crowded them into close-packed manufacturing towns and cities where they had little opportunity for play. The machine was gradually increasing leisure time but failing to provide the means to enjoy it. Now the movies supplied the equivalent of the theatre for every one, no matter how poor; the automobile opened up entirely new recreational possibilities, transforming the whole social scene; and the radio brought entertainment directly into the homes of millions of families the length and breadth of the land.

→≫≪←

THE FIRST moving pictures were the peep-shows which flourished during the 1890's in the phonograph parlors, billiard-rooms, and penny arcades of the cities. One put a nickel in the slot of one of the new-fangled contraptions Mr. Edison had invented, looked eagerly through the peep-hole, and saw the magic of tiny figures actually moving against a dim and blurred background. It might be a man sneezing, a girl dancing, or a baby taking its bath.

It was a brief entertainment, but its novelty brought a steady stream of nickels to the pockets of enterprising showmen.[2]

When the experiments of several inventors (having produced the kinetoscope, Edison largely lost interest in what he regarded as a rather childish toy) succeeded in transferring these moving pictures to a screen where a large number of people could see them at the same time, they were taken up by the variety houses. In New York, Koster and Bial's Music Hall gave the first Broadway exhibition of what was now called the "Vitascope" on April 23, 1896,[3] and soon vaudeville houses everywhere were showing "living pictures" as a star feature on their programs. But these jerky, flickering screen productions had little more than their novelty to commend them to audiences at the better-class vaudeville theatres. They could not offer effective competition to acrobatic dances and popular song hits, and only the cheaper variety houses thought it worth while to keep on showing them. The development of the vitascope was largely left to the proprietors of the penny arcades. They set up their machines in tiny darkened back rooms ("pick-pockets could go through you as easy as an eel through water") and drew in the masses of city workers, often immigrants, who could not afford any better entertainment.[4]

It was not until about 1905 that an important forward step was taken in the presentation of moving pictures. A few years earlier an Electric Theatre had been established in Los Angeles solely for their exhibition, but it was the Nickelodeon that John P. Harris opened in McKeesport, Pennsylvania, just a decade after movies had first been shown that started their real boom.[5] There were perhaps a few hundred little arcade theatres scattered throughout the country in 1905, but the nickelodeons soon numbered as many thousands. Three hundred had opened within the year in New York alone, a writer on the "Nickel Madness" stated in *Harper's Weekly* in 1907. Two hundred thousand people—men, women, and children—were flocking daily 'through the gaudy, blatant entrances." [6]

"In almost every case," reads a contemporary description of these theatres, "a long, narrow room, formerly used for more legitimate purposes, has been made over into what is popularly known as a 'nickelodeon.' At the rear a stage is raised. Across it is swung a white curtain. Before the curtain is placed a piano, which does service for an orchestra. Packed into the room as closely as they can be placed are chairs for the spectators, who number from one hundred to four hundred and fifty. Directly above the entrance is placed the moving picture machine, which flashes its lights and shadows upon the white curtain dropped in front of the stage. Many of the machines are operated by means of a tank filled with gasoline or some similarly inflammable material." [7]

The same story was being repeated not only in every other city in the country but in every town and hamlet. A vast public that had never attended the theatre, even the popular "ten, twent, thirt" melodrama, found in these brief twenty-minute shows entertainment which had never before been within its reach. [8]

The moving picture inevitably had caustic critics. The nickelodeons were called silly and time-wasting, if not actually pernicious. Anthony Comstock found in the darkened theatres intimations of immorality which sent anticipatory shivers up his puritanic spine. Censorship was threatened from the day when social reformers in Atlantic City protested the "hypogastric rhythm" of a peep-show depiction of Dolorita's Passion Dance. "The authorities request us not to show the Houchi Kouchi," the exhibitioner sadly wrote the producer, "so please cancel order for new Dolorita...." [9] When May Irwin and John C. Rice indulged in the kinetoscope's first kiss, an osculation so sensational that it caused nation-wide excitement, the editor of a small Chicago magazine, *The Chap Book*, was especially disapproving. "In a recent play called The Widow Jones," he wrote, "you may remember a famous kiss, which Miss May Irwin bestowed on a certain John C. Rice, and *vice versa*. Neither par-

ticipant is physically attractive, and the spectacle of their prolonged pasturing on each other's lips was hard to bear. When
only life size it was pronounced beastly. But that was nothing
to the present sight. Magnified to Gargantuan proportions and
repeated three times over it is absolutely disgusting.... Such
things call for police interference. Our cities from time to time
have spasms of morality, when they arrest people for displaying
lithographs of ballet-girls; yet they permit, night after night, a
performance which is definitely more degrading. The immorality
of living pictures and bronze statues is nothing to this. The
Irwin kiss is no more than a lyric of the Stock Yards." [10]

A decade later the *Chicago Tribune* attacked the nickelodeons:
"There is no voice raised to defend the majority of five cent
theatres, because they cannot be defended. They are hopelessly
bad." [11] On Christmas Eve of 1908, Mayor McClellan of New
York revoked five hundred and fifty licenses because of objections by the city's pastors. He announced that future permits
would be granted only on agreement not to operate on Sundays
and not to show pictures tending "to degrade the morals of the
community." [12] More generally, however, these show-places were
treated with casual condescension, dismissed as "a harmless diversion of the poor" and "an innocent amusement and a rather
wholesome delirium." [13] Even among the people in the new
motion-picture industry, there were few who could foresee its
expansion or recognize the importance it was so rapidly assuming in the lives of the multitude.

Popular amusements had more generally evolved from diversions that were originally available only to the wealthy. The
theatre in America had at first been primarily class entertainment, the democratic audiences in the large playhouses of the
mid-nineteenth century, as we have seen, offering a marked
contrast to the more exclusive theatre patronage of the colonial
period. And from this gradually democratized theatre had developed the even more popular minstrel shows, burlesque, and
vaudeville. But the first appeal of moving pictures was to the

masses rather than the classes. They were cheap and popular from the very beginning. The support which in time enabled them to raise their standard of entertainment came entirely from their nickel-paying customers.

Their early development along such unashamedly popular lines was not by any means inevitable. It was in part due to the class of people who happened to take them over. The outstanding figures were Jewish garment-workers or fur-traders who bought up the penny arcades, and then the nickelodeons, to merchandise films as they would any other commodity. And their dependence on a mass market led to their continuing to place emphasis on quantity rather than quality. They were not troubled by an artistic conscience, not concerned with culture, in promoting this profitable business. But at the same time what might superficially be dismissed as merely shrewd commercial tactics represented an approach to the development of this new amusement which would not have been possible in any other country. It reflected a democratic concept of the general availability of popular entertainment which was thoroughly American.

In European countries, notably in France, where pioneer work in moving pictures was even more advanced than it was in the United States, developments followed a quite different course. There was nothing comparable to the nickelodeon madness of this country. Instead of appealing to a mass market, the movies essayed the rôle of sophisticated entertainment. Although foreign producers at first made far better films, their efforts to maintain artistic standards lost them the world-wide market that American producers eventually built up because their pictures had a universal appeal.[14] American movies would never have become the outstanding popular entertainment they are to-day had foreign precedents been followed, while a limited market would also have prevented their attaining the technical perfection which has been Hollywood's real contribution to this world-wide amusement. Moving pictures became a leading feature of Amer-

In the Days of the Kinetoscope

A kinetoscope, phonograph, and graphophone arcade in San Francisco. Courtesy of the Museum of Modern Art Film Library.

The Last Word in Picture Theatres

Radio City Music Hall, New York, capacity 6,200, offering elaborate ballet and other stage presentations with feature films. Courtesy of Radio City Music Hall.

Incunabula of the Movies

Left, top to bottom: scene from *Cripple Creek Barroom,* an Edison film of 1898 (Museum of Modern Art Film Library); a daring scene for the nickelodeons about 1910 (Culver Service); William S. Hart in an early Western (Culver Service); Mary Pickford and Owen Moore in *Caprice,* 1913 (Museum of Modern Art Film Library).

Right, top to bottom: scene from a nickelodeon gangster film (Culver Service); Mabel Normand and Mack Sennett in *Barney Oldfield's Race for a Life,* 1913 (Museum of Modern Art Film Library); Charlie Chaplin in *Between Showers,* 1915 (Culver Service); Pearl White in *The Perils of Pauline,* 1914 (Museum of Modern Art Film Library).

ican recreation because they represented the culmination of the democratizing influences in the field of urban entertainment which had been at work for over a century.

→»≫«←

THE FILMS shown in the nickelodeon era represented a striking advance over the flickering glimpses of dancing-girls first seen in the penny-arcade kinetoscopes. Practical difficulties were hard to surmount, and the demand for pictures often outstripped the ability of the producers to supply them, but there was steady progress. With the filming of longer pictures at the close of the century, incidents (man sneezing) had first been elaborated into themes (employer flirting with stenographer). Further stretching out of the picture, to perhaps a thousand feet, then gave a universal popularity to endless variations on the chase motive. The cowboy hero began to track down the western bad man, the city sleuth to pursue bank-robbers and hold-up men. In the simplest form of the latter, the thief was chased through streets crowded with city traffic until the inevitable collision with the fat woman, who felled him with her umbrella and sat on him until the police arrived. The only rival of the chase in this early period was comic relief. The more subtle uses of a banana-peel, of a precariously balanced can of paint, of a small boy with a hose, were developed. The custard pie made its triumphant appearance.

Prize-fights and religious pictures were also introduced, two outstanding events in motion-picture progress being the filming of the Corbett-Fitzsimmons fight and the Oberammergau Passion Play. News and travel had a wide appeal. For Hale's Tours of the World the theatre was darkened, a whistle blew to announce the start of the trip, the seats began to sway through an ingenious system of rockers and brakes, and on the screen were flashed scenes of some distant part of the world taken from the rear platform of a speeding train.[15]

In 1903 an entirely new departure was made with the filming

of *The Great Train Robbery*. Here for the first time the moving picture attempted to tell a story, and the success of the experiment was so immediate that every producer turned to one-reel thrillers.[16] The old melodramas, especially those of the West, were taken over from the popular theatres. By 1908 one magazine writer reported that the magnates of the nickelodeon world were paying from $15 to $30 for a good plot—"or even more"— while these pioneer movie actors received "all the way from $15 to $40 a week." [17]

In most of these films the modern movie-goer would still have felt something strangely lacking. There was no romance, no sex interest. It took time to adapt the formula of boy-meets-girl to the screen, but when the motion pictures had once discovered love, they clung to it. All its various themes were developed— love as sentiment and love as biological instinct. If the latter aspect of the phenomenon was to await fuller exploitation in the 1920's, romance had won a place for itself before the nickelodeon days were over. Among the pictures being shown in Chicago in 1907 were *Cupid's Barometer*, *A Seaside Flirtation*, *Beware, My Husband*, *The Unwritten Law*, *The Course of True Love*, *The Bigamist*, and *The Gaieties of Divorce*.[18]

Culture was not entirely ignored in the popularity of humor, thrills, and love. Shakespeare appeared on the silver screen. The patrons of one theatre were advised that, without any change in the five-cents admission charge, they could see "the superb, soul stirring, heart rending tragedy, Romeo and Juliet ... accompanied with an intensely tragic lecture by Dr. Lamberger."

There were performances of other plays borrowed from the repertory of the legitimate stage. "The actor has a formidable rival in the kinetoscope," the *Theatre Magazine* ominously declared. "The time is not far distant when we will see along Broadway theatrical agencies specially catering to the manufacturers of moving-picture films. The Edison Company of New York, the Vitagraph Company of America, the Pathé Frères of Paris, each has its regular stock company. These men and women, employed at good salaries, are richly costumed for the dramas, and the ballets and fairy tales and the dances that are performed before the machine. It is remarkable to what extent the moving-picture manufacturer will go in his anxiety and determination to obtain realism in his kinetoscopic play." [19]

For some time there were no stars. The best known of the early screen actresses, Florence Lawrence, was known only as "The Biograph Girl." [20] Not until the closing years of the nickelodeon era did feature films and feature players emblazon their starry path across the cinematic skies. "Little Mary" films, first shown in 1909, pointed the way. They enshrined Miss Pickford as America's sweetheart and fastened the star system upon moving pictures even more firmly than it had been fastened on the theatre. Every audience, Keokuk or New York, was convulsed by the antics of John Bunny; held its breath in fear and trembling as Broncho Billy or Tom Mix thundered across the western prairies; and became easy prey (at least its male components) to the charms of Norma Talmadge and the Gish sisters. [21] The nickelodeons had become something far more than "flimsy amusement for the mob." With ten thousand theatres playing to a nation-wide audience of ten million weekly, they were doing a greater volume of business by 1910 than all the legitimate theatres, variety halls, dime museums, lecture bureaus, concert-halls, circuses, and street carnivals combined. [22]

->>><<<-

BEFORE the World War broke out, the movies had graduated from the nickelodeon era. Improvements in the technique of photography, transforming the flickering films of the early days into clear-cut, distinct pictures; the introduction of multireel films; the appearance of a host of new movie stars, and more comfortable, higher-priced theatres were together responsible for a new day in which the triumphs of Biograph, Essanay, and the Mutual Film Corporation were quickly dimmed. One of the new films pointing the way was a comedy Mack Sennett produced in 1914 with Marie Dressler in the star rôle—*Tillie's Punctured Romance*. With Miss Dressler played a newcomer to the movies, an odd little man with baggy pants, a queer waddling walk, and a mustache which was soon to make his face better known than that of any one else in the world.[23] Charlie Chaplin was an immediate success. Within two years, so rapidly were the movies now forging ahead, in no small part owing to his own inimitable appeal, he had accepted a fabulous offer of $670,000 for a year's work.[24]

Incidental to a circulation war among Chicago newspapers, the year 1914 also saw an epidemic of moving-picture serials which proved an almost greater drawing-card than anything else so far produced. A nation-wide public breathlessly followed weekly instalments, released both in the newspapers and on the screen, portraying the thrilling adventures of Dolly of the Dailies, Lucile Love, or the mysterious Florence Gray. The most famous of all the serials was *The Perils of Pauline* with Pearl White:

> Poor Pauline, I pity poor Pauline
> First they tie her to a tree
> Then they send her out to sea. . . .[25]

Still more important, marking as definite an advance in moving-picture production as had *The Great Train Robbery*, was D. W. Griffith's filming of *The Birth of a Nation*. This masterpiece of the screen (it was to earn in all more than $18,000,000) proved once and for all that American movies could provide entertainment which neither the fashionable nor the sophisticated need scorn. It was a great movie because it broke away from the limitations of the stage and utilized the improved motion-picture technique as had no previous film. Its distant scenes, switchbacks, fade-outs, and close-ups revealed what imagination and intelligent direction could really do with this new medium. The producers were able to give a first-run showing of their picture at a legitimate theatre, at legitimate-theatre prices. Here was a far departure from nickelodeon days. While the moving picture remained primarily entertainment for the urban masses, it now began to reach as well a more exacting public.[26]

The growth of more luxurious and higher-priced theatres, slowly driving out the nickelodeons, both reflected and furthered this development. It was again in 1914 that Roxy (Samuel L. Rothafel) took over managership of the Strand, on New York's Broadway, immediately setting a pace in showmanship with which theatres in other cities vainly tried to keep up. The day of large, elaborate, and expensively furnished moving-picture palaces, with pipe-organs and full orchestras replacing the jangling pianos of an earlier day, had arrived. Even neighborhood houses and small-town movies felt this stimulating influence. Comfortable surroundings and higher admission prices were found to pay.

Only six years earlier, Roxy had been showing films in the unused dance-hall above the saloon in Forest City, Pennsylvania, where he worked as a barkeep, but the Strand did not represent the end of the path he was following in raising the exhibition of movies to a fine art. A decade later another theatre, to be known as Roxy's, awed even New York with its gaudy magnificence. This Cathedral of Motion Pictures could seat six thousand people in its immense auditorium, and squads of uniformed ushers kept in order another two thousand waiting in the lobbies for seats. With its musical numbers and ballet-dancing, the show built about the feature picture almost rivaled grand opera.[27]

->>><<<-

THE POST-WAR YEARS found the movies scaling new heights with a reckless abandon which reflected the pervasive extravagance of that astounding era. Production costs sky-rocketed. A million, two million, three million, four million dollars (*The Birth of a Nation* had cost $100,000) were spent on a single spectacle.[28] The ballyhoo about the stars, drawing their ten and twenty thousand dollars a week (Mary Pickford had signed a million-dollar contract for two years' work as early as 1917 [29]), would have filled even P. T. Barnum with envy. And the public loved them all the more because they were such expensive luxuries. A society in which money played such an important rôle basked in their reflected glory.

Hollywood had now become the great center of the movie industry. Jesse Lasky had pointed the way when in 1911 he had rented a barn, for $200 a week, to film *The Squaw Man* against a western background.[30] The advantages of California sunshine had soon become apparent, and the rising film magnates flocked to the Coast. Here the movie world worked and played, and a host of inspired press-agents described with intoxicating detail the fabulous life that centered about the studios. Movie magazines carried to every fan the fascinating, and sometimes lurid, details of Hollywood's loves, marriages, and divorces. The stars became the arbiters of fashions, the molders of popular folkways. Shopgirls and stenographers worshiped dutifully at the Hollywood shrine. Rudolph Valentino, the passionate sheik of millions of love-lorn maidens' dreams, died in 1926. The crowd that waited to see him lying in state at a New York funeral parlor stretched for eleven blocks.[31]

There were good films produced in these years. Mary Pickford was still America's sweetheart; Constance Talmadge and Lillian Gish remained favorites; Gloria Swanson worked havoc with her glamorous charm; Charlie Chaplin continued to lead the field as the screen's greatest actor bar none; Harold Lloyd was winning tremendous popularity for his comedy rôles; the muscular Douglas Fairbanks was a certain drawing-card. . . . The pictures of these stars could usually be counted on, and there were many others—entertainment which from every point of view marked a progressive advance in the standards of the motion-picture industry. But for every *Ben Hur, Covered Wagon, Thief of Bagdad, Gold Rush, Ten Commandments, Beau Geste,* or *Three Musketeers,* scores of movies exploited the more blatant features of the post-war letdown in manners and morals. Their titles were expressive. In one small city there were being simultaneously shown during a single week, to quote the findings of the Lynds' survey in *Middletown,* four such alluring pictures as *The Daring Years, Sinners in Silk, Women Who Give,* and *The Price She Paid.* On another occasion the movie-goers of this same town could choose from among *Rouged Lips, The Queen of Sin,* and *Name the Man—A Story of Betrayed Womanhood.*

"Brilliant men, beautiful jazz babies, champagne baths, midnight revels, petting parties in the purple dawn," advertised the producer of *Alimony,* "all ending in one terrific, smashing climax that makes you gasp." The features of *Flaming Youth* were graphically described: "neckers, petters, white kisses, red kisses, pleasure-mad daughters, sensation-craving mothers, by an author who didn't dare sign his name; the truth, bold, naked, sensational." [32] The cinematic bite was never as bad as its bark (after all, *The Admirable Crichton* was billed as *Male and Female*), but it went deep enough to disturb the guardians of public morals.

This was particularly true in considering the possible effect upon children, who, according to the Payne Fund investigation, made up a third of the nation-wide movie audience. Reformers could not close their eyes to advertisements that invited the youth of the land to learn through the movies "what love really means, its exquisite torture, its overwhelming raptures. . . ." Surveys which showed that the love theme led all others, followed closely by crime and sex; that the heroes of the films, if not "great lovers," were usually gangsters and criminals, led to serious agitation for official censorship that might be more effective than such agencies as the National Board of Review. [33]

When threats from these quarters were added to a storm of disapproval aroused by the revelation of a number of scandals at Hollywood, the motion-picture industry in some trepidation summoned to the rescue Will H. Hays, a politician high in the councils of the Republican party. As czar of the Motion Picture Producers and Exhibitors of America, he issued his ultimatum: "We must have toward the mind of a child, toward that clean and virgin thing, that unmarked slate—we must have toward that the same sense of responsibility, the same care about the impressions made upon it, that the best teacher or the best clergyman, the most inspired teacher of youth would have." At the same time the public was assured that the movies were actually performing a tremendous service for art, education, and international good-will. Despite a little temporary overemphasis on jazz babies and red-hot kisses, Mr. Hays declared that the industry still held Service as its Supreme Purpose.[34]

The producers began to exercise some restraint in their pictures under these circumstances, but it did not go so far as to threaten the box-office appeal of their offerings. The clean-up campaign was successful in averting the threat of further censorship: only six states (Pennsylvania, Ohio, Kansas, Maryland, New York, and Virginia) took legislative action. It somewhat restored the prestige of the industry. Nevertheless sex dramas and ultrasophisticated comedies continued to be turned out in profusion, and there was still a marked emphasis on portrayals of the supposed fast life of high society. Even the news reel did not entirely escape post-war influences, with its inevitable picture of bathing beauties in one-piece suits.

There was no question that the public liked these pictures. Ever greater crowds nightly packed the country's twenty thousand picture houses, from Roxy's to the cheapest second-run village hall.[35] Men and women from every walk of life, but especially those in the working class, found here the vicarious excitement, the thrills, the heart interest, that for a time enabled them to escape the troubles and disappointments of their own lives. The man working all day on the assembly-line in an automobile factory, the tired homeworker leaving the children with a neighbor for her weekly night at the pictures, did not want their entertainment on any higher plane:

> Please don't uplift me when I go
> To see a moving picture show.

"The movie is the art of the millions of American citizens," an English writer in the *Adelphi* discovered, "who are picturesquely called Hicks—the mighty stream of standardized humanity that flows through Main Street.... The cinema is, through and through, a democratic art; the only one." Nor would this commentator have had it otherwise. The attempt to educate the public to higher standards of taste except through the movies' natural evolution in response to a gradually maturing public sentiment was pious humbug. Europe had failed to realize the possibilities of the moving picture and was hiding behind that "singularly putrescent hypocrisy that masquerades as 'artistic culture.'" [36]

-»»»«««-

So THE MOTION PICTURE in the 1920's. But still further triumphs awaited this popular amusement which had so marvelously evolved from the vitascope of only three short decades earlier. In 1928 Warner Brothers released a new film—Al Jolson in *The Jazz Singer*.[37] Science had brought together sight and sound: here was the talkie. There had been several prior talking pictures, but the great success of *The Jazz Singer* marked the turning-point. Within a year their conquest of the silent film was complete. Sound effects were hurriedly inserted in such films as could not be made over, vocal numbers were added when possible, and all-dialogue pictures produced as quickly as the necessary equipment could be obtained. As theatres throughout the country were wired for sound, the talkies whipped up popular appetite for the movies as never before. The industry's annual receipts rose between 1927 and 1929 to the tremendous total of a billion dollars, and weekly attendance jumped to an estimated 110,000,000—the equivalent of four-fifths of the entire population going to a show once a week throughout the entire year.

The depression brought about a drastic decline in these figures as forced economies curtailed all private spending. For a time theatre managers had to watch steadily dwindling audiences, and the industry was almost overwhelmed by its wildly extravagant superstructure of fabulous salaries and expensive production costs. In a frantic attempt to attract greater patronage, the bars were let down on the sex-drama type of picture, double features were inaugurated, and many houses resorted to bank nights and money games—screeno, lucky numbers, and bingo. These enticing lures, combined with partial recovery from the depression, finally succeeded in reversing the downward trend in admissions. In 1935 weekly attendance at the eighteen thousand theatres that had weathered the storm was estimated at 77,000,000, two years later it had risen to 88,000,000, and by the close of the decade it was again approaching the 100,000,000 mark.[38]

The revolution wrought by sound had given rise to a new galaxy of stars and introduced new types of pictures. Many of the familiar figures of the movie world continued in the talkies their success in silent films; a few staged remarkable come-backs after a period of eclipse while they adapted themselves to an unfamiliar technique. Actors and actresses of the legitimate stage, who had often scorned the pantomime of the silent film, made their hopeful way to California in droves, and a good many of them remained. Singers and dancers, for whom the talkies represented an entirely new opportunity, were suddenly in great demand. In a whirl of expanding energy, Hollywood exploited all the means at its disposal to reach the still broader market for popular entertainment now opening up.

The diversity of pictures that sound made possible was the most characteristic feature of the movies in the 1930's. They were filling the democratic rôle that the theatre itself had played a century earlier, and nightly programs often showed a startling resemblance to those of the popular playhouses of that earlier day. As well as straight theatre, the movies offered a modern equivalent for the equestrian melodramas, elaborate burlesques, and variety shows which had once had such wide appeal. At first-run houses there might be seen in quick succession a classical play filmed with all the artistry the producers now commanded, an extravagant girl-and-music show, a detective thriller, a blood-and-thunder western melodrama, a sophisticated comedy, and a slap-stick farce. A single show, again like those of mid-century, invariably included one of these main features; one or more specialities, which might well be a singing or dancing act (the news reel was an innovation for which the theatre had had no parallel); and a comedy short, which took the place of the nineteenth-century afterpiece.

The feature films derived from plays of the legitimate stage ranged from *Camille* to *Petticoat Fever,* from *Pygmalion* to *Idiot's Delight.* Historical romances were elaborately produced: *Disraeli* was a favorite picture one year, and in another *Cimarron,* a story of Oklahoma pioneering. *Gone With the Wind* was a sensation at the close of 1939. Well-known classics were adapted to the screen, with such notable successes as *Captains Courageous* and *David Copperfield.* New possibilities opened up with animated cartoons. The "Silly Symphonies" had a great success, and one of the most popular pictures in 1937-38 was the cartoon fairy-tale (photographed in color) of *Snow White and the Seven Dwarfs.*

The reigning stars during the thirties also revealed how diverse moving-picture entertainment had become. Micky Mouse rivaled Greta Garbo, and the Dionne quintuplets competed with Clark Gable. Lawrence Tibbett and Zazu Pitts, Will Rogers and Jean Harlow, Adolphe Menjou and Shirley Temple, Bette Davis and James Cagney, Mickey Rooney and Vivien Leigh, each had an enthusiastic following.

⊢⟫⟩⟨⟨⊣

THE MOVIES' SUCCESS in reaching such a broad public had long since had a most far-reaching effect on other forms of entertainment. From nickelodeon days they had been gradually drawing off the patrons of the popular melodrama, the devotees of variety and burlesque. They now dominated more completely than ever the whole field of commercial amusement. The people's theatres were either closed or made over into movie palaces, variety shows were so reduced in number that the old two-a-day vaudeville circuit was completely disrupted, and the doors of the local opera houses (unless they too were wired for sound) were everywhere boarded up. The triumph of the movies over the popular theatre was complete.

The legitimate stage which was primarily centered in New York—the theatre of classical drama, sophisticated comedy, problem play, and also musical revue—remained a vital force. It was perhaps more important in some ways than in the nineteenth century. If vaudeville had left it free—or forced it—to go its own way without considering entertainment that would appeal to the urban workers, it was now more than ever the arbiter of its own fashions. It could encourage playwrights—Eugene O'Neill was the country's leading dramatist—who really had something to say. It could present plays dealing with social problems, and musical comedy that deftly satirized the current scene. The 1930's saw a revival of stock companies, especially summer stock; other cities followed the lead of New York with its Theatre Guild and Group Theatre; the International Ladies Garment Workers' Union staged a musical skit which played on Broadway and toured the country; and the Federal Theatre Project became for a time an active force in the theatrical world. Under such stimulating influences there also sprang up a mushroom growth of community theatres with some five hundred thousand amateurs playing before an estimated annual audience of fifteen million.[39]

There were impressive signs here of a striking revival of popular interest in a theatre which was both very much alive and socially conscious. But it was still true that the audience it reached, even when the stock companies and community theatres were taken into account, remained a relatively limited one. In numbers it could not in any way compare with the millions who were *daily* streaming past moving-picture box-offices in every city, town, and village in the land.

Among other forms of amusement that felt the devastating

effect of the movies' competition were the circus and the country fair. The farmer who could drive to town every week and see a motion picture no longer looked forward to circus and fair with the eager anticipation of the day when they represented his one taste of urban entertainment. He often stayed away altogether. The traveling carnival and the amusement park also found themselves overshadowed, while such simple small-town diversions as lodge night, the Grange meeting, and the church social, although by no means extinguished, could hardly match the new entertainment's strident appeal. The movies had become a national habit from which no element in the population was wholly free. Their effect on social life—the home, family relationships, children—was incalculable.

The concern always felt over their influence was naturally heightened by these developments. Their emphasis on the extravagance and artificialities of high society, to say nothing of crime and sex, was believed in many quarters to be thoroughly unhealthy for the body politic. With the letdown in standards during the depression period, public opinion again began to demand some reform, and the protests of such organizations as the Legion of Decency finally convinced the moguls of Hollywood that they would have to put their house in order or have it done for them. Galvanized into action, the Hays organization undertook to coöperate with the reform agencies and established a Production Code which it was prepared to enforce throughout the industry.

This code set up certain standards governing the portrayal of crime, love-making, exposure of the human body, and profanity. There were to be no more scenes of seduction—"the treatment of bedrooms must be governed by good taste." More specifically, as revealed in the correspondence of the code's administrator, film characters were not to kiss savagely, get too drunk, lie around in their underwear, or use such words as "louse" and "floozy." One producer was advised to delete "the business of spraying perfume behind the ears," and another was told to cut out a character's stepping on a cockroach, on the ground "that such action is always offensive to motion picture patrons." Robin Hood was not allowed in the film of that name to kick the sheriff in the stomach; in *Dead End* there was a ban upon "the action of Spit actually expectorating." [40]

Some two per cent of the film output escaped this self-imposed censorship and was bootlegged on "the sex circuit," but otherwise there was a marked improvement after 1934. Too strict control, many critics protested. They found the movies so completely at the mercy of every pressure group in the country that they did not dare call their soul their own. They were compelled to tone down every suggestion of reality. Professor Sawyer Falk caustically declared that he "would rather take a chance on sullying the great American public rather than stultifying it." [41]

-->>><<<--

ENTIRELY apart from questions of morals or good taste, the movies had always been geared to the lowest common denominator of intelligence in the hope of reaching as broad a public as possible. With somewhere between six hundred and eight hundred films being produced annually, by far the greater number relied on the old time-worn formulas—boy meets girl, the Cinderella theme, romance set against an exotic background, the chase, and familiar comedy situations. Producers could not afford to echo the note of dissent with the social scene which was such a striking characteristic of the 1930's, or to deal realistically with any of the problems growing out of the New Deal. There were signs of a less conservative attitude (*They Won't Forget, I Am a Fugitive from a Chain Gang,* and occasionally *The March of Time*) at the very close of the decade, but the movies in general steered a safe course. How far the films were being used as propaganda was another point sometimes raised. Charles and Mary Beard asked some pertinent questions in *America in Midpassage* as to the rôle the movies played in promoting war sentiment through their big navy and aviation films.[42]

Their influence on our civilization could not be ignored. But over against the fears of those who felt it wholly pernicious could be set increasing evidence that there were more "good" films than ever before. Many pictures told with real sensitivity and feeling stories well worth telling, depicted historical events with a validity which carried conviction, or presented scenes of stirring beauty with musical accompaniments at which even the cultured could not cavil. The Beards themselves had no quarrel with *The Story of Pasteur, The Life of Emile Zola,* and *The Good Earth.*

Admitting that the movies were entertainment—not primarily a medium for culture, or education, or propaganda—it was clear that the level of such entertainment could not rise very high if left wholly dependent upon the desires (as interpreted by Hollywood) of a movie-going public which included all elements among the American people. A natural consequence of the democracy of this nation-wide audience was a lag between possible artistic and cultural standards and those which the public would support. But in considering the trend of their development, not only in comparison with the films being shown in the nickelodeon era but against the background of the popular entertainment of the nineteenth century they had so largely replaced, the movies at the close of the 1930's showed many encouraging signs that they were beginning to realize their true potentialities.

Chapter XVIII

A NATION ON WHEELS

THE EARLY HISTORY OF THE AUTOMOBILE, IN SO FAR AS recreation is concerned, could hardly have afforded a more striking contrast to that of the movies. There were in all in this country some three hundred horseless carriages—gasoline buggies, electrics, steam cars—when moving pictures were first thrown on a screen in 1895. When John P. Harris opened his pioneer moving-picture theatre a decade later, there were almost eighty thousand.[1] But though the early period of automobiling coincided so exactly with the years of the nickelodeon madness, the automobile and the movies reached entirely different groups of people.

The movies were for the masses, the automobile for the classes. The distinction could not have been more pronounced. The generalization may be hazarded that none of that vast nickelodeon audience ever even hoped to own or drive a car, while very few of the little band of wealthy automobile owners would have condescended to go to the movies. The first decade of the century witnessed a remarkable expansion in these two new forms of amusement, but it was then impossible to foresee that higher standards of entertainment would soon draw all classes of society into the moving-picture theatres and that the reduced costs of operating an automobile would in time enable all the world to motor. It was not until after 1920 that the movies and motoring could be grouped together as popular forms of recreation in which no class barriers were recognized.

→>>«←

THE RESTRICTION of motoring to the wealthy in the early period of the automobile was not primarily due to the cost of the cars. Although current prices ran as high as $7,000, runabouts could be bought for under $500 and Ford touring-cars for $780 as early as 1911.[2] This was not cheap from the workingman's point of view, but what really made touring such an exclusive prerogative of the rich was the expense of upkeep and operation. The lowest estimate in a magazine series appearing in 1907 was $358 for a six-months' season in which the car-owner drove 3,370 miles. New tires cost $100, minor parts $96, new parts and work on the engine $70, and gasoline $45. A more typical estimate for an expensive car set the total for a year's operating expenses at $3,628. A number of extras were included in this figure: a cape top and glass front, a speedometer, an exhaust-blown horn, and an allowance ($264) for motoring clothes.[3] Nevertheless it graphically reflected the continual drain for repairs and new tires which featured all pre-war motoring. The year's upkeep of a car appears generally to have come very close in these days to its original cost.

The new "automobility" came in for its full share of jokes and jibes, and also bitter denunciation, as the common man watched the newly rich ride proudly through the gates of society in their Cadillacs, Locomobiles, Packards, and Pierce-Arrows. Life parodied "The Charge of the Light Brigade" in 1904:

> Half a block, half a block,
>   Half a block onward,
> All in their automobiles,
>   Rode the Four Hundred.
> 'Forward!' the owners shout,
>   'Racing car!' 'Runabout!'
> Into Fifth Avenue
>   Rode the Four Hundred.[4]

Some three years later, Woodrow Wilson, then president of Princeton University, gravely warned that "nothing has spread socialistic feeling in this country more than the use of the automobile." He declared that to the worker and the farmer the motorist was "a picture of the arrogance of wealth, with all its independence and carelessness." [5]

An expensive amusement not only summed up the general opinion of the automobile in these pioneer years, but appeared to be all that could be expected of it. It was a plaything for the rich. Motoring and automobile racing took a place in the lives of wealthy sportsmen which had formerly been held by coaching; it was regarded as a sport comparable to yachting or riding to hounds. Operating expenses and the inevitability of breakdowns for long shut out any idea of the automobile's more general usefulness, either as a means of transportation in the business and commercial world or as a popular recreation for the people as a whole. As late as 1911 Charles J. Glidden could single out as the primary effect of the advent of the automobile that it had "completely revolutionized the life of well-to-do people." [6]

The sport of motoring was hazardous and exciting as well as costly in the first decade of the century. A long course of instruction was necessary to learn how to drive, the schools providing preliminary practice in gear-shifting and steering behind dummy wheels before the pupil was allowed to venture on the road. He was also taught something about the engine, how to make the necessary repairs and replace parts. Many car-owners became adept at tinkering with the engine, but this phase of motoring was not always considered fun. "The nerve strain of working over those jarring parts, if you have no mechanical instinct," wrote one harassed motorist, "would take away all the pleasure of ownership." [7] One of the most popular automobile jokes was that of the car-owner's ward in the insane asylum. A visitor one day was surprised to find it apparently empty. The physician in charge explained that the patients were all under the cots fixing the slats.

Vast preparations had to be made for a day's run, let alone for the vacation tours which were becoming popular as the automobile very gradually became a more reliable vehicle. Among

Toys for Wealthy

advertisement
...ier's Weekly,
1909.

The Thomas 6 Cyl., 70 H. P. Flyer—Equipped with "Flyabout" Body—$6000
The most Powerful, Complete and Luxurious Stock Car Made
—complete with glass front, top and speedometer.

Thomas 4-60 Flyer $4500
Thomas 6-40 Flyer $3000   **E. R. THOMAS MOTOR CO., Buffalo, N. Y.**   Send 25c in stamps for
Thomas Town Car $3000   Members of Association Licensed Automobile Manufacturers   complete illustrated story
of New York-Paris Race

Cars and Costumes of Pre-War Days

Culver Service.

*Vacationing
on Wheels*

Trailer-camp facilities at Sandusky,
Ohio. Wide World

the items of extra equipment necessary were a full set of tools, elaborate tire-changing apparatus, a pail of water for overheated brakes, extra spark-plugs, tire chains for muddy roads, and a "rear basket with concealed extra gasoline supply." Clothes also were important. In this period the cars were all open, many of them without tops or even wind-shields, and the roads were incredibly dusty. The motorist had to be prepared for all contingencies, laden down with dusters, raincoats, umbrellas, and goggles. A single-breasted duster with eton collar and three patch pockets was recommended for mild weather, but men were further advised to have wind cuffs to be attached to their coat sleeves, caps with visors and adjustable goggles, and leggings for repair work.[8]

For women the problem of the proper motoring clothes was even more important. One had to be fashionable, but everyday styles were hardly adapted to exposure to sun, wind, and dust. Bell-shaped ruffled skirts trailed the ground, and large picture hats were fastened upon imposing pompadours with a multitude of gleaming hat-pins. To motor, all this fine array had to be carefully protected. Long linen dusters were worn, lap-robes tucked securely about the legs, and hats tied down with long veils knotted tightly under the chin.[9]

In 1907 a hundred miles was considered an excellent day's run. There had to be a lot of "sprinting at thirty miles an hour" to get over such a long distance. The average speed was a good deal lower, but fast driving had already become a problem. "The effect of speedy motoring," commented one automobilist, "is that of drinking several cups of strong coffee," [10] and the pre-war generation appears to have had a strong urge to experience this intoxicating sensation. To control these maddened motorists, who frightened horses, upset carriages, and more and more frequently maimed and killed other users of the roads while they escaped uninjured, strict speeding regulations were adopted in a number of states. The law in New York provided a maximum of ten miles an hour in congested areas, fifteen miles an hour in the outlying sections of cities and towns, and twenty miles an hour in the open country.[11]

Driving at night was not a usual practice, but one enthusiast contributed a special article on midnight motoring to the October, 1907, issue of *Country Life*. He painted a glowing picture—the darkness pierced by the flaming arrow of the acetylene headlight, the road opening up like a titanic ribbon spun solely for the motorist's pleasure, the muffled roar of the motor in the deep silence of the night. It was a wonderful sensation as, with hands gripping the seats, hair blown back by the rushing wind, the car plunged "into that big mysterious dark always just ahead, always just beyond reach." One word of warning was given about night running. Should a carriage be encountered, the motorist should be ready to stop at once and attempt to calm the frightened horses by throwing his lap-robe (an essential article of equipment) over the headlights.[12]

Suggestions for driving advised care not only for the safety of the highway, but to combat the prejudice that the automobile still aroused among non-motorists. The horn should be used gingerly because a sudden squeeze was frightening to both horses and pedestrians; headlights should be blown out on city streets; persons having trouble with their horses should be treated courteously, "especially ladies who are apt to be rather helpless in such cases." A final injunction urged special consideration for pedestrians. If they were forced to dodge a speeding car, they were very apt to describe it later, to the ill repute of all motoring, as "one of those (adjective) automobiles." [13]

->>><<<-

By 1914 the motor car had passed well beyond this pioneer stage. There were some two million in the country, and mass production was enabling the manufacturer to turn out cars that could be purchased for as little as $400. More important, the automobile had been so greatly improved that constant breakdowns were no longer the invariable rule of the road, and it was possible to operate a car without the prohibitive expenses of earlier days. Roads also were becoming immeasurably better. An advertisement of one second-hand car gave as the reason for sale that its owner had motored from Illinois and could not return because of bad roads, but the constant pressure of motorists was beginning to take effect in improved highways, macadam and even concrete, throughout the country.

Henry Ford had played a leading part in making the automobile more easily available to a broader public. His Model T was the most familiar of all makes, with half a million of them on the road before the World War. Hundreds of "tin Lizzie" jokes showed the place they had won in the country's life. Do you know what Ford is doing now? was a question the wary learned to ignore. But the answers were legion: enclosing a can-opener with every car so the purchaser could cut out his own doors; painting his cars yellow so that dealers could hang them in bunches and retail them like bananas; providing squirrels to retrieve any nuts that might rattle off. . . . Another story was that of the Illinois farmer who stripped the tin roof off his barn, sent it to the Ford factory, and received a letter saying that "while your car was an exceptionally bad wreck, we shall be able to complete repairs and return it by the first of the week." [14]

The ubiquity of the Ford, as well as of the Ford joke, clearly indicated that the automobile had completely passed through that stage when it could be considered a plaything for the rich or an instigator of socialism. It was reaching the American public —the workingman and the farmer. And throughout the period of the World War this general process of diffusion went on at an increasingly rapid rate. The two million cars of 1914 had become nine million by 1921. In another five years this number had doubled.[15] So great was public interest in the automobile that when Ford brought out a new car in 1927, the formal unveiling of the Model A attracted almost as much attention as a presidential inauguration. Thousands flocked to the Ford show-rooms in Detroit, the mounted police had to be called out in Cleveland, a mob stormed the exhibition at Kansas City, and a million people fought to get a glimpse of the new car at the Ford headquarters in New York.[16]

Succeeding years saw a still further increase in the number of passenger cars on the road. In the 1930's the total rose to over twenty-five million—an automobile for more than two-thirds of the families throughout the country.[17] Such far-reaching improvements had been made that there was now almost no resemblance to the horseless carriage of forty years earlier. The modern car was long and low, showing a definite trend toward stream-lining, and the closed sedan had almost entirely replaced the open touring-car. It could be operated easily and was as nearly foolproof as human ingenuity could make it. It was equipped with such an array of conveniences—from self-starters to heaters—that one could motor with a degree of comfort the pioneer automobilists could not possibly have imagined. Winter motoring—certainly for short trips—was almost as feasible as summer outings. Should anything go wrong, the uniformity of popular models made repairs comparatively easy, but motorists could count so definitely on the dependability of their cars that they hardly knew what was under the hood. It was seldom necessary even to change tires, so greatly had their durability and potential mileage been increased. Everyone could drive a car, and every one did. In the 1890's the tremendous vogue for the bicycle had given the impression that America was a nation on wheels. Half a century later this appeared to be even more true—but on automobile wheels.

->>)<<-

THE SOCIAL CHANGES wrought by the automobile had affected every phase of national life. Transportation was revolutionized, the isolation of the country broken down. No single development ever had a more far-reaching effect in speeding up the tempo of modern living. The entire face of the country was criss-crossed with highways of macadam and cement, lined with filling-stations, lunch-rooms, curio stores, antique shops, hot-dog stands, tourist camps, and signboards. It was the age of the automobile.

Nowhere were the changes more far-reaching than in popular recreation. At least one-quarter of the use of automobiles was estimated by the American Automobile Association to be for pleasure—touring and holiday driving. Equally important was the extent to which it was used as an adjunct to pleasure, as a means of transportation from the country to the amusements of the city and from the city to the sports and outdoor activities of the country. For countless millions the automobile brought the near-by golf-course, tennis-courts, or bathing-beach within practical reach. It opened up the way for holiday picnics in the country and for week-end excursions to fish or hunt. It immensely stimulated the whole outdoor movement, making camping possible for throngs of people to whom woods, mountains, and streams were formerly totally inaccessible. It provided a means of holiday travel for a people whose migratory instinct appeared insatiable, making touring one of the most popular of all amusements.[18]

The delights of a week-end or Sunday motor excursion into the country were spread glowingly over the pages of popular magazines in the advertisements published by manufacturers of popular models. The automobile was "the enricher of life." A midwestern bank president was quoted in one two-page spread in the *Saturday Evening Post* as declaring that "a man who works six days a week and spends the seventh on his own doorstep certainly will not pick up the extra dimes in the great thoroughfare of life." Another advertisement invited the car-owner to make the most of the next sunny Sunday—"tell the family to hurry the packing and get aboard—and be off with smiles down the nearest road—free, loose, and happy—bound for green wonderlands." [19] The suggestion—which innumerable families took—aroused the resentment of those religious elements in the population which believed church-going rather than motoring the way to spend the day, but the automobile finally completed the gradual transformation of the Sabbath from a day of rest and worship to one primarily devoted to recreation.

The pleasures of vacation touring were depicted with even more fulsome praise of the joys of the open road. Every section of the country invited the growing army of motorists to visit it. Chambers of commerce, resort proprietors, and oil companies united in publicizing the attractions of seashore and mountain. New England was a summer vacation land, and Florida a popular winter resort. The national parks and forests, especially those of the West, drew hordes of visitors. In 1910 they had a few hundred thousand; the total in 1935 was thirty-four million.[20] Almost all of them came by automobile. There was an overwhelming response to the slogan *See America First* as the new generation took to the road.

Accommodations to meet the needs of these motorists along the way sprang up quickly. The tourist camp became an institution. Some of them provided comfortable overnight cabins with all modern conveniences; others simply provided facilities for automobile campers. Florida probably had more of them than any other state. In 1925 it reported 178 with accommodations for six hundred thousand people.[21] For the more fashionable there were hotels and inns—there was a rapid growth of them in these years—but the majority of tourists had little money to spend. An overnight cabin or a place where they could stretch a tarpaulin from the side of the car, cooking their own supper at a communal fireplace, was all that most of them demanded.

In the late 1930's the trailer made its appearance as still another boon for those with migratory instincts. The westerner whose forebears had crossed the prairies in a journey of several months trekked back over the old route, in a fraction of the time, with this twentieth-century equivalent of the covered wagon coupled to his car. The number of these vehicles increased rapidly; enthusiasts saw for them a future comparable to that of the automobile itself. In the bright dawn of trailer camping, about 1936, it was wildly stated that there would be a million of them on the road within a year and that a decade would see half the population on wheels. Such fantasies proved illusory; perhaps one hundred thousand passenger trailers, rather than a million, was the total later estimated by *Trailer Travel*.[22]

Some seven hundred manufacturers had rushed into the field. Small machine-shops, bicycle manufacturers, out-of-work carpenters, hoped they had discovered the bootstrap to pull them out of the depression. But the boom faded away as annual production sought levels corresponding to the real demand. For, apart from the expense, new obstacles to further expansion sprang up in strict traffic regulations and bans on trailer parking. Municipalities did not take kindly to the home-on-wheels which could escape taxes and defy housing rules. Nevertheless in a more limited field the trailer provided a new means of touring which had wide appeal, becoming throughout the country a familiar symbol of the life of the highway. Trailer camps were established at the grounds of New York's World Fair, at Florida winter resorts, in the national parks of the Far West.

An important consequence of touring was the growth of a travel industry of immense proportions. In 1935 the American people were reported to have spent almost five per cent of their total income on vacation expenses. More than half this money, or about $1,330,000,000, represented automobile operating expenses that could be fairly allocated to the pleasure use of cars.[23] Here was a sum greater than all moving-picture admissions, greater than the cost of any other form of recreation whatsoever. Add to it all the other expenses of motoring—hotels, tourist camps, restaurants—and some idea may be gained of the importance of the industry that catered to the motorists' needs. Half a century earlier there had been nothing comparable to automobile touring; it had now become an economic as well as social phenomenon of the utmost significance.

Just what a car meant in the lives of countless working-class families, entirely apart from the vogue for touring among those more likely to have summer vacations, was graphically revealed in the comments made by women interviewed in the course of the *Middletown* survey. "The car is the only pleasure we have," one of them stated; another declared, "I'll go without food before I'll see us give up the car"; and a mother of nine children said she would "rather do without clothes than give up the car." [24] An automobile was generally ranked higher than ownership of one's home, before a telephone, electric lighting, or a bathtub. The experience of the depression widely confirmed the general willingness to sacrifice almost everything else in order to keep a car. Generally paid for on the instalment plan, it was the last thing to go. One of the steadiest products on the market was gasoline, bought by countless working-class families heroically economizing on food and clothes to be able to pay for their Sunday spin into the country.

In no other country in the world had motoring for pleasure developed on any such grandiose scale. Everywhere else the use of the automobile for recreation was largely limited, as it had been in the early days in this country, to the more wealthy classes. Only in the United States had a higher standard of living and mass production made possible such general ownership. A car for his family, to be used primarily for pleasure, was accepted as a valid ambition for every member of the American democracy.

->>><<<-

THE EFFECT of the automobile on recreational habits was often decried in the 1930's: the substitution of a passive amusement for something more active; standardization and regimentation; the moral problem of the parked sedan and roadside tourist camp. The Sunday-afternoon drive was devastatingly described —the crowded highways, traffic jams, and accidents; the car windows tightly closed against spring breezes; and whatever beauties the landscape might offer lying hidden behind forbidding lines of advertisements. "One arrives after a motor journey," one eminent sociologist wrote, "all liver and no legs; one's mind is asleep, one's body tired; one is bored, irritable, and listless.[25]

But what such critics forgot was that the great majority of Sunday and holiday motorists, or even vacation tourists, would have been cooped up in crowded towns and cities except for the automobile. The country they saw may at times have been almost blotted out by billboards and the air they breathed tainted by gasoline fumes. But the alternative in many cases would have been the movie, the dance-hall, or the beer-parlor. The steamboat and the railroad began a century ago to open up the world of travel and provide some means of holiday escape from one's immediate environment, but until the coming of the automobile, recreation along these lines was a rare thing. The wealthy could make the fashionable tour in 1825, the well-to-do built up the summer resorts of the 1890's, but every Tom, Dick, and Harry toured the country in the 1930's—thanks to the automobile.

Much of the criticism of the way the automobile was used in leisure-time activities may have been justified, but any general condemnation of its part in national recreation implies that pleasure travel, outdoor life, and many sports should have largely remained the prerogative of the wealthy few who could afford other means of transportation.

Chapter XIX

ON THE AIR

In 1920 THERE WERE SOME FIVE THOUSAND AMATEUR RADIO FANS in the United States. Their chief amusement was picking up on crude, home-made receiving sets the wireless-telephony messages, principally from ships at sea, which symbolized the quarter-century advance in communications since Marconi's experiments in the 1890's.[1] Broadcasting grew out of this amateur activity. When experiments were made in putting news and music on the air, the realization grew that this new medium had startling potentialities for entertainment. They had been foreseen some four years earlier by David Sarnoff, ambitiously planning a "Radio Music Box" for every home, but apart from a few limited demonstrations it was not until 1920 that broadcasting in its modern sense became an actuality.

Among the experiments with music in that year, those of Lester Spangenberg, a former navy radio operator, have been credited with constituting the first regular broadcasting. Volunteer pianists and banjo-players began to meet nightly at the Spangenberg home in Lakeview, New Jersey, and a program was sent out on which hundreds of other amateurs tuned in.[2]

A few months later, enthusiasts who lived near Pittsburgh were also surprised to hear music which was being broadcast—though the word was hardly known—from a plant of the Westinghouse Electric and Manufacturing Company. They liked it; a number of them wrote in suggesting a regular program. One was consequently put on the air—baseball scores and popular music every Wednesday and Saturday night—and soon afterwards a Pittsburgh department store began advertising "approved radio receiving sets for listening to Dr. Conrad's concerts." The Westinghouse officials suddenly realized that they had inadvertently stumbled on something. Here was a way to increase sales of equipment to radio fans by providing entertainment, news reports, and educational features for those who enjoyed listening in.[3]

Arrangements were promptly made to establish the famous KDKA, the first permanent, commercial broadcasting station. It was formally opened on November 2, 1920, to broadcast to a few listeners (some of whom were provided with free receiving sets) the results of the Harding-Cox election. The success of the experiment led to further expansion of KDKA's activities, and within a year to the establishment of other pioneer stations. From that date the rapid expansion of broadcasting and growth of the great invisible audience constituted one of the most amazing phenomena of the post-war decade. When another presidential contest came around in 1924, the news of the election of Coolidge was sent out over a nation-wide hook-up which reached five million homes. Hoover was elected in 1928, and the number of receiving sets had swelled to ten million. They had almost tripled in the next eight years, and the great majority of the people throughout the country first learned of Roosevelt's second election over the air.[4]

→»)«←

WITH the rapid multiplication of broadcasting stations in those first years after 1920, the ether was soon crowded with music, stock-market reports, accounts of sporting events, and bedtime stories. In January, 1921, the rector of the Calvary Episcopal Church in Pittsburgh allowed the first broadcasting of a church service; a few months later Herbert Hoover made the first public address over the air in an appeal for funds to support European relief work.[5] The Dempsey-Carpentier fight was broadcast. The *New York Times* printed an inconspicuous news item referring to it as an interesting experiment in wireless telephony, but a growing army of radio enthusiasts realized that something epochal was taking place.

Before the end of 1922 there were hundreds of broadcasting stations, and a new entertainment industry (WJZ in Newark, New Jersey, was an imaginative pioneer in developing popular programs) was fully launched.[6] "There is radio music in the air, every night, everywhere," wrote a startled newspaper editor in San Francisco. "Anybody can hear it at home on a receiving set, which any boy can put up in an hour." [7] Hundreds of thousands were making the same discovery and rushed to buy radios. President Harding had one installed in his study at the White House. All the world wanted this new device annihilating space and bringing entertainment into the home with the twist of a dial. "The rapidity with which the thing has spread," one astounded observer commented, "has possibly not been equalled in all the centuries of human progress." [8]

There was a great deal more on the air than what might normally fall under the head of entertainment, but radio made its spectacular advance because it was the most novel amusement the American people had ever known. Following the example of the electrical manufacturers who had first supported broadcasting as a means to increase radio sales, other manufacturers, department stores, and newspapers soon seized the opportunity to operate stations which would enable them to get their names before the public in a favorable light. They were not always sure what to do, but at first it did not really matter. The novelty of any broadcast made it a success. Pioneer radio enthusiasts, listening far into the night with head-phones clamped securely to their expectant ears ("ear-muffs" were considered far superior to loud-speakers), were more interested in picking up distant stations than in the quality of near-by music. Involving experiments with new devices, the constant struggle against static, and all-night vigils, radio was originally an exciting sport rather than a passive amusement. It was highly competitive and sometimes quite exhausting.[9]

Broadcasting to the Nation

The Master Control Room of the National Broadcasting Company at Radio City, New York, controlling Stations WEAF and WJZ and the scores of other stations in the Red and Blue Networks. Courtesy of the National Broadcasting Company.

Entertainment for Sunday Evening

Orchestra, chorus, and audience of five thousand at a broadcast of the "Ford Sunday Evening Hour," from Masonic Auditorium, Detroit. Courtesy of the Columbia Broadcasting System

Programs covering the entire day—from setting up exercises at 6:45 A.M. to jazz at midnight—were inaugurated as early as 1923 by such stations as WJZ. Music predominated, soprano solos proving most popular, but there were also informing talks on every conceivable subject and ingenious radio dramas. A trial was made of what were called "omni-oral" productions at which the entire evening's program revolved around a single subject. "A Night Out of the Past" or "A Night in India" was presented with related music and talks.[10]

It was radio's awkward age. Critics concerned about its influence in the transmission of ideas became gravely worried over what was happening. In October, 1924, a writer in the *New Republic* declared that jazz was the principal entertainment on the air, and ninety per cent of everything else was "sheer rubbish." "The development of motion pictures in the United States," he stated, "was held back half a decade because at first it was in the control of fly-by-nights, adventurers and reformed pushcart peddlers, not one in a hundred of whom had reached the social level where one takes off one's hat indoors. Radio broadcasting seems threatened by the same fate." [11] As in the case of the movies, however, radio was destined for popular entertainment even if it meant jazz and rubbish. In attempting to satisfy public taste, commercial-minded though it may have been, the new industry was fulfilling its primary function in providing amusement for the American people as a whole.

Improvements in technique and organization went ahead faster in these years than the quality of entertainment. Nationwide hook-ups were inaugurated in 1924 for the national political conventions. Radio's enthusiasts, listening to the exciting battle between Al Smith and William Gibbs McAdoo in Madison Square Garden (with the persistent Alabama cry—"twenty-four votes for Oscar W. Underwood"), enjoyed more than ever the sport of politics. A few years later, chain broadcasting, linking stations over the entire country, enabled listeners everywhere to hear the same nightly programs. National advertisers, as opposed to local merchants and newspapers, sensed the potentialities of a medium reaching an audience which now numbered many millions. A new era in broadcasting was ushered in with sponsored programs over the new networks, whereby leading manufacturers sought to associate in the mass mind the excellence of the entertainment they provided with the excellent qualities of their tooth pastes, automobiles, mattresses, ginger ales, watches, or cough drops. Performances became more elaborate, radio headliners were developed, and still further impetus given to the contagious craze so rapidly engulfing a great majority of American homes.[12]

Throughout the land orchestras hammered away day and night at "Mister Gallagher and Mister Shean," and then at "Yes, We Have No Bananas," "Barney Google," or "Valencia." "Ol' Man River" kept rolling along. The crooning voice of Rudy Vallee ("I'm Just a Vagabond Lover") stirred millions of feminine hearts; husky-toned torch singers soothed masculine breasts with "Moanin' Low" and "Am I Blue?" Then there were Roxy and his Gang, the Happiness Boys, the A and P Gypsies, the Cliquot Club Eskimos, the Ipana Troubadours....

Saxophones, trombones, ukuleles supplied an orgy of sound such as the world had never known. Writing in 1928, Charles Merz declared that twenty to thirty million Americans were "listening in on the greatest single sweep of synchronized and syncopated rhythm that human ingenuity has yet conceived. This is our counterpart of the drum the black man beats when the night is dark and the jungle lonely. Tom-tom."[13] Tin Pan Alley was rejuvenated. It was no longer the minstrel show, the vaudeville team, or the circus that spread the new songs throughout the country. It was the radio. It gave them an immediate and universal vogue—an almost instantaneous nation-wide popularity.

This music was not the whole show. Classical music—piano recitals, concert singing, symphonies, opera broadcasts—appealed to a small but nevertheless growing public. After 1927 there was general agreement among musicians that radio was definitely serving to improve popular taste.[14] Women particularly favored symphonic music, and national advertisers discovered that concerts as well as dance music might serve the cause of expanding sales. Soon many millions were listening to the Metropolitan Opera every Saturday afternoon and to the New York Philharmonic-Symphony orchestra every Sunday.

An interesting influence was exerted on the phonograph. About 1919 it represented one of the most popular of all home diversions. The American people were spending more on phonographs and equipment, spurred on by an apparently limitless desire for new records, than they were on all other musical instruments, on all books and periodicals, or on all sporting goods. The radio caused an almost immediate collapse in these sales, the total dropping in twelve years from $339,000,000 to $17,000,000.[15] As a general medium of entertainment, the phonograph almost disappeared. But what now happened was that greatly improved and more expensive phonographs, combined with radios, slowly began to make up some of this lost ground, and there was a boom in the sale of recordings of classical music.

The phonograph industry, that is, went through a transformation somewhat comparable to the changes that had developed in theatrical enterprise. The radio supplied the popular product, as vaudeville and then the movies had done for the theatre, and phonographs were largely produced for the more cultured audience which wanted something more than jazz and syncopation. By the 1930's this trend had become very marked, and the parallel between the radio and movies, on the one hand, and phonographs and the legitimate theatre, on the other, was an interesting phenomenon of the amusement world. In time even the piano trade, which also had fallen into the doldrums, felt the quickening effect of a new appreciation for music which the radio inspired but did not wholly satisfy.

Music in general (popular and classical) made up some three-fourths of radio's programs in its early years. Next in popularity were the broadcasts of sporting events—football games, prize-fights, and major-league baseball games.[16] There was for long no more familiar voice in all the land than that of Graham Mc-Namee excitedly describing the winning touchdown, the knock-out blow, or the ninth-inning three-bagger. Radio dramas and skits had also been developed into a new art. There were mystery plays, melodramas, and variety acts. Humorous broadcasts had a great vogue. When stock-market prices began to crash and breadlines lengthen after 1929, literally millions of people turned on their radios every night to listen to the complicated business and domestic affairs of Amos 'n Andy. Other radio head-liners came and went as the great American people took up first one and then another with that penchant for fads which has always been so characteristic of the popular attitude.

At the same time religious services, public functions, political talks, were broadcast regularly. News reports—not only sports and market prices but all foreign and domestic news—featured every program. The radio commentator became a new figure in the world of affairs. Countless lectures falling within the educational field were zealously promoted as sustaining programs. Throughout the day, housewives, half-listening to the radio as they went about their work, were regaled with health talks, fashion hints, recipes, and general household advice. There were children's stories and spelling contests. It all came under the head of entertainment, however serious some of the talks and speeches. The process of taking it in was so completely painless. Should the listener ever become bored, a twist of the dial and he could change his program.[17]

->>)(<<-

WITH further expansion in the 1930's, for the sale of radios did not suffer from the depression as much as many other forms of entertainment, the invisible audience grew still larger. The twelve million sets in use at the opening of the decade had increased to some forty millions by its close.[18] More than four-fifths of the entire population could listen in, and sometimes did, to nation-wide hook-ups on special occasions. There were not only radios in more than twenty-six million private homes, in countless clubs, hotels, schools, and other institutions, but also on railroad trains and in over five million automobiles. It was hard to escape them. Traveling salesmen, cruising taxicab drivers in the cities, even farmers driving their tractors, had radios. They were one of the most commonplace features of American life.

While there had been a continued advance in broadcasting classical music, growing appreciation of folk-songs, new experiments with radio drama, and possibly greater discussion of public affairs, the more popular features of broadcasting still largely filled the air. Tin Pan Alley continued to turn out songs to meet every need; stars of both the stage and the movie world were drafted for radio "appearances"; hillbilly and dance music was always available on a dozen stations. The minstrel show had a belated revival over the air, and vaudeville a new incarnation. Countless thrillers were adapted for broadcasting, and exciting serials were followed as eagerly, and by an even larger audience, as *The Perils of Pauline* had been followed on the screen a quarter-century earlier.

The diversity of entertainment on the air made the attractions of moving-picture theatres appear stereotyped. The program changed generally at fifteen-minute intervals. The listener inadvertently tuning in on "The Woman in White" could hardly discover what was going on before another voice had begun a new chapter in "Aunt Jenny's Story." Melody and Madness succeeded Information, Please; the sketch Blondie was sandwiched between two song recitals; the major-league baseball broadcast (the moment the last man was called out) was followed by a talk on Men and Books; Little Orphan Annie faded out to give way to Science in the News; church hymns were squeezed in after the sketch Valiant Lady; Zinn's Orchestra, Buck Rogers, and Uncle Don followed in quick succession; Mrs. Roosevelt was worked into the Hobby Lobby between two variety shows; the Goldbergs gave way to Life Can Be Beautiful; a Success Session paved the way for the Chicago Symphony; Edwin C. Hill on the news led to Percy Faith's Music; Lowell Thomas followed immediately after the Ink Spot Quartet; the Lone Ranger....[19] It was a mad world. Here was something for all the family, but one had to be quick to catch it.

"The lives of most of my friends," Weare Holbrook wrote in a sketch, "The Ears Have It," in the Herald Tribune Magazine, "seem to be governed by radio programs. In planning any social function, one must allow for the vagaries of the Charlie-McCarthophiles, the Jack-Bennyites, the Eddie-Cantorians, the Information Pleasers, and other devotees of ethereal cults; and the East Teabone Friday Evening Bridge Club has disbanded, simply because it is impossible to get a quorum any more.

"When I hear my host and hostess speaking in a preoccupied manner, and see them glancing surreptitiously at the clock, I no longer feel constrained to say, 'Well, I guess I'd better be running along.' Instead I say, 'How about turning on the radio?' And it is gratifying to observe the eagerness with which they respond to my suggestion." [20]

Objections were sometimes raised as to the way announcements of the remarkable qualities of such-and-such a tooth paste, deodorant, cigarette, automobile, or cathartic broke in on the closing chords of the symphony or interrupted the climax of the western melodrama. But the public generally realized that some one had to support broadcasting. It felt that it was paying a small price for its entertainment in letting the national advertisers have a chance to sell their products. And, after all, it was not necessary to listen to their announcements.

From the economic point of view, the advertising rôle of the radio was even more important than its status as an industry marketing several hundred million dollars' worth ($450,000,000 in 1937) of products annually.[21] Manufacturers reaching a mass market found it an increasingly effective method of promoting sales. Campaigns were geared to radio programs. Merchandisers counted on a flood of orders when announcers told a gullible public (after the heroine had been left hanging over the edge of the cliff, or the swing band had emitted its last squawk) that now was the time to change to winter oil—or underwear—and to take a liver pill for that tired feeling. Never before had entertainment been so closely allied with the operations of big business.

With the near-perfection in the technicalities of broadcasting and reception, if not in the quality of programs, that the industry could now rightfully claim, had radio made its ultimate contribution to the entertainment of the American people? At the close of the decade television appeared over the horizon. It had already been introduced on a limited scale. The millions of visitors who thronged the New York's World Fair in the summer of 1939 had the opportunity not only to hear but to see over the air. The development of this new device had not yet advanced very far beyond the equivalent of the vitascope stage of motion-picture production, but radio engineers promised a phenomenal expansion which in time might revolutionize all broadcasting. (Plastic surgeons in New York were reported opening television hospitals to remodel radio announcers' faces for the future movies of the air.)

As it was, the radio provided more amusement for more people than even the moving picture or the automobile. Every study of how people spent their leisure time in the 1930's placed listening-in high on the list of possible amusements, if not at the very top.[22] Reading was put off, card tables closed up, conversation languished, in favor of the programs of the great broadcasting companies. The local baseball team had few supporters when big-league games came over the air; church entertainments could hardly compete with Broadway stars. In the average household the radio was generally left on for three or four hours a day.[23] From the early-morning weather announcement to the dying strains of the orchestra in some New York night club, it had something to interest or entertain every one. More generally available in urban communities, its invasion of the country (almost seventy per cent of rural families owned radios) was possibly the most important aspect of its growth. The automobile had made it possible for the farmer to get to town occasionally for the movies, breaking down the isolation of the nineteenth century, but the radio brought music and drama into his home whenever he wanted it. There were also the large number of shut-in people—the aged, the sick, the blind—who had never before had anything remotely comparable to the radio to lighten the empty loneliness of their lives.

-->>><<<--

THE BROAD SCOPE of this medium for broadcasting not only entertainment but news and opinion continued to arouse the anxiety over its possible effects on popular thinking expressed in the *New Republic's* caustic editorial of 1924. Church leaders belabored radio for providing so much dance music and so little religion; educators bewailed lost opportunities for raising the cultural level; the social-minded generally coupled the radio with the movies in their worries over standardization, leveling of the public mind, the regimentation of all thought. While mass consumption so completely governed the selection of programs, it was contended that the radio could never have any cultural value or appeal for the sophisticated minority. The dangers of propaganda over the air, in respect to both domestic politics and international affairs, also created very real concern in such a troubled period as the 1930's. With the outbreak of war, broadcasts across national boundaries—the incredible phenomenon of hearing a Hitler actually deliver an address changing the whole course of world events—threw into stark relief the potentialities of the radio for good or evil in a field which went far beyond the boundaries of amusement.

It was left to the future to wrestle with these problems. The American people for the time at least upheld the freedom of the air and would have no governmental restraints thrown about the radio other than supervision of wave-lengths. They were content to leave such censorship as was essential to the broadcasting companies themselves. Their complete dependence upon public good-will was felt to be the greatest possible safeguard against abuse of their tremendous power.

CHAPTER XX

THE GREAT AMERICAN BAND-WAGON

THE AMERICAN PUBLIC THROUGHOUT ITS HISTORY HAS BEEN carried away by successive crazes. The tremendous popularity of dancing in the middle of the eighteenth century was remarked upon by many European visitors, while the Marquis de Chastellux was amazed by Boston's "passion" for whist in the 1780's. The mid-nineteenth century witnessed enthusiastic vogues for phrenology, balloon ascensions, minstrel shows, pedestrian races, and the phenomenon of "Lindomania." In the decades after the Civil War we have seen the fashionable frenzy with which new outdoor pastimes were adopted by society, the epidemics of croquet, roller-skating, and lawn tennis which spread so rapidly over the land. And in the 1890's this same instinct to take up whatever was new or different, to rush hurriedly along untrodden ways, was evident in the tremendous growth of fraternal organizations and women's clubs, in the avidity with which the public welcomed refined vaudeville, and in the interest excited by amateur photography, John L. Sullivan, band concerts, and bicycling.

The twentieth century found an even more susceptible public taking up with still greater vehemence new fads and fancies. Entirely apart from the enthusiastic reception given such major amusements as the movies, automobile touring, or the radio, and the welcome accorded the new sports still to be considered, it rushed through a succession of varied diversions with an intensity born of the feverish pace of modern life. In the ballyhoo years of the 'twenties this zest for novelties had become almost a mania. "One of the most striking characteristics of the era of

Coolidge Prosperity," Frederick Lewis Allen has written in *Only Yesterday*, "was the unparalleled rapidity and unanimity with which millions of men and women turned their attention, their talk, and their emotional interest upon a series of tremendous trifles—a heavyweight boxing match, a murder trial, a new automobile, a transatlantic flight." [1]

As one looks back upon the first forty years of the new century, there is something strange and wonderful about the kaleidoscopic scene. Ragtime burst upon the country to drive out the old-fashioned waltzes and polkas, gave way after its brief rule to jazz, and then in turn jazz surrendered to swing. There was an epidemic of diabolo in 1907, of ping-pong in 1913, of mah-jong in 1923, of cross-word puzzles in 1924, and of miniature golf in 1930. With bewildering rapidity the country also took up (and usually ran into the ground) dance marathons, bathing-beauty contests, bunion derbys, flagpole sitters, comic strips, greyhound-races, and "Yes, We Have No Bananas."

Striking the country with its full force on the eve of the depression, contract bridge almost overnight became the obsession of millions. In a somewhat more sober spirit, the 1930's also found the country taking up gardening, bingo, amateur theatricals, treasure-hunts, monopoly, Chinese checkers, The Game, prize contests, and the big apple. In some cases the fad bit deep enough to become a lasting habit (contract bridge, cross-word puzzles, gardening), but more generally it quickly gave way to something else as with unquestioning enthusiasm everybody climbed aboard the Great American Band-Wagon.

->>><<<-

THE PRE-WAR CRAZE for dancing ushered in by ragtime made it more popular than it had ever been before. The bright particular stars who led this revival were Mr. and Mrs. Vernon Castle. Under the inspiration of their graceful example, hundreds of thousands enthusiastically learned the new dances which the stimulating music of "Alexander's Ragtime Band" had introduced, gliding happily through the mazes of the fox-trot and the hesitation waltz at fashionable *thés dansants* and in public ball-rooms.[2] One of the favorite dance tunes was "Everybody's Doing It"—and it was almost literally true. It was reported that when a young girl was arraigned on a charge of disorderly conduct for turkey-trotting, counsel for defense easily won his case by singing "Everybody's Doing It." The jury joined in the chorus and brought in a quick verdict of acquittal.[3]

The Castles played an influential part in setting the tone of this revival of social dancing. A later commentator wrote that the pre-war craze was "an opening engagement in that revolution in manners and morals which was to excite America during the nineteen twenties,"[4] but music and dancing were far more decorous than in that later decade. The bunny hug, lame duck, and grizzly bear awoke derision and some criticism, but the Castles countered with the tango and maxixe. At the *thés dansants* fashion decreed that actual tea should be served. "Here in America we are just beginning to wake up to the possibilities of dancing," Mr. and Mrs. Castle wrote. "We are beginning to take our place among the nations who enjoy life."[5]

The next step was jazz. There is a natural musical language of jazz, whose esthetic significance may be left to the musicians, but in its popular, commercialized forms it has been loosely defined as "dance music, generally syncopated, played by a small band eccentrically composed."[6] Paul Whiteman termed it "the folk music of the machine age."[7] Known immemorially among the Negroes of the South, it was first brought north about 1914 when various "original" Dixieland Jazz Bands began playing in Chicago night clubs, and then went on to New York jazzing the ragtime blues.[8] The real jazz was played without a score, individual players "faking" their parts, or freely improvising, as they went along. But it was after Whiteman undertook its orchestration—with the development of symphonic jazz—that it really caught on. And then it swept the country like wild-fire. It was so universally the dance music of the 1920's that it gave its name to the decade. "To write fully and adequately about jazz," Mark Sullivan states in *Our Times*, "would be to write the history of much of the generation." [9]

The saxophone was its most essential instrument—"the heart, soul, mind, body and spirit of the jazz orchestra." Everywhere the younger generation fox-trotted to its barbaric yawp, clinging to one another in what one editor described as a "syncopated embrace." [10] Gradually their elders succumbed to the contagion. All the world danced to "Kitten on the Keys," "Crazy Rhythm," "I'm Always Chasing Rainbows," "Tea for Two," "It Ain't Gonna Rain No More," "The Japanese Sandman," "I'll Say She Does," "You're the Cream in My Coffee," "I . Faw Down an' Go Boom." . . .[11]

The violent acrobatics of the Charleston became a new rage:

> We all went to the party, a real high-toned affair
> And then along came Lulu, as wild as any Zulu.
> She started in to 'Charleston,'
> And how the boys did stare. . . .[12]

Jazz set the pace for the hundreds of night clubs, pretentious outgrowth of the first humble speak-easies of these days of Prohibition. At Texas Guinan's, the Embassy Club, Helen Morgan's, and the Cotton Club, New York's fashionable world "made whoopee" in a garish atmosphere spiced with gin and apple-jack.[13] It was the music for the dances of country club, fraternity, and pastime association in the small town. It came over the air for informal dances at a million homes—roll back the rugs, turn on the radio. It ruled supreme at public dance-halls for working men and working girls who had no other opportunity to have their whirl at fox-trot or Charleston. It dominated the cities' growth of taxi dance-halls ("Eureka Dancing Academy—Fifty Beautiful Lady Instructors") where city slickers and country boys, old-line Americans and newly arrived immigrants, found willing partners at a dime a dance.[14] "There are thirty million people who dance in the United States, daily, weekly, or frequently," a magazine writer stated in 1924. "A billion dollars for dancing by rich and poor would be a modest bill." [15]

The type of dancing inspired by jazz awoke a storm of protest from the pure in heart. "The music is sensuous, the embracing of partners—the female only half dressed—is absolutely indecent," the *Catholic Telegraph* declared, "and the motions—they are such as may not be described, with any respect for propriety, in a family newspaper. Suffice it to say that there are certain houses appropriate for such dances; but these houses have been closed by law." Other religious journals united in denouncing the new dances as "impure, polluting, corrupting, debasing, destroying spirituality, increasing carnality." [16]

Jazz and the cheek-to-cheek dancing it inspired were but another manifestation of the post-war upheaval in morals which had set the country, so the reformers sincerely believed, on a downward course that led to chaos and destruction. The younger generation was running wild—short skirts and rolled stockings, bobbed hair, corsets parked in the ladies' dressing-room, the "insidious vintage" of rouge, cigarettes and hip-flasks, petting parties.... It was all a part of the spiritual confusion of an age whose reflex from a war psychosis had led to a mad pursuit of pleasure in which the standards of an earlier day appeared to have gone completely by the board.

The country, even the younger generation, survived. It was perhaps inevitable that with all it had gone through, it should have to let off steam for a time with the throttle wide open and careless disregard of all warning signals. The war had precipitated, made more violent, changes in the social scene which otherwise would have come more slowly. The growing acceptance of the right to play was for a time translated into a popular belief that nothing except play really mattered. The freedom that women were slowly winning became the license characterized, in certain circles of society, by the knee-length skirt and the petting-party. A more healthy balance was in time restored, but the jazz age promoted a freedom in social activities and in the popular attitude toward amusements which really did mark a social revolution.

-»»«<-

EARLY IN THE 1920's another craze hit the country so hard that for a time it appeared that there would be no further playing of the age-old pastime of cards—no more chess, checkers, or dominoes. Mah-jong was a Chinese game which had become popular, with simplified rules, at the English-speaking clubs of Shanghai. In the summer of 1922 the experiment was made of importing a few sets into the United States. The game was publicized with the technique so familiar to the ballyhoo years, and it took hold almost at once. "From fifty thousand tables strewn with green bamboos and fallen Dragons," Charles Merz was writing the next year in the *New Republic,* "comes a nightly chorus, Pung!" [17] American manufacturers began to exploit the market for expensive sets of ivory and bamboo tiles, and despite all the intricacies of the game and bitter disputes over the proper rules of play, mah-jong was all the rage.

It faded away almost as quickly as it had appeared. Soon the Ming box, South Winds, and Red Dragons were forgotten in favor of a new amusement which created even more of a pother and showed greater signs of permanence. For long newspapers had occasionally published cross-word puzzles, and the New York *World* had been running them since 1912. They meant little in the lives of most people, but gradually a group of the intelligentsia—among others Heywood Broun, F.P.A., and Ruth Hale—took them up, and in 1924 it occurred to an editor just embarked on a new publishing venture that a cross-word puzzle book might aid the infant firm in getting started. He appealed to the puzzle editors of the *World* to help him out, and the result was a slim volume, equipped with a pencil, whose sale now became the new publishing firm's major aim. [18]

"We hired halls. We drafted by-laws and rules for amateur cross-word orgies," wrote one of its members. "...we visited

editors, urging them to put cross-word puzzles in the papers.....
Soon we were selling thousands of copies a day and breaking
into the best seller lists." [19] Other puzzle books crowded close
on the heels of the pioneer; newspapers everywhere fell in line
with the idea of printing daily puzzles, and there was a phenomenal demand for dictionaries and copies of Roget's *Thesaurus.*
"The newspapers carried the news that a Pittsburgh pastor had
put the text of his sermon into a puzzle," one commentator wrote.
"The Baltimore and Ohio Railroad placed dictionaries in all the
trains on its main line. A traveler between New York and Boston
reported that 60 per cent of the passengers were trying to fill
up squares in their puzzles, and that in the dining-car five waiters
were trying to think of a five-letter word which meant 'serving
to inspire fear.' Anybody you met on the street could tell you
the name of the Egyptian sun-god or provide you with a two-
letter word which meant a printer's measure." [20] The fad, in short,
was universal.

Supplemented by the vogue they inspired for other somewhat
comparable games, cross-word puzzles appeared to Kathleen
Norris to have opened up entirely new vistas for the American
people. "The newspapers are full of games—words to guess, rimes
to fill in, ingenious autographs to make, novels to identify," she
wrote in the *Ladies' Home Journal* in 1928. "Clerks and plumbers
and school-teachers and school children go home elbow to elbow
in the Subway, muttering five letter words that mean commonplace or trying to supply the laddergram links between Bride and
Groom. Amusement, once the prerogative of royalty and wealth,
is everywhere, now, and with this wave of games the nation gains
a great lifting of the spirit, a sort of universal heightening per
capita of the country's average enjoyment." [21]

Somewhat less happy conclusions were drawn from the same
phenomena by George Jean Nathan. "The games and diversions
that man invents for the pleasure of his leisure hours," he wrote
in the *American Mercury,* "are of such an unbelievable stupidity
and dulness that it is impossible to imagine even the lowest of

God's animals and insects indulging in relatively imbecile re-
laxations." [22]

Whether it may be judged as furthering "a sort of universal
heightening per capita of the country's average enjoyment" or
merely as again demonstrating man's inferiority to the lowest of
God's animals and insects, the next fad that made an impression
upon the country comparable to that of mah-jong or crossword
puzzles was miniature golf. This game involved hitting a ball
across a surface of crushed cotton-seed hulls and through various
tin pipes into a series of holes which represented, as the game's
name implied, a replica of a golf-course. In the summer of 1930
it was hailed, and in the utmost seriousness, as a psychological
and economic answer to the depression which President Hoover's
optimism could no longer conceal was now spreading over the
entire country. Miniature golf was taking the minds of the multitude off the troubles in which their lives seemed enmeshed; it
was creating a demand for cotton-seed hulls and tin pipes which
would revive both the cotton and steel industries.

Thirty thousand courses, valued as high as $125,000,000, sprang
up.[23] They became almost as commonplace along motor roads
as filling-stations or hot-dog stands; they took over the empty
lots of every town and city. Miniature golf was played throughout the day by its devotees; it was played well into the night,
under glaring arc-lights. Its cheapness was in line with the
chastened spirit of the amusement-seekers of 1930, and it filled
the leisure of many who unaccountably found themselves without
jobs. It had a further appeal in its resemblance to golf itself.
Players of the "midget" game could talk as glibly as the country-
club crowd on the difficulties of the fourth hole, of their eagles
and birdies. Men and women, boys and girls, rented putters and
chased balls around the tortuous tin-pipe courses. It was an inexpensive and novel way for the young man to entertain his
girl friend.

The game flourished through that memorable summer like a
green bay tree, and when winter caused the closing of the

courses, it was still confidently expected that the next year would see even further expansion. But by then the public had tired of miniature golf. It had been a one-year phenomenon. A few proprietors of courses hung on, but the motorist no longer stopped for a passing game, and the young man again took his girl friend to a movie—or else they sat on a park bench.

Elmer Davis, writing in December, 1930, when the future of both miniature golf and the economic state of the nation appeared somewhat rosier than events were to prove they actually were, paid his dutiful respects to the sport. "So perhaps miniature golf did its part, and a large part," he said in *Harper's*, "in carrying us past a crisis. Perhaps the business revival would have come sooner if the President, and the Cabinet, and Congress had become miniature golf addicts too." [24]

>>><<<

THE PUTTERS were still being swung at roadside courses when a very considerable part of the population found itself even more absorbed, almost to the exclusion of depression worries, in contract bridge.

Auction had been introduced into this country soon after the opening of the century. Originally devised as a three-handed game by three British civil servants in India who found time hanging heavy on their hands,[25] it had not only taken the place of whist in the social world but had given a new interest to general card-playing. It appealed especially to women of the middle class whose increasing leisure gave them afternoons they often did not quite know how to fill. The bridge club, with its teas and luncheons, had come to represent one of the major social activities of town and suburban life, while informal evening play met the needs of those who desired entertainment without the effort of making conversation. As compared with only one card-party reported in *Middletown's* local press during three months in 1890, the Lynds discovered notices of thirty such affairs in a comparable period for 1923.[26]

Golf on a Vacant Lot

A double midget course in New York. Photograph by Ewing Galloway.

Devotees of Swing

An audience of Bob Crosby's Bob Cats thrilling to hot exploits on the bull
fiddle in a Chicago restaurant. Photograph by Bernard Hoffman, courtesy
of *Life*.

In spite of auction's popularity, the introduction of contract with its more involved play and complicated scoring intensified this craze to an extent which amazed even those who were doing their best to promote it. It had been played in Europe some time earlier but was first brought to this country in 1926. The next year official rules were adopted by the Whist Club, and at first slowly, then with a sudden rush, contract completely supplanted auction.[27] By 1931 enrolment in the new bridge courses started by professional teachers totaled five hundred thousand, and altogether there were estimated to be some twenty million players.[28] The newspapers had bridge columns, magazines were founded to explain the game's fine points, and over a hundred instruction books were on the market. Tournaments attracted the attention usually reserved for championship prize-fights or intercollegiate football games. Bridge had its Four Horsemen as well as football. The entire country hung breathlessly on the outcome of a sensational Battle of the Century between the leading experts. "If contract is not the national game," wrote a contributor describing this "purest of pleasures" for *Harper's* in 1932, "it is second only to golf." [29]

The promotional activities of contract's high priest, Ely Culbertson, revealed a new genius in the art of ballyhoo. He made a card game news as it never had been before. A furor was aroused when he introduced his approach-forcing system of bidding and challenged supporters of the official system to prove that he was not superbly right in everything he said and wrote. The game was played everywhere. If the working class still clung to pedro or five hundred, the social world made contract an almost invariable rule for after-dinner entertainment. Until the effects of the depression somewhat moderated the fever, it was primarily a money game. The stakes ranged from a dollar a point in the fashionable clubs to a tenth of a cent among those who could not afford to gamble. And it was always taken seriously. It seemed almost heresy to many thousands torn with anxiety as to how they should return their partner's lead, lying awake at night smarting under the chagrin of a misleading discard, when the great maestro was quoted as having admitted that "after all, contract is only a game." [30]

-»)«-

DURING the depression years other fads generally reflected the forced economies that most people had to make. One of the most popular, the game of bingo, went a step further. It presented a chance to win something, and all over the country men, women, and children spent long hours trying to fill up a row of numbers on a cardboard square in the hope of taking home a ham, a box of groceries, a tin of coffee, or one of the rare money prizes. Bingo was played at amusement parks, movie theatres, penny arcades, firemen's carnivals, country fairs, Grange suppers, and church socials. It appealed to the gambling instinct of a people always ready for a game of chance. The rewards were never very great, but the risk was even less—thirty-five games for thirty-five cents was the usual charge to play.

It had been a minor carnival attraction, together with beano and keno, for at least thirty years before it was exploited so successfully during the 1930's. How it then started on such a prosperous career remains a mystery, but there was no question that the something-for-nothing motive—or at least something for thirty-five cents—made an appeal which amusement-seekers with little to spend found it hard to resist.[31] When it spread from carnivals and amusement parks to church socials, a storm of controversy arose over the ethics of the gambling involved, but despite all protests it continued to be played as church committees found it the easiest way of raising money.

"Bingo Every Night in the Holy Spirit Room" was the startling announcement of one church presenting it as regular entertainment. And it had warm defenders. "I cannot grow frenzied with the puritanic precisionists who rate the bourgeois pastime of bingo as a major sin," one churchman wrote. "Church bingo parties are a healthy substitute for gossip teas, lovesick movies, and liberal minded lecturers." Outraged ministers of the gospel might declare that "the Kingdom of God cannot be established by shooting craps," but the more realistic among them seemed to feel that bingo was a relatively innocent pastime in comparison with other money games.[32] Many communities, however, finally felt forced to take action against what they considered the dangerous spread of gambling. As a striking throwback to its old blue laws, Connecticut, the land of steady habits, was among those which moved to prohibit the game.

Somewhat analogous to bingo was the craze for prize contests. In newspapers and magazines, over the radio, the public was eloquently urged by interested advertisers to while away the hours and win substantial rewards by completing a limerick extolling some breakfast food or by discovering the name of a facial cream hidden in a cartoon. If reformers again suggested that prize contests came perilously close to lotteries, generally banned since their own vogue early in the nineteenth century, millions nevertheless enjoyed them. And in most cases they accepted with patient resignation their failure to win the offered prizes—an automobile, a trip to Europe, a radio, a bicycle, a diamond pin, and occasionally cash awards as high as a thousand dollars.

It was estimated in 1938 that there had been a thousand per cent increase in prize contests since the advent of the depression. Twenty-five million persons were said to take part in them on an average of twice a year, some individual contests attracting as many as three million entries.[33] The magazine *Win* offered its own selection for addicts whom the national advertisers could not keep busy. Anagrams were puzzled over, missing words filled in, the names of popular songs guessed, cross-word puzzles worked out, verses composed, and candid-camera shots submitted in scores of amateur-photography contests.

Another widespread expression of the gambling spirit (with even less dependence on skill) was the depression-fostered popularity of slot machines, pinball games, punchboards, and jar deals. In an article called "Ten Billion Nickels" a writer in the *Saturday*

Evening Post estimated that the annual take of these gambling devices in 1939 was over $500,000,000, while a Gallup poll the same year reported that one out of every three adults in the country occasionally took a chance on his nickel winning the jackpot. With slot-machine installations in cigar stores, filling stations, lunch counters, drug-stores, and bars, here was a form of petty gambling actually more important than all the betting on horse-races, policy games, and cards.

Along quite different lines, gardening attained a popularity in these years that it had never before experienced. It was hardly a new diversion. A good many centuries earlier Milton had written,

> And add to these retired Leisure,
> That in trim gardens takes his pleasure.

But it appealed to people in the 1930's whose leisure was enforced rather than retired. As the Lynds pointed out in *Middletown Revisited,* there was a rediscovery of the back yard when amusements farther afield seemed impractical that took the form of a "mild mania of flower gardening." [34] Neglected strips of land blossomed out in a profusion of color, and in many cases more economically with carefully weeded rows of vegetables. In the upper reaches of society the growing popularity of this outdoor amusement found expression in the organization of garden clubs, deeply concerned with annual exhibitions in which the rivalry over delphinium and gladioli was as intense as that of the bridge-table. Working-class families were content to cultivate their flowers and vegetables without any such stimulus.

Other hobbies were taken up by the score. So widespread was this development that department stores established hobby sections, newspapers and magazines ran special hobby pages (*The Rotarian* called its page the Hobbyhorse Hitching Post), the radio had its Hobby Lobby, and home-owners made over their cellars into hobby-rooms. Among the rush of books to promote the idea that every man—and woman—should develop some special interest for his leisure hours, one of the most successful was Earnest Elmo Calkin's *The Care and Feeding of Hobby Horses*. Despite the general tendency to take up something that would be as inexpensive as possible, it was estimated in 1937 that the American people were spending anywhere from $50,000,000 to $200,000,000 a year on the craze.[35]

What were the hobbies? Thousands of people took up modeling, water-colors, or wood-carving; collected old bottles, campaign buttons, Indian relics, or match-boxes; built model trains and boats and airplanes; experimented with soap sculpture and puppet shows; studied botany, astronomy, or geology; tried to breed scotties or tropical fish. . . .

-»>>«<<-

WHILE NONE of these minor diversions of the 1930's was in any way quite comparable in sudden and universal popularity to mah-jong, cross-word puzzles, or miniature golf, swing won a distinctive place for itself. As the saxophones blared forth this fresh interpretation of how dance music should be played, a race of "jitterbugs" sprang up to prove that the Great American Band-Wagon was still lumbering along its appointed course for all the bumps and jolts of the depression.

Swing was actually, again to quote the musical theorists, a return to the musical language of jazz, whose original glories had become somewhat dimmed by commercialization. It carried one step further the free improvising that had marked the playing of the first jazz bands. But it too became commercialized as quickly as had jazz after 1914, and in its popular manifestations differed only in degree from music to which America had long since become accustomed.[36] The new orchestras nevertheless created a tremendous stir. They swung the compositions of the great composers; they swung the verses of old nursery rhymes. Although it did not create anything like the excitement of its revolt in the 1920's, the younger generation again kicked up its heels. When Benny Goodman's orchestra first opened in New

York, a theatre audience largely made up of high-school students became so hysterically enthusiastic that staid observers compared the scene to accounts of the children's crusades.

New dances accompanied the upsurge of swing music. At country club and roadhouse, private party and public dance-hall, the generation of the 1930's tried its hand at truckin', took up and then as quickly dropped the big apple, the shag, the Lambeth Walk, and the chestnut tree. The times had not really changed. "If there is anything designed to create more consternation in the national bosom than the new style in women's hats," an editorial writer in the Milwaukee *Journal* observed, "it is undoubtedly the new dances." [37]

Toward the close of the decade the quintessence of harmless idiocy seemed to have been reached in some of the musical fads taken up by night clubs, now legitimately serving the alcoholic drinks which were such an essential part of their entertainment. The café society of New York danced to "Where Is My Little Dog Gone?" and "London Bridge Is Falling Down," played Patty Cake, Patty Cake, and, as the orchestra obligingly swung it, mincingly sang:

> Down in de meddy by de itty bitty poo
> Fam wee itty fitty and a mama fitty, foo.
> 'Fim,' said de mama fitty, 'fim if oo tan'
> And dey fam and dey fam all over de dam. [38]

Chapter XXI

SPORTS FOR ALL

COINCIDENT WITH THE REVOLUTIONARY DEVELOPMENT OF THE movies, automobile, and radio and the rapid progression of popular fads and fancies, there was a no less significant expansion of sports. From prize-fights drawing the largest spectator crowds since the gladiatorial combats of Imperial Rome to a sudden craze for skiing which packed winter excursion trains throughout the North, they boomed as never before. If the American people actually spent more time motoring, going to the movies, and listening to the radio, their interest in sports often appeared to transcend that in anything else.

In 1905 Viscount Bryce had found one of the most noticeable innovations in the life of the American people since his earlier visits "the passion for looking on at and reading about athletic sports." Baseball games and football matches were exciting "an interest greater than any other public events except the Presidential election." [1] Within a few years the expansion of the newspaper sports section intensified this absorption, and as time went on it was still further promoted by moving pictures and radio broadcasts.

But while critics of the American scene declared we were becoming a nation of onlookers, that the sports people watched rather than played were creating a degenerate race getting outdoors only at a stadium or ball park and exercising only in the short walk from the parked sedan to the entrance gate, a less spectacular growth of active sports was actually bringing about a quite opposite development. By the 1920's and 1930's far more people than ever before were themselves taking part in games

347

and athletics. Active sports experienced a post-war revival comparable to the first surge of popular interest in the years following the Civil War. And they had now so expanded that the urban democracy, as well as the middle class and the fashionable world, had regained those opportunities for play which had been largely lost during the industrial changes of the nineteenth century.

The really important development that had taken place since organized sports first won their hold in America was illustrated by the growth of recreational facilities in the cities—playgrounds, athletic fields, softball diamonds, public tennis-courts and golf-links. And almost equally significant was the part played by the automobile in making the country—seashore and mountain—accessible to countless workers who had formerly been completely cut off from it. The millions of visitors at national parks and even greater crowds at bathing-beaches of themselves marked a gain which far outweighed the much more publicized growth of "spectatoritis."

Sensing a need already apparent in the mid-nineteenth century, Walt Whitman had written that "democracy most of all affiliates with the open air." He felt that without access to the revitalizing influence of the open country, America could not develop its "grand races of mechanics, work people, and commonalty...." [2] But not until about 1905 was this issue really taken up. An organized recreation movement then got under way (some twenty years earlier a start had been made with the first provision of public playgrounds for children), and there followed a steady increase in city parks, equipped with all manner of sports facilities, which were available for the use of the general public. [3]

This movement progressed slowly for the next quarter-century and then was given a tremendous impetus by the depression. In the early 1930's, through the Works Progress Administration, the aid of the Federal Government was extended to the municipal recreation programs. By the close of 1937 some $500,000,000 (about ten per cent of the W.P.A.'s total expenditures) had been

Pioneer Sportswomen
Culver Service.

When West Meets East in Football

The crowded Rose Bowl at Pasadena, California, when 91,000 fans saw Duke lose to Southern California on New Year's Day, 1939. Courtesy of Transcontinental and Western Air.

allotted for building 3,700 recreational buildings, 881 new parks, 1,500 athletic fields, 440 swimming-pools, 3,500 tennis-courts, 123 golf-courses, and 28 miles of ski trails.[4] Twelve hundred cities had in all seventeen thousand acres of parks reserved for sports activities, and they were annually spending $60,000,000 on their upkeep. Bathing-beaches and swimming-pools, with an estimated annual attendance of some 200,000,000, were the most popular of their facilities, but there were also 8,800 softball diamonds and 3,600 baseball diamonds at which the player attendance was estimated at 31,000,000; 2,400 ice skating-rinks with an attendance of 13,000,000; 11,000 tennis-courts with an attendance of 11,000,-000; and public golf-courses used by a total of 8,000,000.[5]

Here was the truly democratic approach to this phase of recreation. These millions of urban workers—men, women, and children—were finally enjoying the organized sports that had been introduced by the fashionable world half a century and more earlier. Democracy was making good its right to play the games formerly limited to the small class that had the wealth and leisure to escape the city. No exact totals can possibly be given as to the number of active sports participants in comparison with attendance at sports spectacles in the 1930's. Nobody really knows how many people played softball or tennis, went motor-boating or skiing. But the available evidence clearly shows that in the first forty years of the twentieth century there was a far greater increase in the number of those who played than in the number of those who watched, and there is every reason to believe that in the 1930's the public was spending far more of its leisure—and statistics prove that it was spending four times as much money—on amateur than on professional sports.[6]

In comparison with other countries, more especially those which were under a totalitarian form of government, the promotion of organized outdoor recreation in the United States still lagged. Russia had its great parks of culture and rest, Germany a nation-wide system of people's recreation centers with huge stadia, playing-fields, and swimming-pools. There were such foreign organizations, with which nothing in this country was quite comparable, as the Strength through Joy movement in Germany, the Ready for Work and Defense association in Russia, and Italy's National Leisure-Time Institute.[7] All the difference in the world, however, lay between the totalitarian and the American approach to this form of recreation. The one was a defiant alliance between the need for popular sports and preparedness for war—controlled, ordered, regimented. The other had no connection with military training and was wholly free from any suggestion of compulsion or regimentation. In the totalitarian countries the trend was very definitely toward the obligatory use of leisure time in the interests of the State; in America it was toward broader opportunities for play as the people might choose to take advantage of them in accord with their own needs and interests.

—»»«««-

IN MANY WAYS the outstanding spectator sport of the 1920's and 1930's was intercollegiate football. It had a far larger following than the relatively select crowds that had originally supported it, the short fall season representing for countless sports enthusiasts the climax of the year. The millions who every Saturday afternoon made their way to the games were supplemented by many more millions who hovered over their radios in comfortable steam-heated living-rooms to follow them play by play, and then spent Sunday mornings devouring long accounts in the sports sections of how it all had happened. Football reigned supreme from the opening of early-season practice to the Tournament of Roses. "It is at present a religion," a contributor to *Harper's* stated in 1928 —"sometimes it seems to be almost our national religion."[8]

After the reforms adopted in the 1890's had enabled football to regain a position threatened by professionalism and roughness, it had had to go through still another crisis in 1905. Injuries and even fatalities (the death-roll had reached forty-four in 1903) had become so general that the press was uniformly condemning the game and many colleges were planning to abolish it. Football became a national issue, President Roosevelt inviting its leaders to a White House conference, and public opinion forced a number of reforms. The forward pass, the on-side kick, separation of the rush lines, were devised to make it less dangerous, and these innovations gradually led to a more open—and also more interesting—game.[9]

Crowds of fifty thousand soon began to attend many other contests than those between Harvard, Yale, and Princeton, and in the post-war decade football joyously took part in the dazzling upward movement which characterized everything about those years from women's skirts to stock-market prices. Sensing their opportunity, universities and colleges covered the country with great concrete stadia whose total capacity exceeded two millions. Yale and California had bowls seating eighty thousand; Illinois, Michigan, Ohio State, and several others provided for seventy thousand.[10] Empty almost every day of the year except those fabulous Saturday afternoons in the autumn, the quickened interest of the public then taxed all available facilities. It was estimated that during the season anywhere from ten to thirty millions (attendance generally doubling between 1921 and 1930[11]) watched a game which had been almost entirely taken away from college graduate or undergraduate and given over to a sports-hungry public which supported football as a grandiose commercial amusement.

It was a colorful, exciting show. Every year saw a new sensation: the "praying colonels" of Centre College blazing through the sky like a meteor, and as quickly fading out; Princeton's "Team of Destiny" briefly lighting up the dimmed prestige of the one-time Big Three; the Four Horsemen of Notre Dame galloping down a dozen fields to win new laurels for Knute Rockne; and Red Grange, a team by himself, flashing past all other heroes in football's hall of fame. In this glamorous period the line between intercollegiate football and the newly popular professional game was sometimes hardly distinguishable. Red

Grange was one of those who after playing his last college season definitely stepped over it. While student admirers framed his football jersey at Illinois (also circulating a petition to nominate him for Congress), he joined the Chicago Bears, collected $30,000 in his first game, signed a $300,000 movie contract, and was presented to President Coolidge.[12] Here was fame, and also fortune.

Educators were not wholly pleased with an emphasis on the sport that made the academic standing of their institutions so negligible a factor in comparison with a football championship. Many of them felt that a commercial amusement business, whatever the advertising value of a winning team or the magnitude of the gate receipts, did not fall within the functions of a university. But the general public, and also the greater part of the nation's college alumni, only asked for more victories. Their attitude toward the criticism voiced by the professorial fraternity was aptly expressed in an editorial in *Liberty*. This popular magazine found the protesting faculty members jealous. "The problem is not the elimination or restriction of football," *Liberty* warned, "but how long it will be before red-blooded colleges demand the elimination or the restriction of those afflicted with this inferiority complex." [13]

In 1929 football had to withstand the shock of a distressing disclosure of overemphasis and professionalism in a report of the Carnegie Foundation. But the old fires of controversy as to its place in college life could not be fanned into a very fierce flame. There was too great a vested interest in the game. An influence far more seriously adverse was the depression. It affected the sale of big-game tickets just as severely as that of any market commodity. Nevertheless intercollegiate football withstood these slings of outrageous fortune; it kept its hold on the public. After a few comparatively slim years it was again crowding its stadia to capacity, creating successive generations of national heroes, and monopolizing the radio every Saturday throughout the fall.

Then there was baseball. In the number of persons who actually watched the game, its longer season made it even a little more important. But except for the World Series between the winners in the National and American leagues, there had been since the beginning of the century a relative decline in baseball's popularity. Small-town games had definitely suffered an eclipse from the growth of so many other sports; interest in college baseball was waning; and attendance at professional-league games had not kept pace with the population growth of the cities supporting teams. An actual decline between 1920 and 1930 was reported by several minor leagues. An eleven per cent gain for the majors, to an annual total of ten millions, compared with a twenty per cent population growth in this same period,[14] and in succeeding years attendance did no better than hold these levels.

Nevertheless, the publicity given baseball (its monopolizing of evening-paper head-lines) afforded good evidence that for the public at large it was still the national game. And the World Series remained an event of the greatest importance. Attendance fluctuated. In 1923 it was over 300,000, twice that ten years earlier, but the next decade saw it as low as 164,000 one year, and over 300,000 only once.[15] Baseball had its national heroes. The greatest of them, Babe Ruth, was at the peak of his fame in the 1920's. No athletic figure has ever won greater renown than this Sultan of Swat with his season record of sixty home runs.

More typical of the ballyhoo spirit that characterized professional athletics was prize-fighting. Tex Rickard took over this once disapproved and banned sport, and with a genius for showmanship which rivaled that of P. T. Barnum, he made it at once respectable and glamorous. The fashionable world fought for tickets whose high prices were in themselves proof that prize-fighting had undergone some sort of moral regeneration. Women forgot their traditional scruples in enjoying the ring's primitive combat. The sporting men, who were only a flashier, better-dressed counterpart (with more money to bet) of the nineteenth-century fancy, happily paid whatever the speculators demanded for their ringside seats. Championship bouts came in rapid succession, each occasion being built up with the willing aid of the press to a greater climax than the one before. The public mania for watching sports reached an all-time high in a series of bouts in the 1920's which dwarfed all that had gone before.

There had been a succession of world champions since James J. Corbett (all of eight thousand persons watching the epic encounter) had dethroned the great John L. in 1892: Robert Prometheus Fitzsimmons, James J. Jeffries, Tommy Burns, Jack Johnson, and finally Jess Willard. But the new era in prize-fighting started when Jack Dempsey successfully challenged Willard at Toledo in 1919 and Mr. Rickard added up gate receipts of $452,-000. By the alchemy of clever publicity he had made the nation fight-conscious, and it clamored for bigger and better battles. Georges Carpentier, a handsome, flashy Frenchman, went down before Dempsey's flailing fists at the Battle of the Century at Boyle's Forty Acres in Jersey City, and soon afterwards Luis Angel Firpo, the Wild Bull of the Pampas. Million-dollar gates became the rule for a championship bout—with radio broadcasts, movie rights, testimonials, and other activities building up what had once been an outlawed sport into a big-time industry legalized in fifteen states as "boxing contests." [16]

Gene Tunney, who was to walk with the novelist Thornton Wilder and talk with the literary critic William Lyon Phelps, was the nemesis of the heretofore invincible Mr. Dempsey. The crowd that watched him win the championship at the Philadelphia Sesqui-centennial in 1926 broke all records, but they were shattered again at Chicago in a return bout the next year. Twenty-four special trains rolled into town for the great event. There were 145,000 spectators at Soldiers Field, with two hundred millionaires in the first ten rows. Many of those in the tremendous crowd were so far away from the ring that they could not tell through the fog of cigarette smoke that Tunney had won the fight. It hardly mattered. They had paid $2,650,000 for admission and were happy. Every spectator felt he had watched history being made, and many more—how many millions could hardly be said—heard it being made over the radio. Five listeners to the account of the fight were reported to have dropped dead of heart-failure when Tunney went down in the seventh round.[17]

Prize-fighting could not quite adapt itself to the high standards with which the new champion sought to endow it. He was never popular. And his fortune made (almost $2,000,000 in two years), Tunney retired.[18] The day of million-dollar gates was over—at least for the time being. Not until another colored champion, Joe Louis, arose in the late 1930's (breaking new records by the ease with which he knocked out a succession of second-rate challengers) did prize-fighting recover some of its lost glamour. Even then attendance at his bouts was hardly comparable to that at the epic Dempsey-Tunney encounters.

Other spectator events drew large crowds. The professionalization of new sports, the building of huge arenas, and the extension of night playing (in baseball and football as well as hockey and basketball) contributed to their growing popularity. Race-track attendance exceeded all previous figures in the 1920's, partly owing to the sensational victories of Man o' War, and in 1930 Gallant Fox awoke a fresh enthusiasm with his successive triumphs in the Kentucky Derby, the Preakness, and the Belmont Stakes. Greyhound racing, another old sport, had a sudden revival. The publicity attendant upon the Olympic Games—revived in the 1890's and regularly won by the United States—created widespread interest in athletic meets and the hard-fought races of champion long-distance runners. Six-day bicycle and automobile races retained their old popularity (the crowd at Indianapolis in 1939 was estimated at 145,000); professional hockey and professional football forged ahead; there was new interest in wrestling; and even tennis became a spectator sport. With professional as well as amateur teams in the field—but perhaps most of all because of the high-school craze of the Middle West—basketball was reported to be attracting an even greater aggregate attendance than the more head-lined events.

It was sometimes confusing to find one's way through the maze of sporting news. "This is station KDKAWXJEAZFOW," one magazine writer transcribed a radio station's broadcast for a typical day. "The boys are in top-notch condition and as the first ball was pitched Epinard broke clean and scored two goals on a good mashie pitch that just cleared the rightfield stands and narrowly missed killing Tilden's backhand three inches from the cup when the entire Washington team was awarded to McGraw on points just as the chukker ended. Listen to the cheering!" [19] Whenever international competition entered the picture, public interest was still further heightened by the dramatic conquests of American teams and American players in almost every field of so-called amateur sport. The successive victories in the Olympic Games, in the Davis Cup tennis matches, in the British-American golf matches for the Walker Cup, and in the America's Cup yacht-races all added to the popular excitement.

The country appeared sports-crazy, and every reading of the daily paper confirmed it. In 1919 charges of bribe-taking against the Chicago White Sox created more of a stir than similar charges a few years later against members of the President's Cabinet. In 1928 Tilden's debarment from amateur tennis ranks drove election news, the assassination of Mexico's president-elect, and a search for lost aviators in the Arctic off the front pages of the evening newspapers.[20]

->>><<<-

So MUCH for spectator sports. Among the outdoor activities in which the public participated, hunting and fishing were still leaders. Almost twelve million licenses were being taken out annually for the field sports which had remained since colonial days in a class almost by themselves in American recreation. Interested manufacturers claimed that over eight million men and women remained addicts of the ever-popular amusement of bowling, and there were tremendous numbers of softball players, trap-shooters (with the great popularity of skeet), and tennis-players.[21] But the businessman—hero of the age—had taken over golf in post-war America and made the game his own. It may have been played by fewer people, but it was the fashionable sports leader.

In 1910 the number of courses scattered throughout the country had already grown to several hundred, and there were an estimated half-million players.[22] Golf was no longer regarded as a fad. Its devotees had put away their red coats and leggings; they were seriously getting down to business. Champions on a par with those of England were showing the way—Jerome D. Travis, Francis Ouimet, and W. C. Hagen. More than any other sport so far developed, golf appeared to be the answer to the middle-class need for outdoor exercise. Every year new links were built as the game's advantages became more widely known.

The World War did not interrupt this movement. In 1916 there were 743 courses, in 1930 a total of 5,856—a sevenfold increase in fourteen years. Every town of any size at all boasted at least one. The number of players had risen to two million. Nor was all this golf for the privileged. There were over twelve hundred daily-fee or public courses, and every year clerks and office-workers were taking up the game in greater numbers.[23] "The democracy of golf to-day," Grantland Rice wrote in 1928, "has gone far beyond that of any other sport." [24] But for all the importance of these facts and figures, what gave golf its unique status was the sacred aura that clung about it. Every ambitious member of the white-collar class tried to follow his boss around the links. Golf was a fascinating sport, a healthful outdoor pastime. It was also the ladder to business and social success in the extravagant days that accompanied the recovery from the immediate post-war depression.

Certainly one of the most characteristic social manifestations of the 1920's was the ritual that grew up about this sport. Membership in a country club became a first requisite for the social climber; to be able to play a good game was essential for the young man who wanted to get ahead. It was an era of baggy plus-fours, with tasseled wool stockings; of determined foursomes playing their eighteen-hole matches in a fiercely competitive spirit taken over directly from their business deals; of endless discussions at "the nineteenth hole" about the latest exploits of Bobby Jones, the game's own superchampion.

Women also took up golf. But they played during the week and retired gracefully to club verandahs for tea and bridge when Saturday afternoon brought out their husbands. Men's foursomes were the outstanding feature of country-club life, especially in the suburbs. The weekly handicap tournament was the great event to which hundreds of thousands of commuters looked forward from Monday to Saturday. There was no pretense of observing the Sabbath—the bicycle, motoring, and now golf had stripped it of all semblance of a day of rest. Church was forgotten, the home neglected, wives deserted for the lure of the links.

Golf was expensive. Membership in a club with its heavy outlay for keeping up the course; caddy fees, clubs, and the constant replenishment of balls; all the paraphernalia of such a socially correct activity, resulted in more money being spent on the game than on any other sport. With a nation-wide investment in courses of $850,000,000, it was conservatively estimated in 1929 that the country's golfers were paying $200,000,000 a year for the privilege of enjoying their favorite diversion.[25]

The depression had a devastating effect. Almost every club found itself with greatly reduced membership and many of them opened their onetime exclusive preserves to all comers. Some were forced to close. The end of the era of high-pressure salesmanship, when the stock broker and bond salesman had found the golf-course one of the most profitable fields of operation, took something of the bloom off the ancient and honorable game. But its place in national life was too well established for it to lose its popularity despite its lessened value as an adjunct to business and social life. Public courses increased at the expense of private clubs. In 1935 the total number of golfers was placed at a somewhat lower figure than six years earlier, but there were more players on municipal links. Golf had been

socially deflated, and it was approaching closer to the democratic ideal.[26]

Tennis also had made remarkable progress during these years,
evolving into a game which bore little resemblance to that polite
pastime of the 1890's which was considered so well adapted for
ladies and gentlemen. It became more active, hard-hitting, and
competitive. It was taken up by a continually broadening circle
of players. As the champions of golf, and the publicity given
their matches, served to promote that sport, tournament winners
and Davis Cup players provided the ballyhoo for tennis. And in
the 1920's William T. Tilden became as idolized as Babe Ruth
or Bobby Jones. He was one of the era's bright galaxy of popular
stars.

In costumes which would have horrified her Victorian forebears, the modern woman also played the new tennis. The glamorous Suzanne Lenglen and phenomenal Helen Wills, short-
skirted, bare-legged, developed a game which compared
favorably with that of all but the greatest of the men players.
Thousands of girls followed their lead. More important, they
continued to play far past that age at which the ideal of "female
delicacy" had once decreed embroidery and china-painting as
the only approved pursuits for women, had placed the stamp of
fashion on "the slender, and delicate, and fragile form—the pale,
sallow, and waxen complexion."

Clubs affiliated with the United States Lawn Tennis Association by no means afford a complete picture of what had happened in the world of tennis. Their courts were only a fraction
of a total which included those of country clubs, municipalities,
and private owners. But their increase provides a key to the
game's growing popularity. In 1910 there were 160 member clubs,
and ten years later 294. The next decade saw this figure doubled,
and by 1933 it was almost a thousand. The number of tennis-
players had risen by the 1930's to some three or four millions,
with about a quarter of the total representing players on public
courts.[27]

A new sport that had a great boom in the 1930's was softball. It was a modified form of baseball—the chief difference between the two games being adequately expressed in its name— and its easier, more informal style of play attracted thousands of adults who left the original game to young men and boys. Softball teams were formed by groups representing every element in American society—industrial workers and suburban commuters, church leaguers and employees of the New York Stock Exchange, members of fashionable country clubs and of local village organizations. There were women players, in teams made up of business employees, Y.W.C.A. members, or factory operatives.

The game had been known under various names for some time. It was being played as kitten ball in St. Paul about 1912, and in other places it was called indoor baseball, mush ball, or recreation ball. But its boom followed the organization, in 1933, of the Amateur Softball Association of America. Through its promotional work, sponsorship of regional tournaments, and establishment of an annual world series, softball became a craze which spread over the land much as had the earlier crazes for croquet, roller-skating, and bicycling. The Softball Association soon claimed a membership larger than that of any other amateur sports body in the world, and there were an estimated eight thousand diamonds in some eight hundred cities. In 1938 ten million people—including a greater number of adult players than possibly in any other sport—were reported to have taken up the game.[28]

Industrial plants welcomed it as one of the most practical ways of promoting the nation-wide movement to provide outdoor exercise for employees. It was an outstanding symbol of the twentieth century's approach to recreation, of the recovery for factory-workers of the play opportunities they had so long been lacking. Softball was played on week-ends and holidays, at the lunch hour and after work, on flood-lighted diamonds during the evening.

One of the most interesting developments in these years was

*Factory
Softball*

ata girls in ac-
Wide World
Photos.

ollege Basketball

asium of the Univer-
f California. Courtesy
e Associated Students
News Bureau.

Ski Tracks in the Rockies

The ski-lift on Dollar Mountain, Sun Valley, Idaho. Courtesy of the Union
Pacific Railroad.

On the Be
at Coney Is

A holiday
of bathers, se
sun, in 1939.
World Pho

the rise of skiing. An old sport in northern Europe, it reached the United States by way of Norwegian settlers who organized the country's pioneer ski club at Red Wing, Minnesota, in 1883.[29] It was not until half a century later, however, that it became a fad throughout the northern states, and especially New England, where a combination of snow and mountains made it an ideal winter sport.

The revived interest in the out-of-doors was primarily responsible for its sudden popularity—people could have skied as well in earlier periods. But when about 1929 a few enthusiasts began preaching the gospel of the ski, a public which had hardly heard of the sport found itself carried away. The department stores installed borax slides and imported Austrian instructors; the railroads ran special trains to the skiing country and organized week-end excursions. Quick to sense the unexpected gold in their snow-covered hills, farmers everywhere prepared to rent rooms and provide food for the city skiers who began to dot every good slope. A steadily growing band of fanatics hung on the week-end weather forecasts; argued furiously over waxes, bindings, and the merits of the stem Christy as against the telemark; and then went out to endanger life and limb in hazardous plunges down slope and trail.

Skiing was a limited sport. It could be practised only in certain parts of the country, during a very short season of the year. And though it followed the usual course of gradually reaching a wider and wider public, the expense of equipment and transportation was another restrictive factor. Granted these limitations, its quick rise to a major winter sport nevertheless afforded still another striking illustration of how sport-conscious the country had become, how eager great numbers of people were to take part in sports as well as watch them. In 1930 there were only a handful of skiers in the United States, too few to consider in any survey of recreation. Before a decade had passed, such a holiday as Washington's Birthday found a quarter-million excursionists bound for the hills, and the total number of skiers throughout the country was estimated at two million. In such states as Vermont, New Hampshire, Michigan, Wisconsin, and Idaho (where one of the most elaborate ski centers in the world was established at Sun Valley by the Union Pacific Railroad), skiing had assumed formidable proportions.[30]

->>)&<<-

ALMOST all other sports underwent a tremendous expansion in the post-war years, only temporarily interrupted by the depression. Sailing and boating had a new vogue—a relative decline in yachting but great increase in motor-boating. The outboard motor had opened up for thousands a recreation formerly far beyond their means. It created an entirely new class of water enthusiasts, drawn in great part from those elements in society which a century earlier had lined city water-fronts to watch the regattas of the exclusive boating and yacht clubs. The outdoor movement drew campers, canoeists, hikers, and mountain-climbers into the country. Every summer saw the lakes and trails more crowded with young people discovering for themselves that living in the open, sleeping in log huts or under canvas, and cooking before a camp-fire constituted one of the most satisfying contrasts to the indoor routine of city jobs. There were more fishing and hunting. An unusual revival caused several states to set aside special preserves for bow-and-arrow hunting.

Horseback-riding, fox-hunting, and polo proved that though the horse might be passing in the commercial world, its rôle in the world of sports had become more important. With the democracy taking over so many games, society fell back on these expensive activities for the assurance they provided of social status. It also took up flying—somewhat as it once had motoring and automobile racing—and aviation played the rôle of plutocracy's most exciting and expensive sport.

Both lawn games and indoor games multiplied. Archery and croquet were revived. Field hockey flourished as a game for girls. Badminton was widely taken up, and squash, racquets and handball. Ping-pong flourished mightily in the new guise of table tennis. It was everywhere the same story. Even the traditional country pastime of horseshoe-pitching (although shuffleboard was reported to be taking its place in Florida) felt the quickening urge of the new sports enthusiasm: a National Horseshoe Pitchers Association was organized.[31]

Over everything else, from sheer weight of numbers, stood swimming and bathing. They were the great recreation of millions who did not take up games. The packed beaches of the 1920's and 1930's were a startling demonstration of the changes that had taken place since the nineteenth century. The modern bathing-suit (together with shorts and slacks) had a social significance which could be appreciated only in comparison with the shocked concern over mixed bathing—"the parties always go into the water completely dressed"—in the 1840's. It symbolized the new status of women even more than the short skirts and bobbed hair of the jazz age or the athleticism of the devotees of tennis and golf. It was the final proof of their successful assertion of the right to enjoy whatever recreation they chose, costumed according to the demands of the sport rather than the tabus of an outworn prudery, and to enjoy it in free and natural association with men.

Here was an outdoor recreation more fully open to all classes of people—men and women of whatever age, young people, and children—than any other. The two hundred million attendance at municipal bathing-beaches and swimming-pools (a total almost as large as that of the estimated yearly attendance at *all* spectator sports) did not by any means represent every one who bathed and swam. Their numbers were swelled by throngs of swimmers of which no count could possibly be taken. Nevertheless, even this figure proves how universal a recreation it had become. As a result of changing fashions, a new social interest in recreation, and modern methods of transportation, the democracy had discovered in bathing and swimming a grand chance to affiliate with the open air.

→»《←

ANY ATTEMPT to survey sports in these years is bound to be in adequate. This is implicit in the very fact that opportunities for play had so immeasurably increased in comparison with those of half a century or a quarter-century earlier. In the 1890's the description of the beginnings of half a dozen organized sports could afford a fair idea of this phase of national recreation. In the twentieth century there were innumerable sports. We have only touched on their development, skimmed the surface of outdoor activities. One could add soccer, lacrosse, volley-ball, fencing, rifle-shooting, motorcycling, tobogganing, figure skating, ice-boating, curling, gymnastics. . . . The sports activity of the American people was limitless.

Chapter XXII

THE NEW LEISURE

DURING THE YEARS OF PROSPERITY THAT ENDED SO ABRUPTLY
with the collapse of the stock market in the fall of 1929,
faint voices might be heard asking where the dominance of the
movies, the ballyhoo of sports, the successive crazes for so many
other amusements, were leading the American people. The depression of the 1930's brought this question home with a new
intensity. The further increase in leisure for the great majority of
workers, caused partly by economic circumstance and partly by
governmental action, suddenly awoke the country to the change
that had come over old ideas on the relationship between work
and play. We were fully launched on what James A. Garfield
half a century earlier had said was the second great struggle of
civilization—"What shall we do with our leisure when we get it?"

For three centuries the American tradition had placed an
emphasis on work which made it the chief purpose of existence.
"Business to the American," an Englishman could write even in
the 1920's, "is life's great adventure; it is sport, work, pleasure,
beauty and patriotism rolled into one." [1] Puritanism had imposed
a religious sanction on this concept. Idleness could have no place
in a world where labor was the greatest good. But with the depression the revolutionary transformation wrought by the machine could no longer be ignored. It had not only made leisure
possible for the mass of people, but had imposed it upon them
whether they wanted it or not. Boon or Pandora's box of new
evils, there could be no escaping it. And since it was not in our
nature to accept it easily, gratefully ("Pleasure does make us
Yankees kind o' winch"), we examined it with some foreboding

Leisure became, according to the dictates of our puritan inheritance, not so much an opportunity as a problem.

Despite labor agitation for shorter hours, leisure was primarily a by-product of industrialism rather than anything that had been consciously sought out. Little thought had been given to its ultimate value for the people as a whole through the hurrying years of economic progress. The reduction in hours of work had taken place almost automatically as the application of mechanical power enabled society to satisfy its normal needs in progressively less working time. This was generally true throughout the western world, but the United States particularly was confronted by a condition and not a theory.

The eight-hour day had come into general effect although there were, of course, many exceptions by the 1920's. Statistics for twenty-five forms of manufacture showed the average working-week in this country for both men and women to be forty-eight hours.[2] Shop and office employees fared even better with the more general adoption of both the Saturday half-holiday and the week's or two weeks' summer vacation. The further reduction in this time occasioned by the depression, with the demand for spreading out work and increasing employment, found a forty-hour week suddenly becoming the almost general rule. A full working-day was lopped off through the terms of the National Industrial Recovery Act, and even after the N.R.A. had collapsed, further legislation maintained this shorter working-week as a national objective. Never before had there been such an effective decrease in labor's average working time, considering the country as a whole, in so brief a period.

The average industrial worker at the close of the 1930's enjoyed the equivalent of almost a full day more of weekly leisure than he had had prior to the depression. In comparison with conditions in the 1890's, he had more than twice as much time free for recreational activities. Over the course of a century, prevailing hours of labor had been halved and available leisure was estimated to have increased from about ten hours weekly to some

seventy. It was a startling development whose social significance
could hardly be overestimated.[3]

Since the industrial revolution no people had ever had so much
time for other things besides earning a livelihood. Civilizations of
the past had had many non-working days, more than is generally
realized. In Egypt holidays are said to have amounted to one-
fifth the number of days in the year; there were from fifty to
sixty days of festival in Greece; and in Rome almost a third of
the days in the year were considered "unlucky" for work.[4] But
the factory system had spelled the end of such frequent holidays
and for long imposed just as many hours of daily labor as the
ancient world had known. Now at last, however, the masses enjoyed a measure of weekly leisure which more than made up
for the non-working days and festivals of an earlier age.

The implications of these developments had been seriously
discussed long before the reduction from a forty-eight-hour week
to a forty-hour week. The experience of the depression years,
however, dramatized the situation as never before. The "challenge of the new leisure" became a vital issue. Under such circumstances recreation could no longer be dismissed as a waste of
time or harmless diversion. It could no longer be considered only
a means to restore the capacity to work—part of that endless circle
wherein one worked to gain the opportunity to play and played
to be able to work more effectively. It became for perhaps the
first time in American history something which was represented
as a possible good in itself. The psychologist wrote of the value
of play as an instinctive form of self-expression and emotional
escape-valve; the sociologist stressed its importance in counter-
acting ill health, mental instability, and crime in the urban community.[5]

"The value of leisure-time activities, play and recreation,"
wrote George A. Lundberg, "is usually conceded to lie in the
nervous release which they afford from the customary and co-
ercive activities which the social order imposes upon us. To the
extent, therefore, that the pursuits of our leisure-time tend to

become organized under conventional patterns determined by competitive consumption they lose their unique and primary value as recreation and so become merely another department of activity devoted to the achievement of prestige or status." [6]

The scientific pack was in full cry. There was a sudden burgeoning of committees to study leisure-time activities and of organizations to promote healthful community play. The church intensified its efforts to meet the challenge of commercial amusements, and industry undertook to promote the recreation of its employees along the lines it considered most socially useful. As a phase of the general program for social security, the New Deal reënforced the efforts already being made by municipalities to enable city workers to take part in a broad field of diversions ranging from handball to folk-dancing. It paid out through the W.P.A., as already noted, hundreds of millions of dollars for parks, playgrounds, and recreation centers.

Here was a complete departure from that earlier tradition which had found church and state allied in condemning leisure and amusements. No laws were being passed in the 1930's in detestation of idleness. The energy and resources of the state were employed to implement it. Recognition of a responsibility to promote work had been translated into a responsibility to make leisure worth while.

→>>«←-

ECONOMIC CONSIDERATIONS affected the changed status of leisure in other ways. It was not only that the reduction in hours of labor necessary to produce the goods the people needed had automatically created more free time, or that the efficient working of the factory system demanded healthful recreation to offset the strain of more intensified work. Our whole economy was geared to a necessary consumption of leisure-time goods. The working of the industrial plant had become dependent upon people having the time, and the money, to spend on the commercialized amusements which were the machine age's answer to recreational needs. A large part of our economic activity was the provision of entertainment for the laboring masses. Millions of people were employed in providing amusements for their fellow-workers.

It has been conservatively estimated (many studies giving much higher figures) that the American people spent in 1935 more than eight per cent of their entire income on recreation. The total was something over $4,000,000,000. This was a decline of approximately one-third from the total for 1929, but it was proportionately greater than ever before in our history. The ratio, indeed, was just twice that of a quarter of a century earlier. Vacation travel, dominated by the immense sums spent on automobile touring, accounted for more than half this figure. The remainder was divided almost equally between commercial amusements and so-called recreational products. Motion pictures were far and away the principal item among commercial amusements, but they also included legitimate theatres, amusement parks, billiard parlors and bowling-alleys, public dance-halls, and all spectator sports. Recreational products comprised radios, the lighter books and periodicals, musical instruments, motor boats, games, and all sporting goods and equipment.[7]

These expenditures afford graphic evidence of how accustomed the American democracy had become to digging deep down into its pocket for its amusements. The relative rise in their ratio to national income through the depression years is startling proof of the commercial aspect of popular recreation. The country as a whole appeared every year more willing to buy entertainment, even though it must have meant in countless instances the sacrifice of other things that might normally seem more important. The spirit that induced so many workingmen to give up almost anything else before they let the automobile go was reflected on a broader scale in the whole field of popular diversion.

The large sums recorded by these figures are also impressive in their bearing on the rôle of commercial amusements in national production. That part of the automobile industry which may be statistically allocated to the pleasure use of cars, the motion-picture industry, and the radio industry stand out from the point of view of both value of products and employment as three of America's leading industrial activities. When all other branches of popular entertainment and the economic activities directly dependent upon them are included, the amusement industry as a whole is seen to take its place as an essential cog in the working of the industrial plant as developed during the twentieth century.

If the impossible had happened in the 1930's, if the country had somehow gone back and accepted Puritan concepts of the evil inherent in all amusements, the resulting dislocation in the industries providing popular entertainment would have thrown the entire economic system out of gear. Millions of men and women would have suddenly found themselves without jobs or means of support. No movies, no automobile touring, no radio, no professional sports—the country could hardly have survived! Even the revival of the Puritan Sabbath, with effective blue laws forbidding all Sunday amusements, would have had economic repercussions throwing an army of workers out of employment.

→»«←

ANOTHER ASPECT of recreation under the conditions imposed by the new leisure was its social effects. As any observer of the American scene could easily have foretold, surveys of recreation in the 1930's invariably showed that the radio, movies, and motoring were the most popular and most frequently enjoyed of all diversions. The more simple, unsophisticated leisure-time activities of the home still continued. In point of fact, the forced economies of the depression period introduced a new informality into social life for many people and threw others to a greater extent on their own resources for entertainment than they had been in many years. Some of the surveys revealed that people actually spent more time visiting with their friends than going to the movies. The art of conversation may have died, but people still talked. Nevertheless, almost every questionnaire provided further confirmation that the great amount of time spent by the entire family on machine-made amusements was one of the most significant aspects of contemporary life.[8]

"How does the American adult spend his leisure time?" asked one magazine writer in 1937, who then went on to answer his own question without benefit of scientific surveys. "The chances are eight to ten that he will drive his car along Route 168, watch a 'moom' picture, listen to the Itty Bitty Kiddie Hour, or else enjoy a few inches in the bleachers while some one on the field plays for him." [9]

These new amusements pulled in many different directions. In almost every instance in which the influence of commercialized entertainment could be held unwholesome, almost as good a case could be made out to quite the opposite effect. The movies tended to disrupt family life, but the radio kept people at home. Motoring took away from lawn games and informal back-yard sports; it also opened up larger opportunities for more ambitious outdoor activities. Together these machine amusements led to the decline of many traditional diversions of the small town and countryside. Lodge night, the church social, the Grange picnic, and even the country fair lost something of their old glory, but so did the pool-room, the beer-parlor, the burlesque show, and the shady entertainment palace of metropolis. There was less family-group recreation, but more for the individual regardless of age or sex. A proper balance could not easily be struck in evaluating the change in recreational patterns. The radio's incessant blare brought Beethoven as well as the Jazztown Rubes to its nation-wide audience; the movies offered their millions *Wuthering Heights* as well as *Sinners in Silk*. If conditions of urban life still placed a premium on passive indoor amusements, there was the underlying trend (which the radio and the movies often themselves promoted) toward a wider participation in sports than the country had ever known before.

With modern inventions every one heard the same tunes at the same time over the radio, saw the same movies from coast to coast. Because of the ballyhoo of the entertainment industry, the public took up the same fads and fancies. It played mah-jong one year and miniature golf the next. The American people, it was often charged, were being so closely regimented in their amusements that individuality was doomed. Even for this something might be said on the ground that recreation had become a great unifying force among a very heterogeneous people, an instrument to promote national solidarity at a time when the bonds of church and state had lost their old strength. But how real was this alleged regimentation in comparison with other days or other lands? Its evils were most emphasized by representatives of the class whose leisure and income had always enabled them to enjoy a relatively wide variety of pleasures. Unconsciously, perhaps, they resented the fact that they could no longer maintain an exclusive hold on their amusements. It was disturbing that the new sport could no longer be restricted to the more genteel elements of society, that every fad should be taken up so quickly by the people as a whole.

For the common man the radio, the movies, and the automobile represented recreational opportunities he had never had before. The successive crazes for sports and games introduced a diversity into his life that it had completely lacked. And for him the pattern of these regimented amusements was so complex in comparison with the simple and actually far more uniform diversions of an earlier day that the laments of the sophisticated were incomprehensible. The popularity of an infinite number of hobbies and special interests also seemed to show that individuality had by no means been wholly engulfed in mass entertainment. Millions might listen simultaneously to Bing Crosby or the Singing Lady, crowd the theatres to see *Andy Hardy Gets Spring Fever,* or spend Sunday afternoon motoring in a staggering procession of identical sedans, but vast numbers also grew prize dahlias, played on softball teams, collected stamps, went to legitimate theatres or concert-halls, played checkers and chess, raced outboard motor-boats, worked at amateur carpentry, went on camping trips in the woods, took up bridge, flute-playing, or golf.

No other country, and no other age, had ever had a wider choice of amusements open to the mass of the people. It was overwhelming. Science and the machine had reshaped the traditional patterns of recreation into hundreds of new forms. Working men and working women—factory operatives, plumbers, waitresses, bank clerks, telephone operators, farm-hands, stenographers, storekeepers, nurse-maids, subway guards, mill-hands, garment-workers, office-boys, truck-drivers—found countless pleasures once limited to the privileged few were now theirs for the seeking. The democracy had come into its heritage. It had achieved both leisure and the facilities for its enjoyment.

->>><<<-

DESPITE the demands made for a greater measure of control over popular amusements, the American people continued in the 1930's to maintain the laissez-faire attitude which was felt to be the essence of democracy. Except in so far as Government undertook to provide the increased opportunities for play that it was now felt the community owed its citizens, there was no legislative interference with recreation. It was not officially ordered to promote industrial efficiency, to bind the people to any political system, or to prepare the country for war. The example of the totalitarian states was not followed. Opportunity, not compulsion, symbolized the American way. The wishes of the individual were not sacrificed to the supposed interests of the State, and the theory was generally maintained that public opinion alone should be the arbiter of recreation's rôle in the national life. If its standards were to be raised, it could be done only through popular education.

Such an attitude seemed implicit in the ideals on which American society was based. In an age in which they were being threatened from so many quarters, here was another challenge to everything for which democracy stood.

BIBLIOGRAPHY

THE MATERIALS FOR THE HISTORY OF AMERICAN RECREATION ARE so voluminous that the following bibliographical notes represent only a tentative and very limited guide to the essential sources. There is no encompassing a field which includes laws on colonial and state statute-books, the journals of travelers throughout our history, diaries and autobiographies, newspapers and magazines (their advertisements as well as their news columns), and all extant sports guides, books of games, theatre playbills and programs, circus posters, and general amusement broadsides. It is possible here only to indicate the sources that the present author has found especially useful.

For books dealing with special phases of recreation there are a few helpful bibliographies. Robert W. Henderson has compiled a chronological check-list of books on sports published prior to 1860, *Early American Sports* (New York, 1937); and C. M. Van Sockum a more general bibliography for 1890-1912, *Sport* (New York, 1914). Blanch M. Baker, *Dramatic Bibliography* (New York, 1933), is useful for the theatre, and Leonidas Westervelt, *The Circus in Literature* (New York, 1931), for the circus. The various volumes in *A History of American Life* edited by A. M. Schlesinger and D. R. Fox (12 vols., in progress, New York, 1927–) have bibliographical sections on amusements; and the Russell Sage Foundation has issued two selective bibliographies on modern recreation—Bulletin 151, compiled by Grace P. Thornton, and Bulletin 156, compiled by M. P. Williams. Finally, note should be made of the monthly lists of books on this topic in the magazine *Recreation*, published by the National Recreation Association.

An extensive specialized literature on both the theatre and sports is available, but the only comprehensive attempts to portray the entire theatrical scene are O. S. Coad and Edwin Mims, Jr., *The American Stage* in *The Pageant of America*, Vol. XIV (New Haven, 1929), Arthur A. Hornblow, *History of the American Theatre* (2 vols., Philadelphia, 1919), and John Anderson, *The American Theatre* (New York, 1938); while the only inclusive history of sports is John A. Krout, *Annals of American Sport* in *The Pageant of America*, Vol. XV

(New Haven, 1929). A more recent study in this field designed for student use should also be mentioned, R. B. Weaver, *Amusements and Sports in American Life* (Chicago, 1939), but here again the field is more limited than that which the present book attempts to cover. All these books have lists of sources, and though the following notes are somewhat more comprehensive, it should again be emphasized that they constitute an arbitrary and highly selective bibliography which makes no pretense of including all available material.

NEWSPAPERS AND PERIODICALS

The most important primary source on recreation is newspapers and periodicals. Scattered notices in the colonial papers afford such evidence as is available on the beginnings of the theatre, and, in the first half of the nineteenth century advertisements are still the most valuable clue for all commercial entertainment. The rise of organized sports may also best be traced through newspaper columns and magazine articles. After 1850 this material becomes voluminous, and by the close of the century the special theatre and sports sections have come into being. Through its rôle as a center for amusements, the papers of New York are perhaps most valuable, with the *Tribune* and the *Herald* providing the most readily available sources. Those of other cities also reflect the changing scene, however, while small-town papers throughout the country throw a revealing light through their local notices on the character of non-commercial entertainment.

The first important magazine to be devoted to amusements (although it had been preceded by *The American Turf Register,* founded in 1829) was *The Spirit of the Times, a Chronicle of the Turf, Field Sports, Literature and the Stage.* It was established in 1835 and was variously known as *Porter's Spirit of the Times* and *Wilkes' Spirit of the Times. The National Police Gazette* (1845) also dealt with amusements, and *The New York Clipper* (1853) was the first exclusively sporting journal. Through these magazines more than in any other way the early beginnings of commercial amusements and organized sports may be traced. *Outing,* first called *The Wheelman,* was established in 1882 and gave more attention to amateur sports. Many other magazines devoted to athletics now sprang up (see Frank Luther Mott, *A History of American Magazines,* 5 vols., in progress, New York and Cambridge, 1930–), and as early as 1887 this group of periodicals included *The Ball Players' Chronicle, Sports and Games, Sporting Life, The American Angler, The American Canoeist, The*

American Cricketeer, Bicycle World, The Mirror of Sports, Field and Stream, Sporting Life.... By the twentieth century their number is legion.

The most useful journal devoted to the theatre, after mid-nineteenth century, was *The New York Dramatic Mirror,* founded in 1879. It carried full reports of theatrical activities throughout the country, with extensive lists of shows on the road. Many publications devoted to the stage have subsequently been established, ranging from *Theatre Arts Monthly* to *Variety.*

Articles on various phases of recreation are also found after 1850 in almost every magazine published. The most useful are the illustrated weeklies, notably *Harper's .Weekly, Frank Leslie's Illustrated Newspaper,* and *Gleason's Pictorial and Drawing-Room Companion.* Among the monthlies occasional articles were published in *The Atlantic Monthly, Harper's, Scribner's, Godey's Lady's Book, Century,* and *The North American Review.* In later years such material is often most conveniently found in *The Literary Digest,* but the files of such magazines as *The Saturday Evening Post, Collier's, The American Magazine, McClure's, The Ladies' Home Journal, The American Mercury,* and *Country Life* yield much information that cannot be found elsewhere.

The appended chapter notes will show more adequately where the material for the present book has been gathered. In addition to the magazines noted, its sources have ranged from an article on trolley parks in *The Street Railway Review* to a study of church entertainment in *The Forum,* from a description of parlor games in *Good Housekeeping* to an analysis of "the recreational dollar" in *Business Week.*

COLONIAL SOURCES

Among the scattered primary sources for colonial recreation a few contemporary diaries and travel journals stand out with special prominence. Samuel Sewall, *Diary, Massachusetts Historical Society Collections,* Ser. 5, Vols. V-VII, 1878-82 (also available in abridged form, edited by Mark Van Doren, New York, 1927), is invaluable for New England in the period from 1674 through 1729, and for the latter half of the eighteenth century the diaries of John Adams, in *Works,* II (Boston, 1850); John Quincy Adams, in *Life in a New England Town* (Boston, 1903); Nathaniel Ames, in *Jacobin and Junto* (Charles Warren, editor, Cambridge, 1931), and Joseph Bennett, in *Proceedings of the Massachusetts Historical Society,* 1861. An interesting

New York diary is John Sharp, *A Journal of My Life-Exteriour*, in *Pennsylvania Magazine of History and Biography*, XL (1916), while an incomparable source for recreation on a southern plantation is Philip Vickers Fithian, *Journal and Letters* (Princeton, 1900). There is also some account of southern amusements in such sources as William Byrd's *The History of the Dividing Line* (Richmond, 1866) and *The Diaries of George Washington* (4 vols., Boston, 1925).

Among many travel accounts of the eighteenth century, the most useful for recreation are John Bernard, *Retrospections of America 1797-1811* (New York, 1887); Andrew Burnaby, *Travels Through the Middle Settlements in North-America* (London, 1775); Marquis de Chastellux, *Travels in North America* (New York, 1827); Captain Francis Goelet, *Journal*, in *New England Historical and Genealogical Register*, XXIV (1870); Dr. Alexander Hamilton, *Itinerarium* (edited by A. B. Hart, St. Louis, 1907); Hugh Jones, *The Present State of Virginia* (London, 1724; reprinted New York, 1865); Sarah Kemble Knight, *Private Journal* (Albany, 1865); and Henry Wansey, *An Excursion to the United States* (Salisbury, 1798).

There is a wealth of secondary sources. Interest in how the early settlers lived has always been so great that recreation in the colonial era has received more adequate treatment than in any other period until the twentieth century. Among general social histories some material has been brought together, although very briefly, in such books as Charles M. Andrews, *Colonial Folkways* in *Chronicles of America*, VI (New Haven, 1918); Thomas J. Wertenbaker, *The First Americans* in *A History of American Life*, II (New York, 1929); and James Truslow Adams, *Provincial Society* in *A History of American Life*, III (New York, 1936). More useful are a number of books dealing with specialized topics. A highly selective list would include Philip Alexander Bruce, *Social Life in Virginia in the Seventeenth Century* (Richmond, 1907); Mary N. Stannard, *Colonial Virginia* (Philadelphia, 1917); Robert M. Lawrence, *New England Colonial Life* (Cambridge, 1927); Mary Caroline Crawford, *Social Life in Old New England* (Boston, 1914); George Francis Dow, *Every Day Life in the Massachusetts Bay Colony* (Boston, 1935); Esther Singleton, *Social New York Under the Georges* (New York, 1902); Sydney George Fisher, *Men, Women and Manners in Colonial Times* (2 vols., Philadelphia, 1898); and, with even more marked attention to recreation as revealed in contemporary sources, the various books of Alice Morse Earle: *Colonial Days in Old New York* (New York, 1896), *Colonial Dames and Goodwives* (Boston, 1895), *Home Life in Co-*

lonial Days (New York, 1898), and *Child Life in Colonial Days* (New York, 1899).

For amusements in the cities, apart from books dealing specifically with the theatre which are listed under that topic, there is also interesting material, among other local histories, in Martha J. Lamb, *History of the City of New York* (2 vols., New York, 1877); James Grant Wilson, *The Memorial History of New York* (3 vols., New York, 1893); J. F. Watson, *Annals of New York* (Philadelphia, 1846); J. Thomas Scharf and Thompson Westcott, *History of Philadelphia* (3 vols., Philadelphia, 1884); J. F. Watson, *Annals of Philadelphia* (Philadelphia, 1857); Lyon G. Tyler, *Williamsburg* (Richmond, 1907); E. S. Riley, *The Ancient City* (Annapolis, 1887); Justin Winsor, *Memorial History of Boston* (3 vols., Boston, 1880-81); and Carl Bridenbaugh, *Cities in the Wilderness* (New York, 1939).

Note may also be made, among still more special studies, of Edward Field, *The Colonial Tavern* (Providence, 1897); Walter Tittle, *Colonial Holidays* (New York, 1910); and Richardson Wright, *Hawkers and Walkers in Early America* (Philadelphia, 1927).

Nineteenth-Century Travelers

An important source of the nineteenth century that deserves special mention is the host of travel books of that period. Apart from newspaper and magazine material, such revealing diaries as that of Philip Hone (edited by Allan Nevins, 2 vols., New York, 1927), or such occasional descriptive records as Emerson Davis, *The Half Century* (Boston, 1851); Timothy Dwight, *Travels in New England* (4 vols., London, 1823); Anne Royall, *Sketches of History, Life and Manners of the United States* (New Haven, 1826); and George Makepeace Towle, *American Society* (2 vols., London, 1870), the impressionistic travel journals published by English visitors to the United States between 1820 and 1860 provide the clearest picture of the recreational scene in those years. They are most conveniently listed in Allan Nevins (editor), *American Social History as Recorded by British Travellers* (New York, 1923), but a few of the most helpful for this special topic may be singled out.

Such a specialized list would include W. E. Baxter, *America and the Americans* (London, 1855); Alfred Bunn, *Old England and New England* (2 vols., London, 1853); George Combe, *Notes on the United States* (3 vols., Edinburgh, 1841); Charles Dickens, *American Notes* (London, 1842); Emily Faithfull, *Three Visits to America*

(Edinburgh, 1884); James Flint, *Letters from America* (Edinburgh, 1822); Thomas Colley Grattan, *Civilized America* (2 vols., London, 1859); Francis J. Grund, *The Americans* (Boston, 1837); Francis Hall, *Travels in Canada and the United States* (London, 1818); Basil Hall, *Travels in North America* (3 vols., London, 1829); Mrs. Basil Hall, *The Aristocratic Journey* (New York, 1931); Thomas Hamilton, *Men and Manners* (2 vols., Philadelphia, 1833); Frances Anne Kemble, *Journal* (2 vols., Philadelphia, 1835); Charles Lyell, *Travels in North America* (2 vols., New York, 1852); Alexander Mackay, *The Western World* (3 vols., London, 1850); Harriet Martineau, *Society in America* (3 vols., London, 1838); Captain Frederick Marryat, *A Diary in America* (2 vols., Philadelphia, 1839); T. L. Nichols, *Forty Years of American Life* (London, 1874); James Stuart, *Three Years in North America* (2 vols., London, 1833); Frances M. Trollope, *Domestic Manners of the Americans* (2 vols., London, 1832); and Frances Wright D'Arusmont, *Views of Society and Manners in America* (New York, 1821).

A number of French travel accounts also (for bibliography see Frank Monaghan, *French Travellers in the United States, 1765-1932*, New York, 1933) are useful for the early nineteenth century: Michael Chevalier, *Society, Manners and Politics in the United States* (Boston, 1839); Achille Murat, *A Moral and Political Sketch of the United States* (London, 1833); Alexis de Tocqueville, *Democracy in America* (1834-41) (2 vols., Boston, 1876); and, somewhat later, Paul Blouet (Max O'Rell), *Jonathan and His Continent* (New York, 1884); Paul de Rousiers, *American Life* (New York, 1892); and S. C. de Soisson, *A Parisian in America* (Boston, 1896).

THE THEATRE

Apart from scattered newspaper notices, contemporary records of the theatre are not generally available until after 1800. For subsequent years there are many extensive collections of play bills, theatre programs, and other memorabilia, two of the largest being the Harvard University Collection and the Robinson Locke Collection of Dramatic Scrapbooks in the New York Public Library. Among books the most important primary sources for the early nineteenth century are William Dunlap, *History of the American Theatre* (London, 1833); William B. Wood, *Personal Recollections of the Stage* (Philadelphia, 1855); Joseph Norton Ireland, *Records of the New York Stage, 1750-1860* (2 vols., New York, 1866-67); William W. Clapp,

A *Record of the Boston Stage* (Boston, 1853); N. M. Ludlow, *Dramatic Life as I Found It* (St. Louis, 1880); and Sol Smith, *Theatrical Management in the West and South for Thirty Years* (New York, 1868). They are supplemented by a number of autobiographies, among which the more important are William Davidge, *Footlight Flashes* (New York, 1867); *The Autobiography of Joseph Jefferson* (New York, 1889); Anna C. Mowatt (Mrs. A. C. Ritchie), *Autobiography of an Actress* (Boston, 1853); Tyrone Power, *Impressions of America* (2 vols., London, 1836); Olive Logan, *Apropos of Women and the Theatre* (New York, 1869); James E. Murdoch, *The Stage* (Philadelphia, 1880); and the journal of Harry Watkins (*One Man in His Time*), edited by Maud and Otis Skinner (Philadelphia, 1938).

Primary sources for the second half of the nineteenth century embrace the complete records of the stage now available in newspapers and magazines, an increasing number of autobiographies, and the reminiscences of several well-known critics. An even more selective list of books covering these years would include Lester Wallack, *Memories of Fifty Years* (New York, 1889); Daniel Frohman, *Memoirs of a Manager* (Garden City, 1911); John Rankin Towse, *Sixty Years of the Theatre* (New York, 1916); Henry Austin Clapp, *Reminiscences of a Dramatic Critic* (Boston, 1902); William Winter, *The Wallet of Time* (2 vols., New York, 1916); E. H. Sothern, *The Melancholy Tale of Me* (New York, 1910); De Wolfe Hopper, *Once a Clown Always a Clown* (Boston, 1927); and George M. Cohan, *Twenty Years on Broadway* (New York, 1925).

Modern writers have treated the history of the theatre from every possible angle. Its beginnings in colonial America are traced in Charles P. Daly, *First Theatre in America, Dunlap Society Publications,* New Series, No. I (New York, 1896); Eola Willis, *The Charleston Stage in the Eighteenth Century* (Columbia, 1924); Paul Leicester Ford, *Washington and the Theatre, Dunlap Society Publications,* New Series, No. VIII (New York, 1899); George O. Seilhammer, *The History of the American Theatre* (3 vols., Philadelphia, 1888-91), an ambitious project which carries the story only through the eighteenth century. The development of the theatre through the years, as already noted, is the subject of such general histories as those by Arthur A. Hornblow, O. S. Coad and Edwin Mims, Jr., and John Anderson. Other specialized studies include A. H. Quinn, *History of the American Drama* (2 vols., New York, 1927); Montrose J. Moses and John Mason Brown, *The American Theatre as Seen by Its Critics 1752-1934* (New York, 1934); R. C. Dimmick, *Our Theatre*

Today and Yesterday (New York, 1913); Mary C. Crawford, *The Romance of the American Theatre* (Boston, 1925); Lawrence Hutton, *Curiosities of the American Stage* (London, 1891); Constance Rourke, *Troupers of the Gold Coast* (New York, 1928); Norman Hapgood, *The Stage in America 1897-1900* (New York, 1901); W. L. Phelps, *The Twentieth Century Theatre* (New York, 1918); O. M. Sayles, *Our American Theatre* (New York, 1913); Sheldon Cheney, *The New Movement in the Theatre* (New York, 1914); Albert McCleery and Carl Glick, *Curtains Going Up* (New York, 1939); Esther C. Dunn, *Shakespeare in America* (New York, 1939).

Possibly more important are a number of local histories of the theatre. Foremost among such books, and an invaluable source for the period it covers, is the monumental work of George C. D. Odell, *Annals of the New York Stage*, of which the ten volumes already published (New York, 1927–) carry the story through 1875. Two interesting volumes on the Philadelphia stage are valuable for that city: Reese D. James, *Old Drury of Philadelphia* (Philadelphia, 1932), and Arthur H. Wilson, *A History of the Philadelphia Theatre, 1835 to 1855* (Philadelphia, 1935). There are also Eugene Tompkins and Quincy Kilby, *History of the Boston Theatre* (Boston, 1908); H. P. Phelps, *Players of a Century* (Albany, 1880); George O. Willard, *History of the Providence Stage, 1762-1891* (Providence, c. 1891); Douglas L. Hunt, "The Nashville Theatre," *Birmingham-Southern College Bulletin*, XXVIII, No. 3 (1935); and, for the St. Louis stage, William G. B. Carson, *The Theatre on the Frontier* (Chicago, 1932).

A few of the more important biographical studies may also be mentioned. They include Montrose J. Moses, *Famous Actor Families in America* (New York, 1906); Lewis C. Strang, *Players and Plays of the Last Quarter Century* (2 vols., Boston, 1903); Montrose J. Moses, *The Fabulous Forrest* (Boston, 1929); Asa B. Clarke, *The Elder and Younger Booth* (Boston, 1882); Leota S. Driver, *Fanny Kemble* (Chapel Hill, 1933); Francis Joseph Daly, *The Life of Augustin Daly* (New York, 1917); William Winter, *The Life and Art of Joseph Jefferson* (New York, 1914).

OTHER COMMERCIAL ENTERTAINMENT

The opera and the concert platform have their own literature, but as they have not received extended treatment in the text, the following books alone are noted as outlining their general development: O. G. Sonneck, *Early Opera in America* (Boston, 1915), and *Early Concert-*

Life in America (Leipzig, 1907); Henry C. Lahee, *Annals of Music in America* (Boston, 1922); Louis C. Elson, *The History of American Music* (New York, 1925); John T. Howard, *Our American Music* (New York, 1931); Henry E. Krehbiel, *Chapters of Opera* (New York, 1909); and Irving Kolodin, *The Metropolitan Opera* (New York, 1936).

Material on minstrelsy is largely scattered through the contemporary magazines, but it has also had its historians. Carl Wittke, *Tambo and Bones* (Durham, N. C., 1930), and Dailey Paskman and Sigmund Spaeth, *"Gentlemen, Be Seated!"* (New York, 1928), are the two leading books on this topic, but the subject is also taken up in Francis Pendleton Gaines, *The Southern Plantation* (New York, 1924), while John Tasker Howard has written an interesting biography of minstrelsy's greatest composer, *Stephen Foster, America's Troubadour* (New York, 1934).

Source material for the variety stage and circus is found in a number of autobiographies. Outstanding among them is the autobiography of P. T. Barnum, first issued as *The Life of P. T. Barnum, Written by Himself* (New York, 1855). Other such books include Gil Robinson, *Old Wagon Shows Days* (Cincinnati, 1925); W. C. Coup, *Sawdust and Spangles* (Chicago, 1901); J. J. Jennings, *Theatrical and Circus Life* (Chicago, 1893); Ralph Keeler, *Vagabond Adventures* (Boston, 1872); and M. B. Leavitt, *Fifty Years in Theatrical Management* (New York, 1912).

These forms of commercial entertainment have not received from modern writers comparable treatment to that given the theatre—although Professor Odell includes all entertainment in his *Annals of the New York Stage*. For the origins of the American circus, however, a valuable compilation of early notices is R. W. G. Vail, "Random Notes on the History of the Early American Circus," *Proceedings of the American Antiquarian Society*, April, 1933 (reprint, Worcester, 1934). Leonidas Westervelt has also gathered together some of this material in *The Circus in Literature* (New York, 1931). Another comparable book, although it carries the story only through 1835, is Isaac J. Greenwood, *The Circus* (New York, 1898), while a more general account is Earl Chapin May, *The Circus from Rome to Ringling* (New York, 1932). There is also much material on this subject in M. R. Werner, *Barnum* (New York, 1927).

The development of the variety stage is discussed in Caroline Coffin, *Vaudeville* (New York, 1914), and that of burlesque in Bernard Sobel, *Burleycue* (New York, 1931).

The Frontier and Far West

Contemporary accounts of the amusements of the pioneers are found in a number of travel books. A valuable compilation of such journals, carefully indexed, is Reuben Gold Thwaites, *Early Western Travels 1748-1846* (32 vols., Cleveland, 1907). A highly selective list of other primary sources would include John James Audubon, *Delineations of American Scenery and Character* (1834), (New York, 1926); H. M. Brackenridge, *Recollections of Persons and Places in the Far West* (Philadelphia, 1868); Peter Cartwright, *Autobiography* (New York, 1857); *The Life of Davy Crockett, Written by Himself* (Philadelphia, 1860); Joseph Doddridge, *Notes on the Settlement and Indian Wars* (Albany, 1876); Timothy Flint, *Recollections of the Last Ten Years* (Boston, 1826); James B. Finley, *Autobiography* (Cincinnati, 1854); Baynard Rush Hall, *The New Purchase* (New York, 1855); James Hall, *Sketches of History, Life and Manners in the West* (2 vols., Philadelphia, 1835); William H. Milburn, *The Rifle, Axe and Saddle-Bags* (New York, 1857). For the West of a somewhat later period (the prairie states) there are many records, but among them all one stands out with special prominence—Hamlin Garland, *A Son of the Middle Border* (New York, 1917). And it is best supplemented by the same author's *Boy Life on the Prairie* (New York, 1899).

Among secondary accounts of frontier life, Everett Dick, *The Sod-House Frontier, 1854-1890* (New York, 1937); Bessie Louise Pierce, *A History of Chicago*, Vol. I (New York, 1937); Thomas D. Clark, *The Rampaging Frontier* (Indianapolis, 1939); Bernard De Voto, *Mark Twain's America* (Boston, 1932), and E. E. Calkins, *They Broke the Prairie* (New York, 1937), take up recreation and amusements in considerable detail.

For the Far West, Samuel L. Clemens (Mark Twain), *Roughing It* (2 vols., New York, 1899), is a classic. Some account of amusements is found also in such books as A. K. McClure, *Three Thousand Miles through the Rockies* (Philadelphia, 1869); Samuel Bowles, *Across the Continent* (Springfield, 1865); J. H. Cook, *Fifty Years on the Old Frontier* (New Haven, 1923); T. A. McNeal, *When Kansas Was Young* (New York, 1922); R. M. Wright, *Dodge City* (Dodge City, 1913); William Wright (Dan De Quille), *The Big Bonanza* (Hartford, 1876); Wells Drury, *An Editor on the Comstock Lode* (New York, 1934). Two books with interesting chapters on the amusements of the cowboy are Emerson Hough, *The Story of the*

Cowboy (New York, 1897), and Philip Ashton Rollins, *The Cowboy* (New York, 1922), while a more colorful record is *We Pointed Them North*, by E. C. Abbott ("Teddy Blue") and Helen Huntington Smith (New York, 1939). The authentic flavor of this country is also preserved in John A. and Alan Lomax, *Cowboy Songs* (New York, 1938).

THE ANTE-BELLUM SOUTH

The distinctive character of recreation in the ante-bellum South demands some special mention of the primary sources in this field. Two interesting journals of northerners describing plantation life are Henry Barnard, "The South Atlantic States," in *The Maryland Historical Magazine*, XIII, and A. DePuy Van Buren, *Jottings of a Year's Sojourn in the South* (Battle Creek, Mich., 1859), while among many reminiscences of pre-war days are Susan Dabney Smedes, *Memorials of a Southern Planter* (Baltimore, 1887); Herbert Ravenel Sass, *A Carolina Rice Plantation in the Fifties* (New York, 1936); Eliza Ripley, *Social Life in Old New Orleans* (New York, 1912); F. D. Srygley, *Seventy Years in Dixie* (Nashville, 1893); and Thomas Nelson Page, *Social Life in Old Virginia* (New York, 1897). Quite a different phase of southern life, with descriptions of amusements in the backwoods, is taken up in two memorable literary records: Joseph G. Baldwin, *The Flush Times of Alabama and Mississippi* (New York, 1854), and Augustus B. Longstreet, *Georgia Scenes* (Augusta, 1835). Two of the best contemporary social studies are D. R. Hundley, *Social Relations in Our Southern States* (New York, 1860), and Frederick Law Olmsted, *The Cotton Kingdom* (2 vols., New York, 1862).

Secondary sources that may be singled out for their material bearing on recreation are U. B. Phillips, *Life and Labor in the Old South* (Boston, 1929); Francis P. Gaines, *The Southern Plantation* (New York, 1924); Guion Griffis Johnson, *Ante-Bellum North Carolina* (Chapel Hill, 1937); and Minnie Clare Boyd, *Alabama in the Fifties* (New York, 1931).

THE RISE OF SPORTS

On the broad subject of the rise of sports the most valuable material is found in contemporary magazines, such manuals and guides as those of Spalding's Athletic Library, published by the American Sports Publishing Company, and other memorabilia in the extensive A. G. Spalding Collection in the New York Public Library. But a number of early books on sports would also qualify as primary sources: Horatio Smith, *Festivals, Games and Amusement* (New York, 1833); Charles A. Peverelly, *The Book of American Pastimes* (New York, 1866); J. H. Walsh, *Encyclopedia of Rural Sports* (Philadelphia, 1874); *The Tribune Book of Open-Air Sports* (New York, 1887); William Patten (editor), *The Book of Sport* (New York, 1901); and J. Parmly Paret, *The Woman's Book of Sports* (New York, 1901). There are also many books on hunting and field sports. While in general not of much value to the historian, two exceptions are H. W. Herbert (Frank Forester), *Field Sports of the United States and British Provinces* (2 vols., New York, 1848), and B. H. Revail, *Shooting and Fishing in the Rivers, Provinces and Backwoods of America* (London, 1865).

Among the many personal records of individual sportsmen, there may be mentioned Hiram Woodruff, *The Trotting Horse of America* (New York, 1871); John J. McGraw, *My Thirty Years in Baseball* (New York, 1923); J. J. Corbett, *The Roar of the Crowd* (New York, 1925); Ed Geer, *Ed Geer's Experience with Trotters and Pacers* (Buffalo, 1901); William R. Wister, *Some Reminiscences of Cricket in Philadelphia before 1861* (Philadelphia, 1904); L. H. Porter, *Wheels and Wheeling* (New York, 1892); Walter G. Kendall, *Four Score Years of Sport* (Boston, 1933); Charles Evans, Jr., *Chick Evans' Golf Book* (Chicago, 1921); J. D. Travers and J. R. Crowell, *The Fifth Estate, Thirty Years of Golf* (New York, 1926); and A. A. Stagg and W. W. Stout, *Touchdown* (New York, 1927).

The only comprehensive record of American sports among the secondary authorities, as already noted, is John A. Krout, *Annals of American Sport;* but Herbert Manchester, *Four Centuries of Sport in America 1490-1890* (New York, 1931), has a broad sweep, and there is a stimulating essay, "The Rise of American Sports," by F. L. Paxson in the *Mississippi Valley Historical Review,* IV. Jennie Holliman has made a careful study for a limited period in *American Sports 1785-1835* (Durham, N. C., 1931), and note should also be made of Emmett A. Rice, *A Brief History of Physical Education* (New York, 1929); C. E. Rainwater, *The Play Movement in the United States* (Chicago, 1921); John R. Tunis, *Sports, Heroics and Hysterics* (New York, 1928); and Paul Gallico, *Farewell to Sport* (New York, 1938). There is also considerable material in R. B. Weaver's previously cited *Amusements and Sports in American Life.*

Among individual sports, yachting has an extensive literature, two of the best accounts being F. S. Cozzens, *Yachts and Yachting* (New

York, 1888), and W. P. Stephens, *American Yachting* (New York, 1904). Horse-racing has had many histories, among which may be mentioned John H. Wallace, *The Horse of America* (New York, 1897); W. S. Vosburgh, *Racing in America 1866-1921* (New York, 1922); F. G. Griswold, *Race Horses and Racing* (New York, 1926); and, especially useful, Dwight Akers, *Drivers Up: the Story of American Harness Racing* (New York, 1938), and Charles B. Parmer, *For Gold and Glory: The Story of Thoroughbred Racing in America* (New York, 1939).

Baseball has had several historians also. The principal authority is A. G. Spalding, *America's National Game* (New York, 1911), although its account of the origin of baseball is now superseded by the article of R. W. Henderson in the April, 1939, issue of the *Bulletin of the New York Public Library*. Other supplementary records include Francis C. Richter, *History and Records of Baseball* (Philadelphia, 1914); John M. Ward, *Baseball* (Philadelphia, 1889); A. H. Spink, *The National Game* (St. Louis, 1910); and G. L. Moreland, *Balldom* (New York, 1914). Parke H. Davis has written the leading history of football in *Football, the Intercollegiate Game* (New York, 1911). Other less valuable accounts are Walter Camp and Lorin F. Deland, *Football* (New York, 1896), and A. M. Weyand, *American Football* (New York, 1926).

A few other interesting books in their respective fields are Alexander Johnston, *Ten—And Out!* (New York, 1936), a history of prize-fighting; Robert F. Kelley, *American Rowing* (New York, 1932); H. F. Leonard, *A Handbook of Wrestling* (New York, 1877); Robert P. Elmer, *Archery* (Philadelphia, 1926); Frederick W. Jannsen, *A History of American Amateur Athletics and Aquatics* (New York, 1888); James Naismith and L. Gulick, *Basketball* (New York, 1894); Samuel Crowther and Arthur Ruhl, *Rowing and Track Athletics* (New York, 1905); J. P. Paret, *Lawn Tennis* (New York, 1912); *Fifty Years of Lawn Tennis in the United States* (New York, 1931); H. B. Martin, *Fifty Years of American Golf* (New York, 1936). Interesting data on all sports may be found in the various editions of the *All-Sports Record Book* and the *Encyclopedia of Sports*, both edited by Frank G. Menke.

The Movies, Radio, and Automobile

The primary material for the growth of motion pictures, the recreational use of the automobile, and radio is found in newspapers and magazines, both the more general publications to which reference has already been made and various special magazines. *The Motion Picture News* and *Film Daily* are especially useful for the movies, the *Film Daily Yearbook* providing a valuable annual summary. Among publications devoted to the automobile, *Facts and Figures of the Automobile Industry,* issued annually by the National Automobile Chamber of Commerce, is an indispensable factual record of the industry's expansion. *Radio Broadcast* and *Radio Today* provide a running commentary on developments in broadcasting. There have been many special studies of the influence and social significance of the movies and radio—reports, among many others, of the Motion Picture Research Council and of both the National Broadcasting Company and the Columbia Broadcasting Company. Also, many autobiographies of screen stars have appeared in recent years. No attempt at a bibliography has been made in listing the following selected sources.

The best account of the early development of motion pictures in book form is Terry Ramsaye, *A Million and One Nights* (2 vols., New York, 1926). Other sources include Ben J. Lubschez, *The Story of the Motion Picture* (New York, 1920); Benjamin B. Hampton, *A History of the Movies* (New York, 1931); H. B. Franklin, *Sound Motion Pictures* (Garden City, 1920); F. A. Talbot, *Moving Pictures* (Philadelphia, 1912); Will Irwin, *The House That Shadows Built* (New York, 1927); W. M. Seabury, *The Public and the Motion Picture Industry* (New York, 1926); Lewis Jacobs, *The Rise of the American Film* (New York, 1939), with an extensive bibliography; Margaret F. Thorp, *America at the Movies* (New Haven, 1939); and, among other studies of the Payne Fund, Edgar Dale, *The Content of Motion Pictures* (New York, 1935).

Books on the automobile are largely concerned with its industrial importance rather than the recreational aspects of motoring, but among the more useful histories Hiram Percy Maxim, *Horseless Carriage Days* (New York, 1937); R. C. Epstein, *The Automobile Industry* (Chicago, 1928); H. L. Barber, *The Story of the Automobile* (Chicago, 1927); Arthur Pound, *The Turning Wheel* (New York, 1934), should be mentioned. There are many books about Henry Ford. Two to be noted are *My Life and Work,* written by Henry Ford in collaboration with Samuel Crowther (Garden City, 1922), and Charles Merz, *And Then Came Ford* (New York, 1929).

Paul Schubert's *The Electric Word: the Rise of Radio* (New York, 1929) is a general history of this form of communications and entertainment. Other accounts are A. N. Goldsmith and A. C. Lescarboura,

This Thing Called Broadcasting (New York, 1930); Gleason L. Archer, *History of Radio* (New York, 1938); Alvin F. Harlow, *Old Wires and New Waves* (New York, 1936); Samuel L. Rothafel and R. F. Yates, *Broadcasting—Its New Day* (New York, 1925); and Hadley Cantril and Gordon W. Allport, *The Psychology of Radio* (New York, 1935). There is also interesting material in Alfred P. Morgan, *The Pageant of Electricity* (New York, 1939).

GENERAL TWENTIETH-CENTURY SOURCES

While the primary sources and special studies already noted provide the basic data for any discussion of recreation in the twentieth century, two other groups of books of a more general nature remain to be noted. The first comprises contemporary records of American civilization. Foremost among them in its treatment of the people at play is Mark Sullivan, *Our Times: The United States 1900-1925* (6 vols., New York, 1925-35). There is a stimulating chapter on entertainment in Charles A. and Mary Beard, *America in Midpassage* (New York, 1939), and unusually valuable material in both *Middletown* (New York, 1929) and *Middletown in Transition* (New York, 1937), by Robert S. and Helen Merrell Lynd. Stuart Chase has a chapter on "Play" in *Whither Mankind* (Charles Beard, editor, New York, 1928), and John R. Tunis one on "The Business of American Sport" in *America as Americans See It* (New York, 1932). Among many others two especially helpful books in this field are Charles Merz, *The Great American Bandwagon* (New York, 1925), and Frederick Lewis Allen, *Only Yesterday* (New York, 1931).

The second group of books includes a large number of sociological studies of leisure and recreation. This literature is listed in the bibliographies of the Russell Sage Foundation, and only a few titles can be noted here. The most important for the purposes of this study is Jesse F. Steiner, *Americans at Play* (New York, 1938), a monograph from which the material was derived for the chapter on recreation in *Recent Social Trends,* Report of the President's Research Committee on Social Trends (2 vols., New York, 1933). Special note should also be made of Julius Weinberger, *Economic Aspects of Recreation* (Harvard Business Review reprint, Cambridge, 1937), the best of several studies of this nature; the annual *Recreation Yearbook* of the magazine *Recreation;* and the articles on recreation, play, amusements, leisure, etc., in the *Encyclopedia of the Social Sciences.* A highly selective list of books on the modern "problem of leisure" would include C. DeLisle Burns, *Leisure in the Modern World* (New York, 1932); C. E. M. Joad, *Diogenes; or The Future of Leisure* (London, 1928); Arthur N. Pack, *The Challenge of Leisure* (New York, 1934); G. B. Cutten, *The Threat of Leisure* (New Haven, 1926); George A. Lundberg, *Leisure—A Suburban Study* (New York, 1934); Herbert L. May and Dorothy Petgen, *Leisure and Its Uses* (New York, 1928); M. H. and E. S. Neumeyer, *Leisure and Recreation* (New York, 1936), a textbook; and Jay B. Nash, *Spectatoritis* (New York, 1932). There are also many analytical studies of the use of leisure and recreational habits in specific communities, and an extensive periodical literature on this general topic.

NOTES

CHAPTER I

"In Detestation of Idleness"

1. Ralph Hamor, *A True Discourse of the Present Estate of Virginia* (London, 1615; reprint Richmond, 1860), 26.
2. Edward Winslow (December 11, 1621), quoted in Alice Morse Earl, *Child Life in Colonial Days* (New York, 1899), 217.
3. Thomas Morton, *The New English Canaan* (London, 1637; reprint *Prince Society Publications*, XIV, Boston, 1883), 279.
4. William Bradford, *History of Plymouth Plantation*, in J. F. Jameson (editor), *Original Narratives of Early American History* (New York, 1908), 238.
5. Peter Force, *Tracts and Other Papers* (4 vols., Washington, 1836-46), III, 2, 16.
6. Bradford, *loc. cit.*, 238; *Records of the Court of Assistants of the Colony of Massachusetts Bay* (Boston, 1904), II, 37.
7. Alexander Brown, *The Genesis of the United States* (Boston, 1890), I, 70.
8. Edward Channing, *A History of the United States* (6 vols., New York, 1905-25), I, 200.
9. Quoted in George C. D. Odell, *Annals of the New York Stage* (New York, 1927–), I, 3.
10. Philip Bruce, *Institutional History of Virginia in the Seventeenth Century* (New York, 1910), I, 528.
11. *Records of the Governor and Company of Massachusetts Bay* (Boston, 1853), I, 405.
12. *Ibid.*, II, 195; *Public Records of the Colony of Connecticut* (Hartford, 1850), I, 527.
13. *Records of the Court of Assistants . . . of Massachusetts Bay*, II, 37; *Public Records of . . . Connecticut*, I, 528.
14. See *Records of the Governor . . . of Massachusetts Bay*, II, 70, 180; William B. Weeden, *Economic and Social History of New England* (Boston, 1890), I, 224-25; *Documents and Records Relating to the Province of New Hampshire* (Concord, 1867), I, 391; Walter F. Prince, "An Examination of Peter's 'Blue Laws,'" *American Historical Association Annual Report*, 1898, 97ff.
15. *Massachusetts Historical Society Collections*, Ser. 2, Vol. X, 183-84.
16. *Records of the Governor . . . of Massachusetts Bay*, III, 224.
17. Gustavus Myers, *Ye Olden Blue Laws* (New York, 1921), 211; Arthur A. Hornblow, *History of the American Theatre* (Philadelphia, 1919), I, 24.

18. John Winthrop, *History of New England*, in J. F. Jameson (editor), *Original Narratives of Early American History* (New York, 1908), I, 325-27.

19. *Records of the Court of Assistants of . . . Massachusetts Bay*, II, 87; Alexander Young, *Chronicles of the First Planters of the Massachusetts Bay Colony* (Boston, 1846), 413.

20. Force, *Tracts*, III, 2, 10; Alexander Brown, *The First Republic in America* (Boston, 1898), 278; Bruce, *Institutional History of Virginia*, I, 37.

21. *Records of the Court of Assistants . . . of Massachusetts Bay*, III, 316-17; *Public Records of . . . Connecticut*, II, 280; *Documents . . . of New Hampshire*, I, 388.

22. *Records of the Court Assistants . . . of Massachusetts Bay*, III, 316-17.

23. Frances M. Caulkins, *History of New London* (New London, 1895), 250.

24. Charles Francis Adams, "Some Phases of Sexual Morality and Church Discipline in Colonial New England," *Proceedings of the Massachusetts Historical Society*, Ser. 2, Vol. VI (1891), 496.

25. See Thomas Cuming Hall, *The Religious Background of American Culture* (Boston, 1930), Chap. I.

26. Edward Eggleston, *The Beginnings of a Nation* (New York, 1897), 124-34.

27. *The King's Majesties Declaration to his subjects concerning Lawful Sports to be used* (London, 1618; reprinted Philadelphia, 1866).

28. H. D. Traill (editor), *Social England* (London, 1895), IV, 167.

29. See Cotton Mather, *Magnalia Christi Americana* (Hartford, 1820), I, 240, quoted in Thomas J. Wertenbaker, *The First Americans* (*A History of American Life*, II), (New York, 1929), 92.

30. Bradford, *loc. cit.*, 126-27.

31. Samuel Sewall, *Diary, Massachusetts Historical Society Collections*, Ser. 5, Vols. V-VII (1878-82), and in abridged form, Mark Van Doren, editor (New York, 1927). See also N. H. Chamberlain, *Samuel Sewall and the World He Lived in* (Boston, 1897).

32. Sewall, *Diary* (Van Doren edition), 218.

33. *Ibid.*, 24-25, 27, 46.

34. *Ibid.*, 22, 177, 209, 255-56, 263.

35. *Ibid.* (*Massachusetts Historical Society* edition), VII, 171.

36. *Ibid.* (Van Doren edition), 151, 138.

37. Alice Morse Earle, *Customs and Fashions in Old New England* (New York, 1893). 164ff.

38. *Ibid.*, 168ff.; Wertenbaker, *The First Americans*, 200ff.

39. Winthrop, *loc. cit.*, I, 120.

40. Cotton Mather, *Diary* (March 18, 1710-11), *Massachusetts Historical Society Collections*, Ser. 7, Vols. VII-VIII (1911-12), VII, 51.

41. *Records of the Governor . . . of Massachusetts Bay*, V, 63, quoted in James Duncan Phillips, *Salem in the Seventeenth Century* (Boston, 1933), 244.

42. Quoted in Wertenbaker, *The First Americans*, 196.

43. *The Statutes at Large of Virginia, 1619-1792* (Philadelphia, 1823), II, 361. See also John A. Krout, *Origins of Prohibition* (New York, 1925), 6-7.

44. Quoted in Myers, *Ye Olden Blue Laws*, 147.
45. *Ibid.*, 158.
46. Earle, *Customs and Fashions*, 256; Weeden, *Economic and Social History*, I, 294.
47. Quoted in Wertenbaker, *The First Americans*, 196-97.
48. Sarah Kemble Knight, *Private Journal* (Albany, 1865), 50. For further discussion of this point see John Dunton, *Letters from New England, Prince Society Publications*, IV; Edward Ward, *A Trip to New England* (London, 1699); Charles Francis Adams, *loc. cit.*, 477-516; and Wertenbaker, *The First Americans*, 196-200.

CHAPTER II

Husking-Bees and Tavern Sports

1. Ralph Hamor, *A True Discourse of the Present Estate of Virginia* (London, 1615; reprint Richmond, 1860); 20-21.
2. Joseph Seccombe, "A discourse utter'd in Part at Ammauskeeg-Falls, in the Fishing Season, 1739" (Boston, 1743), 17.
3. John Sharp, *A Journal of My Life-Exteriour*, in *Pennsylvania Magazine of History and Biography*, XL (1916), 286, 294, 295, 296.
4. Esther Singleton, *Social New York Under the Georges* (New York, 1902), 262.
5. Quoted in Mary N. Stannard, *Colonial Virginia* (Philadelphia, 1917), 259.
6. John Bernard, *Retrospections of America 1797-1811* (New York, 1877), 206.
7. George Alsop, *A Character of the Province of Mary-land* (London, 1666; reprinted, N. D. Mereness, editor, Cleveland, 1902), 58.
8. Charles Warren, *Jacobin and Junto* (Cambridge, 1931), 29.
9. Quoted in Ray Palmer Baker, "The Poetry of Jacob Bailey, Loyalist," *New England Quarterly*, II (1929), 67-69.
10. William B. Weeden, *Economic and Social History of New England*, I, 230.
11. Quoted in Captain Frederick Marryat, *Diary in America* (Philadelphia, 1839), I, 125-26.
12. Andrew Burnaby, *Travels Through the Middle Settlements in North-America* (London, 1775), 144-45; Bernard, *Retrospections of America*, 89. See also H. R. Stiles, *Bundling, Its Origin, Progress and Decline* (Albany, 1869).
13. Quoted in James Truslow Adams, *Provincial Society* (*A History of American Life*, II) (New York, 1936), 159.
14. Sydney George Fisher, *Men, Women and Manners in Colonial Times* (Philadelphia, 1898), I, 287ff.
15. Knight, *Private Journal* (Albany, 1865), 52-53.
16. Samuel Sewall, *Diary* (Van Doren edition), 163.
17. Ebenezer Cook, *The Sot-Weed Factor* (B. C. Steiner, editor), *Maryland Historical Society Fund Publications*, No. 36 (1900), 22.
18. Alice Morse Earle, *Colonial Dames and Goodwives* (Boston, 1895), 207-208; Stannard, *Colonial Virginia*, 153, 258-59.

19. Philip Vickers Fithian, *Journal and Letters* (Princeton, 1900), 42-43.
20. See Samuel Eliot Morison, *Three Centuries of Harvard* (Cambridge, 1936), 121-22.
21. George Francis Dow, *Every Day Life in the Massachusetts Bay Colony* (Boston, 1935), 112-14.
22. *Ibid.*, 114 for instances of these sports; Singleton, *Social New York Under the Georges*, 267; Alice Morse Earle, *Customs and Fashions in Old New England* (New York, 1893), 237; Martha J. Lamb, *History of the City of New York* (2 vols., New York, 1877-80), II, 453; J. Thomas Scharf and Thompson Westcott, *History of Philadelphia* (Philadelphia, 1884), II, 939*ff*; Jennie Holliman, *American Sports 1785-1835* (Durham, North Carolina, 1931), 127.
23. William Winterbotham, *An Historical View of the United States* (New York, 1796), II, 17; Earle, *Customs and Fashions*, 19.
24. Quoted in Albert Bushnell Hart, *Commonwealth History of Massachusetts* (5 vols., New York, 1927-30), II, 280.
25. William B. Bentley, *Diary* (Salem, 1905), I, 254.
26. Edward Channing, *A History of the United States*, I (New York, 1905), 536.
27. Daniel Denton, *A Brief Description of New York* (London, 1670), in William Gowans, *Biblioteca Americana* (New York, 1845), 3-4.
28. Alice Morse Earle, *Colonial Days in Old New York* (New York, 1896), 20; Herbert Ingraham Priestley, *The Coming of the White Man* (A History of American Life, I) (New York, 1930), 338-39.
29. Stannard, *Colonial Virginia*, 257.
30. Thomas J. Wertenbaker, *The First Americans* (A History of American Life, II) (New York, 1929), 263.
31. Hugh Jones, *The Present State of Virginia* (London, 1724; reprinted New York, 1865), 48.
32. Bernard, *Retrospections of America*, 155-56.
33. Elkanah Watson, *Men and Times of the Revolution* (New York, 1856), 262.
34. Jones, *The Present State of Virginia*, 48.
35. Marquis de Chastellux, *Travels in North America* (New York, 1827), 293.
36. Ruth E. Painter, "Tavern Amusements in Eighteenth Century America," *Americana*, XI (1916), 92*ff*. See also Edward Field, *The Colonial Tavern* (Providence, 1897).
37. John Adams, *Diary*, in *Works* (10 vols., Boston, 1850-56), II, 125.
38. Quoted in Earle, *Customs and Fashions*, 240.
39. Quoted in Lamb, *History of the City of New York*, II, 465.
40. Earle, *Customs and Fashions*, 238.
41. *Ibid.*, 163.
42. Winterbotham, *An Historical View of the United States*, II, 17.
43. Stannard, *Colonial Virginia*, 141.
44. Burnaby, *Travels* (reprint New York, 1904), 57-58.
45. Bernard, *Retrospections of America*, 208-209.
46. Dow, *Every Day Life*, 115.
47. Samuel Sewall, *Diary*, Massachusetts Historical Society Collections, Ser. 5, Vol. VII, 1.

48. R. W. G. Vail, "Random Notes on the History of the Early American Circus," *Proceedings of the American Antiquarian Society*, April, 1933 (reprint, Worcester, 1934), 6-7; Scharf and Westcott, *History of Philadelphia*, II, 864; Odell, *Annals of the New York Stage*, I, 10.
49. Earle, *Customs and Fashions*, 243; Odell, I, 18, 44.
50. Sewall, *Diary*, V, 196.
51. Odell, *Annals of the New York Stage*, I, 10.
52. *Ibid.*, I, 48-49; Singleton, *Social New York Under the Georges*, 317.
53. Scharf and Westcott, *History of Philadelphia*, II, 863.
54. Dow, *Every Day Life*, 117.
55. Odell, *Annals of the New York Stage*, I, 23-24, 27, 30.
56. Scharf and Westcott, *History of Philadelphia*, II, 950.
57. *The Pope's Kingdom*, Book IV, translated from the Latin of Thomas Neogeorgus by Barnaby Googe, 1570, quoted in Joseph Strutt, *The Sports and Pastimes of the People of England* (London, 1831), lv.

CHAPTER III

The Colonial Aristocracy

1. John Adams, *Works*, II, 59.
2. *Ibid.*, II, 62, 10, 289.
3. *Quaint Advertisements*, Old Times Series, No. 4.
4. John Quincy Adams, *Life in a New England Town* (Boston, 1903), 46.
5. *Ibid.*, 77, 97.
6. *Ibid.*, 88, 91, 78.
7. Joseph Bennett, *Diary, Proceedings of the Massachusetts Historical Society*, 1861, 125.
8. Quoted in Justin Winsor, *Memorial History of Boston* (3 vols., Boston, 1880-81), I, 458.
9. Bennett, *Diary*, 125.
10. Dr. Alexander Hamilton, *Itinerarium* (A. B. Hart, editor) (St. Louis, 1907), 178-79.
11. Captain Francis Goelet, *Journal, New England Historical and Genealogical Register*, XXIV (1870), 53.
12. Anne Hulton, *Letters of a Loyalist Lady* (Cambridge, 1927), *passim*.
13. Walter Tittle, *Colonial Holidays* (New York, 1910), 28.
14. Marquis de Chastellux, *Travels in North America* (New York, 1827), 334-35.
15. Quoted in Winsor, *Memorial History of Boston*, I, 479.
16. Charles Warren, *Jacobin and Junto* (Cambridge, 1931), 20.
17. *Ibid.*, 26.
18. O. G. Sonneck, *Early Concert-Life in America* (Leipzig, 1907), 19, 250, 253.
19. Peter Kalm, quoted in Martha J. Lamb, *History of the City of New York* (2 vols., New York, 1877-80), II, 633.
20. J. F. Watson, *Annals of New York* (Philadelphia, 1846), 264.
21. Lamb, *History of the City of New York*, II, 633ff.
22. Andrew Burnaby, *Travels Through the Middle Settlements in North-America* (London, 1775), 114.

23. Sarah Kemble Knight, *Private Journal* (Albany, 1865), 70-71.
24. Alexander Macraby, quoted in Alice Morse Earle, *Colonial Dames and Goodwives* (Boston, 1895), 220.
25. Alice Morse Earle, *Colonial Days in Old New York* (New York, 1896), 220-21.
26. *Ibid.*, 221.
27. Esther Singleton, *Social New York Under the Georges* (New York, 1902), 265-66.
28. John Sharp, *A Journal of My Life-Exteriour*, in *Pennsylvania Magazine of History and Biography*, XL (1916), 420, 425.
29. Quoted in Singleton, *Social New York Under the Georges*, 303. See also George C. D. Odell, *Annals of the New York Stage* (New York, 1927–) I, 27.
30. Singleton, *Social New York Under the Georges*, 307, 308.
31. Quoted in Earle, *Colonial Days in Old New York*, 216.
32. *New York Gazette*, January 6-13, 1735-36, quoted in Odell, *Annals of the New York Stage*, I, 17. See also Sonneck, *Early Concert-Life*, 159-72.
33. Foster Rhea Dulles, *Eastward Ho* (Boston, 1930), 137.
34. Odell, *Annals of the New York Stage*, I, 5-7, 10-11, 21. For further discussion see Charles L. Daly, *The First Theatre in America;* Oscar L. Wegelin, *The Beginnings of the Drama in America*.
35. Odell, *Annals of the New York Stage*, I, 32*ff*.
36. *Ibid.*, 114-15.
37. *New York Gazette*, quoted in Watson, *Annals of New York*, 264.
38. Quoted in Odell, *Annals of the New York Stage*, I, 111. See also William Dunlap, *History of the American Theatre* (London, 1833), 51.
39. Odell, *Annals of the New York Stage*, I, 110-45 *passim;* Dunlap, *History of the American Theatre*, 51*ff*; Singleton, *Social New York Under the Georges*, 272-95; O. G. Sonneck, *Early Opera in America* (Boston, 1915), 77*ff*.
40. Burnaby, *Travels*, 31.
41. Marquis de Chastellux, quoted in George Morgan, *Patrick Henry* (Philadelphia, 1929), 55.
42. Philip Vickers Fithian, *Journal and Letters* (Princeton, 1900), 50, 296.
43. *Ibid.*, 202.
44. *Ibid.*, 58, 143, 144, 181, 218.
45. *Ibid.*, 59.
46. *Ibid.*, 223-24.
47. *Ibid.*, 96, 97, 185, 192-93.
48. George Washington, *Diaries* (4 vols., Boston, 1925), I, 299*ff*.
49. *Ibid.*, I, 126.
50. Sarah N. Randolph, *The Domestic Life of Thomas Jefferson* (New York, 1871), 26*ff*.
51. Paul Leicester Ford, *Washington and the Theatre, Dunlap Society Publications*, New Series, No. 8 (New York, 1899), 20-22.
52. *Ibid.*, 5-9; Odell, *Annals of the New York Stage*, I, 9, 20; Lyon G. Tyler, *Williamsburg* (Richmond, 1907), 224-26; Eola Willis, *The Charleston Stage in the Eighteenth Century* (Columbia, 1924), 25-26.
53. Tyler, *Williamsburg*, 230.

54. Josiah Quincy, *Memoir of the Life of Josiah Quincy, jun.* (Boston, 1825), 96.
55. Willis, *The Charleston Stage*, 59-77.
56. Alexis de Tocqueville, *Democracy in America* (Boston, 1876), I, 243
57. Hamilton, *Itinerarium*, 50.
58. Burnaby, *Travels*, 87.
59. James Truslow Adams, *Provincial Society* (*A History of American Life*, II) (New York, 1936), 261-62; Singleton, *Social New York Under the Georges*, 311.
60. Carl Bridenbaugh, "Colonial Newport as a Summer Resort," *Rhode Island Historical Society*, XXVI (1933), I, 4.
61. *Ibid.*, 14, 16-18.
62. Quoted in George O. Willard, *History of the Providence Stage* (Providence, 1891), 8-9.
63. *Ibid.*, 14-15.
64. Quoted in Ford, *Washington and the Theatre*, 24.

CHAPTER IV

The Frontier

1. Frances Trollope, *Domestic Manners of the Americans* (London, 1832), I, 248.
2. William Faux, *Memorable Days in America* (London, 1823), in Reuben Gold Thwaites, *Early Western Travels 1748-1846* (Cleveland, 1907), XI, 210.
3. John James Audubon, *Delineations of American Scenery and Character* (1834; reprinted New York, 1926), 59-62; John Woods, *Two Years Residence in the Illinois Country* (London, 1822), in Thwaites, *Early Western Travels*, X, 249, 318; John Bradbury, *Travels in the Interior of America* (London, 1819), in *ibid.*, V, 280; Thomas D. Clark, *The Rampaging Frontier* (Indianapolis, 1939), 31.
4. David Crockett, *An Account of Colonel Crockett's Tour Written by Himself* (Philadelphia, 1837), 176ff. See also Edmund Flagg, *The Far West* (New York, 1838), in Thwaites, *Early Western Travels*, XXVI, 360-61; William N. Blane, *An Excursion Through the United States* (London, 1824), 302; Baynard Rush Hall, *The New Purchase* (New York, 1855), 104-12.
5. John Bernard, *Retrospections of America 1797-1811* (New York, 1877), 181.
6. H. M. Brackenridge, *Recollections of Persons and Places in the West* (Philadelphia, 1868), 60-63.
7. Albert Beveridge, *Abraham Lincoln* (Boston, 1928), I, 111.
8. Samuel L. Clemens (Mark Twain), *Life on the Mississippi* (1874) (Hartford, 1899), 32-33.
9. Timothy Flint, *Recollections of the Last Ten Years* (Boston, 1826), 98.
10. Thomas Ashe, *Travels in America* (London, 1808), quoted in John A. Krout, *Annals of American Sport* (*Pageant of America*, XV) (New Haven, 1929), 28.

398   AMERICA LEARNS TO PLAY

11. William H. Herndon and Jesse W. Weik, *Life of Lincoln* (New York, 1896), I, 108-9.
12. Quoted in Marquis James, *Andrew Jackson: the Border Captain* (Indianapolis, 1933), 19. See also James Parton, *Life of Andrew Jackson* (New York, 1860), I, 253.
13. Faux, *Memorable Days in America*, in Thwaites, *Early Western Travels*, XI, 196; Woods, *Two Years Residence*, in *ibid.*, X, 264, 346; Richard Flower, *Letters from Lexington and Illinois* (London, 1819), in *ibid.*, X, 125.
14. Bessie Louise Pierce, *A History of Chicago* (New York, 1937), I, 208.
15. Flower, *Letters from Lexington and Illinois*, in Thwaites, *Early Western Travels*, X, 300.
16. Crockett, *An Account of Colonel Crockett's Tour*, 34.
17. Audubon, *Delineations of American Scenery*, 244.
18. Everett Dick, *The Sod-House Frontier, 1854-1890* (New York, 1937), 75, 266, 281.
19. William H. Milburn, *The Rifle, Axe and Saddle-Bags* (New York, 1857), 46-51; Hall, *The New Purchase*, 426-28.
20. Beveridge, *Abraham Lincoln*, I, 92.
21. Bernard De Voto, *Mark Twain's America* (Boston, 1932), 104*ff.*
22. James Stuart, *Three Years in North America* (New York, 1833), II, 174-75.
23. James Flint, *Letters from America* (Edinburgh, 1822), in Thwaites, *Early Western Travels*, IX, 261-62.
24. Peter Cartwright, *Autobiography* (New York, 1857), 121.
25. James B. Finley, *Autobiography* (Cincinnati, 1854), 364.
26. Cartwright, *Autobiography*, 48.
27. Herndon and Weik, *Life of Lincoln*, 11-12.

CHAPTER V

A Changing Society

1. Timothy Dwight, *Travels in New England and New York* (London, 1823), IV, 343-44.
2. Bureau of the Census, as cited in *Statistical Abstract*, 1935 (Washington, 1936), 6.
3. Michael Chevalier, *Society, Manners and Politics in the United State* (Boston, 1839), 473.
4. Quoted in George B. Cutten, *The Threat of Leisure* (New Haven, 1926).
5. T. L. Nichols, *Forty Years of American Life* (London, 1874), 206.
6. Charles Lyell, *A Second Visit to United States* (New York, 1849) quoted in Allan Nevins, *American Social History as Recorded b British Travellers* (New York, 1932), 333. See also Charles Dickens *American Notes* (Fireside Edition), 68, 99-100; Frances Trollope *Domestic Manners of the Americans* (London, 1832), II, 82, 142 193; Basil Hall, *Travels in North America* (London, 1829), 258 Thomas Hamilton, *Men and Manners* (Philadelphia, 1833), 70 Frances J. Grund, *The Americans* (Boston, 1837), 119.

7. Trollope, *Domestic Manners of the Americans,* II, 142, 193.

8. Dickens, *American Notes,* 170.

9. *Ibid.,* 99, 100.

10. Quoted in Arthur A. Hornblow, *History of the American Theatre* (Philadelphia, 1919), I, 24.

11. Henry Ward Beecher, *Addresses to Young Men* (1844) (Philadelphia, 1893), 242, 253, 259. See also Dickens, *American Notes,* 68; Grund, *The Americans,* 120; Alfred Bunn, *Old England and New England* (London, 1853), II, 110-11.

12. See Edward Channing, *A History of the United States* (6 vols., New York, 1905-25), V, 175*ff;* John Bach McMaster, *History of the People of the United States* (8 vols., New York, 1883-1913), IV, 531*ff;* John A. Krout, *Origins of Prohibition* (New York, 1925).

13. Anne Royall, *Sketches of History, Life and Manners of the United States* (New Haven, 1826), 299.

14. *Voice of Industry,* March 20, 1846, quoted in Norman Ware, *The Industrial Worker, 1840-60* (Boston, 1924), 127. See also John R. Commons, *A Documentary History of American Industrial Society* (Cleveland, 1910), VI, 97.

15. Henry Wansey, *An Excursion to the United States* (Salisbury, 1798), 24; McMaster, *History of the People of the United States,* V, 575.

16. Emerson Davis, *The Half Century* (Boston, 1851), 188.

17. Nichols, *Forty Years of American Life,* 43.

18. *Democratic Press,* June 14, 1827, quoted in Commons, *Documentary History,* V, 80.

19. *The American Lyceum* (Boston, 1829), reprint, *Old South Leaflets,* VI, No. 139; Cecil B. Hayes, "The American Lyceum," Bureau of U. S. Education Bulletin No. 12 (1932), 7-9, 22.

20. Philip Hone, *Diary* (edited by Allan Nevins, New York, 1927), 515, 572-73.

21. Chevalier, *Society, Manners and Politics,* 128-29.

22. Harriet H. Robinson, *Loom and Spindle* (New York, 1898), 75.

23. Dickens, *American Notes,* 78*ff.* See also Lucy Larcom, "Among Lowell Mill Girls," *Atlantic Monthly,* XLVIII (1881), 600; "Leisure for Mill Girls," *Lowell Offering,* 11, 65*ff;* Basil Hall, *Travels in North America,* 287; David Crockett, *Life of* (Philadelphia, 1860), 92; James Silk Buckingham, *The Eastern and Western States of America* (London, 1842), I, 295*ff.*

24. *Lowell Offering,* I, 5.

25. George Combe, *Notes on the United States* (Edinburgh, 1841), I, 120.

26. See Frances Wright D'Arusmont, *Views of Society and Manners in America* (New York, 1821), 120.

27. Achille Murat, *A Moral and Political Sketch of the United States* (London, 1833), 356. See also Combe, *Notes on the United States,* II, 126; Trollope, *Domestic Manners of the Americans,* I, 166, 214, 216; Alexander Mackay, *The Western World* (London, 1850), I, 228.

28. Hamilton, *Men and Manners,* 81.

29. *Spalding Skating Guide* (New York, 1862), 51; Arthur Charles Cole, *The Irrepressible Conflict* (*A History of American Life,* VII) (New York, 1934), 189.

30. *Lowell Offering*, I, 61.
31. Basil Hall, *Travels in North America*, 195, 294; Mrs. Basil Hall, *The Aristocratic Journey* (New York, 1931), 125.
32. James Stuart, *Three Years in North America* (London, 1833), I, 497.
33. Charles William Day, *Hints on Etiquette* (New York, 1843).
34. Captain Frederick Marryat, *A Diary in America* (Philadelphia, 1839), quoted in Dixon Wecter, *The Saga of American Society* (New York, 1937), 317.
35. Trollope, *Domestic Manners of the Americans*, I, 189.

CHAPTER VI

The Theatre Comes of Age

1. William Davidge, *Footlight Flashes* (New York, 1867), 202.
2. *Arcturus*, II (1841), 29, quoted in Frank Luther Mott, *A History of American Magazines* (New York and Cambridge, 1930–), I (1741-1850), 430.
3. John Bach McMaster, *History of the People of the United States* (8 vols., New York, 1883-1913), VII, 92ff.
4. Reese D. James, *Old Drury of Philadelphia* (Philadelphia, 1932), 24, 66; George C. D. Odell, *Annals of the New York Stage* (New York, 1927–), II, 460; Henry Austin Clapp, *Reminiscences of a Dramatic Critic* (Boston, 1902), 134.
5. George M. Edward, *Some Earlier Public Amusements of Rochester* (Rochester, 1894), 4; John Bernard, *Retrospections of America 1797-1811* (New York, 1877), 318; Joseph B. Felt, *Annals of Salem* (Salem, 1845), II, 43-45.
6. See N. M. Ludlow, *Dramatic Life as I Found It* (St. Louis, 1880); Frances C. Wemyss, *Chronology of the American Stage from 1752 to 1852* (New York, c. 1852), 11, 14; and article on Samuel Drake in *Dictionary of American Biography*.
7. Tyrone Power, *Impressions of America* (London, 1836), I, 66, 87, 123, 141, 210, 351-52; II, 172, 191.
8. Carl Russell Fish, *The Rise of the Common Man* (*A History of American Life*, VI) (New York, 1937), 145.
9. Odell, *Annals of the New York Stage*, IV, 603; James, *Old Drury of Philadelphia*, 40-41; Arthur A. Hornblow, *History of the American Theatre* (Philadelphia, 1919), II, 26, 161; William G. B. Carson, *The Theatre on the Frontier* (Chicago, 1932), 180.
10. *New York Daily Advertiser*, quoted in Odell, *Annals of the New York Stage*, II, 8. See also *ibid.*, IV, 603; Hornblow, *History of the American Theatre*, II, 77, 443; Clapp, *Reminiscences*, 366, 493; Arthur Herman Wilson, *A History of the Philadelphia Theatre, 1835 to 1855* (Philadelphia, 1935), 38; William B. Wood, *Personal Recollections of the Stage* (Philadelphia, 1855), 299; Alfred Bunn, *Old England and New England* (London, 1853), II, 105.
11. James Silk Buckingham (1838), quoted in Dixon Wecter, *The Saga of American Society* (New York, 1937), 466.
12. Hornblow. *History of the American Theatre*, II, 143.

13. T. Allston Brown, *A History of the New York Stage* (New York, 1903), I, 415-18; Philip Hone, *Diary* (edited by Allan Nevins, New York, 1927), 870; Harry Watkins, *Journal* (*One Man in His Time*, edited by Maud and Otis Skinner, Philadelphia, 1938), 73-74.
14. Wemyss, *Chronology of the American Stage*, 178.
15. Richard Grant White, quoted in Hornblow, *History of the American Theatre*, II, 167-68.
16. Frances Trollope, *Domestic Manners of the Americans* (London, 1832), I, 187; II, 162-63. See also Odell, *Annals of the New York Stage*, VII, 655.
17. *New York Herald*, November 2, 1864, quoted in Odell, *Annals of the New York Stage*, VII, 658-59.
18. Richard Grant White, quoted in Hornblow, *History of the American Theatre*, II, 167-68.
19. Quoted in Montrose J. Moses and John Mason Brown, *The American Theatre as Seen by Its Critics 1752-1934* (New York, 1934), 40ff.
20. James, *Old Drury of Philadelphia*, 31; Odell, *Annals of the New York Stage*, II, 517; V, 485; III, 183; VII, 236-37.
21. William Dunlap, *History of the American Theatre* (London, 1833), 407ff.
22. Carson, *The Theatre on the Frontier*, 309.
23. *New York Herald*, September 19, 1838. See also *Plain Dealer*, December 3, 1836, and Francis Joseph Daly, *The Life of Augustin Daly* (New York, 1917), quoted in Hornblow, *History of the American Theatre*, II, 168.
24. Joseph Jefferson, *Autobiography* (New York, 1889), 54, 30.
25. Ludlow, *Dramatic Life as I Found It*, 64-68.
26. Sol Smith, *Theatrical Management in the West and South for Thirty Years* (New York, 1868), 79.
27. Watkins, *Journal*, 67, 103, 39.
28. *Ibid.*, 141.
29. *Ibid.*, 55-56; Clapp, *Reminiscences*, 221-36, 278.
30. Watkins, *Journal*, 83.
31. Carson, *The Theatre on the Frontier*, 311, 319, 328-30; Wilson, *A History of the Philadelphia Theatre*, 18-19, 130-31; Douglas L. Hunt, "The Nashville Theatre, 1830-1840," *Birmingham-Southern College Bulletin*, XXVIII, No. 3 (1935), 54; Watkins, *Journal*, 151.
32. Watkins, *Journal*, 230.
33. Program collection, New York Public Library.
34. Watkins, *Journal*, 68; Odell, *Annals of the New York Stage*, V, 578.
35. *New York Herald*, September 3, 1852, quoted in Moses and Brown, *The American Theatre*, 73-75.
36. Quoted in Meade Minnigerode, *The Fabulous Forties* (New York, 1924), 174-77.
37. "Durang's History of the Philadelphia Stage," *Philadelphia Sunday Dispatch*, May 17, 1854, quoted in James, *Old Drury of Philadelphia*, 26-27; Odell, *Annals of the New York Stage*, III, 21, 215, IV, 163.
38. Odell, *Annals of the New York Stage*, IV, 614.
39. Achille Murat, *A Moral and Political Sketch of the United States* (London, 1833), 367. See also *Appleton's Journal*, VIII, 580.

40. *New York Herald,* May 15, 1840, in Odell, *Annals of the New York Stage,* IV, 359.
41. Hornblow, *History of the American Theatre,* II, 143.
42. Hone, *Diary,* 480.
43. Lawrence Hutton, *Curiosities of the American Stage* (London, 1891), 157-58, 165; Odell, *Annals of the New York Stage,* V, 529*ff.* See also Olive Logan, *Apropos of Women and the Theatre* (New York, 1869), 134-37; Hornblow, *History of the American Theatre,* II, 101.
44. Odell, *Annals of the New York Stage,* V, 378*ff,* 401*ff.*
45. *New York Tribune,* December 1, 1847; *New York Herald,* March 1, 1848.
46. Quoted in Minnigerode, *The Fabulous Forties,* 144.
47. Quoted in Mary C. Crawford, *The Romance of the American Theatre* (Boston, 1925), 450-51.
48. Odell, *Annals of the New York Stage,* IV, 664.
49. *Ibid.,* V, 495.
50. Moses and Brown, *The American Theatre,* 70-71.
51. Hone, *Diary,* 573.
52. Odell, *Annals of the New York Stage,* II, 466; Hornblow, *History of the American Theatre,* I, 299.
53. Mott, *A History of American Magazines,* II, 198.
54. Quoted in James E. Murdoch, *The Stage* (Philadelphia, 1880), 429.

CHAPTER VII

Mr. Barnum Shows the Way

1. M. R. Werner, *Barnum* (New York, 1927), 52.
2. Broadside advertisement, New York Public Library.
3. Werner, *Barnum,* 65.
4. "Sights and Wonders in New York" (pamphlet, New York, 1849); P. T. Barnum, *Life . . . Written by Himself* (New York, 1855), 225.
5. Philip Hone, *Diary* (edited by Allan Nevins, New York, 1927), 12-13, 795.
6. Barnum, *Life,* 148*ff,* 242*ff,* 350*ff.*
7. George C. D. Odell, *Annals of New York Stage* (New York, 1927–), IV, 669. See also Harry Watkins, *Journal* (*One Man in His Time,* edited by Maud and Otis Skinner, Philadelphia, 1938), 225*ff.*
8. Watkins, *Journal,* 91.
9. Barnum, *Life,* 343. See also contemporary magazine comments in Frank Luther Mott, *A History of American Magazines* (New York and Cambridge, 1930–), II, 194-95.
10. N. P. Willis, *Memoranda of the Life of Jenny Lind* (Philadelphia, 1851), 95-97.
11. *Ibid.,* 126.
12. Barnum, *Life,* 343.
13. William Davidge, *Footlight Flashes* (New York, 1867), 127.
14. Lawrence Hutton, *Curiosities of the American Stage* (London, 1891), 124-26; Carl Wittke, *Tambo and Bones* (Durham, N. C., 1930), 45; Francis Pendleton Gaines, *The Southern Plantation* (New York, 1924), 100-101.

15. Hutton, *Curiosities*, 115-19; N. M. Ludlow, *Dramatic Life as I Found It* (St. Louis, 1880), 392-93; Robert P. Nevin, "Stephen C. Foster and Negro Minstrelsy," *Atlantic Monthly*, XX (1867), 608.

16. Joseph Jefferson, *Autobiography* (New York, 1889), 7.

17. *Holden's Dollar Magazine*, I (1848), quoted in Mott, *History of American Magazines*, I, 433.

18. Wittke, *Tambo and Bones*, 57, 58-60; Davidge, *Footlight Flashes*, 127-28; Ralph Keeler, *Vagabond Adventures* (Boston, 1872), 132.

19. See Dailey Paskman and Sigmund Spaeth, *"Gentlemen, Be Seated!"* (New York, 1928), 47ff.

20. Quoted in Albert J. Beveridge, *Abraham Lincoln*, II, 536, 597. See also Wittke, *Tambo and Bones*, 209; and Nevin, *loc. cit.*, 608.

21. Earl Chapin May, *The Circus from Rome to Ringling* (New York, 1932), 25-27; W. C. Coup, *Sawdust and Spangles* (Chicago, 1901), 141; R. W. G. Vail, "Random Notes on the History of the Early American Circus," *Proceedings of the American Antiquarian Society*, April, 1933 (reprint; Worcester, 1934), 17.

22. Vail, *loc. cit.*, 29; Joseph B. Felt, *Annals of Salem* (Salem, 1845), II, 92.

23. Isaac J. Greenwood, *The Circus* (New York, 1898), 113-14.

24. *Ibid.*, 64ff; Vail, *loc. cit.*, 35; Barnum, *Life*, 177ff; Gil Robinson, *Old Wagon Show Days* (Cincinnati, 1925), 20.

25. Greenwood, *The Circus*, 64ff; Vail, *loc. cit.*, 64-68; Odell, *Annals of the New York Stage*, II, 491.

26. Vail, *loc. cit.*, 32-40; Coup, *Sawdust and Spangles*, 140-41.

27. E. E. Calkins, *They Broke the Prairie* (New York, 1937), 245; Bessie Louise Pierce, *A History of Chicago* (New York, 1937), I, 209; Greenwood, *The Circus*, 116; May, *The Circus*, 77-79; Vail, *loc. cit.*, 35.

28. Edmund Flagg, *The Far West* (New York, 1838), in Thwaites, *Early Western Travels*, XXVI, 225.

29. Hiram Fuller, *Belle Brittan on Tour* (New York, 1858), 160.

30. Barnum, *Life*, 348-49.

CHAPTER VIII

The Beginning of Spectator Sports

1. *Atlantic Monthly*, I (1858), 881.

2. Jennie Holliman, *American Sports 1785-1835* (Durham, N. C., 1931), 158. See also Philip Hone, *Diary* (edited by Allan Nevins, New York, 1927), 156.

3. James Silk Buckingham, *The Eastern and Western States of America* (London, 1842), I, 22.

4. P. T. Barnum, *Life . . . Written by Himself* (New York, 1855), 352-55.

5. *Spirit of the Times*, November 8, 1856.

6. *Frank Leslie's Illustrated Newspaper*, June 28, 1856.

7. William N. Blane, *An Excursion Through the United States* (London, 1824), 315-17; Josiah Quincy, *Figures of the Past* (Boston, 1883), 97; Charles H. Haswell, *Reminiscences of an Octogenarian of the City of New York* (New York, 1896), 140-44. See also Ralph Henry

Gabriel, *The Evolution of Long Island* (New Haven, 1921), 169; and Max Farrand, "The Great Race—Eclipse Against the World," *Scribner's*, LXX (1921), 457-64.

8. *New York Herald*, May 13, 1845. See also article on William Ransome Johnson, "Napoleon of the Turf," in *Dictionary of American Biography*, and Gabriel, *Evolution of Long Island*, 169.

9. Hone, *Diary*, 601.

10. Marquis James, *Andrew Jackson: The Border Captain* (Indianapolis, 1933), 118.

11. Quoted in Everett Dick, *The Sod-House Frontier, 1854-1890* (New York, 1937), 279.

12. *Spirit of the Times*, November 1, 1856.

13. Hiram Woodruff, *The Trotting Horse of America* (New York, 1871), 283; Dwight Akers, *Drivers Up* (New York, 1938), 73-89.

14. *Frank Leslie's Illustrated Newspaper*, May 17, 1853, 357; Charles A. Peverelly, *The Book of American Pastimes* (New York, 1866), 164, 249.

15. Peverelly, *Book of American Pastimes*, 244ff; Holliman, *American Sports*, 158; *Frank Leslie's Illustrated Newspaper*, April 28, 1860, March 17, 1860; *New York Herald*, August 9, 1838, September 11, 1838.

16. Quoted (December 9, 1829) in Holliman, *American Sports*, 158.

17. *Frank Leslie's Illustrated Newspaper*, July 13, 1857, 28.

18. *New York Clipper*, October 18, 1856, July 18, 1857.

19. *Spirit of the Times*, July 20, 1839.

20. *Ibid.*, July 13, 1837.

21. Hone, *Diary*, 156-57; Holliman, *American Sports*, 154.

22. *New York Clipper*, April 26, May 31, June 28, 1856.

23. *Niles' Weekly Register*, XIII (1817), 128, quoted in Holliman, *American Sports*, 143.

24. Hone, *Diary*, 620.

25. *Ibid.*, 620.

26. *Spirit of the Times*, April 7, March 17, 1860; Holliman, *American Sports*, 143ff; Alexander Johnston, *Ten—And Out!* (New York, 1936), 24-30.

27. *Vanity Fair*, I (1860), 45, quoted in Frank Luther Mott, *A History of American Magazines* (New York and Cambridge, 1930–), II, 202.

28. *Spirit of the Times*, April 28, 1860.

29. *Ibid.*, September 1, 1860; *Cleveland Plain Dealer*, August 1, 1860, quoted in Arthur C. Cole, *The Irrepressible Conflict* (*A History of American Life*, VII) (New York, 1934), 191.

CHAPTER IX

Mid-Century

1. Philip Hone, *Diary* (edited by Allan Nevins, New York, 1927), 588.

2. *The American Farmer* (Baltimore), VI (1824-25), 271, 349. See also Arthur C. Cole, *The Irrepressible Conflict* (*A History of American Life*, VII) (New York, 1934), 190.

3. Timothy Flint, *Recollections of the Last Ten Years* (Boston, 1826), 386.

4. Francis J. Grund, *The Americans* (Boston, 1837), 323.

5. Fred A. Wilson, *Some Annals of Nahant* (Boston, 1928), 72; *New York Herald* (1853), quoted in Jefferson Williamson, *The American Hotel* (New York, 1930), 238; "Poem on the Mineral Waters of Ballston and Saratoga" (Ballston Spa, 1819). See also G. M. Davison, *The Fashionable Tour* (Saratoga Springs, 1825).

6. William Gregg, *Essays on Domestic Industry* (1845), in D. A. Tomkins, *Cotton Mill, Commercial Feature* (Charlotteville, N. C., 1899).

7. Quoted in Dixon Wecter, *The Saga of American Society* (New York, 1937), 437.

8. Flint, *Recollections*, 393-94.

9. Hone, *Diary*, 415.

10. Eliza Ripley, *Social Life in Old New Orleans* (New York, 1912), 142.

11. Achille Murat, *A Moral and Political Sketch of the United States* (London, 1833), 358.

12. Michael Chevalier, *Society, Manners and Politics in the United States* (Boston, 1839), 315-16.

13. Murat, *A Moral and Political Sketch*, 367.

14. Quoted in Meade Minnigerode, *The Fabulous Forties* (New York, 1924), 213-14.

15. Henry Wansey, *An Excursion to the United States* (Salisbury, 1798), 211.

16. Wilson, *Some Annals of Nahant*, 77.

17. James Stuart, *Three Years in North America* (London, 1833), I, 280.

18. *Frank Leslie's Illustrated Newspaper*, August 22, 1857.

19. Amelia M. Murray, *Letters from the United States* (London, 1856), I, 37, quoted in Cole, *The Irrepressible Conflict*, 201.

20. *New York Herald*, July 19, 1853, quoted in Williamson, *The American Hotel*, 236-37.

21. Joseph Doddridge, *Notes on the Settlement and Indian Wars* (Albany, 1876), 201.

22. William Makepeace Thackeray, *Roundabout Papers* (London, 1863), 273. See also Mark Twain, *Life on the Mississippi*.

23. Herbert Asbury, *Sucker's Progress* (New York, 1938), 229.

24. *Ibid.*, 232.

25. Thomas Clark, *The Rampaging Frontier* (Indianapolis, 1939), 244.

26. George H. Devol, *Forty Years a Gambler on the Mississippi* (New York, 1926), 27, 37, 43.

27. Harry Watkins, *Journal* (*One Man in His Time*, edited by Maud and Otis Skinner), 162-63.

28. E. E. Calkins, *They Broke the Prairie* (New York, 1937), 243-45.

29. *New York Herald*, February 21, 1848; George C. D. Odell, *Annals of the New York Stage* (New York, 1927—), IV, 43, 49. See also Cole, *The Irrepressible Conflict*, 239.

30. Everett Dick, *The Sod-House Frontier, 1854-1890* (New York, 1937), 285, 286.

31. Thomas Nelson Page, *Social Life in Old Virginia* (New York, 1897), 107.

32. A. DePuy Van Buren, *Jottings of a Year's Sojourn in the South* (Battle Creek, Mich., 1859), 88.

33. Henry Barnard, "The South Atlantic States," *Maryland Historical Magazine*, XIII, 295ff, 318. See also U. B. Phillips, *Life and Labor in the Old South* (Boston, 1929), 229, 335.

34. Susan Dabney Smedes, *Memorials of a Southern Planter* (Baltimore, 1887), 180.

35. Herbert Ravenel Sass, *A Carolina Rice Plantation in the Fifties* (New York, 1936).

36. *Agriculture of the United States in 1860* (Eighth Census), 247, quoted in Cole, *The Irrepressible Conflict*, 34.

37. Van Buren, *Jottings of a Year's Sojourn in the South*, 118.

38. U. B. Phillips, *American Negro Slavery* (New York, 1918), 314-15.

39. *American Historical Review*, III, 41.

40. D. R. Hundley, *Social Relations in Our Southern States* (New York, 1860), 263.

41. Phillips, *Life and Labor in the Old South*, 339ff.

42. Guion Griffis Johnson, *Ante-Bellum North Carolina* (Chapel Hill, 1937), 91-104, 180.

43. *Ibid.*, 111.

44. Augustus Baldwin Longstreet, *Georgia Scenes* (New York, 1840), 14, 119.

45. Frederick Law Olmstead, *The Cotton Kingdom* (New York, 1862), II, 73.

46. Frances Anne Kemble, *Journal* (Philadelphia, 1835), I, 83-84n.

47. Samuel Dexter Ward, *Diary, New York Historical Society Quarterly Bulletin*, XXI (1937), 114-15.

48. Charles Lyell, *Travels in North America* (New York, 1852), I, 58. See also Grund, *The Americans*, 323.

49. *New York Daily Tribune*, May 27, 1851, quoted in Norman Ware, *The Industrial Worker, 1840-60* (Boston, 1924), 33.

50. *New York Herald*, July 4, 1838; July 6, 1845; July 12, 1845; August 27, 1838.

51. Eric Adolphus Dime, "America's First Aeronaut," *Air Travel*, January, 1918, 214ff. See also Cole, *The Irrepressible Conflict*, 195-96.

52. Gabriel Furman, "How New York City Used to Celebrate Independence Day," *New York Historical Society Quarterly Bulletin*, July, 1937, 93-94; Charles H. Haswell, *Reminiscences of an Octogenarian of the City of New York* (New York, 1896), 62.

53. *New York Herald*, March 3, 1838; January 4, 17, 28, 1845.

54. *Frank Leslie's Illustrated Newspaper*, December 15, 1855; *New York Herald*, November 3, 1857; *New York Clipper*, June 14, 1856.

55. *New York Herald*, July 6, 1838.

CHAPTER X

Cow-Towns and Mining-Camps

1. E. C. Abbott ("Teddy Blue") and Helen H. Smith, *We Pointed Them North* (New York, 1939), 257.

2. See John A. and Alan Lomax, *Cowboy Songs* (New York, 1938).
3. William Wright (Dan De Quille), *The Big Bonanza* (Hartford, 1876), 438.
4. *Ibid.*, 29-30.
5. Allan Nevins, *The Emergence of Modern America* (*A History of American Life*, VIII) (New York, 1927), 137.
6. Samuel L. Clemens (Mark Twain), *Roughing It* (New York, 1899), II, 27-28.
7. Philip Ashton Rollins, *The Cowboy* (New York, 1922), 80.
8. Herbert Asbury, *Sucker's Progress* (New York, 1938), 316.
9. A. K. McClure, *Three Thousand Miles Through the Rockies* (Philadelphia, 1869), 412, 414.
10. Wells Drury, *An Editor on the Comstock Lode* (New York, 1936), 88.
11. McClure, *Three Thousand Miles Through the Rockies*, 424-25.
12. Drury, *An Editor on the Comstock Lode*, 91.
13. Quoted *ibid.*, 299-300.
14. Constance Rourke, *Troupers of the Gold Coast* (New York, 1928), 57.
15. *Ibid.*, 43.
16. *Ibid.*, *passim*.
17. Drury, *An Editor on the Comstock Lode*, 54-61; Bernard De Voto, *Mark Twain's America* (Boston, 1932), 123-26.
18. George D. Lyman, *The Saga of the Comstock Lode* (New York, 1934), 270ff.
19. Rollins, *The Cowboy*, 40.
20. *Ibid.*, 174ff; Hough, *The Story of the Cowboy*, 225ff.
21. Lomax, *Cowboy Songs*, xvi.
22. Rollins, *The Cowboy*, 172; Lomax, *Cowboy Songs*, 5; Abbott and Smith, *We Pointed Them North*, 260.
23. Rollins, *The Cowboy*, 174-89; Hough, *The Story of the Cowboy*, 221-36.
24. Hough, *The Story of the Cowboy*, 238.
25. Rollins, *The Cowboy*, 296-97.
26. Hough, *The Story of the Cowboy*, 261.
27. Abbott and Smith, *We Pointed Them North*, 123.
28. *Ibid.*, 126.
29. *Ibid.*, 9.
30. Hough, *The Story of the Cowboy*, 252-53.
31. Robert M. Wright, *Dodge City* (Dodge City, 1913), 149.
32. Lomax, *Cowboy Songs*, 169.

CHAPTER XI

The Rise of Sports

1. *The Nation*, III, 115.
2. Pamphlet material on James L. Plimpton, New York Public Library.
3. Arthur C. Cole, *The Irrepressible Conflict* (*A History of American Life*, VII) (New York, 1934), 187. See also *Lowell Offering*, I, 61.
4. Quoted in D. R. Hundley, *Social Relations in Our Southern States* (New York, 1860), 41.

5. Thomas Wentworth Higginson, "Saints and Their Bodies," *Atlantic Monthly,* I (1858), 587.

6. *New York Clipper,* July 5, 1856; Edward Everett, *Orations and Speeches on Various Occasions* (Boston, 1856-72), III, 407, quoted in Cole, *The Irrepressible Conflict,* 188.

7. *Harper's Monthly,* XIII (1856), 642, 646.

8. *Atlantic Monthly,* I (1858), 881.

9. *New York Herald,* July 12, 1858, quoted in Cole, *The Irrepressible Conflict,* 189.

10. Frederick L. Paxson, "The Rise of Sports," *Mississippi Valley Historical Review,* IV, 143-68.

11. *Outing,* II (1883), 468.

12. *Independent,* LII (1900), 1361.

13. W. E. Baxter, *America and the Americans* (London, 1855), 99, quoted in Cole, *The Irrepressible Conflict,* 188.

14. Robert W. Henderson, "How Baseball Began," *Bulletin of New York Public Library,* XLI (1937), 288, and "Baseball and Rounders," *ibid.,* XLIII (1939), 303-14; Jane Austen, *Northanger Abbey* (Boston, 1898), 8.

15. Horatio Smith, *Festivals, Games and Amusements* (New York, 1833), 330.

16. William R. Wister, *Some Reminiscences of Cricket in Philadelphia before 1861* (Philadelphia, 1904), 6-9; Charles A. Peverelly, *The Book of American Pastimes* (New York, 1866), 529ff; *Spirit of the Times,* January 24, 1857.

17. In addition to articles by R. W. Henderson, cited above, see Ralph E. Renaud, "Baseball's Centenary," *New York Times Magazine,* June 11, 1939, 11ff; A. G. Spalding, *America's National Game* (New York, 1911), 19-23, 29-41; Francis C. Richter, *History and Records of Baseball* (Philadelphia, 1914), 17-31; John M. Ward, *Baseball* (Philadelphia, 1889), 9-34; George Wright, "Sketch of the National Game of Baseball," *Records of the Columbia Historical Society,* XXIII (1920), 80ff.

18. "By-Laws of Knickerbocker Club," in Spalding Collection, New York Public Library.

19. Quoted in Richter, *History and Records of Baseball,* 32.

20. *Spirit of the Times,* January 10, 1857; Peverelly, *The Book of American Pastimes,* 461; article on Alfred J. Reach in *Dictionary of American Biography.*

21. *Spirit of the Times,* December 27, 1856; *New York Clipper,* July 19, 1856.

22. Article on Henry Wright in *Dictionary of American Biography.*

23. *Spirit of the Times,* March 24, 1860; Peverelly, *The Book of American Pastimes,* 353.

24. *Spirit of the Times,* December 6, 1856; *Frank Leslie's Illustrated Newspaper,* April 26, 1856.

25. Spalding, *America's National Game,* 71; A. H. Spink, *The National Game* (St. Louis, 1910), 3.

26. *Spirit of the Times,* July 28, October 6, September 8, 1860; Spalding, *America's National Game,* 80-81.

27. Peverelly, *The Book of American Pastimes,* 508, 337; *The Galaxy,* VI (1868), 563, and *Sports and Games,* III (1872), 112, quoted in Frank Luther Mott, *A History of American Magazines* (New York and Cambridge, 1930–), III, 217.

28. Richter, *History and Records of Baseball,* 37-39; Spalding, *America's National Game,* 137-39.

29. Spalding, *America's National Game,* 210-14; Richter, *History and Records of Baseball,* 40.

30. Samuel L. Clemens (Mark Twain), *Speeches* (1923), 145.

31. George Makepeace Towle, *American Society* (London, 1870), II, 40; *Frank Leslie's Illustrated Newspaper,* quoted in Lloyd Lewis and Henry Justin Smith, *Oscar Wilde Discovers America* (New York, 1936), 381.

32. *How to Play Field and Parlor Croquet* (1865).

33. Towle, *American Society,* II, 39.

34. *The Nation,* III, 115.

35. *Harper's Weekly,* September 13, 1879, quoted in John A. Krout, *Annals of American Sport* (*The Pageant of America,* XV) (New Haven, 1929), 164.

36. *Outing,* II, 468.

37. William Patten (editor), *The Book of Sport* (New York, 1901), 309*ff.*

38. Pamphlet material on James L. Plimpton in the New York Public Library.

39. *Spalding's Manual,* 1884.

40. *San Francisco Evening Bulletin,* January 10, 1891.

41. *Harper's Weekly,* XXXIII (1889), 463.

42. *Outing* (*The Wheelman*), I (1882), 22-29, 69-70, IX, 390; *Tribune Book of Open-Air Sports* (New York, 1887), 455; L. H. Porter, *Wheels and Wheeling* (New York, 1892), 36-96.

43. *Harper's Monthly,* July, 1881, 285.

44. *Outing,* IV, 471; Walter G. Kendall, *Four Score Years of Sport* (Boston, 1933), 79*ff.*

45. *Outing* (*The Wheelman*), I (1882), 22-29.

46. *Ibid.,* I, 57.

47. *World Almanac,* 1890, 182-84.

48. Professor Hoffman, *Tips to Tricyclists.*

49. Porter, *Wheels and Wheeling,* advertisements.

50. *Outing* (*The Wheelman*), I (1882), 29.

51. Andrew M. F. Davis, "College Athletics," *Atlantic Monthly,* May, 1883, 677-84.

52. Quoted in *Outing,* XLVII (1905), 247.

53. William Saltonstall Scudder, "An Historical Sketch of the Oneida Football Club of Boston 1862-65," deposited with the Massachusetts Historical Society, 1926.

54. Parke H. Davis, *Football, the Intercollegiate Game* (New York, 1911), 42.

55. *Ibid.,* 35-37.

56. *Ibid.,* 65-72; Walter Camp and Lorin F. Deland, *Football* (New York, 1896), 63-76.

57. Davis, *Football,* 72.

58. Ira N. Hollis, "Intercollegiate Athletics," *Atlantic Monthly*, XC (1902), 534-44; Frederick L. Paxson, "The Rise of Sports," *Mississippi Valley Historical Review*, IV, 143-68; John A. Krout, "Some Reflections on the Rise of Sport," *Proceedings of the Association of History Teachers of the Middle States and Maryland*, No. 26 (1928), 84n.

CHAPTER XII

The New Order

1. *Outing*, XVII, 229.
2. William H. Nugent, "The Sports Section," *American Mercury*, XVI (1929), 336-37. See also unpublished study of newspaper content 1878-1898, Arthur M. Schlesinger, *The Rise of the City* (A History of American Life, X) (New York, 1933), 199.
3. James F. Muirhead, *The Land of Contrasts* (Boston, 1898), 107-10.
4. *Outing*, IV, 470, 476; VI, 614.
5. *New York Tribune*, May, 1890.
6. *Godey's Lady's Book*, July, 1890.
7. George Makepeace Towle, *American Society* (London, 1870), II, 87. See also *ibid.*, II, 15, 22, 40, 151.
8. James Bryce, *The American Commonwealth* (New York, 1888), II, 665, 666.
9. Paul de Rousiers, *American Life* (New York, 1892), 330.
10. Paul Blouet (Max O'Rell), *Jonathan and His Continent* (New York, 1884), 51.
11. Nathaniel H. Egleston, *Villages and Village Life* (New York, 1878), 307-08.
12. Mark Sullivan, *Our Times* (New York, 1925-35), II, 24-25.
13. J. W. Buel, *Metropolitan Life Unveiled* (San Francisco, 1883), 26.
14. Josiah W. Leeds, *The Theatre* (Philadelphia, 1884), 70, 82.
15. Quoted in Wilbert L. Anderson, *The Country Town* (New York, 1914) 281-82.
16. *Literary Digest*, XII (December 21, 1895), 228.
17. Josiah Strong, *The Challenge of the City* (New York, 1907), 222-23.
18. N. S. Shaler, *The United States of America* (New York, 1894), II, 467.
19. Towle, *American Society*, II, 25; William Bayard Hale, "A Study of Church Entertainment," *Forum*, XX (1896), 570-77. See also article in *North American Review*, quoted in *Literary Digest*, XIV (January 9, 1897), 307.
20. Hale, *loc. cit.*, 571.
21. Leeds, *The Theatre*, 78, 81.
22. Bryce, *The American Commonwealth*, II, 572.
23. Schlesinger, *The Rise of the City*, 335.
24. Samuel Lane Loomis, *Modern Cities* (New York, 1887), 104.
25. Quoted in Leeds, *The Theatre*, 67-68.
26. Quoted in Allan Nevins (editor), *American Social History as Recorded by British Travellers* (New York, 1923), 498.

27. Horace Greeley, *Recollections of a Busy Life* (New York, 1873), 118.
28. Quoted in Jesse Lyman Hurlbut, *The Story of Chautauqua* (New York, 1921), 184.

CHAPTER XIII

Metropolis

1. *Fifteenth Census of the United States,* I, 8, 9, 18-19.
2. Arthur M. Schlesinger, *The Rise of the City* (*A History of American Life,* X) (New York, 1933), 65, 72-73.
3. *Ibid.,* 67-70.
4. Quoted in George C. D. Odell, *Annals of the New York Stage* (New York, 1927–), VII, 236-37.
5. Alvin F. Harlow, *Old Bowery Days* (New York, 1931), 465.
6. *Harper's Weekly,* May 10, 1890, 370-72.
7. *Chicago by Day and Night, The Pleasure Seeker's Guide to the Paris of America* (Chicago, 1892), 34-42.
8. Owen Davis, *I'd Like to Do It Again* (New York, 1931), 105.
9. Harlow, *Old Bowery Days,* 459.
10. Henry Collins Brown, *New York in the Elegant Eighties, Valentine's Manual of New York* (New York, 1927), 138-39.
11. Richard J. Walsh, *The Making of Buffalo Bill* (Indianapolis, 1928), 181, 227*ff*.
12. *Punchinello,* I (1870), 116, quoted in Frank Luther Mott, *A History of American Magazines* (New York and Cambridge, 1930–), III, 208.
13. George Makepeace Towle, *American Society* (London, 1870), II, 21; Olive Logan, *Apropos of Women and the Theatre* (New York, 1869), 136.
14. Schlesinger, *The Rise of the City,* 300*n*.
15. Edwin Milton Royle, "The Vaudeville Theatre," *Scribner's,* XXVI (1899).
16. M. B. Leavitt, *Fifty Years in Theatrical Management* (New York, 1912), 185.
17. *Ibid.,* 209.
18. Harlow, *Old Bowery Days,* 466.
19. Leavitt, *Fifty Years in Theatrical Management,* 194*ff*. See also articles on B. F. Keith and F. F. Proctor in *Dictionary of American Biography.*
20. Royle, *loc cit.,* 495.
21. Harlow, *Old Bowery Days,* 456-59.
22. *Variety,* December 16, 1905. See also article on B. F. Keith in *Dictionary of American Biography.*
23. Harlow, *Old Bowery Days,* 473.
24. *Chicago by Day and Night.*
25. Harlow, *Old Bowery Days,* 454.
26. *Harper's Weekly,* XL (1896), 757-58; Henry Collins Brown, *The Golden Nineties, Valentine's Manual of New York* (New York, 1928), 57.

27. *Harper's Weekly*, XXXIII (1889), 746.
28. J. A. Dacus and James W. Buel, *A Tour of St. Louis* (St. Louis, 1878), 383.
29. "The Trolley Park," *Cosmopolitan*, XXXIII (1902), 265-72; *Street Railway Review*, XVI (1906), 121-22.
30. See article on George C. Tilyou in *Dictionary of American Biography*.
31. Quoted in A. G. Spalding, *America's National Game* (New York, 1911), 451.
32. *Harper's Weekly*, XXX (1886), 202.
33. *Ibid.*, XXXIV (1890), 356.
34. Spalding, *America's National Game*, 224-25.
35. *Ibid.*, 269-81.
36. Quoted *ibid.*, 467.
37. *Ibid.*, 251-61.
38. *Ibid.*, 442.
39. Brown, *The Golden Nineties*, 331-32.
40. Robert F. Kelley, *American Rowing* (New York, 1932), 37*ff.*
41. James F. Muirhead, *The Land of Contrasts* (Boston, 1898), 158.
42. See R. F. Dibble, *John L. Sullivan* (Boston, 1925).
43. *Ibid.*, 59.
44. *Ibid.*, 42-43.
45. Quoted in Brown, *The Golden Nineties*, 382.
46. Quoted in *Literary Digest*, VIII (December 23, 1893), 152.
47. Josiah Strong, *The Challenge of the City* (New York, 1907), 115.

CHAPTER XIV

World of Fashion

1. George Makepeace Towle, *American Society* (London, 1870), I, 292*ff.*
2. Mrs. John King Van Rensselaer, *The Social Ladder* (New York, 1924), 173.
3. Frederick Townsend Martin, *The Passing of the Idle Rich* (New York, 1911), 51-52.
4. Emily Faithfull, *Three Visits to America* (Edinburgh, 1884), 216-17, quoted in Arthur M. Schlesinger, *The Rise of the City* (A History of American Life, X) (New York, 1933), 151.
5. George D. Lyman, *The Saga of the Comstock Lode* (New York, 1934), 217.
6. Dixon Wecter, *The Saga of American Society* (New York, 1937), 338-39.
7. Ward McAllister, *Society as I Have Found It* (New York, 1890) *passim*.
8. *Ibid.*, 350.
9. Quoted in *Literary Digest*, XII (November 30, 1895), 146.
10. McAllister, *Society as I Have Found It*, 369-81.
11. Martin, *The Passing of the Idle Rich*, 30-31.
12. Wecter, *The Saga of American Society*, 369-71; Henry Collins Brown, *The Golden Nineties, Valentine's Manual of New York* (New York, 1928), 71. See also Charles A. and Mary Beard, *The Rise of American Civilization* (New York, 1927), II, 392-93.

13. Brown, *The Golden Nineties,* 108-15; Paul Blouet (Max O'Rell) *Jonathan and His Continent* (New York, 1884), 165-67; Francis Joseph Daly, *The Life of Augustin Daly* (New York, 1917), 119; George C. D. Odell, *Annals of the New York Stage* (New York, 1927–), VIII, 429, 559, IX, 392.

14. John Rankin Towse, *Sixty Years of the Theatre* (New York, 1916), 96-88; Henry Austin Clapp, *Reminiscences of a Dramatic Critic* (Boston, 1902), 50*ff;* Arthur A. Hornblow, *History of the American Theatre* (Philadelphia, 1919), II, 318-19; Odell, *Annals of the New York Stage,* VII, 203, X, 570.

15. *Harper's Weekly,* XXXIII (1889), 463; *Atlantic Monthly,* XLIII (1879), 453-58; Hornblow, *History of the American Theatre,* II, 318-19; William Winter, *The Wallet of Time* (New York, 1916), I, 27-29; Odell, *Annals of the New York Stage,* VIII, 559.

16. See Norman Hapgood, *The Stage in America,* 1897-1900 (New York, 1901).

17. Odell, *Annals of the New York Stage,* X, 592, 614, 651, 694.

18. Henry E. Krehbiel, *Chapters of Opera* (New York, 1909), 86.

19. Irving Kolodin, *The Metropolitan Opera* (New York, 1936), 12.

20. *Ibid.,* 2-3.

21. Quoted *ibid.,* 15-16.

22. Henry C. Lahee, *Annals of Music in America* (Boston, 1922), 67.

23. See Don C. Seitz, *The James Gordon Bennetts* (New York, 1928).

24. *Outing,* III, 354.

25. Robert P. Elmer, *Archery* (Philadelphia, 1923), 135.

26. *Tribune Book of Open-Air Sports,* 106.

27. Wecter, *The Saga of American Society,* 439.

28. *Scribner's,* XVII (1895), 692*ff; Harper's Weekly,* XXXIX (1895), 63.

29. Wecter, *The Saga of American Society,* 440.

30. Caspar Whitney, "Evolution of the Country Club," *Harper's,* XC (1894), 16*ff;* Robert Dunn, "The Country Club," *Outing,* XLVII (1905), 160-73.

31. Jerome D. Travers and James R. Crowell, *The Fifth Estate* (New York, 1936), 22.

32. H. C. Chatfield-Taylor, "The Middle West Discovers Outdoors," *Outing,* XLV (1904), 441-49; *Harper's Weekly,* XL (1896), 761-62.

33. *Century,* XLIV (1892), 602; *Scribner's,* XVII (1895), 531*ff; Outing,* XXX, 249.

34. *New York Tribune,* November, 28, 1890.

35. *Harper's Weekly,* XXXVII (1893), 1184.

36. William H. Nugent, "The Sports Section," *American Mercury,* XVI (1929), 337.

37. A. M. Weyand, *American Football* (New York, 1926), 45*ff.*

38. *The Nation,* November 20, 1890, 51.

39. Quoted in *Literary Digest,* XII (November 30, 1895), 128.

40. James F. Muirhead, *The Land of Contrasts* (Boston, 1898), 114-16.

41. Quoted in *Literary Digest,* VIII (1894), 428.

42. *Harper's Weekly,* XXXVII (1893), 1236.

43. Weyand, *American Football,* 79*ff.*

CHAPTER XV

Main Street

1. William Allen White, "A Typical Kansas Community," *Atlantic Monthly*, LXXX (1897), 171-77.
2. *Chelsea Telegraph Pioneer*, September 25, 1875, March 4, 1876.
3. *North American Review*, quoted in *Literary Digest*, XIV (January 9, 1897), 307.
4. *Eighty Pleasant Evenings*, Boston, 1898.
5. Robert S. and Helen Merrell Lynd, *Middletown* (New York, 1929), 280.
6. Leger D. Mayne (William B. Dick), *What Shall We Do Tonight* (New York, 1873); Lucretia Peabody Hale, *Fagots for the Fireside* (New York, 1895).
7. S. C. de Soisson, *A Parisian in America* (Boston, 1896), 186, quoted in Arthur M. Schlesinger, *The Rise of the City* (*A History of American Life*, X) (New York, 1933), 305.
8. For interesting discussion of these popular songs, and many specimens see Mark Sullivan, *Our Times* (New York, 1925-35), II, 154-83 and also Sigmund Spaeth, *Read 'Em and Weep* (Garden City, 1926) and *Weep Some More, My Lady* (Garden City, 1927).
9. Sullivan, *Our Times*, III, 399.
10. John Philip Sousa, *Marching Along* (Boston, 1928), Chap. iv.
11. Albert G. Stevens, *The Cyclopædia of Fraternities* (New York, 1899) v; B. H. Meyer, "Fraternal Beneficiary Societies in the United States," *American Journal of Sociology*, VI (1901), 646-61.
12. See Charles W. Ferguson, *Fifty Million Brothers* (New York, 1937).
13. H. C. Merwin, "A National Vice," *Atlantic Monthly*, LXXI (1893) 769; W. B. Hill, "The Great American Safety Valve," *Century* XLIV (1892), 383-84.
14. Paul de Rousiers, *American Life* (New York, 1892), 356.
15. J. C. Croly, *The History of the Women's Club Movement* (New York, 1898), 15, 88; *Nineteenth Century*, XLVII, 847.
16. *Atlantic Monthly*, XLVI (1880), 724-25.
17. Therese Blanc, *The Condition of Women in the United States* (Boston, 1895), 107, quoted in Schlesinger, *The Rise of the City*, 143.
18. "Ready-made Housekeeping," *Good Housekeeping*, V (1887), 266 quoted in Schlesinger, *The Rise of the City*, 132-33.
19. *New York Dramatic Mirror*, January 11, 1890.
20. Jesse Lyman Hurlbut, *The Story of Chautauqua* (New York, 1921) 247, 384-86.
21. Quoted in Gay MacLaren, *Morally We Roll Along* (Boston, 1938), 78.
22. *Ibid.*, 151, 169.
23. Schlesinger, *The Rise of the City*, 174. See also James B. Pond, *Eccentricities of Genius* (New York, 1900), 5ff.
24. Schlesinger, *The Rise of the City*, 291ff; *New York Dramatic Mirror* March 25, 1899.
25. *New York Dramatic Mirror*, December 10, 1898.
26. White, *loc. cit.*, 174.

27. *New York Dramatic Mirror,* January 11, 1890.

28. Marie Dressler, *My Own Story* (Boston, 1934), 40*ff.*

29. J. Frank Davies, "Tom Shows," *Scribner's,* LXXVII (1925), 350.

30. W. W. Stout, "Little Eva Is Seventy-Five," *Saturday Evening Post,* CC (October 8, 1927), 10*ff.*

31. Lynd and Lynd, *Middletown,* 266.

32. Everett Dick, *The Sod-House Frontier, 1854-1890* (New York, 1937), 280-81.

33. James A. Naismith, "Basketball," in *Encyclopædia Britannica.*

34. *Outing,* XXXI, 224.

35. Booth Tarkington, *The Gentleman from Indiana* (New York, 1899), 92.

36. *Twelfth Census of the United States,* X, 328, cited in Schlesinger, *The Rise of the City,* 313.

37. L. H. Porter, *Wheels and Wheeling* (New York, 1892), 9.

38. "The Rule of the Bicycle," *Scribner's,* XIX (1896), 783-84.

39. Joseph R. Bishop, "Social and Economic Influence of the Bicycle," *Forum,* XXI (1896), 680-89.

40. *Literary Digest,* XIII (1896), 361.

41. Lillian Campbell Davidson, *Handbook for Lady Cyclists* (London, 1896), 27.

42. *Godey's Lady's Book,* CXX (1890), 338; Dr. Henry J. Garrigues, "Woman and the Bicycle," *Forum,* XX (1896), 583; *Outing,* XVII (1891), 305; *Harper's Weekly,* XXXVIII (1894), 710.

43. *Scribner's,* XIX (1896), 783.

44. *Twelfth Census of the United States,* X, 329, cited in Schlesinger, *The Rise of the City,* 314.

45. *Vermont Phœnix* (Brattleboro), January 21, 1898.

CHAPTER XVI

Farm and Countryside

1. Nathaniel H. Egleston, *Villages and Village Life* (New York, 1878), 35, 42.

2. Quoted *ibid.,* 25.

3. See series of articles in the *Atlantic Monthly:* "The Problems of Rural New England," LXXIX (1897), 577-98, and "The Future of Rural New England," LXXIX (1897), 74-83.

4. Hamlin Garland, *A Son of the Middle Border* (New York, 1917), 21, 123, 209.

5. Allan Nevins, *The Emergence of Modern America* (*A History of American Life,* VIII) (New York, 1927), 169-71.

6. Everett Dick, *The Sod-House Frontier, 1854-1890* (New York, 1937), 384.

7. Garland, *A Son of the Middle Border,* 94. See also Grant Showerman, *A Country Chronicle* (New York, 1916), 46-52.

8. Mark Sullivan, *Our Times* (New York, 1925-35), II, 166.

9. Philip Morgan, "The Problems of Rural New England," *Atlantic Monthly,* LXXIX (1897), 377-88.

10. Sullivan, *Our Times*, II, 210-11.
11. Garland, *A Son of the Middle Border*, 165-66.
12. *Ibid.*, 165-66.
13. *Nauvoo* (Illinois) *Rustler*, July 1, 1890.
14. Henry Wheeler Shaw, *Josh Billings on Ice and Other Things* (New York, 1868), quoted in Wayne Caldwell Neely, *The Agricultura Fair* (New York, 1935), 193.
15. Neely, *The Agricultural Fair*, 83, 89, 96. See also article on Elkanah Watson in *Dictionary of American Biography*.
16. John A. Krout, *Annals of American Sport* (*The Pageant of America*, XV) (New Haven, 1929), 51-53.
17. Quoted in Neely, *The Agricultural Fair*, 204.
18. Alvan F. Sanborn, "The Problems of Rural New England," *Atlantic Monthly*, LXXIX (1897), 595.
19. Neely, *The Agricultural Fair*, 107.
20. Garland, *A Son of the Middle Border*, 167-68.
21. Nelson Lloyd, "The County Fair," *Scribner's Magazine*, XXXIV (1903) 129-47.
22. Earl Chapin May, *The Circus from Rome to Ringling* (New York, 1932), 113-14.
23. P. T. Barnum, *Struggles and Triumphs* (Buffalo, 1889), 284; M. R. Werner, *Barnum* (New York, 1927), 306-10; May, *The Circus*, 113-17.
24. Barnum, *Struggles and Triumphs*, 284, 331, 334.
25. *Ibid.*, 356.
26. *Ibid.*, 332*ff*; Werner, *Barnum*, 333*ff*.
27. May, *The Circus*, 224*ff*; *New York Dramatic Mirror*, 1890, advertisements.
28. *Nauvoo* (Illinois) *Rustler*, June 17, 1890.
29. *Carson Appeal*, May 29, 1875, quoted in Wells Drury, *An Editor on the Comstock Lode* (New York, 1936), 303.
30. For two colorful contemporary descriptions of circus day see Booth Tarkington, *A Gentleman from Indiana* (New York, 1899), 177-43 *passim;* Hamlin Garland, *Boy Life on the Prairie* (New York, 1899), 231-51 *passim.*
31. Quoted in Sullivan, *Our Times*, II, 171.
32. Garland, *A Son of the Middle Border*, 135-37.

CHAPTER XVII

The Growth of the Movies

1. Ben J. Lubschez, *The Story of the Motion Picture* (New York, 1920), 43; *Outing*, LXIV (July, 1914), 499-505; Paul Schubert, *The Electric Word* (New York, 1928), 3*ff*.
2. Benjamin B. Hampton, *A History of the Movies* (New York, 1931), 7.
3. *Ibid.*, 11; Terry Ramsaye, *A Million and One Nights* (New York, 1926), 233; "The Motion Picture in Its Economic and Social Aspects," *Annals of the American Academy of Political and Social Science*, CXXVIII (1926), 7.

4. Hampton, *A History of the Movies,* 12.
5. *Ibid.,* 44-45; Ramsaye, *A Million and One Nights,* 429-30.
6. Barton W. Currie, "The Nickel Madness," *Harper's Weekly,* LI (1907), 1246-47; George E. Walsh, "Moving Picture Drama for the Multitude," *Independent,* LXIV (February 6, 1908).
7. Quoted in Mark Sullivan, *Our Times* (New York, 1925-35), III, 552-53.
8. Hampton, *A History of the Movies,* 57; Walsh, *loc. cit.,* 306.
9. Ramsaye, *A Million and One Nights,* 256.
10. *Ibid.,* 259.
11. *Ibid.,* 473ff.
12. Sullivan, *Our Times,* III, 551-52.
13. Currie, *loc. cit.,* 1247; *Review of Reviews,* XXXVIII (December, 1908), 744.
14. Hampton, *A History of the Movies,* 29-39.
15. Walsh, *loc. cit.,* 307; Lubschez, *Story of the Motion Picture,* 58; *Annals of American Academy of Political and Social Science,* CXXVIII (1926), 10; Ramsaye, *A Million and One Nights,* 281-89, 363-78, 429.
16. Hampton, *A History of the Movies,* 31; Ramsaye, *A Million and One Nights,* 416ff.
17. Walsh, *loc. cit.,* 307-08.
18. Ramsaye, *A Million and One Nights,* 474.
19. Sullivan, *Our Times,* III, 553.
20. *Annals of the American Academy of Political and Social Science,* CXXVIII (1926), 11.
21. Hampton, *A History of the Movies,* 86ff; Ramsaye, *A Million and One Nights,* 544-45, 547-49, 605.
22. Hampton, *A History of the Movies,* 57, 92.
23. Ramsaye, *A Million and One Nights,* 645ff; Marie Dressler, *My Own Story* (Boston, 1934), 168-69.
24. Ramsaye, *A Million and One Nights,* 734.
25. *Ibid.,* 661; Pearl White, *Just Me* (New York, 1919).
26. Hampton, *A History of the Movies,* 130; Ramsaye, *A Million and One Nights,* 635ff.
27. Ramsaye, *A Million and One Nights,* 675-77; Hampton, *A History of the Movies,* 333.
28. Hampton, *A History of the Movies,* 342.
29. Ramsaye, *A Million and One Nights,* 748.
30. *Ibid.,* 625.
31. Frederick Lewis Allen, *Only Yesterday* (New York, 1931), 101.
32. Robert S. and Helen Merrell Lynd, *Middletown* (New York, 1929), 266.
33. Edgar Dale, *The Content of Motion Pictures* (New York, 1935), 17, 227.
34. Allen, *Only Yesterday,* 102; Will H. Hays, "The Motion Picture Industry," *Review of Reviews,* LXVII (1923), 65-80.
35. Hampton, *A History of the Movies,* 362.
36. Quoted *ibid.,* 354-55.
37. *Ibid.,* 387ff.

38. Julius Weinberger, "Economic Aspects of Recreation," reprint from *Harvard Business Review*, Summer, 1937, 450, 454; Preston W. Slosson, *The Great Crusade and After* (*A History of American Life*, XII) (New York, 1931), 394; Hampton, *A History of the Movies*, 362; *Film Daily Yearbook*, 1939.

39. Albert McCleery and Carl Glick, *Curtains Going Up* (New York, 1939), 332.

40. "The Hay's Office," *Fortune*, XVIII (December, 1938), 68*ff*; Ben Ray Redman, in *Saturday Review of Literature*, XIX (December 31, 1938), 3; J. P. McEvoy, "The Back of Me Hand to You," *Saturday Evening Post*, CCXI (December 24, 1938), 8*ff*.

41. *Current History*, L (March, 1939), 47.

42. Charles A. and Mary Beard, *America in Midpassage* (New York, 1939), 595*ff*.

CHAPTER XVIII

A Nation on Wheels

1. Mark Sullivan, *Our Times* (New York, 1925-35), I, 497.
2. *Country Life*, XIX (January, 1911), advertisements.
3. *Ibid.*, XII (1907), 76, 552.
4. Sullivan, *Our Times*, I, 497.
5. *Ibid.*, III, 431.
6. *Country Life*, XIX (January, 1911), 241-42.
7. *Ibid.*, XII (May, 1907), 76.
8. *Ibid.*, X (October, 1906), 702; XII (June, 1907), 198.
9. Harold Underwood Faulkner, *The Quest for Social Justice* (*A History of American Life*, XI) (New York, 1931), 170.
10. *Country Life*, XII (June, 1907), 198.
11. Sullivan, *Our Times*, I, 501.
12. *Country Life*, XII (October, 1907), 683-84.
13. *Ibid.*, XII (October, 1907), 684.
14. Sullivan, *Our Times*, IV, 63, 64.
15. *Automobile Facts and Figures*, 1939.
16. Frederick Lewis Allen, *Only Yesterday* (New York, 1931), 163.
17. *Automobile Facts and Figures*, 1939.
18. Preston W. Slosson, *The Great Crusade and After* (*A History of American Life*, XII) (New York, 1931), 238-39; *Recent Social Trends in the United States*, Report of the President's Research Committee (New York, 1933), II, 921, 950*ff*.
19. Robert S. and Helen Merrell Lynd, *Middletown* (New York, 1929), 259.
20. *Recent Social Trends*, II, 920; Jesse F. Steiner, "Research Memorandum on Recreation in the Depression," *Social Science Research Council Bulletin*, No. 32, 1937, 64.
21. Slosson, *The Great Crusade and After*, 237-38.
22. "Automobile Trailers," *The Index* (New York Trust Company), XVII (1937), 63*ff*.
23. Julius Weinberger, "Economic Aspects of Recreation," *Harvard Business Review*, Summer, 1937, 455-56.
24. Lynd and Lynd, *Middletown*, 255-56.

25. C. E. M. Joad, *Diogenes; or the Future of Leisure* (London, 1928), 42, quoted in George A. Lundberg, *Leisure—A Suburban Study* (New York, 1934), 63.

CHAPTER XIX

On the Air

1. Paul Schubert, *The Electric Word: the Rise of Radio* (New York, 1928), 194-95.
2. Alfred P. Morgan, *The Pageant of Electricity* (New York, 1939), 323-27.
3. Schubert, *The Electric Word*, 197*ff*; Preston W. Slosson, *The Great Crusade and After* (*A History of American Life*, XII) (New York, 1931), 389.
4. Julius Weinberger, "Economic Aspects of Recreation," *Harvard Business Review*, Summer, 1937, 450.
5. Slosson, *The Great Crusade and After*, 389n.
6. A. N. Goldsmith and A. C. Lescarboura, *This Thing Called Broadcasting* (New York, 1930), 42.
7. Quoted in Frederick Lewis Allen, *Only Yesterday* (New York, 1931), 78.
8. "'Listening In,' Our New National Pastime," *Review of Reviews*, LXVII (1923), 52.
9. Orange Edward McMeans, "The Great Audience Invisible," *Scribner's*, LXXIII (1923), 410-16.
10. Goldsmith and Lescarboura, *This Thing Called Broadcasting*, 99-101; Samuel L. Rothafel and R. F. Yates, *Broadcasting—Its New Day* (New York, 1925) *passim*.
11. *New Republic*, XL (October 8, 1924), 135-36.
12. Goldsmith and Lescarboura, *This Thing Called Broadcasting*, 177*ff*; Slosson, *The Great Crusade and After*, 390-92.
13. Charles Merz, *The Great American Bandwagon* (New York, 1925), 50.
14. Goldsmith and Lescarboura, *This Thing Called Broadcasting*, 189.
15. Weinberger, *loc. cit.*, 452.
16. Goldsmith and Lescarboura, *This Thing Called Broadcasting*, 209*ff*.
17. For studies of radio programs see George A. Lundberg, "The Content of Radio Programs," *Social Forces*, VII (1928), 58-60; Hadley Cantril and Gordon W. Allport, *The Psychology of Radio* (New York, 1935), 75-76.
18. Cantril and Allport, *Psychology of Radio*, 85; Weinberger, *loc. cit.*, 450.
19. *New York Herald Tribune*, July 30, 1939, vi, 8.
20. *New York Herald Tribune Magazine*, July 30, 1939, 9.
21. Weinberger, *loc. cit.*, 452.
22. *The Leisure of 5,000 People, A Report of a Study of Leisure Time Activities and Desires*, National Recreation Association (1934), 4.
23. Cantril and Allport, *Psychology of Radio*, 87-88.

CHAPTER XX

The Great American Band-Wagon

1. Frederick Lewis Allen, *Only Yesterday* (New York, 1931), 186.
2. Mr. and Mrs. Vernon Castle, *Modern Dancing* (New York, 1914), 37*ff*, 155*ff*.
3. Frederick Lewis Allen, "When America Learned to Dance," *Scribner's*, CII (1937), 11-17.
4. *Ibid.*, 17.
5. Mr. and Mrs. Vernon Castle, *Modern Dancing*, 38.
6. Wilder Hobson, *American Jazz Music* (New York, 1939), 15; Henry O. Osgood, *So This Is Jazz* (Boston, 1926), 10.
7. Paul Whiteman, "In Defense of Jazz," *New York Times*, March 13, 1927, quoted in Preston W. Slosson, *The Great Crusade and After* (*A History of American Life*, XII) (New York, 1931), 283.
8. Paul Whiteman, *Jazz* (New York, 1926), 17*ff*; Hobson, *American Jazz Music*, 92*ff*.
9. Mark Sullivan, *Our Times*, VI (New York, 1925-35), 479-80.
10. Quoted in Allen, *Only Yesterday*, 90.
11. Sullivan, *Our Times*, VI, 444*ff*.
12. *Ibid.*, VI, 489.
13. Stanley Walker, *The Night Club Era* (New York, 1933), *passim*.
14. Paul G. Cressy, *The Taxi Dance Hall* (Chicago, 1932), 109*ff*.
15. Walter S. Hiatt, "Billions—Just for Fun," *Colliers*, LXXIV (October 25, 1924), 31.
16. Quoted in Allen, *Only Yesterday*, 90.
17. *New Republic*, XXXV (August 1, 1923), 255-56.
18. Prosper Buranelli and Margaret Petherbridge, "How the Crossword Craze Started," *Colliers*, LXXV (January 31, 1925), 12.
19. Beatrice Barmby, "What It Means to be a Book Publisher at 29," *McClure's*, LIX (1927), 63, quoted in Slosson, *The Great Crusade and After*, 285.
20. Allen, *Only Yesterday*, 191-92.
21. Kathleen Norris, "I Know a Game," *Ladies' Home Journal*, XLV (September, 1928), 14.
22. *American Mercury*, VI, 234.
23. Elmer Davis, "Miniature Golf to the Rescue," *Harper's*, CLXII (December, 1930), 5.
24. *Ibid.*, 14.
25. Elmer Davis, "Purest of Pleasures: Contract," *Harper's*, CLXV (1932), 287-95.
26. Robert S. and Helen Merrell Lynd, *Middletown* (New York, 1929), 282.
27. Milton C. Work, *Contract Bridge* (Philadelphia, 1927), 1-3.
28. Ely Culbertson, "North West East South," *American Magazine*, CXIII (1932), 30.
29. Davis, "Purest of Pleasures," 287.
30. *Literary Digest*, October 17, 1931, 31.

31. Catherine Brody, "With Benefit of Clergy," *Collier's*, CI (May 7, 1938), 14*ff.*

32. *Literary Digest*, CXXV (January 1, 1938), 32-33.

33. Thurlow Reed, "Our Great American Sweepstakes," *Commonweal*, XXVIII (May 13, 1938), 67.

34. Lynd and Lynd, *Middletown*, 251.

35. "Hobbyhorse Hitching Post," *Rotarian*; Julius Weinberger, "Economic Aspects of Recreation," *Harvard Business Review*, Summer, 1937, 453.

36. Larry Clinton, "Swing Grows Up," *Good Housekeeping*, CVII (October, 1938), 13.

37. *Current History*, August, 1939, 52.

38. *Life*, July 24, 1939, 50.

CHAPTER XXI

Sports for All

1. James Bryce, "America Revisited—Changes of a Quarter Century," *Outlook*, March 25, 1905, in Allan Nevins (editor), *American Social History as Recorded by British Travellers* (New York, 1923), 542.

2. Quoted in Lee F. Hanmer, *Public Recreation* (*Regional Plan of New York*, V) (New York, 1928).

3. C. E. Rainwater, *The Play Movement in the United States* (Chicago, 1921), 44*ff*; Charles M. Robinson, *The Improvement of Towns and Cities* (New York, 1901), 156*ff*; *Recent Social Trends in the United States*, Report of the President's Research Committee (New York, 1933), II, 915*ff*; "Public Recreation Facilities," *Annals of the American Academy of Political and Social Science*, XXXV (March, 1910).

4. *Report on Progress of the Works Progress Administration Program*, June 20, 1938, 20-24, 51.

5. *Recreation Yearbook* (*Recreation*, XXXIII, June, 1939), 124*ff*.

6. For attendance figures and expenditure estimates on sports, see *Recent Social Trends*, II, 947*ff*; Julius Weinberger, "Economic Aspects of Recreation," *Harvard Business Review*, Summer, 1937, 452*ff*; "The "Recreational Dollar," *Business Week*, July 13, 1932; "The Sports Industry," *The Index* (New York Trust Company), XVI (1936), 127*ff*; John R. Tunis, *Sports, Heroes, and Hysterics* (New York, 1928); Frank G. Menke (editor), *All Sports Record Book* (New York, 1935), and *Encyclopedia of Sports* (1938).

7. L. H. Weir, *Europe at Play* (New York, 1937), *passim*.

8. John R. Tunis, "The Great God Football," *Harper's*, CLVII (1928), 743.

9. Harold Underwood Faulkner, *The Quest for Social Justice* (*A History of American Life*, XI) (New York, 1931), 291.

10. *Recent Social Trends*, II, 930.

11. *Ibid.*, II, 930; Preston W. Slosson, *The Great Crusade and After* (*A History of American Life*, XII) (New York, 1931), 274.

12. Frederick Lewis Allen, *Only Yesterday* (New York, 1931), 208-09.

13. *Liberty*, III (July 17, 1926), quoted in Slosson, *The Great Crusade and After*, 276.
14. *Recent Social Trends*, II, 931-32.
15. *World Almanac*, 1939.
16. William Cunningham, "No Wonder They Want to Fight," *Collier's*, LXXIV (September 13, 1924), 14; H. W. Clune, "Palookas and Plutocrats," *North American Review*, CCXXVII (1929), 49-55. See also article on Tex Rickard in *Dictionary of American Biography*.
17. Allen, *Only Yesterday*, 210-11.
18. Article on "Prize-Fighting" (by Gene Tunney) in *Encyclopædia Britannica*.
19. *Literary Digest*, LXXXIII (October 4, 1924), 77.
20. Slosson, *The Great Crusade and After*, 271.
21. *Recent Social Trends*, II, 923; John R. Tunis, "Changing Trends in Sports," *Harper's*, CLXX (1934), 85. See also *Encyclopedia of Sports*.
22. Arthur B. Reeves, "What America Spends for Sports," *Outing*, LVII (1910), 304-05.
23. *Recent Social Trends*, II, 927; Robert C. Duffus, "The Age of Play," *Independent*, CXII (December 20, 1924), 539-40.
24. Grantland Rice, "The National Rash," *Collier's*, LXXXII (October 20, 1928), 10.
25. *Recent Social Trends*, II, 927.
26. *Encyclopedia of Sports*.
27. *Recent Social Trends*, II, 927-28; *Encyclopedia of Sports*.
28. "Softball," *Literary Digest*, September 11, 1937, 32-33; Frank J. Taylor, "Fast and Pretty," *Collier's*, CII (August 20, 1938), 22ff.
29. Arthur M. Schlesinger, *The Rise of the City* (*A History of American Life*, X) (New York, 1933), 315.
30. John Kieran, "The Ski's the Limit," *American Magazine*, CXXIII (February, 1937), 28.
31. Tunis, "Changing Trends in Sports," 75-86; but see also same author's "A Nation of Onlookers?" *Atlantic Monthly*, CLX (1937), 141-50.

CHAPTER XXII

The New Leisure

1. C. E. M. Joad, *Diogenes; or the Future of Leisure* (London, 1928), 65.
2. Jesse F. Steiner, "Research Memorandum on Recreation in the Depression," *Social Science Research Council Bulletin*, No. 32 (1937), 29. See also *Recent Social Trends in the United States*, Report of the President's Research Committee (New York, 1933), II, 828-29.
3. Steiner, *loc. cit.*, 29-30; *Report of New York Committee on the Use of Leisure Time*, National Recovery Administration (1934).
4. C. Delisle Burns, *Leisure in the Modern World* (New York, 1932), 260.
5. See Jay B. Nash, *Spectatoritis* (New York, 1932); Arthur N. Pack, *The Challenge of Leisure* (New York, 1934); G. B. Cutten, *The*

Threat of Leisure (New Haven, 1926); George A. Lundberg, *Leisure—A Suburban Study* (New York, 1934); Herbert L. May and Dorothy Petgen, *Leisure and Its Uses* (New York, 1928); M. H. and E. S. Neumeyer, *Leisure and Recreation* (New York, 1936); Jesse F. Steiner, *Americans at Play* (New York, 1933); *Encyclopedia of the Social Sciences* (articles on leisure, play, recreation, etc.); Stuart Chase, "Play," in Charles A. Beard (editor), *Whither Mankind* (New York, 1928); John R. Tunis, "The Business of American Sport," in *America as Americans See It* (New York, 1932).

6. Lundberg, *Leisure,* 17.

7. Julius Weinberger, "Economic Aspects of Recreation," *Harvard Business Review,* Summer, 1937, 452*ff.* For other discussions on this point see *Recent Social Trends,* II, 949; Edwin E. Slosson, "The Amusement Business," *Independent,* LVII (July 21, 1904), 134*ff;* Arthur B. Reeve, "What America Spends for Sport," *Outing,* LVII (December, 1910), 300*ff;* Walter S. Hiatt, "Billions—Just for Fun," *Collier's,* LXXIV (October 25, 1924), 31; "The Amusement Industry," *The Index* (New York Trust Company), XVII (1937), 200*ff;* Chase, "Play," *loc. cit.,* 337.

8. *The Leisure Hours of 5,000 People, A Report of a Study of Leisure Time Activities and Desires,* National Recreation Association (1934). See also Robert S. and Helen Merrell Lynd, *Middletown in Transition* (New York, 1937).

9. John R. Tunis, "A Nation of Onlookers," *Atlantic Monthly,* CLX (1937), 147.

INDEX

425

Cincinnati, amusements described by Frances Trollope, 67

Circus, origin and early development, 131-35; as rural diversion in 1890's, 282-86; overshadowed by moving pictures, 305

Cities (*see also* Urban amusements), influence on recreation of growth of, 84-85, 136-38, 204, 211-13

Coaching, 182, 239, 241

Coasting, 34

Cock-fighting, in colonial New England, 33; in colonial South, 35, 57, 58, 65; in middle colonies, 50, 52; on frontier, 75; in mid-nineteenth century, 138, 159; in Far West, 172

Cock-skailing, 14

Cody, William F., as theatrical producer, 216-17

Cohan, George, actor, 218

College sports (*see also* Football), 197

Colonies, early bans on amusements in, 4ff.; sports of yeomanry of, 26, 31-37; country dances in, 30, 33, 37-39; social life of aristocracy of, 44-66; theatre in, 53-57, 62-63, 64-65

Combe, George, quoted, 93

Comic strips, 333

Commencement exercises, colonial, 31

Comstock, Anthony, attitude toward early movies, 290

Concert-saloons, 98, 221

Concerts, in colonial period, 49, 50, 53; of Jenny Lind, 126-27; in 1890's, 237-38; in 1930's, 372

Coney Island, 164, 223

Connecticut, colonial blue laws in, 6

Conrad, Dr. Frank, initiates broadcasting, 321

Contrast, The, 29, 56

Conway, Russell H., lecturer, 257

Cook, Ebenezer, his "Sot-Weed Factor" quoted, 30

Cook, George Frederick, actor, 109, 110

Corbett, James J., prize-fighter, 228, 244, 354

Costs of recreation, 301, 317, 345, 348-49, 368-70

Cotton, John, views on "mixed" dancing, 6

Count of Monte Cristo, The, 236

Country clubs, 241, 357

Country fairs, in colonial period, 26, 30; growth and expansion in nineteenth century, 279-82

County Fair, The, 236

Coup, William C., circus owner, 282

Courtney, Charles E., professional sculler, 226

Covered Wagon, The, 298

Cowboys, amusements on the range, 174-77; in town, 177-81

Crabtree, Lotta, actress, 173

Cricket, in colonial period, 33, 52; on frontier, 75; in Philadelphia, 186; overshadowed by baseball, 188

Crockett, David, on shooting contests, 72; on dancing, 76-77; tall tales of, 80

Croquet, introduced to United States, 191-92; at summer resorts, 202; declining importance in 1890's, 264-65; modern revival, 362

Crosby, Bing, radio singer, 372

Cross-word puzzles, 333; book publication of, 337-38

Crowninshield, Captain David, imports first elephant, 40

Culbertson, Ely, promotes bridge, 341, 342

Curling, 364

Cushman, Charlotte, actress, 109, 121

Cyrano de Bergerac, 236

Park Theatre (New York), first, 101, 103; second, 103, 105, 106, 120, 142

Parker, Elisha, 52

Parlor-games, in colonial period, 46; in 1890's, 249; modern, 338

Parties. *See* Balls, Farm festivals, small town parties.

Pastor, Tony, initiates refined vaudeville, 218

Patti, Adelina, concert artist, 237

Peck's Bad Boy, 218

Perils of Pauline, The, 296

Petticoat Fever, 303

Peverelly, Charles A., quoted, 189

Peytona, horse, 140

Philadelphia, as colonial capital, 50

Phonograph, 252, 325

Photography. *See* Amateur photography.

Pickford, Mary, moving-picture actress, 295, 297, 298

Picnicking, in colonial period, 51; in *ante-bellum* South, 157, 162; in rural areas, 277-78

Pinafore, 237

Pinero, Sir Arthur Wing, 236

Ping-pong, 333, 363

Pitts, Zazu, moving-picture actress, 303

Pittsburgh, horse racing in, 73

Pizarro, 108

Placide, Henry, actor, 109

Plays. *See* Theatre, and under individual titles.

Plimpton, James L., introduces roller-skating, 193

Ploughboy, horse, 141

Plymouth, first Thanksgiving at, 3; sports in, 13; drinking in, 17

Poker, 154, 170, 176

Polka, introduced, 151

Polo, introduced, 240, 241; modern sport, 362

Pool-rooms (*see also* Billiards), 371

Popular songs. *See* Songs.

Power, Tyrone, actor, 102

Princeton, colonial commencement of, 31; and intercollegiate football, 197, 198

Prisoner of Zenda, The, 236

Prize contests, 333, 343

Prize-fighting, early development, 144-47; in Virginia City, 171, 172; in the 1890's, 226-28; as modern sport, 353-55

Proctor, F. F., vaudeville producer, 219

Professionalization of sports (*see also* Baseball, Prize-fighting, Running, Spectator sports), 200-201, 355

Punch and Judy shows, 164

Puritanism (*see also* Sabbath observance), repressive influence in colonial period, 4ff., 12-13, 16, 18-21, 66, 204, 365; attitude toward theatre, 6, 64-65, 101, 205; origin of attitude toward amusements, 8-12; attitude as revealed in Sewall's diary, 13-15; modern influence of, 21, 365-66, 370; revival of, in nineteenth century, 86

Putnam, the Iron Son of '76, 115, 236

Pygmalion, 303

Pynchon, William, 48

Quakers, 23

Quarter-racing, 35, 72-73

Quincy, Josiah, Jr., quoted, 63

Quoits, 6, 64, 73, 75

Racing. *See* Horse racing.

Racquets, 363

Radio, invention of, 287; early development of, 320-21; becomes popular fad, 321-26; popular programs of, 324, 327-28; effect on

Scouts of the Plains, The, 216

Sculling. *See* Rowing.

Sears, R. D., tennis player, 193

Seccombe, Joseph, quoted, 25

Secret Service, 236

Sennett, Mack, moving-picture actor, 295

Sewall, Samuel, quotations from diary of, 13-15, 25, 39, 40; attends Boston training day, 29

Sharp, John, on cock-fighting, 25

Shakespearean drama (*see also* under individual plays), popularity in colonial period, 57, 62-63, 65; in nineteenth-century theatres, 110-12, 116; in Far West, 172, 173; at popular theatres of 1890's, 219; on legitimate stage, 236-37; in early movies, 294

Shaw, Bernard, playwright, 236

She Stoops to Conquer, 57

Shenandoah, 236

Sherlock Holmes, 236

Shooting galleries, 220, 223

Shooting matches, in colonial period, 26, 29, 36-37, 43, 52; on frontier, 71-72; in ante-bellum South, 160

Shore Acres, 236

Show-boats, 153-54

Shuffle-board, in colonial period, 6, 36; as modern sport, 363

Simpson, Edmund, theatrical producer, 107

Singing (*see also* Songs), in colonial period, 15, 26, 30, 46; on western prairies, 175-76; in small town of 1890's, 252-54

Sinners in Silk, 299, 371

Sir Henry, horse, 140, 143

Six-day bicycle races, 355

Skating, in colonial New York, 34; in mid-nineteenth century, 96-97, 184; in 1890's, 269: as modern sport, 364

Skeet, 356

Skiing, 360-62

Skinner, Otis, actor, 237

Slaves, amusements of, 158-60

Sleighing, 33, 51, 148, 269

Slot machines, 343-44

Small town parties, in colonial days, 45-46; in 1890's, 251-52

Smedes, Susan Dabney, quoted, 158, 161

Smith, Sol, theatrical producer, 108

Snow White and the Seven Dwarfs, 303

Soccer, 364

Social clubs (*see also* Fraternal orders, Women's clubs), in colonial period, 63-64

Society, in colonies, 44-66; at mid-nineteenth-century summer resorts, 148-52; sponsors sports, 184-85, 187, 192, 239-42, 362; in 1890's, 230-34; takes up motoring, 309ff.

Softball, 356, 360

Songs, minstrel, 130; cowboy, 175-76; "old favorites," 252-54, 276-77; circus, 285; popular, 324, 335

Sothern, E. H., actor, 236

Sousa, John Philip, introduces two-step, 254

South, the, sports in colonial period, 24, 26, 30, 35; social life of colonial aristocracy, 57-63; theatres in, 62-63, 102; amusements of ante-bellum days, 156-62

Spangenberg, Lester, pioneer broadcaster, 320

Spaulding, A. G., on world baseball tour, 226

Speakeasies, 335

Spectator sports (*see also* Baseball, Intercollegiate football, Prize-fighting), as developed in early nineteenth century, 98, 136-47; in 1890's, 200-202, 223-28; in twentieth century, 347, 350-56

Spectre Bridegroom, The, 107

Spencer, Herbert, quoted, 209